Western Union and the Creation of the American Corporate Order, 1845–1893

This work chronicles the rise of Western Union Telegraph from its origins in the helter-skelter ferment of antebellum capitalism to its apogee as the first corporation to monopolize an industry on a national scale. The battles that raged over Western Union's monopoly on nineteenth century American telecommunications – in Congress, in courts, and in the press – illuminate the fierce tensions over the rising power of corporations after the Civil War and the reshaping of American political economy. The telegraph debate reveals that what we understand as the normative relationship between private capital and public interest is the product of a historical process that was neither inevitable nor uncontested. Western Union's monopoly was not the result of market logic or a managerial revolution, but the conscious creation of entrepreneurs protecting their investments. In the process, these entrepreneurs elevated economic liberalism above traditional republican principles of public interest and helped create a new corporate order.

Joshua D. Wolff completed a PhD in history at Columbia University, where he has also served as a lecturer in history. He is an associate for a global management consulting firm.

Western Union and the Creation of the American Corporate Order, 1845–1893

JOSHUA D. WOLFF

CAMBRIDGE
UNIVERSITY PRESS

CAMBRIDGE UNIVERSITY PRESS
Cambridge, New York, Melbourne, Madrid, Cape Town,
Singapore, São Paulo, Delhi, Mexico City

Cambridge University Press
32 Avenue of the Americas, New York, NY 10013-2473, USA

www.cambridge.org
Information on this title: www.cambridge.org/9781107012288

First published 2013

Printed in the United States of America

A catalog record for this publication is available from the British Library.

Library of Congress Cataloging in Publication data
Wolff, Joshua D., 1976–
Western Union and the creation of the American corporate order,
1845–1893 / Joshua D. Wolff
pages cm
Includes index.
ISBN 978-1-107-01228-8 (hardback)
1. Western Union Telegraph Company. 2. Telegraph – United States –
History – 19th century. 3. Telecommunication – United States – Management –
History – 19th century. 4. Monopolies – United States – History – 19th
century. 5. Corporations – United States – History – 19th century. I. Title.
HE7797.W53W65 2012
384.10973'09034 – dc23 2013000569

ISBN 978-1-107-01228-8 Hardback

For Melissa

Contents

Acknowledgments

This book has followed a long and twisted path through graduate school, in and out of academic jobs, and concurrent with a series of life events typical of the transition from quarter- to mid-life and not particularly conducive to the speedy completion of a manuscript. Over time the list of people and institutions deserving of acknowledgment has grown lengthy indeed, and this is a mere digest of the major players.

I am greatly indebted to my colleagues and mentors in the history department at Columbia University. Among my colleagues, a few names feature prominently in the "I would not have made it through graduate school if it weren't for X" category, notably Kevin Murphy, Jeremy Derfner, and Emily Lieb (who agreed with me whenever I argued that I *should* give up, and yet maintained a firm confidence that I would not). Eric Wakin returned to Columbia at just the right moment to provide a fresh perspective and a new voice of encouragement. Among the faculty, Herb Sloan was an early and stalwart supporter who never failed to inspire and instigate and always treated me like a potential colleague. I can scarcely express in this small space how much I owe to Elizabeth Blackmar as a teacher, guide, and friend. Her generosity and selfless commitment to her students exemplifies the very best traditions in graduate education. This book began as a sprawling series of questions raised in marathon chats in her office, and though I am afraid the answers are not all here, her inspiration can nonetheless be found on many a page. It was my great fortune that Eric Foner agreed to serve as advisor when this book was in its dissertation phase. My comments can do little to add to his reputation as an outstanding teacher and scholar, but let me say as one of his students that one could not ask for a better mentor. Thanks as well to the members of my dissertation committee: Foner, Blackmar, Kim Phillips-Fein, Anders Stephanson, and David Weiman.

My students at Columbia also played an indispensable role for which I am grateful. On the face of things, they kept me distracted when too much time on the book would surely have produced diminishing returns. More importantly, they kept me sharp and engaged. The vitality, good humor, and intellectual challenges they brought to my classroom and my gabled cell in Hamilton Hall filled me with vigor in a way that solitary scholarship did not. I owe a special thanks to the students who braved my history of capitalism seminar, my laboratory for experimenting with many of the themes in this book.

My entry into the world of telegraph scholarship began with a lucky break when I met Alison Oswald at the Archive Center at the Smithsonian Institution's National Museum of American History. Alison introduced me to both the rich, massive Western Union Collection and to several of the scholars who have made use of it. Her suggestion that I get in touch with Richard John proved particularly auspicious. Richard's willingness to share his time, wisdom, and encyclopedic knowledge of this topic enormously influenced my research. Alison also introduced me to David Hochfelder, who has been similarly generous with his knowledge of all matters telegraphic.

During the research and writing of this manuscript, I enjoyed material support from several sources. I began my research as a Richard Hofstadter Fellow in the Columbia University Department of History. Travel funds were provided in a Lemelson Center Short-Term Visitor Fellowship at the Smithsonian and a Filson Fellowship at the Filson Historical Society in Louisville. Pete Daniel sponsored me as a Visiting Scholar at the Smithsonian, providing me with office space and greater access to the wonderfully helpful staff of the Archive Center at the National Museum of American History. The Doris G. Quinn Foundation provided valuable backing with a dissertation completion grant. The Bancroft Dissertation Prize helped with the transition from dissertation to book. Cambridge University Press graciously accepted my manuscript when it was still very close to the original dissertation. I am grateful to the editors who saw potential in the rough draft and for the readers whose keen criticism helped light the path toward a better book.

I received a great deal of support for my work from outside the boundaries of "the guild." Seth Kamil and Big Onion Walking Tours provided both financial sustenance and a sense of professional purpose while constantly renewing my love for New York. The many friends who have been force-fed obscure points about Western Union over the years and nonetheless claimed that they looked forward to the book merit greater thanks than I can offer here, but one deserves special mention: Jeff Tapick provided not only steadfast friendship but also a room in his apartment in Washington, turning what might have been a lonely year away from home into a very pleasant sojourn.

Of all my friends and colleagues, Andrew Edwards invested the most time and energy in the book. My former student, research assistant, free-lance editor, and "dissertation therapist," Andrew came to the rescue at a critical time, bringing fresh questions, arguments, and inspiration when I was running low. No less importantly, he cruelly cut thousands of words from the manuscript when self-indulgence stayed my hand. Every reader of this book should be grateful to Andrew, but none so much as I.

Last, but absolutely not least, I owe tremendous thanks to my family. My wife Melissa supported me in this endeavor from start to finish, sharing her life with this book and its voracious demands for attention and space (no small sacrifice in New York apartments). Her encouragement and patience appeared never to flag, even when my own did. My daughter arrived fairly late in the process and her contributions have been entirely without her knowledge or consent. One day I will explain to her why the telegraph trumped the playground on some weekends, and how that tradeoff was another powerful motivator to get this project completed. My sister pursued a PhD at Columbia at the same time that I did, and we were very lucky to travel this winding road together. My parents cheered me along throughout my graduate career and in the years since very kindly refrained from asking about my progress on the book any more often than convention required. My father's career in the telecommunications industry informed my thinking about the telegraph in countless ways. For years he and I have enjoyed an ongoing conversation about communications policy, technology, and business. I hope this book, now that it is finished, will start our conversation anew.

Introduction

"We, of Western Union, are accustomed to thinking of ourselves as shapers of history," company president Russell McFall declared in a 1971 address to the Newcomen Society. McFall surely knew that this statement – which he intended to refer to Western Union's legacy of technological achievement – was as ironic as it was bold. In 1971, Western Union was not shaping history so much as fading into it.

Yet the description of Western Union as a shaper of history is appropriate. Almost a century earlier, Western Union had emerged as one of the largest, most powerful firms in an era so marked by the spectacular growth of corporations that historians often refer to it as a "Second Industrial Revolution." Henry Adams observed in his celebrated memoir how in the late nineteenth century "Trusts and Corporations" had created "new power" in the United States. With their "vigorous and unscrupulous energy," they had troubled "all the old conventions and values, as the screws of ocean steamers must trouble a school of herring."[1] When Adams was a boy in the 1840s, most firms employed only a few workers, and except for textile mills and the fledgling railroads, few commanded substantial sums of capital. By the 1870s, industrial corporations had transformed the economic order of the United States. Backed by tens of millions of dollars of capital, employing thousands of workers, and reaching beyond state and regional boundaries, industrial corporations changed the way Americans worked, consumed, traveled, and, crucially, communicated. On the face of it, this was an economic and technological

[1] Henry Adams, *The Education of Henry Adams* (New York: The Modern Library, 1996), 500.

revolution. But as Adams observed, the disruptive force of the rising "Trusts and Corporations" went well beyond the marketplace. Firms such as Western Union represented not merely a new form of business organization, but also new loci of social and political power.

Western Union rode in the vanguard of this corporate revolution. Launched by a small group of Rochester entrepreneurs in 1851, Western Union gobbled up allies and rivals alike at a dizzying pace. By 1866 the company had seized control of the largest telegraph network in the world, becoming the first American private corporation to monopolize a national industry. A few railroad companies commanded greater sums of capital, but none controlled the rails entirely. With Western Union's ascendance, monopoly, which had long been the prerogative of sovereigns and states alone to grant, became a market phenomenon – albeit one tacitly supported by the state through patents and court enforcement of exclusive contracts for telegraph rights-of-way.

The American resistance to monopolies in all their forms ranked high among the "old conventions and values" most threatened by the rise of "Trusts and Corporations." In antebellum America, antimonopolists railed against state-granted franchises in industries such as banking and transportation. Andrew Jackson had made antimonopolism a central plank of the Democratic Party and devoted much of his presidency to attacking the paper-money system and the Bank of the United States, monstrous symbols of "monopoly and exclusive privileges."[2] In economic terms, monopoly grants stymied the salubrious effects of vigorous competition, choking off the spirit of free enterprise. In political terms, they reeked of corruption and encouraged the abuse of government power.

Western Union's emergence as a monopoly in 1866 was thus surprising, disruptive, and contrary to both economic and political norms. Looking back from 1971, McFall celebrated his predecessors for founding Western Union "with 550 miles of wire, and a concept": that the public would be better served by "a unified telegraph system."[3] However, if Western Union's founders had any far-reaching strategy, it was that telegraph *investors*, not customers, could be better served by a market free from competition. None of the telegraph entrepreneurs of the 1850s envisioned a private telegraph system managed by a single firm.

---

[2] Sean Wilentz, *The Rise of American Democracy: Jefferson to Lincoln* (New York: W. W. Norton, 2005), 454.
[3] Russell W. McFall, *Making History by Responding to Its Forces* (New York: Newcomen Society in North America, 1971).

Though Western Union's share of the American telegraph market rarely rose above 90 percent, critics and partners alike regularly attached the pejorative term "monopoly" to the company after 1866. At the time and for many decades to follow, Americans routinely labeled private corporations with any hint of "bigness" as "monopolies." As historian Ellis Hawley noted in his account of the New Deal, for most Americans the term "monopoly" reflected concern "with the question of power, with the development, in particular, of private concentrations of economic power and with the implications of this development for a democratic society."[4] But Western Union was hardly just another big company with suspiciously antidemocratic tendencies. For most of two decades the company effectively *controlled* the national telegraph market – that Western Union's share fell short of 100 percent made the monopoly designation no less apt. Communication, particularly rapid communication, has always been associated with power, and in America, this power was Western Union's to grant or deny.

Western Union's domination of the industry persisted despite the popular belief that the telegraph had a special civic purpose – perhaps even a providential design. Some contemporaries who lauded inventor Samuel F. B. Morse believed he had been divinely inspired and his invention would usher in an era of peace and universal communication.[5] In 1873 an early telegraph historian declared that this technology, "more than any other agency," had bound "the nations of the earth in a brotherhood" and seemed "like the herald of a millennial era."[6] Later generations of historians have been no less admiring, often citing the invention of the electromagnetic telegraph as a pivotal achievement in a nineteenth-century "communication revolution."[7] In his recent survey of U.S. history from

---

[4] Ellis Hawley, *The New Deal and the Problem of Monopoly: A Study in Economic Ambivalence* (Princeton, N.J.: Princeton University Press, 1966), 4.

[5] Richard R. John, "Private Enterprise, Public Good? Communications Deregulation as a National Political Issue, 1839–1851," in *Beyond the Founders: New Approaches to the Political History of the Early American Republic*, ed. Jeffrey L. Pasley, Andrew W. Robertson, and David Waldstreicher (Chapel Hill, N.C.: The University of North Carolina Press, 2004), 340.

[6] Benjamin J. Lossing, "Professor Morse and the Telegraph," in *Lightning Flashes and Electric Dashes: A Volume of Choice Telegraphic Literature, Humor, Fun, Wit & Wisdom*, ed. W. J. Johnston (New York: W. J. Johnston, 1877), 26. The article was first published in *Scribner's Monthly* in March 1873.

[7] Robert Albion coined this expression in 1932 with the intent of separating the changes brought by steam, rails, and telegraphy from the Industrial Revolution. Robert G. Albion, "The 'Communication Revolution'," *American Historical Review* 37, no. 4 (1932).

1815 to 1848, Daniel Walker Howe employed Morse's invention and his immortal first message, "What hath God wrought," as a central metaphor for "the transformation of America."[8]

Samuel Morse embraced grandiose claims for the telegraph, but he also shared some of his contemporaries' misgivings about control of the wires. Morse shared the faith first articulated by James Madison in *The Federalist* in the power of technology to bind the nation together through improved communication.[9] He saw an obvious connection between the telegraph and the post office, an institution so important to the health of the republic that the Constitution mandated its creation and ordained it a government entity. The telegraph, Morse explained to Congress, had the same "principal object" as the mail: "the rapid and regular transmission of intelligence."[10] Yet Morse also expressed a common anxiety toward the antidemocratic nature of concentrated power. In his 1838 appeal to Congress for funds to build an experimental telegraph line, Morse argued that such an "instrument of immense power, to be wielded for good or evil," should belong first to the government. But fearing that a government monopoly "might become a means of working vast mischief to the republic," Morse proposed a dual system in which the government would operate the telegraph as part of the postal system but also license the technology to promote private competition. The "enterprising character" of Americans would soon see the whole surface of the country "channeled" with telegraph wires, "those *nerves* which are to diffuse, with the speed of thought, a knowledge of all that is occurring throughout the land; making, in fact, a *neighborhood* of the whole country."[11]

The symbolic importance of the telegraph to the unity of the republic can scarcely be exaggerated. The inaugural messages sent over the newly completed transcontinental telegraph line announced that California and Utah would remain with the Union in the Civil War. In John Gast's iconic 1872 painting *American Progress*, the angelic, allegorical figure of America unspools a telegraph wire behind her as she soars into the frontier. In 1884, Colorado Senator Nathaniel Hill insisted the American

---

[8] Daniel Walker Howe, *What Hath God Wrought: The Transformation of America, 1815–1848* (New York: Oxford University Press, 2007).

[9] John F. Kasson, *Civilizing the Machine: Technology and Republican Values in America, 1776–1900* (New York: Hill and Wang, 1976), 35.

[10] "Electro-Magnetic Telegraphs," Report No. 753, House of Representatives, 25th Congress, 2nd Session, 7.

[11] "Electro-Magnetic Telegraphs," Report No. 753, House of Representatives, 25th Congress, 2nd Session, 8–9.

people were "entitled" to the telegraph as an "enlightened public service" because of its "benefits of stimulating trade, diffusing intelligence, and strengthening social and family ties."[12] Nor should the real importance of telegraph communications be denied. European governments established state telegraph networks as a public service and strategic necessity. Only England eschewed a government system for competitive private telegraphy, and that proved temporary: in 1868 Parliament nationalized the telegraph companies.

In the United States, Congress ignored Morse's exhortations and declined to purchase his patent. By the 1850s the private American telegraph industry consisted of a patchwork of rival networks operating under competing patents. In 1857 the six strongest regional companies united in an anticompetitive cartel that lasted only until Western Union absorbed its partners and took charge of the industry in 1866. The unified telegraph that McFall touted a century later as Western Union's great achievement was subordinate to the company's primary goal: the elimination of competition.

Historians have more readily accepted Western Union managers' arguments that the public interest demanded telegraph consolidation than many of the managers' contemporaries did. Historian Alfred D. Chandler, Jr. echoed McFall in *The Visible Hand*, his seminal account of the second industrial revolution. To manage valuable intercity "through traffic," Chandler suggested that the telegraph industry marched unavoidably through stages of "competition, cooperation, and consolidation" even faster than the railroads. The technical requirements of the telegraph necessarily gave birth to Western Union, "the first nationwide multiunit modern business enterprise in the United States."[13] Robert Luther Thompson, a twentieth-century historian who wrote an exhaustive, pioneering monograph of the early telegraph industry similarly concluded that Western Union's march to monopoly had been inevitable.[14] Even Morse, who had seen his hopes for a government telegraph dashed, noted that although Western Union was "doubtless a *monopoly*," a unified private telegraph was a "public advantage" if properly managed.[15]

---

[12] Nathaniel Peter Hill, *Speeches and Papers on the Silver, Postal Telegraph, and Other Economic Questions* (Colorado Springs: The Gazette Printing Company, 1890), 232.
[13] Alfred D. Chandler, *The Visible Hand: The Managerial Revolution in American Business* (Cambridge, Mass.: Belknap Press of Harvard University Press, 1977), 197.
[14] Robert Luther Thompson, *Wiring a Continent: The History of the Telegraph Industry in the United States, 1832–1866* (Princeton, N.J.: Princeton University Press, 1947).
[15] Samuel Morse to Amos Kendall, 19 March 1866, Morse Papers. Emphasis in the original.

Nonetheless, the telegraph was not what political economists later called a "natural monopoly" – an industry in which costs persistently decline as volume increases so that a single firm serves the whole market more efficiently than competing firms.[16] Railroads, for example, had large capital requirements, high fixed costs, and substantial debt obligations, all of which became proportionately less onerous as the volume of traffic increased. But unlike railroads, telegraph lines were inexpensive to build, and, for the first several decades, most operating costs increased in proportion to message volume. Until the advent of multiplex and automatic telegraph in the late 1870s, every message required a dedicated wire, two operators, keys, batteries, and stationery. Labor, a variable cost, accounted for more than half the cost per message. Through cooperative ventures with railroads, hotels, and other points requiring a wire, telegraph companies kept fixed costs down, often paying little or no rent for their offices and in some cases not even paying for line construction. For most of the first forty years of telegraphy, doubling the number of messages nearly doubled expenses. The telegraph was subject to powerful network effects – the value of the network increased with additional nodes at a greater than linear rate. However, this did not preclude efficient competition between large firms or between cooperative networks of small firms.

Western Union was thus an unnatural monopoly. The telegraph monopoly was not a technical inevitability but a deliberate, creative act, forged through years of aggressive maneuvering and maintained against fierce opposition. Telegraph companies pursued anticompetitive strategies as the way to generate profits despite poor construction, weak management, and, too often, fraudulent capitalization. Eliminating competition proved the easiest way to overcome these defects and earn a return for pioneer holders of telegraph stock – securities so risky that one major holder likened his stake to a bet in a faro game.

The self-serving Western Union argument that only a single company could afford to conduct the nation's telegraph business had a profound and lasting effect on telecommunications policy. The emergence of a new communications technology brings with it a set of "constitutive choices" about the "general legal and normative rules" of operation, the "structure of networks," and "organization of the industry."[17] For the telegraph,

[16] Jonathan E. Nuechterlein and Philip J. Weiser, *Digital Crossroads: American Telecommunications Policy in the Internet Age* (Cambridge, Mass.: The MIT Press, 2005), 12.

[17] Paul Starr, *The Creation of the Media: Political Origins of Modern Communications* (New York: Basic Books, 2004), 5.

Western Union employed enough political and economic power to sub-jugate the public policy concerns to the interests of private capital – specifically to the self-perpetuation of Western Union and the interest of its shareholders. In this, Western Union was a leader in one of the most significant and peculiar elements of the new finance capitalism: the transition of capital from an enabler of productive business to an enabler of its own growth – from businesses making money to money making money.[18]

Critics claimed the unchecked telegraph monopoly offered unlimited potential for corruption. They accused the company of manipulating the news, tampering with elections, disclosing the contents of messages, and exploiting market information. Yet the evidence suggests that such venal corruption was exceedingly rare and usually attributable to dishonest individuals.[19] But Western Union engaged in a deeper *systematic* corruption, manipulating both the press and the political system, destroying competition and resisting efforts to democratize the telegraph through regulation or the creation of a public telegraph. The question of whether a private telegraph served the public interest could not be answered without prejudice so long as Western Union wielded an overwhelming influence over the discourse. An 1881 *Puck* cartoon depicting Jay Gould and William H. Vanderbilt torturing Uncle Sam on a rack fashioned out of a Western Union telegraph pole exaggerated the company's power, but only slightly. "They can stretch him to any extent they please," explained *Puck*.[20] Indeed, when it came to the question of control of the telegraph, capital was mostly free to determine what was best.

---

[18] Richard White explores similar themes in *Railroaded*, which he published while this manuscript was in revision. Telegraph companies, like railroads, often made a great deal of money for finance capitalists even as they delivered poor service or failed as concerns. Richard White, *Railroaded: The Transcontinentals and the Making of Modern America* (New York: W. W. Norton, 2011), xviii.

[19] Economic historian John Joseph Wallis divides corruption into "venal" and "systematic" corruption. Venal corruption "denotes the pursuit of private economic interests through the political process," while systematic corruption is the manipulation of the economy in a manner intended to keep a political group in power. I have modified these definitions slightly. Venal corruption in this case involves the use of the wires to steal or manipulate information for profit, while systematic corruption involves manipulation of the government and political system to protect the interests of private investors. In Wallis' view, venal corruption is perpetual and "small potatoes," while systematic corruption has far-reaching and more damaging effects. John Joseph Wallis, "The Concept of Systematic Corruption in American History," in *Corruption and Reform: Lessons from America's Economic History*, ed. Edward L. Glaeser and Claudia Goldin (Chicago: University of Chicago Press, 2006), 25, 52.

[20] "The Two Philanthropists," *Puck*, 23 February 1881, 414, 420.

Western Union defined the "best" telegraph as one that provided a fast, premium service to primarily business customers. This made for a profoundly undemocratic communications revolution. Monopoly rates gave the advantage to large firms over small, concentrated information in urban centers, and encouraged monopolies in news and market information. Forty years after Samuel Morse opened the first telegraph line, Western Union managers claimed that only 2 percent of Americans used the telegraph each year and the lion's share of messages concerned "stock-jobbing," bucket shops (wherein customers gambled on stock prices without buying or selling shares), commodities futures, and race-tracks.[21] "The Telegraph is essentially an adjunct of commerce," Western Union president Norvin Green told the Speaker of the House in 1883, "and most complaints are by people who never use it and never would at any price except in case of death. What farmer or mechanic ever wants to use the Telegraph in any other case?"[22]

Such claims that high rates reflected a lack of customer demand for cheaper service were disingenuous at best. Though it is reasonable to wonder why a "farmer or mechanic" required telegraph service in place of the inexpensive, reliable post office, technologies that are first deployed at high prices and embraced only by the business community are often used widely by the general public after prices are reduced. Long-distance telephone service, mobile phones, computers, and e-mail were all once mere "adjuncts of commerce" that all Americans came to use, often in unexpectedly productive and empowering ways. Western Union managers gradually realized that when rates went down, volume increased substantially, suggesting a deep unfulfilled demand for telegraphy. The English experience certainly bore this out: in the two years after Parliament nationalized the telegraph, the number of messages carried on the English network nearly *doubled* to ten million per year, about the same number sent in the United States, though the latter had twice the population.[23]

At a moment in American history when private property became more intensely concentrated than ever before and the question of whether and how to limit corporate power was thrust to the fore of the national debate, Western Union helped to define core elements of the market triumphalism that persists to the present: that governments are corrupt and

[21] Norvin Green, "Postal Telegraph Facilities," 28 February 1890, WUC, 4.
[22] Norvin Green to J. G. Carlisle, 15 December 1883, WUC.
[23] "Postal Telegraph System in Europe," House of Representatives Misc. Doc. No. 36, 41st Congress, 3rd Session, 3.

markets are pure; that public solutions cost more and provide less than private solutions; and that civic needs are best served by private interests. Large-scale telecommunications companies were perhaps preferable to small, disconnected firms, but Western Union distorted the need for unity into a justification for monopoly, and then developed a political constituency and an ideology to explain and perpetuate itself. The telegraph giant became interlinked with other large-scale businesses, compounding the advantages of large-scale firms and the power of concentrated capital in other industries.

Russell McFall was right – probably more so than he realized – when he described Western Union as a shaper of history. Critics of the old trope of the "robber barons" argue that the so-called barons were merely rational, visionary actors behaving within the limits of the system. But the story of Western Union shows how industrial and finance capitalists *created* the system, justified it, and reinforced it. The reshaping of the American political economy by corporations untethered from traditional obligations to the public welfare was not a technical inevitability but a deliberate and historically contingent process.

I

The Meanest Property in the World

On a breezy afternoon in June 1871, ten thousand of New York's leading citizens gathered near the elm-lined mall on the east side of Central Park. At the front of the crowd a statue obscured by draped American flags stood on a seven-foot granite pedestal. The governor of New York addressed the throng, the band struck up "The Star-Spangled Banner," and the flags fell away to reveal a heroic bronze effigy of Samuel F. B. Morse, the Father of the Telegraph. The tribute to Professor Morse continued that night in a celebration at the Academy of Music, the city's finest hall. Leading figures in government and business, several Civil War generals, and public luminaries such as Henry Ward Beecher and Horace Greeley sat on the crowded stage before a sold-out audience. Finally, Morse himself, eighty years old and frail, entered to cheers and waving handkerchiefs and took his place upon the stage.

Speaker after speaker hailed Morse as the peacemaker of the age, an American genius equal to Franklin, Fulton, and Watt, the inventor "of the greatest instrument of power over earth which the ages of human history have revealed." After an hour of paeans, young telegraph operator Sadie Cornwell walked to a table at the center of the stage and took her station at a key purportedly connected to all the wires in America. "Greetings and thanks to the telegraph fraternity throughout the world," she tapped. "Glory to God in the highest, on Earth peace, goodwill to men." Then Morse took his place at the key, and in a house suddenly hushed, he "signed" the message in the code that bore his name. The audience erupted in cheers, and when at last they had subsided, William Orton, the chairman of the evening's ceremony and president of the Western

Union Telegraph Company, somberly announced, "Thus the Father of the Telegraph bids farewell to his children."[1] "Telegraph" and "Morse" are virtually synonymous today, and so it was for Americans in 1871. However, "Morse" was not the only name inextricably linked to the telegraph – "Western Union" was just as closely connected. In 1871 Western Union owned more than two-thirds of the 180,000 miles of telegraph wire in the United States and transmitted 90 percent of the messages.[2] Western Union sponsored the tribute to Morse, commissioned the $5,000 bronze statue, and arranged for its prominent placement in recently opened Central Park. Western Union operators and managers pledged contributions to the memorial over company wires.[3] At the gala in his honor, Morse shared the stage with several former Western Union executives. The event committee included the entire Western Union board of directors and the railroad mogul who had recently taken a controlling interest in the company, Cornelius Vanderbilt. When Morse shuffled to center stage to send his "farewell" message, the president of Western Union steered him by the arm.[4]

Ironically, the great corporation hosting the tribute and the telegraph pioneers whom Morse praised in a brief address of gratitude had been no friends to Morse in the telegraph's formative years. Morse had once judged these same men who now glorified him as upstarts and traitors threatening to destroy his legacy. Western Union had in fact been created with the express purpose of breaking Morse's patent monopoly. Yet Morse's veneration of the men once set against him was hardly the most unexpected development in the evolution of the American telegraph. More surprising was that the regional entrepreneurs who built the nation's lines had surrendered control of the wires to railroad magnates and stock operators, that a single corporation dominated the telegraph in every corner of the nation, and indeed that *any* private corporation could achieve such a scale. Though the tribute was for Morse, the triumph belonged entirely to Western Union, a uniquely big business at the dawn of an era of big businesses.

[1] *Journal of the Telegraph*, 15 June 1871, 162–8.
[2] Richard B. Du Boff, "The Telegraph and the Structure of Markets in the United States, 1845–1890," *Research in Economic History* 8 (1983): 256. Du Boff's figures involve some interpolation based on Western Union's market share in other years. The very limited extension of opposition lines at the time suggests that Du Boff's estimate is accurate.
[3] Kenneth Silverman, *Lightning Man: The Accursed Life of Samuel F. B. Morse* (New York: Alfred A. Knopf, 2003), 430–1.
[4] *Journal of the Telegraph*, 15 June 1871, 162–8.

When Western Union was launched in 1851 as the New York & Mississippi Valley Printing Telegraph Company, small, single-unit, owner-managed proprietorships conducted most of the business in the United States. Not only was large-scale private enterprise impractical, but the very idea was also alien to American businessmen.[5] Except for railroads, textile mills, and armories, industrial firms resembled workshops more than factories. Even large businesses were usually partnerships in which a small number of investors were personally responsible for their companies' liabilities. In the late 1840s, new general incorporation laws allowed for the charter of limited liability corporations for strictly business purposes. The number of business corporations remained small before the Civil War, as did the capital markets that supported them. Manufacturers had little access to national or international credit and capital markets. They generally financed their firms with personal assets or retained earnings, or they formed small corporations with fixed capital and sought the backing of wealthy merchants and other local businessmen.[6] Early railroads relied on state support and capital subscriptions from the same local sources as manufacturers and were locally controlled, geographically limited, and rarely interconnected. Railroad finance only gradually concentrated in New York and Boston, and railroads did not rely on bonded debt from European investors until the rail boom of the 1850s.[7] The corporate economy remained so limited in size and extent that railroad stocks and bonds represented half the nation's negotiable securities at mid-century.[8]

The transformation of the telegraph from an industry crowded with small regional competitors to one dominated by a single national firm foreshadowed the big business revolution of the postwar period. For the

---

[5] Richard John has argued that not until the 1840s was large-scale private enterprise even considered a possibility, and the "perceptual shift" that occurred on these lines is "often overlooked." See Richard R. John, "Private Enterprise, Public Good? Communications Deregulation as a National Political Issue, 1839–1851," in *Beyond the Founders: New Approaches to the Political History of the Early American Republic*, ed. Jeffrey L. Pasley, Andrew W. Robertson, and David Waldstreicher (Chapel Hill, N.C.: The University of North Carolina Press, 2004), 331.

[6] Glenn Porter and Harold C. Livesay, *Merchants and Manufacturers: Studies in the Changing Structure of Nineteenth-Century Marketing* (Chicago: Ivan R. Dee, 1971), 65–70.

[7] Lawrence E. Mitchell, *The Speculation Economy: How Finance Triumphed over Industry* (San Francisco: Berrett-Koehler 1997), 282–3; Sarah Gordon, *Passage to Union: How the Railroads Transformed American Life, 1829–1929* (Chicago: Ivan R. Dee, 1997), 53.

[8] John Steele Gordon, *An Empire of Wealth: The Epic History of American Economic Power* (New York: HarperCollins, 2004), 148–9.

entrepreneurs involved, however, the unification of the telegraph industry did not presage a revolution. Instead, the creation of a national anticompetitive telegraph cartel and then a single unified monopoly were creative acts. Constructing a big business – large not just in terms of invested capital, like the railroads, but a unified anticompetitive venture on a national scale – was an inspired and original attempt to make perilous investments in the telegraph pay off.

The course that telegraph entrepreneurs steered through consolidation, cartel, and ultimately, to national monopoly, was not only fundamentally new, but it was also contrary to the prevailing antimonopoly ideology that opposed any overwhelming power concentrated in private hands as an obstacle to the natural functioning of the economy.[9] The major bugbear for antebellum antimonopolists was the state-granted charter of incorporation for public purposes such as banking and transportation. State legislatures often created such public–private "mixed corporations" with special privileges: subsidies and grants of localized monopoly.[10] Jacksonian Democrats, who came to power with the 1828 presidential election of Tennessean Andrew Jackson, demanded democratized laws of general incorporation to end the practice of creating corporations with special government protections.[11]

Early telegraph entrepreneurs knew these antimonopoly principles well – they frequently employed antimonopoly rhetoric in debates in the press and in Congress, and several of the leading telegraph monopolists were themselves Jacksonian Democrats. They were manufacturers, merchants, and newspaper publishers – there was scarcely a banker or financial adventurer among them, and most of them could fairly be described as "self-made" men. Yet these archetypical antebellum businessmen created an entirely new kind of enterprise – a private, market-driven monopoly cartel – that was contrary to their own philosophy of political economy and a generation before the corporate revolution of the Gilded Age.

Historians such as Alfred Chandler have often seen the problem of telegraph competition as analogous to that of railroad competition. The railroads passed through similar stages of competition, cooperation, and

---

[9] Arthur P. Dudden, "Antimonopolism, 1865–1890: The Historical Background and Intellectual Origins of the Antitrust Movement in the United States" (Dissertation, University of Michigan, 1950), 49.

[10] Daniel Walker Howe, *What Hath God Wrought: The Transformation of America, 1815–1848* (New York: Oxford University Press, 2007), 557–8.

[11] Herbert Hovenkamp, *Enterprise and American Law, 1836–1937* (Cambridge, Mass.: Harvard University Press, 1991), 37–40.

consolidation, though in telegraphy these transitions occurred more than twenty years faster.[12] However, unlike the railroad, the early telegraph had few economies of scale (every single message required two operators and a dedicated line) and demanded relatively little capital. Except for patents – which were usually purchased with stock rather than in bonded debt requiring interest payments – telegraph lines required minimal direct investment. Railroads, the most capital-intensive enterprises of the era, cost more than ten times as much per mile as telegraph lines – roads constructed in New York in the 1850s cost an average of $45,000 per mile, compared to generally much less than $400 per mile for the telegraph.[13] In a telling letter, early telegraph entrepreneur Jeptha Wade estimated that the nominal capital outlay for telegraph lines was *three to six times greater* than the actual price of the material and instruments, making it easy to "forget how remunerative the business is, upon the actual cash cost of the material property." The telegraph appeared to be capital intensive only because companies doled out so much stock to contractors and patent holders and then issued still more stock for mergers, often in princely sums paid for poorly built and redundant lines. Wade concluded that all the nation's "good and well regulated lines" could be replaced with the net profits from a single year of operations.[14]

Minimal capital requirements, an array of contending patents, poorly constructed lines, and managerial incompetence created a telegraphy industry that was fiercely competitive and generally dysfunctional. The challenge facing the telegraph pioneers was how to make order out of this chaos and create a functioning, profitable network in a tempest of entrepreneurial enthusiasm. The solution they discovered, the creation of a single unified system, was anything but novel – there was already a unified national network in the form of the U.S. Post Office. But creating a unified national system in private hands was novel, and moreover, private monopoly made the telegraph *pay*.

The founding story of Western Union, the first national big business, is foremost about entrepreneurs discovering monopoly as a safe harbor from competition, a haven in capitalism's storm of creative destruction. As telegraph entrepreneur Norvin Green put it, why expose the family fortune to "the tossing waves of the great sea of commercial investment"

---

[12] Alfred D. Chandler, *The Visible Hand: The Managerial Revolution in American Business* (Cambridge, Mass.: Belknap Press of Harvard University Press, 1977), 189, 197.
[13] Henry V. Poor, ed., *American Railroad Journal*, vol. 27 (New York: J. H. Schultz, 1854), 124.
[14] Jeptha Wade to Isaac Elwood, 24 January 1861, Sibley Papers (Addition).

when it could be "engulfed in a moment by the great whirlpool of panic"?[15] Monopoly promised to calm the telegraphic storm. The entrepreneurs who built the telegraph monopoly in the 1850s recast their anticompetitive policies as a public good. "Unity" became a stalking horse for anticompetitive cartels and, ultimately, for a single-firm monopoly. Even after interfirm cooperative agreements made possible a consistent, high-volume flow of traffic between urban centers, anticompetitive collusion and consolidations continued. As was often the case in the "Great Merger Movement" of the 1890s, efficiency and quality were secondary to sheltering invested capital from competition.[16] And in its infancy, telegraph stock was a particularly precarious investment – one early investor called it the "meanest property in the world."[17]

In the early decades of the nineteenth century, even without the telegraph, news traveled faster than at any point in history. By the 1850s the post office could carry a letter by road and rail from New York to New Orleans in just five days, a trip that had taken more than two weeks a generation earlier.[18] Visionaries contemplated schemes for even faster communication, with several falling under the rubric of "telegraph." The word "telegraph" was spun out of Greek for "writing at a distance" some forty years before the invention of the electromagnetic telegraph. It first applied to the French "optical telegraph," a network of towers fanning out from Paris that relayed messages by manipulating the towers' massive arms in a visual code. Though limited by fog, darkness, and capacity constraints, the French system was remarkably effective and eventually extended 2,900 miles.[19] Dozens of inventors attempted to improve on the optical telegraph by developing an electromagnetic telegraph that might transmit a greater volume of messages faster, day and night, and – in principle – in all weather.[20]

[15] Norvin Green to Martha Green, 6 March 1859 and 20 March 1859, Green Papers (U.K.).
[16] Naomi R. Lamoreaux, *The Great Merger Movement in American Business, 1895–1904* (New York: Cambridge University Press, 1985), 188.
[17] Norvin Green to Wife, 10 April 1859, Green Papers (U.K.).
[18] Chandler, *The Visible Hand*, 84–5.
[19] Alexander James Field, "French Optical Telegraphy, 1793–1855: Hardware, Software, Administration," *Technology and Culture* 35, April (1994); Richard R. John, *Network Nation: Inventing American Telecommunication* (Cambridge, Mass.: Belknap Press, 2010), 14.
[20] David Hochfelder estimates that there were sixty telegraph inventors working prior to 1840. See David Paul Hochfelder, "Taming the Lightning: American Telegraphy as a

Samuel F. B. Morse, a painter and professor at New York University, began experimenting with a magnetic telegraph of his own design in 1832. Later hailed as the man who wrested electricity from nature and "made it a Missionary in the cause of human progress," Morse was not a passive participant in his rise to global fame.[21] Rather than waiting for history to anoint him the inventor of the telegraph, he seized the mantle and secured it though court decisions and the aggressive campaigning of his supporters and business partners.

Morse envisioned a nationalized telegraph network entirely covered by his patent and unified as an extension of the postal service. To Morse the telegraph was merely "another mode" for "the rapid and regular transmission of intelligence," and thus the government's constitutional authority to transmit the mail extended to the telegraph as well.[22] Congress rejected his proposal in 1838 but five years later awarded Morse $30,000 to build a pilot line between Washington and Baltimore.[23] On May 24, 1844, Morse transmitted the first telegraph message – "What hath God wrought" – from the chamber of the Supreme Court to the Mount Clare depot in Baltimore. Thus the age of electrical communication formally began on lines sponsored by the federal government. The election of 1844 returned the Democrats to the White House and renewed opposition in Congress to federal spending on internal improvements such as a national telegraph system, putting Morse's plans in danger.

However, Morse soon found prominent political allies who believed telegraphy was a federal responsibility.[24] Postmaster General Cave Johnson championed the cause in a report to Congress in 1845.[25]

Revolutionary Technology, 1832–1860" (Case Western Reserve University, 1999), 172. Paul Israel argues that the invention of the telegraph was a collaborative effort, but Morse may be seen as a "team leader." See Paul Israel, *From Machine Shop to Industrial Laboratory: Telegraphy and the Changing Context of American Invention, 1830–1920* (Baltimore: Johns Hopkins University Press, 1992), 37.

[21] Chase is quoted in James D. Reid, *The Telegraph in America: Its Founders, Promoters, and Noted Men*, 1st ed. (New York: Derby Brothers, 1879), 699.

[22] "Electro-Magnetic Telegraphs," Report No. 753, House of Representatives, 25th Congress, 2nd Session, 7.

[23] Benjamin J. Lossing, "Professor Morse and the Telegraph," in *Lightning Flashes and Electric Dashes: A Volume of Choice Telegraphic Literature, Humor, Fun, Wit & Wisdom*, ed. W. J. Johnston (New York: W. J. Johnston, 1877), 24. Lossing related a story that Morse himself promoted that the bill passed in the last five minutes of the session – a dramatic tale contrary to both his own letters and Congressional records. See George P. Oslin, *The Story of Telecommunications* (Macon, Ga.: Mercer University Press, 1992), 21.

[24] Howe, *What Hath God Wrought*, 694.

[25] John, "Private Enterprise, Public Good?" 342–6.

For Johnson the question was not *whether* the government should be involved in telegraphy, but only to *what extent* it should share the task with private enterprise. The telegraph would be a "potent instrument" for speculators who might unjustly "rob the many" and concentrate wealth and power in the clutches of the oligarchs. "The use of an instrument so powerful for good or evil cannot, with safety to the people, be left in the hands of private individuals, uncontrolled by law," Johnson concluded.²⁶ As a Democrat, Johnson's advocacy of a government telegraph was unexpected, but the fears he expressed were widespread. Kentuckian Henry Clay, the perennial Whig presidential candidate and power broker, provided a more politically predictable call for "exclusive" government control of the telegraph, warning that in private hands it might be used "to monopolize intelligence" for speculative purposes.²⁷

Morse's most vigorous advocate was Amos Kendall, his business agent in the sale of his patent. Kendall was a lawyer and newspaper editor who had served as Andrew Jackson's Postmaster General and was a member of Jackson's "kitchen cabinet," a group of informal but influential advisers. Scurrilous rumors alleged that the shadowy Kendall had wielded the power behind Jackson's throne in the days of his political ascendancy, but by 1845 Kendall had fallen on hard times.²⁸ Morse and his telegraph offered a lifeline of sorts. At first Kendall tried to buy Morse's patent himself for $100,000, but since he was nearly broke, he subsequently set his sights instead on securing a buyer with pockets deep enough to both pay a hefty price for the patent and deploy the technology: the federal government.²⁹ Despite Kendall's campaigning, Congress adjourned in March 1845 without acting on Morse's offer to sell his patent for $100,000.

The increasingly poor prospects for a government buyout placed Morse and the partners who shared his patent interest in a quandary.³⁰ Fearing that competing telegraph technology would soon emerge, the patentees quarreled about whether to try again to sell to the government

---

²⁶ Cave Johnson, Appendix to the Congressional Globe, 29th Cong., 1st Session, 22.

²⁷ Clay is quoted in Robert Vincent Remini, *Henry Clay: Statesman for the Union* (New York: W. W. Norton, 1991), 643–4.

²⁸ Donald B. Cole, "Kendall, Amos," in *American National Biography*, ed. John A. Garraty and Mark C. Carnes (New York: Oxford University Press, 1999), 556.

²⁹ Donald B. Cole, *A Jackson Man: Amos Kendall and the Rise of American Democracy* (Baton Rouge: Louisiana State University Press, 2004), 247.

³⁰ Richard John describes Morse's failure to sell the telegraph to the government as the result of "bad luck, technical setbacks, personality conflicts, and a tacit refusal on the part of Congress to increase the patronage that would be at the disposal of the party in power." See Richard John, "Politics of Innovation," 197–8.

or seek private investors instead. Former Maine Congressman Francis O. J. Smith, owner of one-quarter of the Morse patent, adamantly held that the patentees could make four or five times as much through a private sale. The determined and unscrupulous Smith had served on the committee evaluating Morse's request for a federal appropriation while already a secret partner in Morse's venture. Not surprisingly, he had reported favorably on Morse's proposal. Now he chastised Kendall for his democratic pretensions. Kendall assured Smith that he had no "special love for the people" and preferred "to make the most money in the shortest time we can honestly."[31]

Despite public excitement about Morse's invention after the successful demonstration in 1844, investors shied away from the telegraph. Promotional endeavors for the unproven technology were often more spectacle than substance, and it remained to be seen whether there was a market sufficient to make telegraphy profitable. The experimental line between Washington and Baltimore struggled, offering scant promise that revenues would ever exceed expenses.[32] A demonstration line in New York charged twenty-five cents for a look, a carnival approach that another promoter dismissed as "a strange way to enlist capital."[33]

Kendall determined that local investors who sought the utility of the telegraph for their communities might provide the critical capital resources that large investors and the federal government withheld from the unproven technology.[34] Even the railroads, which would one day enlist a flood of European capital, initially depended on daring local investors who saw the railroad as a regional "lever of growth" rather than a surefire bet on its own.[35] However, in Kendall's vision, the telegraph would have an important difference from locally funded early railroads: The Morse patent would unite the entire system in a national network of companies operating as spokes with New York City as the hub.[36] The "one *sine qua non*" of the telegraph was "*the unity of the lines.*"[37] Regional Morse

---

[31] Kendall is quoted in Cole, *A Jackson Man*, 249.
[32] James D. Reid, *The Telegraph in America and Morse Memorial*, 2d ed. (New York: John Polhemus, 1884), 108.
[33] Reid, *Telegraph in America*, 114.
[34] Gerald W. Brock, *The Telecommunications Industry: The Dynamics of Market Structure* (Cambridge, Mass.: Harvard University Press, 1981), 62–3.
[35] Steven W. Usselman, *Regulating Railroad Innovation: Business, Technology, and Politics in America* (New York: Cambridge University Press, 2002), 13.
[36] Robert Luther Thompson, *Wiring a Continent: The History of the Telegraph Industry in the United States, 1832–1866* (Princeton, N.J.: Princeton University Press, 1947), 39.
[37] Kendall is quoted in Cole, *A Jackson Man*, 251.

telegraph companies would cooperate in their common interest, and the Morse patent holders would retain half the capital stock of each company, gluing the whole system together. In 1845 Kendall founded the first such private telegraph firm, the Magnetic Telegraph Company, chartered to build a line between New York and Philadelphia.

The financing of the Magnetic's line set a precedent for telegraph companies' investment structure. Investors received $2 in capital stock for every dollar paid in cash, and the Morse patentees received a share of stock for every share issued to investors. In total, the company issued $60,000 in stock on only $15,000 of invested capital.[38] The scheme's originality proved another challenge for investors. In nineteenth-century securities law, capital stock represented the actual value of an enterprise based on its physical assets and patents, rather than its potential earnings, and one-quarter of the Magnetic's capital had no asset basis at all. Simultaneously the $30,000 in stock granted to the Morse patentees seemed a hefty sum given that the *entire* patent interest had recently been offered for sale at $500,000.[39] "Each man feared to be the first fool," recalled J. D. Reid, an early telegraph promoter and the industry's first historian. In the end, raising $15,000 required more than two dozen subscribers.[40]

By the end of 1845 Kendall had arranged for new companies to build trunk lines between most major cities. The lines went up quickly, but the unity Kendall had hoped for proved elusive. In practice, not even the Magnetic Company itself exhibited much unity – internal squabbles and "jealousies" contributed to problems with promotion, construction, finances, and "scientific ignorance" of Morse's technology.[41] Local investors and ambitious speculators had begun to pour money into regional telegraph companies, but the whole was decidedly less than the sum of its parts. Reid, a pioneer of these first lines, aptly characterized the spate of building as "methodless enthusiasm."[42]

To invest in lines with such uncertain promise required more than a little daring, and the telegraph attracted some colorful personalities. One such character was Henry O'Rielly, an Irish immigrant, Jacksonian Democrat, and newspaper publisher. As Postmaster General, Kendall had

[38] Thompson, *Wiring a Continent*, 41–2.
[39] David L. Dodd, *Stock Watering: The Judicial Valuation of Property for Stock-Issue Purposes* (New York: Columbia University Press, 1930), 10.
[40] Reid, *Telegraph in America*, 115–16.
[41] Thompson, *Wiring a Continent*, 55.
[42] Reid, *The Telegraph in America*, 530.

appointed O'Rielly the postmaster of Rochester in 1837, where O'Rielly proved himself an energetic public servant and a tireless pursuer of mail robbers.[43] In 1845, O'Rielly entered into a vague contract with Kendall and the Morse patentees to build telegraph lines from the termini of the Eastern seaboard lines to all points in the West. Kendall expected him to build a unified Western telegraph company, but the democratically inclined O'Rielly founded several independent companies instead. Reid, who initially served as one of his lieutenants, admired O'Rielly's intelligence and energy, but found he cared more for "personal fame than wealth" and lacked the patience and "veneration for contracts" required of a successful businessman.[44] O'Rielly proved a gifted promoter. As a former publisher, he recognized the potential importance of the telegraph to newspapers – particularly those far afield from Eastern urban centers – and vice versa. He cultivated friendly editors with subsidies and used their pages to attract hundreds of small investors.[45] With these investors' capital, O'Rielly commenced building lines, but soon ran afoul of Morse partner F. O. J. Smith, who had his own plans for Western expansion. Despite the New Yorker's initial successes, Smith convinced Kendall to void O'Rielly's contract and redistribute his valuable territory.[46]

The intrigues over the O'Rielly contracts illustrated the peculiar position Kendall found himself in as the chief promoter of the Morse patent: After a political career as a Jacksonian opponent of state-sponsored monopoly – particularly the monstrous state-granted monopoly of the Bank of the United States – Kendall now became an ardent defender of the patent monopoly the state had granted Morse and his associates.[47] Under the Patent Act of 1836, the Patent Office scrutinized applications for originality, providing a stamp of legitimacy for the patent holder to secure his property rights. This encouraged a market for patents to be

[43] The spelling of Henry O'Rielly's name is a problem. O'Rielly himself used "O'Rielly" during part of his life and several historians have favored this spelling. However, the collections of his papers at the Rochester Historical Society and the New York Historical Society both employ the "O'Reilly" spelling, as did O'Rielly's contemporaries. I have chosen to use "O'Rielly" throughout. Thompson, *Wiring a Continent*, 70–1.

[44] Reid, *The Telegraph in America*, 153.

[45] Menahem Blondheim, *News over the Wires: The Telegraph and the Flow of Public Information in America, 1844–1897* (Cambridge, Mass.: Harvard University Press, 1994), 42–3.

[46] Thompson, *Wiring a Continent*, 76–89.

[47] Brooke Hindle offers an excellent discussion of the contradictions inherent in trying to promote ingenuity by granting patent monopolies in Brooke Hindle, *Emulation and Invention* (New York: W. W. Norton, 1983).

traded, subdivided, and sold to multiple assignees to raise capital for deployment of inventions.[48] However, the validity of a patent could still be challenged in court, and the volume of patent litigation increased steadily throughout the century alongside the number of patents.[49] As Kendall and Morse worked to attract investment and increase deployment of Morse's invention, they also developed a plan to increase the value and security of Morse's patent by expanding the original application and filing for a second patent to cover the Morse receiving magnet.[50] In their broad claims for Morse's invention – Morse later claimed he had invented a "genus" (communication by electric signal) and not merely a "species" (telegraphy) – they designed the reissued Morse patent of 1846 to cover virtually the *entire* process of electromagnetic transmission of intelligence regardless of the device employed.[51]

In 1848, Kendall attempted to secure the Morse patent monopoly by suing O'Rielly for infringement. After Kendall revoked his Morse contract, O'Rielly had continued pursuing his grand plan for a Western network with a modified telegraph that circumvented the Morse patent. Kendall condemned O'Rielly for "piracy."[52] O'Rielly accused the Morse interest of seeking "an exclusive monopoly of the great general principle of Telegraphing by Electricity."[53] Even after the Morse interests defeated him in court, O'Rielly persisted in his operation until U.S. Marshals cut his lines and seized his property.[54]

O'Rielly was not the only entrepreneur in pursuit of an alternative to Morse's patent. By 1848 two significant new telegraph systems challenged the Morse monopoly. Scottish scientist Alexander Bain's telegraph employed clockwork and a metal stylus to mark a paper ribbon treated with potassium prussiate, leaving blue marks that could be translated

---

[48] Naomi R. Lamoreaux, "Did Insecure Property Rights Slow Economic Development? Some Lessons from Economic History," *The Journal of Policy History* 18, no. 1 (2006): 158; B. Zorina Khan, *The Democratization of Invention: Patents and Copyrights in American Economic Development, 1790–1920* (New York: Cambridge University Press, 2005), 60–1.

[49] Lawrence M. Friedman, *A History of American Law*, 2d ed. (New York: Simon & Schuster, 1985), 435.

[50] Cole, *A Jackson Man*, 254.

[51] Hochfelder, "Taming the Lightning," 173–5, 80–1.

[52] Amos Kendall, *Morse's Patent: Full Exposure of Dr. Chas. T. Jackson's Pretentions to the Invention of the American Electro-Magnetic Telegraph* (Washington: J. T. Towers, 1852), 16.

[53] Henry O'Reilly, "Letter of Henry O'Reilly to Professor Morse, concerning the attempted, Telegraph Monopoly, &c." 14 April 1848, Henry O'Reilly Papers (RHS).

[54] Hochfelder, "Taming the Lightning," 202.

into alphanumeric characters. Bain's telegraph was faster than Morse's, but it had several significant drawbacks, including torment for the operators who inhaled chemical fumes while straining to read the ribbon's tiny spiral markings.[55] Because the Morse system similarly used a tape and simple code markings – the more efficient method of receiving code by sound was not part of Morse's original design – the Bain telegraph provided an easy target for an infringement suit. In 1851 Morse and Kendall's Magnetic Company successfully sued a prosperous Bain line between New York and Washington. Within a year, the Morse patentees absorbed nearly all the rival Bain lines between several major cities.

Another competing system, the House printing telegraph, proved a hardier opponent. In 1848 Royal E. House of Vermont patented a telegraph that could print twenty-six Roman characters, eliminating the need for translating code. The House telegraph employed two synchronized sending and receiving mechanisms. The operator typed a message into a keyboard producing printed messages at much greater speeds than the Morse telegraph. The House telegraph transmitted messages electromagnetically, but it used compressed air to print them, a crucial difference from the Morse patent. The House telegraph had several shortcomings – it was ineffective over long distances, and if the transmitter and receiver were even slightly out of sync, the message became garbled.[56] But such limitations were not enough to dissuade Morse's competitors. When Morse and his partners sued the first successful House line, the court ruled that the House telegraph did not infringe upon the Morse patent.[57] Now the Morse monopoly faced its first real competitors, one of whom would found the company that would devour them all.

In April 1851, a Rochester entrepreneur named Hiram Sibley inspired a group of local businessmen to form a House telegraph company, the New York & Mississippi Valley Printing Telegraph Company. Sibley, the Democratic sheriff of Monroe County, had built a prosperous manufacturing establishment with a sawmill, a foundry, and a factory for wool carding accompanied by "Sibleyville," an employee village.[58] Even a person

---

[55] Thompson, *Wiring a Continent*, 156–7.
[56] For technical discussion of the House printing method, see George B. Prescott, *Electricity and the Electric Telegraph*, Eighth ed., 2 vols., vol. 2 (New York: D. Appleton and Company, 1892), 605–9.
[57] For discussion of the House court case, see Hochfelder, "Taming the Lightning," 207–16.
[58] William F. Peck, *History of Rochester and Monroe County*, 2 vols., vol. 1 (New York: Pioneer Publishing Company, 1908), 716.

with ambitions as grand as Sibley's could not have imagined that the New York & Mississippi Valley would one day grow into Western Union, but Sibley later claimed that from the very beginning he at least recognized the telegraph as "priceless to civilization – the stupendous discovery of the age."[59] Like Morse and Kendall, Sibley backed the New York & Mississippi Valley with a little cash and a lot of stock. The company had a nominal capital of $360,000, but the thirteen founders contributed only $83,000 in cash to the scheme.[60] They assigned the remaining stock to the contractors who would build the lines and the House patent holders, creating a crucial divide between the "cash men" and the "patentees" commonly found in early telegraph companies. The company planned to stretch a line from Buffalo to St. Louis, running along the shore of Lake Erie to Cleveland and then southwest via Columbus, Cincinnati, and Louisville. But this proved too ambitious for the poorly capitalized firm. By the end of 1853 the New York & Mississippi Valley ran no further west than Louisville and operated only a single wire – at a loss.[61]

Two things may justly be said about the early telegraph industry – the era of methodless enthusiasm: first, the prospects for this world-changing device were boundless, at least in the minds of those who promoted it, and second, the telegraph was as functionally limited in practice as it was grand in potential. Under the right conditions across a short distance between two fixed points, the telegraph worked well enough. But its true promise required it to function over long distances and in a cohesive network, which the hodgepodge of firms operating with only minimal cooperation and competing incompatible systems could scarcely deliver. "Never was an enterprise of equal extent conducted in a looser manner," complained one of the industry's first trade publications.[62] The lack of cooperation led to clumsiness in passing messages between the various regional firms, which clung tenaciously to what an industry insider generously called "the independence and local pride of small organizations."

[59] Jane Marsh Parker, "How the Men of Rochester Saved the Telegraph," in *The Rochester Historical Society Publication Fund Series*, ed. Edward R. Foreman (Rochester: Rochester Historical Society, 1926), 122–3; Hiram Sibley, "Memories of Hiram Sibley," in *Publication Fund Series*, ed. Edward R. Foreman (Rochester, N.Y.: The Rochester Historical Society, 1923), 127.
[60] Reid, *The Telegraph in America*, 465.
[61] Thompson, *Wiring a Continent*, 269.
[62] "National Telegraph Convention at Washington, in March," *American Telegraph Magazine*, January 1853, 152.

Many companies simply refused to take responsibility for sending messages beyond their lines, and even within each company errors in transmission were common.[63] Sloppy construction and insufficiently insulated wires compounded unreliable service. Poor weather interfered with telegraph signals and storms and falling trees severed lines altogether.[64] Understandably, public confidence in the telegraph was low.[65] Frustrated customers refused to pay for delayed dispatches. A telegraph manager complained in 1854 that money spent on the telegraph "was considered worse than thrown away."[66]

The shortcomings of the telegraph were in stark contrast to recent improvements in mail service. Americans came to expect such consistency and celerity from the postal mail that most of the expressions of praise for the telegraph – such as the "annihilation of time and space" – had already been used to describe the postal system.[67] Thanks to substantial price reductions in the Post Office Acts of 1845 and 1851 and improvements in speed via steamboats and railroads, the mail presented an attractive alternative to the finicky, expensive telegraph. Ideally a telegram could beat a letter from Richmond to Boston, New York, and Philadelphia by four, three, and two days respectively – but not consistently.[68] A telegram from Boston to Chicago, for example, might be copied and handed off between different regional companies at New York, Buffalo, and Detroit with delays at each step, and a response might not arrive until the second or third day.[69] Even when messages were not delayed, their cost remained a problem. In 1852 a ten-word telegram from Washington to New York cost $0.50, to Chicago $1.25, and to New Orleans $2.20.[70] Alternatively, a letter of great length and detail could travel to any point in the United States for a mere three cents per half ounce.[71]

Not surprisingly, few Americans chose to use the telegraph. Henry David Thoreau criticized the demand for fast communication, writing in *Walden*, "We are in great haste to construct a magnetic telegraph from

---

[63] Reid, *The Telegraph in America*, 427.
[64] Hochfelder, "Taming the Lightning," 276–7.
[65] S. A. Strong to Ezra Cornell, 1 August 1853, Cornell Papers.
[66] J. Murray to Ezra Cornell, 13 September 1854, Cornell Papers.
[67] Richard R. John, *Spreading the News: The American Postal System from Franklin to Morse* (Cambridge, Mass.: Harvard University Press, 1995), 10–11.
[68] Du Boff, "The Telegraph and the Structure of Markets," 263.
[69] E. B. Grant, *The Western Union Company: Its Past, Present and Future* (New York: Hotchkiss, Burnham, 1883), 4.
[70] Thompson, *Wiring a Continent*, 245.
[71] John, *Spreading the News*, 160.

Maine to Texas; but Maine and Texas, it may be, have nothing important to communicate."[72] Though Thoreau's quip referred primarily to sectional politics, most Mainers and Texans probably *didn't* have much to communicate that was worthy of the telegraph price premium. Though in 1860 telegraph lines carried five million messages, or one for every six people, it was not until 1880 that the annual total of telegraph messages equaled the number of letters sent through the post office in 1840.[73] For the press, businessmen and speculators, the telegraph offered an indispensable competitive advantage over the mail, but for most Americans lightning messages were impractical.[74]

For telegraph entrepreneurs, the practical limitations of the telegraph were less vexing than the lack of profits. Some twenty-three thousand miles of wire zigzagged the American landscape by 1852, and total mileage more than doubled by 1860.[75] But as one line builder contended in 1852, though the telegraph had attracted enough investment to connect "almost every town and village in the United States," in aggregate the lines had "paid comparatively nothing."[76] At least thirty telegraph firms had been launched by 1855, but only two or three were even self-sustaining.[77] The profusion of competing, incompatible lines was at least partially to blame. Kendall's Magnetic Company, for example, reportedly earned a 20 percent profit between Washington and New York in 1848. But by 1851, rival lines competing in parallel erased this margin.[78]

---

[72] Henry David Thoreau, *Walden* (New York: Thomas Y. Crowell & Co., 1910), 67.
[73] Du Boff, "The Telegraph and the Structure of Markets," 256; Richard R. John, "Recasting the Information Infrastructure for the Industrial Age," in *A Nation Transformed by Information: How Information Has Shaped the United States from Colonial Times to the Present*, ed. Alfred D. Chandler and James W. Cortada (New York: Oxford University Press, 2000), 80.
[74] Richard John has noted that there has been little systematic study of how the telegraph changed American business, and there is similarly little published work quantifying the telegraph's economic impact. Notable exceptions include articles by Richard DuBoff and Alexander Field. Richard R. John, "Elaborations, Revisions, Dissents: Alfred D. Chandler, Jr.'s the Visible Hand after Twenty Years," *Business History Review* 71, no. 2 (1997): 186; Du Boff, "The Telegraph and the Structure of Markets"; Alexander James Field, "The Magnetic Telegraph, Price and Quantity Data, and the New Management of Capital," *The Journal of Economic History* 52, no. 2 (1992): 404.
[75] Cole, *A Jackson Man*, 262; Du Boff, "The Telegraph and the Structure of Markets," 256.
[76] Sanford J. Smith to Hiram Sibley and Isaac R. Elwood, 17 November 1852, Sibley Papers (Addition).
[77] Grant, *The Western Union Company: Its Past, Present and Future*, 4.
[78] Alvin F. Harlow, *Old Wires and New Waves: The History of the Telegraph, Telephone, and Wireless* (New York: D. Appleton-Century Company, 1936), 244.

Investors and managers often identified the lack of cooperation between firms as the root cause of telegraph losses. The "large fortunes and profits" the telegraph had been expected to produce had been undermined – in the words of one investor – by the companies "*constantly quarreling with each other*, instead of amicably combining to work for the mutual interest of all."[79] Calling the problem a lack of "amicable" combination understated the ferocity of competition. One entrepreneur described the industry's progress as a "history of wars." Indeed "war" was a metaphor often invoked by telegraphers, and the spirit of the industry encouraged – some even might say demanded – pugnacity.[80] A prominent backer of the New York & Mississippi Valley advised Hiram Sibley that the "Telegraph business" required "the most stringent and active meanness."[81] Norvin Green, a Kentucky investor in the successful Southwestern Telegraph Company, promised his wife that he would sell his telegraph investment and buy land rather than remain in such a bloody fight. "Telegraph stock is the meanest property in the world," he explained, adding that its "uncertainty and dependence upon trickery and chance" made it as risky an investment as "stock in a faro bank."[82] Even Kendall, who sowed more than his share of discord, sounded a note of regret when he admitted, "These quarrels kill the telegraph."[83]

Even *within* firms cooperation was often lacking, as the divided investment structure pioneered by Morse and Kendall led to competing interests between the two major shareholder groups, the cash men and the patentees. At the New York & Mississippi Valley Printing Telegraph, the House patentees stubbornly insisted that the superior House technology would inevitably dominate American telegraphy and discouraged cooperation with firms using competing methods. But the "cash men" who had paid for the company's lines advocated any profitable connection with another company – even those employing a rival patent. To their cash backers, the patent holders' claims were prejudice at the expense of profit. One investor complained that the elegance of the House telegraph's

[79] Cambridge Livingston to Ezra Cornell, 20 September 1854, Cornell Papers. Emphasis in the original.
[80] Ezra Cornell to Mary Ann Cornell, 24 April 1853, Cornell Papers.
[81] R. W. Russell to Hiram Sibley, 17 June 1854, Sibley Papers (Addition). Which definition of "meanness" Russell intended cannot be known for sure, but it would certainly be in his character to suggest vicious and aggressive behavior, rather than an unwillingness to share.
[82] Norvin Green to Wife, 10 April 1859, Green Papers (U.K.).
[83] Amos Kendall to Ezra Cornell, 24 March 1854, Cornell Papers.

transmissions in plain English instead of code meant little to the public, which did not care if messages went "through in characters, Hebrew, German or English" as long as they went quickly.[84] The cash men insisted that survival of the House lines required some "treaty of peace" with the Morse lines – particularly after Kendall's legal assault on the Bain patent wiped out the Bain companies – a position the patentees could not accept.[85] The result was disaster. The two factions' strategic deadlock and the ensuing paralysis threatened to drive the New York & Mississippi Valley into bankruptcy in 1853.[86] The company's managers were lucky to receive even partial payment of their salaries, and many outside investors believed they were "doomed to ruin."[87] They were "whistling around what seemed the grave-yard of buried hopes," Reid recalled.[88]

When New York & Mississippi Valley founder Hiram Sibley considered the grim state of telegraphic affairs in the 1850s, he saw opportunity rather than ruin. Where other backers panicked as their ventures failed, Sibley increased his stake. Rather than continue the quarrel with his patent holders, he capitalized on the deadlock and loss of investor confidence at his own firm by purchasing all the outstanding rights to the House patent at discount. But Sibley, like the strict cash men, had no allegiance to the House system, or any system. He sought to control not only the House lines in the Great Lakes region, but *all* the telegraph lines. He would create a profitable telegraph company by amalgamating the failures. It was a bold plan and perhaps a reckless one. Even his allies referred to it as "Sibley's crazy scheme."[89]

In 1853 and 1854 Sibley pursued this "crazy scheme" for a regional monopoly with characteristic verve. But for his plan to work he needed a fresh infusion of cash for the Mississippi Valley Printing Telegraph; after buying out the House patent holders Sibley was "all in" and mortgaged to boot. Never one to shy from promotion, he called his Rochester

---

[84] Sanford J. Smith to Hiram Sibley and Isaac R. Elwood, 17 November 1852, Sibley Papers (Addition).

[85] The House party even sought to retain a patent attorney who was regarded as particularly dangerous to keep him from working on behalf of the Morse patent. See Cambridge Livingston to Hiram Sibley, 4 June 1852, Sibley Papers (Addition).

[86] Isaac Butts to Hiram Sibley, 9 January 1852, Sibley Papers (Addition); Cambridge Livingston to Hiram Sibley, 4 April 1853, Sibley Papers (Addition).

[87] Cambridge Livingston to Hiram Sibley, 23 April 1853, Sibley Papers (Addition).

[88] Reid, *The Telegraph in America*, 471.

[89] Parker, "How the Men of Rochester Saved the Telegraph," 128; Reid, *The Telegraph in America*, 464.

business associates to his office to sway them to back the scheme for regional consolidation, but even Sibley could not hide the telegraph's abysmal record as an investment. One skeptic likened the consolidation of failing telegraph companies to collecting all the county's paupers into one organization in the absurd hope that it would "insure their success and make them men of fortune."[90] Another associate agreed to buy a $5,000 share on condition of anonymity, so as not to tarnish his reputation with a foolish deal. But Sibley's enthusiasm proved convincing, or at least compelling, enough. He raised an additional $90,000 for the New York & Mississippi Valley Telegraph, bringing the total cash invested in the venture to $170,000.[91] In January 1854 the company reorganized under control of the cash men.[92]

With his new capital Sibley went to work buying lines west of Buffalo. According to telegraph lore, he wandered the region on "line forages" with a bag full of money, snapping up failing lines for pennies on the dollar.[93] Whenever possible he paid for lines with stock instead of his newly acquired cash, a strategy that yielded growth at little cost. In one such case, $50,000 in freshly minted stock certificates bought six hundred miles of line without a penny paid in cash.[94]

Another method of building lines without direct monetary investment exploited the cooperation of the railroads. Though telegraph lines would eventually become a commonplace on American railroads, railroad and telegraph companies were reluctant partners in the 1850s. Railroad managers preferred "time and rule-based protocols" to dispatch their trains. The telegraph was considered unreliable for signaling and hazardous to trains and tracks. However, as the railroads grew more extensive, managers warmed to the value of running telegraphs along their routes, though they lacked the patents and technical expertise to operate lines of their own.[95] Telegraph entrepreneurs, mindful of the opportunity, stepped in

---

[90] "Telegraph History," *New York Evening Post*, 27 February 1885. The quotes may not be strictly reliable, but they address valid themes. This article was quoted first by Robert Luther Thompson. Substantial details are confirmed by J. D. Reid. There is also evidence for Sibley's fundraising effort in letters stating opposition to it. See Robert W. Russell to Hiram Sibley, 20 March 1854, Sibley Papers (Addition).

[91] This brought the total to 29 investors. Sibley himself was the third-largest shareholder, behind Isaac Elwood and H. S. Potter, both of Rochester. For a full list of shareholders, see Thompson, *Wiring a Continent*, 271.

[92] Reid, *The Telegraph in America*, 465

[93] Parker, "How the Men of Rochester Saved the Telegraph," 131.

[94] Reid, *The Telegraph in America*, 467.

[95] Benjamin Sidney Michael Schwantes, "Fallible Guardian: The Social Construction of Railroad Telegraphy in 19th-Century America" (University of Delaware, 2008), 10–12.

to fill the gap. Ohioans Jeptha Wade and his partner John J. Speed signed agreements with new railroads west of the Great Lakes, securing nearly two thousand miles in railroad contracts in 1853 alone.[96] Anson Stager, a Sibley deputy, took his cue from Wade and negotiated with three railroads to establish telegraph connections to Detroit and Chicago. The contracts were "highly favorable" to the telegraph company, particularly an exclusive clause that barred rival telegraphs from building along the road.[97] The railroad companies constructed the lines according to precise specifications and then turned them over to the telegraph company in exchange for free telegraph service and $125 per mile in telegraph stock.

The success of this railroad strategy was most evident in the Erie & Michigan Telegraph Company, a line controlled by Speed, Wade, and Ezra Cornell. The Erie & Michigan controlled the Morse patent in the region west of the New York & Mississippi Valley Telegraph's lines and had locked up exclusive railroad connections, creating a formidable obstacle to Sibley's ambition to monopolize Northwestern telegraphy.[98] But the Erie & Michigan also presented a dilemma. The Morse patent would expire in 1854 unless Congress granted an extension. If Sibley bought out the Erie & Michigan and the Morse patent expired, new patent-free competitors would enter the market and destroy Sibley's hard-earned monopoly. But if Sibley could not combine with the Erie & Michigan and the Morse patent were renewed, the superior Erie & Michigan would block the New York & Mississippi Valley from using the House patent on railroads to the west.[99] Even mounting a *successful* competing line would likely have been more expensive than buying the Erie & Michigan outright, but Sibley's new associates balked at the high asking price.[100]

Fortunately for Sibley, the personal enmity so common among partners in the telegraph industry worked in his favor at Erie & Michigan Telegraph. Wade and Speed, it turned out, were eager to end their association with Cornell, whose "strong convictions" and "pertinacity" made him a stubborn and disagreeable partner.[101] Indeed Cornell was combative even beyond telegraph industry norms, vowing in one letter that the Erie & Michigan would blow "the House army" to "atoms."[102]

[96] Anson Stager to Hiram Sibley, 28 August 1853, Sibley Papers (Addition).
[97] Thompson, *Wiring a Continent*, 275.
[98] Anson Stager to Hiram Sibley, 1 January 1854, Sibley Papers (Addition).
[99] Robert W. Russell to Hiram Sibley, 19 February 1854, Sibley Papers (Addition).
[100] Anson Stager to Hiram Sibley, 9 April 1854, Sibley Papers (Addition).
[101] Reid, *The Telegraph in America*, 299.
[102] Ezra Cornell to J. J. Speed, 8 July 1852, Cornell Papers.

His self-righteousness and parsimony infuriated Wade, who sarcastically praised Cornell for being "the only *infallible* Telegrapher living." Cornell's notion of "economy" led him to abandon his administrative duties to travel miles "on foot, alone, knee deep in mud" carrying a twenty-four-foot ladder "when some *foolish, extravagant* Presidents would have paid an Irishman $12 a month for doing the same thing."[103]

By the time Sibley finally convinced his partners to buy or break the Erie & Michigan, Wade and Speed were ready to sell out Cornell. When Wade happened upon the New York & Mississippi Valley's Anson Stager at an "eating counter" in Ohio, a deal was quick to follow. Over pork and beans, the two men admitted to each other the dire circumstances of their respective firms, and Wade agreed to travel to Rochester to sell his stake in the Erie & Michigan.[104] For $50,000 in new stock, the New York & Mississippi Valley Company took control of the Morse patent rights for much of the country west of Buffalo and in effect brought Wade and Speed's lines into the fold in mid-1854. Cornell raged against his partners' treachery, condemning the perfidious Wade as an "arch Traitor" and "modern Judas."[105] An associate of Sibley explained the plot to Cornell in the simplest terms: "Our object is to make money," he wrote, and Cornell would profit if he cooperated.[106]

The New York & Mississippi Valley issued a public circular celebrating the union as the end to the "great confusion and imperfection" the competing patent interests had created in the West. No more would public business be "badly done" and the stockholders "poorly paid." Consolidation would bring "harmony."[107] Cornell, however, insisted his patent rights had been stolen and vowed to fight on.[108] For several months, he operated a piece of the former Wade–Speed–Cornell combination under pressure from "the venom" of his "open enemies and false friends."[109] Despite

---

[103] Jeptha Wade to Ezra Cornell, 27 November 1853, Cornell Papers. Wade took so much pride in his clever harangue that he forwarded a copy to Kendall, who shared it with Morse and reported that he and "the Professor" had "a hearty laugh over the hard but very genteel wits" that Wade dished out. Amos Kendall to J. H. Wade, 30 March 1854, Wade Papers.

[104] Reid, *The Telegraph in America*, 471.

[105] Ezra Cornell to Lucien Barbour, 8 May 1854, Cornell Papers; Ezra Cornell to Mary Ann Cornell, 1 June 1854, Cornell Papers.

[106] Cambridge Livingston to Ezra Cornell, 12 May 1854, Cornell Papers.

[107] "Telegraph Consolidation, Union of House, Morse, Speed and Wade Lines," Circular, 1854, Wade Papers.

[108] Ezra Cornell, Circular, 22 June 1854, Caton Papers.

[109] Ezra Cornell to Mary Ann Cornell, 8 September 1854, Cornell Papers.

warnings from his managers that his line was sinking fast, Cornell contended that he could "stand a siege" and the House interest would have "to mount 'bigger guns.'"[110] But the "guns" arrayed against him proved big enough; Cornell's opponents cut off his business and, Cornell claimed, bribed his employees to shirk their duties or abandon their posts.[111] After Sibley announced the "Union Telegraph Consolidation of House, Morse, O'Rielly and Wade Lines," a Cornell manager complained, "Folks begin to think there are no other lines left."[112]

Cornell finally surrendered in the fall of 1855. For his doggedness he was rewarded with $150,000 in newly created New York & Mississippi Valley stock – almost a third of the company's total capital. Cornell's acquiescence gave Sibley's Rochester party undisputed exclusive rights to the Morse patent in most of the territory north and west of the Ohio River.[113] The name "New York & Mississippi Valley *Printing Telegraph* Company" was no longer adequate. With rights to the Morse patent the firm could abandon the House printing telegraph, which was less reliable over long distances and slower than the new Morse technique of receiving messages by sound.[114] Cornell also deemed "New York & Mississippi Valley" an insufficient moniker for the consolidated company. He urged the adoption of the name "Western Union," which he had used in his former combination with Speed and Wade.[115] On April 4, 1856, the state legislature of New York approved the new name, and the Western Union Telegraph Company was born.[116]

The creation of Western Union marked a sea-change in the history of the American telegraph as the erratic building and cutthroat competition

---

[110] Ezra Cornell to Frank Cornell, 31 January 1855, Ezra Cornell Papers.
[111] Ezra Cornell to J. D. Caton, 1 November 1854, Caton Papers; Ezra Cornell to J. D. Caton, 16 November 1854, Caton Papers. Amos Kendall apparently affirmed that such tricks had been used against Cornell. Kendall to Ezra Cornell, 15 December 1854, Cornell Papers.
[112] N. A. Breach to Ezra Cornell, 30 March 1855, Cornell Papers.
[113] Thompson, *Wiring a Continent*, 284. The territory included Ohio, Indiana, Illinois, Michigan, Wisconsin, Iowa, and Minnesota.
[114] Hochfelder, *Taming the Lightning*, 240.
[115] He must have had a particular fondness for the name, because he insisted on it over Speed's objection that even though "*Union*" was a "very good word," it had been "most awfully abused" and now had "about as much meaning to it as 'Democracy' when applied to the Loco Foco party." Ezra Cornell to John J. Speed, 8 July 1852, Cornell Papers; J. J. Speed to Ezra Cornell, 28 July 1852, Cornell Papers.
[116] "An Act to change the name of the New York and Mississippi Valley Printing Telegraph Company," 4 April 1856, Caton Papers.

of "methodless enthusiasm" gave way to an era of tense cooperation.[117] In later years, Western Union officials often described how disunity and "ruinous competition" caused unnecessary delays, forced up costs, and "threatened to destroy the telegraphic property of the whole country," a self-serving narrative intended to deflect criticism from the telegraph monopoly that nonetheless contained a grain of truth about the short-comings of a divided system.[118] To provide fast, long-distance communi-cation, regional firms had to be able to exchange messages without delays or additional charges, and that required combination, a path eventually followed by the railroads.[119]

In 1853, Amos Kendall created the American Telegraph Confederation, inviting representatives of the major Morse lines – but not the competing House lines – to convene in Washington. The delegates forged policies for routing messages between companies, established an executive commit-tee, and appointed a secretary and purchasing agent.[120] The Confederation was intended to "promote the welfare" of the industry, but its nonbinding resolutions had no power over the management of its members. In prac-tice, the Confederation proved too weak even to enforce cooperation, and its exclusion of the non-Morse telegraph companies proved a major mistake.[121]

When Kendall's attempt at cooperation met with little success, a few substantial stakeholders in the telegraph industry cautiously advanced grander visions of consolidation instead. Consolidation promised not just to realize the telegraph's potential in an organized network, but as Sibley had realized, to make telegraph investments *pay* by eliminating compe-tition. Better service and an integrated national network were second-ary to ending costly rivalries. Whatever their ideological preference for free enterprise might have been, telegraph investors developed a taste for monopoly.

Jeptha Wade exhibited this thinking in 1852 when he merged his company with Ezra Cornell's. Wade publicly informed shareholders that consolidation would lead to "business being better done, with less delay, fewer mistakes, and at less than half the expense," thus doubling or tri-pling the public appetite for telegraphy.[122] But when he privately wooed

[117] Thompson, *Wiring a Continent*, 259.
[118] Grant, *The Western Union Company: Its Past, Present and Future*, 4.
[119] Chandler, *The Visible Hand*, 134–7.
[120] Reid, *The Telegraph in America*, 429.
[121] Thompson, *Wiring a Continent*, 260–4.
[122] Jeptha Wade, "Proceedings of the Third Annual Meeting of the Stockholders of the Cleveland and Cincinnati Telegraph Company," 28 June 1852, Wade Papers.

Cornell, Wade emphasized the *profitability* of a unified system that would force competitors to join or perish. "It's perfectly clear to me that consolidation is the only way to make anything, and put ourselves on an independent basis," he wrote to Cornell. With consolidation, Wade predicted, *"we are all rich."* [123]

No one believed more strongly in building a telegraph enterprise by merging with competitors than Hiram Sibley. By 1854, Sibley already looked beyond the parochial interests of the Morse and House patentees and proposed to the American Telegraph Confederation's secretary Tal Shaffner a general peace through consolidation. Shaffner agreed that the resulting yields would be "a balm in Gilead" for profit-starved telegraph investors. [124] Robert Russell, an English telegraph backer based in New York City, encouraged Sibley to pursue a *total* consolidation of the telegraph. Russell feared that new telegraph technologies could render both the House and Morse patents worthless in much the same way the House telegraph had undermined the original Morse monopoly. Russell proposed "a strong combination," a cartel that would purchase and monopolize every new telegraph patent – what would later be called a patent pool. I. M. Singer & Co. created such a patent pool for sewing machines in 1856 and railroad patent associations emerged in the 1870s, but Russell was ahead of the trend. [125] He warned Sibley that "consolidation alone" would save their property from a "shipwreck." [126] In Russell's view the rationale for telegraph consolidation could not be any simpler: "A great monopoly of the Telegraph business will pay well." [127]

Effecting such a consolidation, however, would not be easy. Russell believed that cooperation, not conquest, was the answer. He proposed offering generous terms to rivals and abandoning the "erroneous" policy of trying to "beat down" the opposition. [128] Russell suggested creating a trusteeship to control the entire telegraph industry. A neutral party would negotiate the "surrender" of both the House and Morse interests, which would lease their entire properties to the new trustees. In this way, they could be rid of the "old fogies" Morse and Kendall and at last solve "the great Telegraph problem" with a monopoly. Yet to compensate

---

[123] Jeptha Wade to Ezra Cornell, 22 July 1852, Cornell Papers. Emphasis is in the original.

[124] Taliaferro P. Shaffner to Hiram Sibley, 31 January 1854, Sibley Papers (Addition).

[125] Ruth Brandon, *A Capitalist Romance: Singer and the Sewing Machine* (Philadelphia: J. B. Lippincott Company, 1977), 98–9; Usselman, *Regulating Railroad Innovation*.

[126] Robert W. Russell to Hiram Sibley, 9 June 1854, Sibley Papers (Addition).

[127] Robert W. Russell to Hiram Sibley, 14 June 1854, Sibley Papers (Addition).

[128] Russell to Sibley, 19 June 1854, Sibley Papers (Addition).

shareholders for all their telegraph stock, the trustees of such a lease would require substantially greater wealth than most of the principal telegraph investors commanded. Russell believed the scheme demanded the backing of New York City "Capitalists." If the "Capitalists" took over the telegraph, they would end wasteful competition, lawsuits, and interminable quarrels once and for all.[129]

Though he may have been a visionary, Russell was no diplomat. His associates and rivals alike described him as uncouth, obnoxious, and duplicitous. One colleague deemed him "more dangerous as a friend than as an enemy," and a foe routinely described him as a crook and a "dishonest 'Old English Hog.'"[130] However, a more substantial obstacle to Russell's plan was the demand from Sibley and his associates for a handsome rate of profit to lease their lines. Russell dismissed such demands as localism and arrogant "folly." He scolded Sibley that Rochester would never be the center of the nation's telegraph interests. "Redemption" for the industry would only come through a grand consolidation in New York.[131]

In July 1855, representatives from the major telegraph companies, both Morse and House, gathered in New York City to discuss cooperation and consolidation. Competing agendas, personal rancor, and mutual distrust undermined the negotiations from the start. Russell believed his plan for a consolidated trusteeship would advance with the aid of Cyrus Field, the conference chair, whom Russell had commissioned to discreetly investigate at what price Morse and Kendall would surrender their telegraph interests.[132] Though Field was only thirty-six years old, he had already made a fortune in the paper and printing supply business and had only recently turned his entrepreneurial zeal to the telegraph. Russell may have been willing to trust him because Field had set his sights well beyond the domestic market on a telegraph cable that would span the Atlantic Ocean.

Field's cable project faced formidable challenges. In the early 1850s, underwater telegraphy was still in its technological infancy. Field had no prior experience operating a telegraph company, but he and his partners

[129] Robert W. Russell to Hiram Sibley, 4 August 1854, Sibley Papers (Addition); Robert W. Russell to Hiram Sibley, 26 December 1854, Sibley Papers (Addition); Robert W. Russell to Hiram Sibley, 6 January 1855, Sibley Papers (Addition).

[130] Jeptha H. Wade to Hiram Sibley, 13 June 1856, Wade Papers; Daniel H. Craig to Hiram Sibley, 28 May 1855, Sibley Papers (Addition).

[131] Robert W. Russell to Hiram Sibley, 30 April 1855, Sibley Papers (Addition).

[132] Robert W. Russell to Hiram Sibley, 28 July 1855, Sibley Papers (Addition).

had something many of the early telegraph entrepreneurs did not: large sums of capital. Field's principal collaborator was his Gramercy Park neighbor Peter Cooper, a prosperous and eminent inventor and the era's "quintessential industrialist."[133] Field and Cooper were joined by a group of wealthy merchants who had lately moved their fortunes into banking and transportation.[134]

The first step in the cable project was to build a line to Newfoundland, where the cable would eventually make landfall. In 1854, Field and Cooper launched the Newfoundland & London Electric Telegraph Company to connect St. Johns, at the island's far-eastern tip, to the United States. This first link in the transatlantic chain carried news from ships arriving at St. Johns to New York – cutting forty-eight hours off the information transit time from Europe. But news from Newfoundland had to pass through a bottleneck of overpriced, poor quality lines belonging to New England telegraph companies with exclusive patent rights.[135] To guarantee the rapid dissemination of European market news to American business centers, Field hoped to lease the property and patents of the New England telegraph companies and later add trunk lines to Buffalo, Washington, and New Orleans. Morse himself blessed the project and encouraged the Northeastern companies to enter into a general agreement with Field when they gathered in New York .[136]

But at the conference Field's ambition for a Northeastern combination and new lines to the South and West collided with the plans of the other telegraph entrepreneurs. In New England, the Morse patent rights belonged to Morse and Kendall's erstwhile partner, the notoriously greedy F. O. J. Smith, who would not concede to any but the most generous terms. Field's plan for a New York to Buffalo trunk line required the cooperation of either the New York, Albany & Buffalo – a Morse company – or the New York State Printing Telegraph – a House company controlled

---

[133] Sven Beckert, *The Monied Metropolis: New York City and the Consolidation of the American Bourgeoisie, 1850–1896* (New York: Cambridge University Press, 1993), 249.

[134] These included Wilson G. Hunt, a successful cloth merchant, Marshall O. Roberts, who made a fortune in naval supplies and had recently taken command of a steamship company, and Moses Taylor, a sugar merchant who had become the city's leading investment banker. Thomas Kessner, *Capital City: New York City and the Men Behind America's Rise to Economic Dominance, 1860–1900* (New York: Simon & Schuster, 2003), 19–20; Reid, *Telegraph in America*, 401.

[135] Thompson, *Wiring a Continent*, 301–2.

[136] Peter Cooper to Samuel F. B. Morse, 10 March 1857, Morse Papers; Robert W. Russell to Hiram Sibley, 28 July 1855, Sibley Papers (Addition).

by Sibley's Rochester party. Sibley rejected Field's terms and demanded a ransom for his Buffalo line.[137] A Field ally pleaded with Sibley to be "just" and not play the *"trickster,"*[138] but Sibley had other plans for the meeting. He abandoned Field's proposition and leased his Buffalo line at a higher price to a competitor, the New York, Albany & Buffalo, giving Western Union and its new partner a monopoly on both the Morse and House patents from New York City to Buffalo and across the Great Lakes region. After weeks of negotiations and machinations, the conference ended in failure. Field and Cooper withdrew their offers to lease the New England lines.[139] Sibley's Western New York monopoly alliance of Morse and House lines strained the tenuous accord of the Morse companies, and Kendall's Morse-only American Telegraph Confederation collapsed soon thereafter.

Field and Cooper nonetheless pursued their plan to create a domestic link in their proposed chain across the Atlantic. In November 1855, they organized the American Telegraph Company. Because they designed the new corporation to carry news to and from the Atlantic cable, they chartered it in New York, the only state with a law granting press dispatches special priority on the wires. The New York Associated Press (AP), a consortium of newspapers seeking to monopolize the nation's wire news, supported the new firm. Field and Cooper's failure to consolidate the New England Morse companies would have required their company to employ the outmoded House telegraph. But the American Telegraph Company boasted a new technology: the Hughes type-printing telegraph.

D. H. Craig, the general agent for the AP, discovered the wondrous invention of David E. Hughes, a Kentucky music professor. The Hughes telegraph employed synchronous spinning wheels to print messages on plain paper. It promised rapid transmission on circuits up to 250 miles long and required one-tenth of the battery power of the House telegraph.[140] More importantly, a company with rights to the Hughes patent could build *anywhere* without infringing on the Morse or House patent monopolies – precisely the danger of new technologies that Russell had tried to impress upon Sibley. Field and Cooper understood the opportunity – the

---

[137] Robert W. Russell to Hiram Sibley, 3 August 1855, Sibley Papers (Addition).

[138] Daniel H. Craig to Hiram Sibley, 9 August 1855, Sibley Papers (Addition). Emphasis is in the original.

[139] Thompson, *Wiring a Continent*, 303.

[140] Reid, *The Telegraph in America*, 405. For a full technical explanation of the Hughes system, see Prescott, *Electricity and the Electric Telegraph*, 609–42.

American Telegraph Company paid $100,000 for North American rights to the Hughes telegraph.[141] Craig advised Sibley that the rumors about the new device were "*positively true,*" and he would not give Sibley "*eighteen pence*" for the House and Morse patents.[142] Though the Hughes required substantial refinement before it could be used commercially – in 1855 it did not even have a patent approved – Kendall warned Morse that the American Telegraph Company would hold it "in *terrorem*" over their heads and force them to lease their lines at a reduced rent.[143] Unfettered by infringement suits, existing contracts, or interfirm quarrels, the superior Hughes telegraph threatened to sweep away the feuding Morse and House companies – if it could be made to work.

By 1856 a small number of players had reshaped the disjointed American telegraph industry. Morse and Kendall's Magnetic Company, the oldest telegraph firm in the nation, ran Morse lines from New York to Philadelphia and Washington. To block the American Telegraph Company from connecting to the South, the Magnetic had merged with another Morse company, thereby adding lines from New York to New Orleans. Meanwhile, Western Union and its allies reached west from New York to St. Louis, operating both Morse and House equipment. The newly created American Telegraph Company operated House lines from New York to Newfoundland, with imminent plans to lay the first cable to Europe.

The American Telegraph Company, with its new technology, grand plans, and Cooper's financial backing, posed a serious threat to its competitors, but its success depended on developing the capability to carry high-priced European news to points beyond New York. The AP pummeled the Morse interests in the press in a "war of nerves" intended to convince the Morse companies' stockholders to lease their lines to the American Telegraph Company. Morse demanded that Field and Cooper publicly repudiate the AP, but they insisted they were not responsible for the press campaign.[144] Morse accused Field and Cooper of betraying him by acquiring the Hughes patent. Cooper responded that some other party would have bought the Hughes instead and destroyed them all, and

[141] Reid, *The Telegraph in America*, 406.
[142] Daniel H. Craig to Hiram Sibley, 25 October 1855, Sibley Papers (Addition). Emphasis is in the original.
[143] Kendall is quoted in Thompson, *Wiring a Continent*, 304.
[144] Morse apparently made this demand in January 1857, and Cooper refused in March 1857. Peter Cooper to Samuel F. B. Morse, 10 March 1857, Morse Papers.

the American Telegraph Company was actually trying to *protect* Morse's interests.[145]

The American Telegraph Company's growing strength threatened Western Union as well. If the Atlantic cable succeeded, the American Telegraph Company could demand virtually any terms for connections to its network.[146] One Western Union officer feared that the "heavy capitalists" backing the American Telegraph Company made it a formidable foe even without the Atlantic cable, whereas if the cable succeeded, "The whole Telegraph interest in this country will be almost at their mercy." Combination was the "only security" against the Hughes telegraph and domination by the American Telegraph Company.[147]

In early 1857 Sibley met with Kendall, whom he privately referred to as the "Old Fox." Sibley found Kendall "anxious to sell" but unwilling to offer a "reasonable" price.[148] Despite the growing strength of the American Telegraph Company, the Old Fox still had enough power to spoil any general agreement of telegraph interests, so Sibley continued to court him. Sibley pressed for a second conference of the major telegraph companies that summer to bring the American Telegraph Company into the fold and establish "general arrangements for the mutual protection of existing lines."[149] Kendall reluctantly agreed to the conference, but Sibley was certain the Old Fox was more interested in protecting his investments than creating a permanent accord between the warring telegraph companies. Determined to "spike" Kendall's agenda, Sibley decided to arrive at the conference early to make a "definite arrangement" with the American Telegraph Company and its "heavy capitalists" before the Old Fox appeared.[150] The stage was set for what one historian called a "revolt of second generation telegraphers against the pioneers."[151]

The convention, meeting in late June 1857, resolved that the best interests of the public, investors, and patent holders required "an amicable arrangement" among the telegraph companies to produce a return on the "large amounts of money" expended in constructing the nation's

[145] Peter Cooper to Samuel F. B. Morse, 10 March 1857, Morse Papers.
[146] Jeptha H. Wade to Hiram Sibley, 28 April 1857, Wade Papers.
[147] Isaac R. Elwood to J. D. Caton, 5 June 1857, Caton Papers.
[148] Hiram Sibley to Jeptha H. Wade, 15 January 1857, Wade Papers.
[149] Hiram Sibley to Amos Kendall, 8 June 1857, Wade Papers; Amos Kendall to Samuel Morse, 27 August 1857, Morse Papers.
[150] Hiram Sibley to Jeptha H. Wade, 20 June 1857, Wade Papers.
[151] Thompson, *Wiring a Continent*, 313.

lines.[152] The proposed plan required the companies to connect exclusively with each other, to divide their business at points of competition, and to appoint a board of control to make rules and settle disputes. Significantly, the companies were to promise to use "all proper means [to] discourage new competing lines." Writing to Morse, who was in England promoting the Atlantic cable project, Kendall praised the proposal as "equal and impartial" and without room for "dissent."

However, like Sibley, Cooper and Field had more than just "friendly relations on equal terms" as their object. They threatened to withdraw from the talks and kill the agreement unless the other companies contributed $60,000 in payment for the Hughes rights. The other companies balked, and the meeting adjourned without an official settlement. But after the other delegates left, Norvin Green of the Southwestern Company and Hiram Sibley negotiated a separate peace with the American Telegraph Company that excluded Kendall's Magnetic Company.

On August 10, 1857, delegates signed the "The Six Party Contract, or the Treaty of the Six Nations" – a deliberate reference to the Iroquois Confederacy of Sibley's northwestern New York. The agreement demarcated the "sovereign" territory of each company, entitling the six signers to "exclusive enjoyment of all telegraph business" within their region and requiring each to connect exclusively with other members of the pact. Delegates from the Six Nations would convene annually during the contract's thirty-year term and committees would settle disputes.[153] Because both Kendall's Magnetic Telegraph Company and F. O. J. Smith's New England companies remained outside the agreement, the Six Nations did not control the Morse patent on most of the Eastern seaboard and thus did not have a total monopoly on telegraphy. Still, the combination of the six firms was closer to telegraph unity than had been seen at any point since Morse began licensing patent rights.[154] When he heard of it, the Old Fox declared the agreement a revolting "act of perfidy" and lamented that the traitors would share the Hughes patent and "parcel out the United States among them as if no Morse telegraph ever existed."[155] Kendall vowed to Morse that he would not "abandon the Telegraph to

---

[152] "Proceedings of a Meeting of the Representatives of a Number of Principal Telegraph Companies in the United States," 30 June and 1 July 1857, Wade Papers.

[153] The agreement is reprinted in full in Thompson, *Wiring a Continent*, 504–15.

[154] J. D. Reid includes the purchase of Morse and Smith's interest as an explicit goal of the Six Party Contract, a claim which I have not been able to verify. Reid, *The Telegraph in America*, 430.

[155] Amos Kendall to Samuel Morse, 27 August 1857, Morse Papers.

those unscrupulous men who for love of gain would rob you not only of your property but of a just and enviable fame."[156]

At the first annual meeting of the Six Nations – thenceforth known as the North American Telegraph Association – in New York in October 1858, the confederation determined that its "chief object" was to "advance the interests of the respective companies" and to "guard against" competition. The telegraph could not be both competitive and profitable. In a tortured reversal of free market orthodoxy, the committee concluded that competition was also bad for consumers. "Sharp competition" led to badly run, poorly maintained lines, a burden that ultimately fell "in some shape on the public." Thus "the interests of the public" demanded that the Six Nations form a monopoly so that they could "afford" to provide a prompt, satisfactory, and cheaper service. Because eliminating competition had typically led to higher prices, not lower, this claim was dubious. The Association would make competition "profitless" by requiring exclusive connections between member "nations," limiting the ability of outside companies to pass messages to Association lines, and sharing the cost of rate wars against outside companies.[157]

The Six Nations' competitors were not willing to give up without a fight. Kendall forged an alliance with Smith to harass and discredit the Telegraph Association. Their target was the projected Atlantic cable, potentially the Association's most valuable strategic asset. But the Association had already established a daunting lead. The American Telegraph Company had sought monopoly rights from legislatures in Maine and Massachusetts to prevent competing cables from landing in New England.[158] Massachusetts rejected the request, but Maine awarded the American Telegraph Company a twenty-five-year monopoly on all lines connecting directly or indirectly to Europe. Other governments were even more generous. Newfoundland not only assigned Cooper and Field the exclusive right to a cable landing for fifty years, but offered a cash subsidy and land grants as well.[159] The U.S. Congress promised $70,000 per year until the cable earned 6 percent net profits, and $50,000 per year

---

[156] Amos Kendall to Samuel Morse, 23 October 1857, Morse Papers.

[157] "Proceedings of the Annual Meeting of the North American Telegraph Association, Held in the City of New York, October, 1858," 21 October 1858, Wade Papers.

[158] "A Remonstrance Against the Petition of Peter Cooper and Others, Respecting Exclusive Privileges in Relation to a Sub-Marine Telegraph Cable between Europe and America," 20 March 1857, Wade Papers.

[159] *The Atlantic Telegraph: Its History...* (London: Bacon and Co., 1866), 12.

thereafter for twenty-five years, and the English Parliament offered 14,000 and 10,000 pounds sterling on the same conditions. Both governments provided ships for laying cables and escorts for the convoy.

The subsidies and monopoly grants cast telegraph competition into the political realm, Kendall's former domain. In 1857, Tal Shaffner, the former secretary of the defunct American Telegraph Confederation and a former partner in Fields's cable project, appealed to Congress to extend the bounty promised to Field's Atlantic Cable Company to *any* party that successfully landed a cable. Shaffner had been pursuing his own quixotic scheme to wrap telegraph wire around the globe until the earth was *"girdled with one continuous and unbroken flame of electric light."* [160] He won support from several European leaders for a projected series of cables connecting Denmark, the Faroe Islands, Iceland, Greenland, and North America. Shaffner urged Congress to pass a "general law" for ocean telegraphs to curtail the "reckless speculators" interested in their own gain rather than the "ultimate honor and the good of their fellow men." [161] Congress ignored Shaffner's request, but Kendall, the Old Fox, saw it as a potential political opportunity. He embraced Shaffner's plan and urged Morse and the Magnetic Company to support it. [162]

Employing the logic of the Shaffner plan, Kendall seized on the grants promised to Field's cable project to launch a political attack on the Telegraph Association as a wicked, state-sponsored monopoly such as those that had been opposed by Democratic antimonopolists for decades. Kendall appealed to Congress in 1858, claiming that the Telegraph Association companies had entered into a combination to force the legitimate holders of the Morse patent to sell out or see their property's value destroyed. The Atlantic cable, once "a noble enterprise," had been "converted into an enormous scheme of monopoly" to control global telegraphy and secure "inordinate gains to a few individuals." In the 1857 Atlantic Cable Act, Congress had guaranteed equal rights of cable access to all citizens, but the *exclusive* Six Party Contract made this proviso "wholly illusory," Kendall argued. He offered a solution: Congress should pass a general telegraph law to prohibit monopoly combinations and require connections between all lines "on terms of

---

[160] Taliaferro P. Shaffner, "Memorial of Taliaferro P. Shaffner," 3 March 1857, 35th Congress, 1st Session, Misc. Doc. No. 263, 46. Emphasis in the original.

[161] Taliaferro P. Shaffner, "Memorial of Taliaferro P. Shaffner," 3 March 1857, 35th Congress, 1st Session, Misc. Doc. No. 263, 8. Shaffner insisted that the provisions in the Atlantic Cable Act were written in such a way that only Field's company could fulfill them.

[162] Thompson, *Wiring a Continent*, 321.

perfect equality."[163] Such a law would essentially eliminate the advantages secured by the Six Party Contract. Kendall, an ardent defender of the Morse patent monopoly as encompassing *all* electromagnetic communication, had suddenly returned to his Jacksonian, antimonopoly roots.

Why requires little speculation. Cooper and Wilson Hunt of the American Telegraph Company exposed Kendall's hypocrisy in their response to his memorial to Congress. For years Kendall had made "every effort" to prevent competition, they wrote. Now Kendall's sought to "compel the enterprising" to share their "well-earned reward" with the losers of the contest. After repeatedly refusing to strike a bargain with the American Telegraph Company, Kendall's "patriotism and solicitude" were finally excited because his financial interest was at risk.[164]

The two appeals raised vital questions about the government's authority and responsibility to regulate the telegraph industry. Kendall's proposed antimonopoly general telegraph federalized a regulatory responsibility that had thus far belonged to the states – since 1845, every state but Arkansas and Iowa had passed some type of telegraph regulation.[165] Cooper and Hunt – and presumably their allies in the Telegraph Association – opposed the creation of any federal regulatory authority and questioned its legitimacy. Did the Constitution's authority to regulate "commerce" apply to the telegraph?[166]

The Senate Judiciary Committee took up this question two months after the Cooper and Hunt memorial, issuing a report in June 1858 that shrugged off federal responsibility for telegraph regulation. The committee determined that each state had "full authority" to "control and regulate" telegraph companies within its borders. The committee conceded that by nature such companies tended to be "more or less monopolies," but

[163] Amos Kendall et al, "Memorial of the Magnetic Telegraph Company and the of the New England Union Telegraph Company, 10 March 1858, 35th Congress, 1st Session, Misc. Doc. No. 227.

[164] Peter Cooper and Wilson Hunt, "Memorial of the American Telegraph Company in Answer to the Memorial of the Magnetic Telegraph Company and the New England Union..." 20 April 1858, 35th Congress, 1st Session, Misc. Doc., No. 245.

[165] Arkansas passed its first telegraph law in 1859, Iowa followed in 1860. Tomas Nonnenmacher, "State Promotion and Regulation of the Telegraph Industry, 1845–1860," *The Journal of Economic History* 61(2001): 21–2.

[166] Peter Cooper and Wilson Hunt, "Memorial of the American Telegraph Company in Answer to the Memorial of the Magnetic Telegraph Company and the New England Union..." 20 April 1858, 35th Congress, 1st Session, Misc. Doc., No. 245.

the states had enough power to protect the public. In fact, the landmark 1837 Supreme Court decision *Charles River Bridge v. Warren Bridge* had affirmed the power of the states to break up monopolies that threatened economic growth.[167] Particularly before the Civil War, the federal government had neither the institutional resources nor the inclination to interfere with or regulate what were ostensibly local businesses.[168] But in the presumption that the telegraph was something akin to an intrastate road or bridge, the senators revealed an acute lack of understanding of the scale of the corporations coming to dominate the industry. Telegraphy had become a much bigger business than they realized.

For a few thrilling days in August 1858, Cyrus Field's Atlantic cable appeared to be a triumph. Field had attempted to lay a cable in 1857, but three hundred miles into the expedition the cable snapped and sank in water two thousand fathoms deep.[169] Undaunted, Field tried again the following summer. Breakages plagued the second attempt, and newspapers reported each setback to anxious readers. But mechanical improvements and a few skillful splices kept hopes alive. On August 4, the U.S.S. *Niagara* reached Newfoundland with one end of the cable, while the H.M.S. *Agamemnon* anchored off the coast of Ireland with the other. On August 14, the first message passed between the continents: "Europe and America are united in telegraph communication. 'Glory to God in the highest, and on earth peace, goodwill towards men.'" Messages between Queen Victoria and President James Buchanan followed, promising "perpetual peace and friendship."[170]

The public excitement about the cable cannot be overstated. Newspapers covered the story for weeks – headlines declared it "The Great Event of the Age."[171] In New York, flags flew throughout the city in celebration, jewelers sold charms fashioned from bits of cable, and the *Times* reported, "Everybody shook hands with everybody, and pledged the Telegraph in their own fashion."[172] Across the nation, one-hundred-gun

---

[167] Report of the Senate Committee on the Judiciary, 9 June 1858, 35th Congress, 1st Session, Rep. Com. No. 313.
[168] Kutler, Stanley I. *Privilege and Creative Destruction: The Charles River Bridge Case.* John Hopkins paperbacks ed. (Baltimore: John Hopkins University Press, 1990), 131.
[169] W. H. Russell, *The Atlantic Telegraph* (London: Day & Son Limited, 1866), 22.
[170] Russell, *The Atlantic Telegraph*, 26–7.
[171] "The Great Event of the Age," *The New York Times*, 6 August 1858, 1.
[172] "Atlantic Telegraph," *The New York Times*, 7 August 1858, 5.

salutes, bonfires, speeches and sermons celebrated the cable as "an omen of promise for Christian progress."[173] George Templeton Strong, Field's neighbor in Gramercy Park, described in his diary how the jubilation ran amok. "The triumphant pyrotechnics with which our city fathers celebrated this final and complete subjugation by man of all the powers of nature – space and time included – set City Hall on fire, burned up its cupola and half its roof, and came near destroying the County Clerk's office." he recorded.[174]

The jubilation proved premature. The cable never worked as hoped – the first fourteen-word message took thirty-seven minutes to transmit, and the greeting from Queen Victoria to President Buchanan required sixteen hours, a rate of ten minutes per word.[175] Two weeks later, transmissions ceased entirely. Field later recalled that "joy turned into mourning" when the cable "went out like a spark in the mighty waters."[176] The hopes for the American Telegraph Company's dominance of transatlantic communication lay dead at the bottom of the sea.

In October 1858, the Six Nations met in New York to plot a buyout of Smith and Kendall's competing lines. Representatives agreed upon a blueprint for consolidation: the American Telegraph Company would absorb the Magnetic Company and Smith's New England interest, and the other members of the confederation would pay for the portions of the purchased lines in their respective territories. When all the Morse lines were in the fold, the Six Nations would aggressively lobby for a seven-year renewal of the Morse magnetic relay patent, which would expire in 1860. The Telegraph Association would thus secure a monopoly over the Morse, House and Hughes telegraphs, essentially eliminating competition. But, as usual, self-interested stakeholders rife with personal and commercial strife did not easily yield to consolidation.[177] As a Western Union director warned the ever-recalcitrant Ezra Cornell, "No one should hold back in

---

[173] Joseph A. Copp, *The Atlantic Telegraph: As Illustrating the Providence and Benevolent Designs of God: A Discourse Preached in the Broadway Church, Chelsea, August 8, 1858.* (Boston: T. R. Marvin & Son, 1858), 14.

[174] George Templeton Strong, *The Diary of George Templeton Strong*, 4 vols., vol. 2 (New York: The Macmillan Company, 1952), 410.

[175] John Steele Gordon, *A Thread across the Ocean: The Heroic Story of the Transatlantic Cable* (New York: Walker & Co., 2002), 137–8.

[176] New York Chamber of Commerce, *The Atlantic Telegraph* (New York: J. W. Amerman, 1866), 18; Commerce, *The Atlantic Telegraph*.

[177] Hiram Sibley to J. H. Wade, 23 November 1858, Wade Papers.

the hopes of making a better bargain *for himself* and thus jeopardize the whole matter."[178] Yet this is precisely what occurred.

Each time the great consolidation seemed certain, some new complication stymied the plan. Smith demanded $300,000 for his stocks and patent interest, an outrageous price that many parties in the Association were nonetheless willing to pay to eliminate him.[179] Kendall behaved with characteristic duplicity and obstructionism – Sibley complained that the nickname "Old Fox" was inadequate, and it would take "a *skunk* to complete the figure."[180] But the failure of the Six Nations to agree with *each other* posed at least as great an obstacle. Russell, representing the American Telegraph Company, was reportedly a "self-willed" and "unpleasant" negotiator.[181] From Russell's perspective, the chief difficulty was that the Western members of the Association insisted on driving "a hard bargain" when they should have paid any price to put an end to competition.[182] Sibley believed that Russell had secretly encouraged Kendall and Smith to demand greater payments. In March 1859 Sibley invited all the parties except Russell to a clandestine meeting that produced a consolidation commitment.[183] But, as one of Sibley's colleagues warned, the possibility remained for "many a slip between the cup and the lip," and the compact collapsed again.[184]

Negotiations among the Association, Kendall, and Smith continued intermittently, because all parties believed the value of telegraph stock depended upon consolidation. The Southwestern Company's Norvin Green wrote to his wife that with "general confederation and harmony" would come "permanent and increased value" of telegraph stock, and without it, the stock's "almost total sacrifice."[185] Although all the companies needed to work together, Western Union and the American Telegraph Company, competitors acknowledged, held the key positions on the "telegraphic chessboard" and would determine "whether the game be lost or won."[186]

---

[178] Isaac R. Elwood to Ezra Cornell, 26 November 1858, Sibley Papers (Addition).
[179] Hiram Sibley to Jeptha Wade, 16 December 1858, Wade Papers.
[180] Hiram Sibley to Jeptha Wade, 17 September 1859, Wade Papers.
[181] E. D. L. Sweet to J. D. Caton, 9 April 1859, Caton Papers; J. J. Speed to J. D. Caton, 29 June 1859, Caton Papers.
[182] Robert Russell to Isaac R. Elwood, 22 January 1859, Wade Papers.
[183] Hiram Sibley to Jeptha Wade, 27 December 1858, Wade Papers; Isaac Elwood to Hiram Sibley, 7 March 1859, Wade Papers.
[184] Hiram Sibley to Isaac Elwood, 18 March 1859, Wade Papers; Isaac Elwood to Jeptha Wade, 19 March 1859, Wade Papers.
[185] Norvin Green to Martha Green, 10 April 1859, Green Papers (U.K.).
[186] Hiram O. Alden to Hiram Sibley, 28 February 1859, Sibley Papers (Addition).

Though they preferred cooperation, both companies prepared for the alternative. Sibley admitted to a colleague that he would "concede much for the sake of peace," but if negotiations failed, Western Union would "go for a fight such as never was before."[187]

The Six Nations met again in New York in September 1859 and negotiations dragged on for weeks.[188] The Telegraph Association finally agreed to buy both Smith's New England companies and the Magnetic Telegraph Company.[189] Morse and Kendall joined the board of the American Telegraph Company, which paid for the lion's share of the Magnetic, and a former Magnetic manager became the American Telegraph Company's new president. Cyrus Field, who had lost $300,000 in his two bids to build an Atlantic cable and another $100,000 in the panic of 1857, sold his stake in the American Telegraph Company.[190]

The telegraph peace of 1859 was promising, but restive. If the united companies could win an extension for the patent on the Morse receiving magnet in 1860, no competitor could enter the field for seven years without some new patentable device. In a circular the American Telegraph Company pledged that the telegraphing public would "be better served" by the cartel and boasted openly of the Six Party Contract's provisions for "extinguishing competition" by undercutting the rates of any future competitor.[191] However, with the competing Magnetic Telegraph eliminated, the American Telegraph Company raised its rates over objections from its partners that the hike would provoke new competing lines and excite opposition to the patent renewal. The American Telegraph Company acquiesced to cartel pressure and lowered rates but suspicion lingered.[192] Though the "outside" companies had been eliminated, a renewed conflict between the American Telegraph Company and Western Union appeared inevitable as leaders of each firm wondered if they had granted too much

[187] Hiram Sibley to J. H. Wade, 17 September 1859, Wade Papers.

[188] "Proceedings of the North American Telegraph Association, 1858–1859 & 1860," Wade Papers.

[189] Reid, *The Telegraph in America*, 418; Thompson, *Wiring a Continent*, 329.

[190] Hiram Sibley to D. A. Watson, 27 October, 1857, Wade Papers; Cyrus Field to [unknown], 27 December 1860, Cyrus Field Papers. Russell had been a large holder in the American Telegraph Company since February 1859, when the American Telegraph Company purchased Russell's New York & Washington Printing Telegraph Company in a stock deal. The threat of the American competing on the Magnetic's chief route with the House patent probably forced Kendall to accept a settlement the next fall. Reid, *The Telegraph in America*, 417.

[191] "Statistics, Etc. of The American Telegraph Company," 20 August 1860, WUC.

[192] Isaac Elwood to Jeptha Wade, 22 November 1859, Wade Papers; Isaac Elwood to J. H. Wade, 21 December 1859, Wade Papers.

to their rivals and feared their new partners intended to encroach on their territory.[193]

After a dozen years of unceasing competition and personal conflict, there is little wonder that the telegraph pioneers were eager to take shelter in the safe harbor of a cartel. The six companies did not attempt to monopolize the telegraph to make electricity a "missionary to human progress." They hoped to perform a bit of business alchemy, to turn the worthless stock of haphazardly built and poorly managed telegraph lines into gold, to make a great success from a "consolidation of failures." But the North American Telegraph Association contained the seeds of its own destruction – the same self-interested, anticompetitive motives that had spurred its creation would tear it apart.

[193] Isaac Elwood to Jeptha Wade, 21 December 1859, Wade Papers. Elwood told Wade a plan for Western Union to absorb the Albany & Ohio Telegraph Company was already underway.

2

Midwife to Monopoly

In March 1890, *Omaha Bee* editor Edward Rosewater offered a history
lesson to a House of Representatives committee contemplating a government takeover of private telegraph lines. Rosewater had worked in
the telegraph industry for thirteen years and had served in the United
States Military Telegraph Corps during the Civil War. He alleged that
during the war, Western Union infiltrated the War Department to profit
from the Military Telegraph. Rosewater insisted that the North American
Telegraph Association had manipulated the federal government "to yield
the largest revenue," spending millions in public money on military telegraph facilities later appropriated by the telegraph companies. Norvin
Green, Western Union's president in 1890, flatly denied Rosewater's
charges. Yet the essence of Rosewater's condemnation was close to the
truth: the cartel companies had "actively co-operated to protect the interests of each other, regardless of the interests of the Government" during
the Civil War, doing their best to profit and expand during the conflict.[1]
Most impressively, they had enjoyed the partnership and protection of
both belligerent governments.

As members of a monopoly cartel, the six companies in the North
American Telegraph Association had positioned themselves well to take
advantage of the war boom in business. In a sense the cartel fostered an
alliance between two institutions with continental ambitions, the North
American Telegraph Association and the U.S. government itself. At the
urging of Western Union executives Hiram Sibley and Anson Stager, the
War Department turned over responsibility for military telegraphing to

---

[1] "Postal Telegraph Facilities," 18 March 1890, WUC, 1–3.

the cartel's own leaders, allowing them to operate the Military Telegraph Corps as a quasi-private service answerable only to the Secretary of War himself. Only the Six Nations cartel made this near unification of the Military Telegraph Corps and the private companies possible. Had Stager pursued Western Union's agenda to the detriment of the American Telegraph Company or his other allies, had there been no agreement about a common "telegraph interest," the quarrels that were so common in the 1850s would probably have scotched the warm partnership between the industry and the War Department.

The Military Telegraph Corps, though a great contributor to the Union war effort in its own right, played a dual role reflecting its public-private status. While laying thousands of miles of telegraph line along the Union advance, it also became the guarantor that the private property of the telegraph companies would be protected – indeed, *enhanced* – during the war, and that the companies would operate profitably throughout. In the Civil War the federal government generally did not nationalize private industries to generate the resources required for the war, relying on private enterprise.[2] But by having its own managers take charge of the military lines, the telegraph cartel achieved the reverse – it, in effect, privatized part of the military. The cartel's alliance with the War Department protected more than the Six Nations' Northern interests. Its close relationship with the federal government led to the almost entirely unencumbered restoration of the companies' Southern holdings, even though the Southern lines had profitably served the Confederacy in both commercial and military capacities.

The Military Telegraph Corps was not the only way the telegraph companies allied themselves directly with the state. Two great projects bookending the war years linked the Association, and Western Union specifically, to the federal government: the Pacific Telegraph and what became known as "Collins' Overland Line" – an attempt to route a telegraph line across the Bering Strait to Europe.[3] In both, patriotism

---

[2] Richard Franklin Bensel, *Yankee Leviathan: The Origins of Central State Authority in America, 1859–1877* (New York: Cambridge University Press, 1990), 188.
[3] I will not argue in this chapter that Western Union is an early piece of the military–industrial complex. Although Western Union's close relationship with the military advanced the company's interests, Western Union did not seek to perpetuate that relationship; managers expedited the exit of the government from the telegraph industry. Robert Angevine notes that finding antecedents for the modern military–industrial complex has preoccupied military historians, and he finds "roots" in the military's relationship with the railroads during the Civil War. I think in the case of the telegraph, however, there

and the national interest aligned neatly with Western Union's interest – Rosewater's accusation of mercenary motives notwithstanding. As one Senate committee insisted, the United States could simultaneously "suppress rebellion at home" and "extend her great commercial and scientific power all over the earth."[4]

The rise of the Republican Party made this cooperation possible. The new Republican majority favored government support for internal improvements, negating long-standing opposition from Democrats, many of whom had left Congress when their states left the Union. Many Republicans held that the government should not interfere in the natural harmony of the economy, and the best managers of infrastructure development projects were those whose money was at risk.[5] These tenets paved the way for Western Union to develop the Pacific telegraph with government aid but essentially free from government control. The same convictions helped foster the relationship between the federal government and the private telegraph companies during the war. Thus, the federal government unintentionally played midwife to the birth of the telegraph monopoly.

In 1857 the North American Telegraph Association had divided the United States into six "sovereign" sections (and soon added a seventh "nation" – the Montreal Company), but California and the Western territories remained unclaimed and unconnected to the Association's Eastern network. California's boomtowns connected to each other with a growing web of lines built with the same "reckless abandon" typical in early telegraph construction in the East.[6] The vast region from St. Louis to the Sierra Nevada Mountains, however, remained unconquered by the telegraph and, more importantly, by telegraph entrepreneurs. A line from the Missouri River to the Pacific coast posed unacceptable risks to investors. Even in the densely populated East, the telegraph had proved fragile, unreliable, and often unprofitable. Only the most ambitious – or foolhardy – entrepreneurs envisioned constructing a line through a wilderness

may be a contribution to the creation of a relationship pattern between the military and industry, but not of an actual relationship between the military and the telegraph industry. See Robert G. Angevine, *The Railroad and the State: War, Politics, and Technology in Nineteenth-Century America* (Stanford, Calif.: Stanford University Press, 2004), xvii.

[4] Senate Report No. 13, 37th Congress, 2nd Session, 17 February 1862.

[5] Heather Cox Richardson, *The Greatest Nation of the Earth: Republican Economic Policies During the Civil War* (Cambridge, Mass.: Harvard University Press, 1997), 28.

[6] Robert Luther Thompson, *Wiring a Continent: The History of the Telegraph Industry in the United States, 1832–1866* (Princeton, N.J.: Princeton University Press, 1947), 347.

without roads and full of hostile Indians. But when it came to the telegraph, such men were in abundance.

The most persistent proposition for a transcontinental telegraph came
from the industry's enduring promoter of farfetched schemes: Henry
O'Rielly. Beginning in 1847, O'Rielly proposed a Pacific line in a grand
design for a national telegraph "range." An 1849 convention of eight
hundred Western railroad and telegraph promoters in St. Louis embraced
O'Rielly as the standard-bearer for the Western telegraph. In 1852 Illinois
Senator Stephen A. Douglas signed on to O'Reilly's plan for a national
military and post road protected by a chain of stockades every twenty
miles, garrisoned by small units of dragoons and squads of riders to carry
the mail. The national military road would create "one of the best and
quickest mail lines in the world" while "furnishing the protection" for a
telegraph line from Missouri to California. True to his Jacksonian roots,
O'Rielly refused any government funds or favors for his telegraph line,
promising he would build a telegraph *and* leave the right-of-way "open
to free competition."[7]

O'Rielly was an exception; those who dared to dream of coast-to-coast
telegraphy usually assumed generous aid from Congress in their reveries.
In 1851, the Atlantic & Pacific Telegraph Company – a speculative venture without any established telegraph lines – promised to build a line on a
Southern route in eighteen months if Congress would provide a $350,000
subsidy. Despite the project's poor prospects, the Senate Committee on Post
Office and Post Roads embraced the plan with the credulity upon which
telegraph speculators so often depended. The Atlantic and Pacific coasts
would "become as one," and intelligence between them would "follow the
path of the lightning" and "scatter wealth and civilization in its course."
Similar proposals soon followed, including two by leading figures in the
American Telegraph Company for lines funded by federal land grants.

By the mid-1850s, the drumbeat for improved communication with
the West had grown loud and steady. A House Select Committee concluded in 1856 that the necessity for transcontinental railroad and telegraph lines was "conceded by everyone." But sectional conflict prevented
Congressional action. Any proposal that specified a Northern or Southern
route met with blistering opposition from the opposite section.[8] O'Rielly,

---

[7] Henry O'Reilly, "Memorial of Henry O'Reilly..." 6 April 1852, 32d. Congress, 1st Session,
Misc. Doc. No. 67, 2–11.
[8] David M. Potter, *The Impending Crisis, 1848–1861*, ed. Don E. Fehrenbacher (New York:
Harper & Row, 1976), 146.

by now a sort of telegraph activist, tried to evade sectional politics by modifying his proposal to include both a Northern *and* a Southern mail and telegraph route.[9] As usual he was ahead of his time. Douglas presented O'Rielly's plan to the Senate in 1858 and 1859, but opposition from Southern senators and a dispute within the California delegation defeated it.[10]

Skeptics of a transcontinental line abounded outside of Congress, too. Hiram Sibley, by then president of Western Union, attempted to ignite interest in his own plan for a transcontinental line in 1857 at a meeting of the North American Telegraph Association, only to have it met with a "universal shout of derision." His plan seemed as likely to succeed as "a line to the moon."[11] Yet Sibley believed that a transcontinental telegraph was inevitable – the principal question was not if a line could be built, but who would control it.[12] His insight was not unique. Although no company in the cartel would assume the risk of building a line, each sought to secure the greatest advantage from its construction.[13]

The member of the confederation that controlled the Pacific line – much as the American Telegraph Company had intended to control the Atlantic cable – threatened to dominate its partners.[14] The site of the line's Eastern terminus became the chief point of dispute between the Six Nations, much as it was in Congress, with the east–west-oriented Western Union favoring St. Louis and the north–south-oriented American Telegraph Company preferring New Orleans. In October 1858 the Telegraph Association finally appointed a committee to seek aid from Congress for a transcontinental line, but the committee procrastinated. Sibley, following O'Rielly's lead, offered a revised plan for both a Northern line and a

---

[9] Henry O'Reilly, "Memorial of Henry O'Reilly," 12 January 1854, 35th Congress, 1st Session, Misc. Doc. No. 134.

[10] "A Bill to Facilitate Communication between the Atlantic and Pacific States by Electric Telegraph," 24 May 1858, S. 401, 35th Congress, 1st Session, Norvin Green to Isaac R. Elwood, 23 January 1859, Wade Papers.

[11] Charles T. Porter, "Lecture Delivered before the Mechanical Engineers' Association of the Sibley College of Mechanical Arts, Cornell University," 4 December 1885, reprinted in Hiram Sibley, "Memories of Hiram Sibley," in *Publication Fund Series*, ed. Edward R. Foreman (Rochester, N.Y.: The Rochester Historical Society, 1923), 133.

[12] Sibley to Norvin Green, 3 April 1858, Green Papers (FHS).

[13] For example, Norvin Green told his wife in 1859 that he intended to lobby for the "Pacific Telegraph bill now before the Senate" to get it "in such shape as to throw its immense business to our lines." Green to Martha Green, 14 January 1859, Green Papers (U.K.).

[14] James D. Reid, *The Telegraph in America: Its Founders, Promoters, and Noted Men*, 1st ed. (New York: Derby Brothers, 1879), 489–90.

Southern line, but as one Western Union director noted, with a great deal of "congressional plunder" at stake, the route question would not be so easily settled.[15]

How much "plunder" the Pacific line might yield remained an open question. California promised a bounty of $6,000 per year for ten years for the first line to reach the state and $4,000 per year for the second.[16] Sibley hoped for a greater prize from Congress. In January 1860 he took up residence at Willard's Hotel in Washington to lobby full time. There, he cultivated an alliance with California Senator William Gwin, "a true man for his State."[17] Gwin introduced a bill authorizing the Postmaster General to contract for government telegraph business of $50,000 per year for ten years on a line to be constructed by the brothers Frederic and Albert Bee via a northern route from San Francisco to Washington that would connect to Western Union's lines.[18] Sibley begged his allies in the Telegraph Association to come to Washington and use their influence to promote Gwin's bill.[19] His effort, it turned out, was not proceeding unopposed. While Sibley coaxed members to vote for the bill, O'Rielly lobbied to keep the Pacific line out of the clutches of the Six Nations monopoly, to "reserve the country from the greatest injustice."[20]

The gravest threat to Sibley's plans came from within the Association itself. Robert Russell, the English investor who allied with Sibley when it suited him, had acquired a large enough stake in the American Telegraph Company to take control of the company's board, and had submitted his own proposal, denouncing Sibley's.[21] The infuriated Sibley accused Russell of menacing the confederation and threatening its most valuable enterprise.[22] But Sibley was in luck. While tussling with Sibley over the Pacific line, Russell was also competing for control of the American Telegraph Company's board, which had postponed its 1860 election to

---

[15] Isaac Elwood to Sibley, 26 January 1860, Wade Papers.
[16] Thompson, *Wiring a Continent*, 349.
[17] Sibley to Isaac Elwood, 29 January 1860, Sibley Papers (Addition).
[18] "A Bill to Facilitate Communication Between the Atlantic and Pacific States by Electric Telegraph," S. 84, 36th Congress, 1st Session.
[19] Sibley to Elwood, 5 February 1860, Wade Papers.
[20] Sibley quotes O'Reilly in Sibley to Isaac Elwood, 7 February 1860, Wade Papers.
[21] Sibley to Isaac Elwood, 31 January 1860, Sibley Papers (Addition); Hiram Sibley to Isaac Elwood, 1 January 1860, Sibley Papers (Addition); Hiram Sibley to Isaac Elwood, 29 January 1860, Sibley Papers (Addition).
[22] Sibley to Elwood, 16 February 1860, Sibley Papers (Addition); Sibley to Wilson Hunt, 21 February 1860, Sibley Papers (Addition). It is possible that Sibley did not send this letter.

thwart Russell's coup. In the midst of the struggle, Russell made the critical error of picking a fight with the New York Associated Press (AP). The New York AP had been the American Telegraph Company's first patron, and the American Telegraph Company had an exclusive arrangement with the press cartel, transmitting the AP's consolidated reports at special reduced rates and "dropping" them at multiple sites. Newspapers paid a low price to receive the AP's reports, while fees for non-AP news were dramatically higher. Now Russell condemned the AP as a dangerous monopoly and proposed that the American Telegraph Company should accept reports from *all* newspapers at equal rates that would be 75 to 150 percent higher than those presently paid by the AP.[23] The new price structure, Russell argued, would create a competitive market for news reports and encourage the proliferation of press associations – a windfall for the telegraph companies, which would do more business at higher rates. In retaliation, the AP's general agent, D. H. Craig, who had done much to help create the American Telegraph Company, waged a public campaign against Russell, whom he denounced as a "soulless vampire."[24] Russell's policy divided the American Telegraph Company's board, which settled into a stalemate.[25]

For Sibley a divided American Telegraph Company was better than one united against Western Union, and he seized the advantage. Over Russell's objections the Telegraph Association agreed to back Sibley's Pacific telegraph bill.[26] Sibley marshaled supporters at Willard's Hotel and "made out lists" of Congressmen to lobby for both his bill and a special extension of the Morse patent long sought by the cartel.[27] With a divisive election looming, the Senate approved the Pacific telegraph bill in late March 1860 despite Southern opposition – twelve of fifteen "nays" came from Southern Senators.[28] A tough battle loomed in the House.[29]

The press at first supported Sibley's Pacific telegraph bill, but Horace Greeley, then an editor in the AP, warned Sibley that Russell's attack on the AP would generate press opposition to the Telegraph Association's

---

[23] Thompson, *Wiring a Continent*, 336–7.

[24] This collection of epithets may be found in Menahem Blondheim, *News over the Wires: The Telegraph and the Flow of Public Information in America, 1844–1897* (Cambridge, Mass.: Harvard University Press, 1994), 122.

[25] Sibley to Elwood, 11 March 1860, Wade Papers.

[26] "Proceedings of the North American Telegraph Association, 1858–1859 & 1860," Wade Papers.

[27] Sibley to Elwood, 11 March 1860, Wade Papers.

[28] Senate Journal, 36th Congress, 295.

[29] Thompson, *Wiring a Continent*, 352.

agenda in Congress.[30] The Boston *Daily Advertiser* reminded readers that the consolidating Magnetic and American Telegraph Companies had promised *lower* rates, and given that the American Telegraph Company now monopolized the telegraph on the East Coast, the 150 percent hike on press rates was "sheer extortion."[31] Given that an extension of the Morse patent and a transcontinental line would *expand* the Telegraph Association's monopoly, such reports were the last thing Sibley wanted to see in the press.

Henry O'Rielly, meanwhile, waged his own public battle against the cartel in Congress. He issued a circular condemning the Telegraph Association as a greater evil than even the Bank of the United States, the original bête noire of Jacksonian Democrats, as a "MONOPOLY *more extensive – more intimately interwoven with the business and social relations of the whole people –* more *dangerous...*than any that ever existed before." The "only remedy" and the sole way to provide the "cheap telegraphing" that was, like cheap postage, the right of the American people, was *"fair and healthy competition."* O'Rielly repeated his vow to build a line to California without "spoils" or "special favors" from Congress.[32] He appeared before the House committee considering Sibley's bill and succeeded in pushing down the guarantee of government business on the transcontinental line by 20 percent. In addition, Congress set the maximum rate for *all* business on the Pacific line at $3 for ten words, a price at which one Sibley associate deemed the line "not worth having."[33] O'Rielly also railed against the patent extension Morse had filed for in 1860 on his telegraph receiving magnet, a device necessary for carrying signals any distance on the era's poorly insulated lines, arguing that it would perpetuate "an odious and tyrannical monopoly" injurious to both "private interest and the public welfare."[34]

The House of Representatives debated the Pacific telegraph bill in April. Opponents challenged the bill in terms reflecting O'Rielly's appeal

[30] Emory Cobb to Hiram Sibley, 31 March 1860, Sibley Family Papers (Addition); Sibley to Elwood, 11 March 1860, Wade Papers.

[31] Sibley to J. D. Caton, 9 April 1860, Caton Papers.

[32] Henry O'Rielly and John J. Speed, "A Few Suggestions respectfully Submitted Concerning the Senate Bill Now Pending in the House of Representative: A Bill Virtually Creating Monopoly and High Prices in Telegraphing between the Atlantic and Pacific States," O'Reilly Papers (RHS).

[33] Sibley to Isaac Elwood, 4 April 1860, Sibley Papers (Addition), Norvin Green to Hiram Sibley, 16 May 1860, Sibley Papers (Addition).

[34] Henry O'Reilly, "Argument of Henry O'Reilly against the Extension of Prof. Morse's Second Patent," May 1860, O'Reilly Papers (RHS).

for telegraphic democracy. Kentucky Democrat Henry Burnett questioned the constitutionality of federal support for the telegraph and grants of "such gigantic powers of monopoly upon private individuals."[35] Competitors would have no legitimate chance against a corporation to which the government had given such great advantages, and the leaders of the Telegraph Association had "agreed among themselves" to "destroy and prevent all competition."[36] Burnett amended the bill, removing the names of Sibley and his allies and opening the project to competitive bidding. Despite Sibley's best efforts to kill the competitive provision, both houses approved the amended bill.[37] In an ominous sign for Sibley's designs, the threat of a "huge monopoly" had been successfully worked against him.[38] Morse's requested extension for his receiving magnet, however, fared better: concerted lobbying by the Telegraph Association and Morse's personal testimony led to a seven-year extension.[39]

When the Telegraph Association convened its annual meeting in New York in August 1860, Western Union and the American Telegraph Company clashed over the Pacific Telegraph Act. Russell demanded that the convention condemn the Act and wait for a "favorable" bill subsidizing both a Northern and a Southern line.[40] The convention approved Russell's resolution with Western Union's support, but this move proved to be a "wheel within the wheel." Western Union proposed a resolution stating that though the *cartel* rejected the Pacific Telegraph Act, the *individual* companies could bid on the federal contract – provided the line connected exclusively with the Six Nations. Western Union would bid as a defensive measure against any "outside" party that might seek the franchise from Congress. The resolution passed, and the door opened wide for Western Union to go it alone to the Pacific.[41]

By refusing to cooperate with Sibley on the Pacific Telegraph Act, Russell had inadvertently handed the franchise to Western Union. Sibley considered a "magnificent scheme" to buy the American Telegraph

---

[35] Congressional Globe, 36th Congress, 1st Session, 1694.

[36] Congressional Globe, 36th Congress, 1st Session, 2252.

[37] Hiram Sibley to Jeptha Wade, 13 June 1860, Jeptha Wade Papers; "An Act to Facilitate Communication between the Atlantic and Pacific States by Electric Telegraph," 36th Congress, 1st Session, Chapter 137.

[38] Bridges to E. Cobb, 19 June 1860, Sibley Papers (Addition).

[39] Kenneth Silverman, *Lightning Man: The Accursed Life of Samuel F.B. Morse* (New York: Alfred A. Knopf, 2003), 381–2.

[40] "Proceedings of the North American Telegraph Association, 1858–1859 & 1860," Wade Papers, 108.

[41] Thomas Bassnett, "Report on Telegraph Convention," August 1860, Caton Papers.

Company and oust the troublesome Russell, but at least one Western Union director dissented that the combined company would be "too large a concern to manage with economy."[42] Moreover, Sibley feared that he might pay a premium to be rid of Russell only to find him back in business with an opposition company.[43] Russell's own appointees to the American Telegraph Company's board of directors settled the issue by switching sides. By the end of 1860, they had expelled Russell and the American Telegraph Company had restored the peace and signed a new contract with the New York AP.

The terms of the Pacific Telegraph Act required the line to be completed by July 31, 1862. To most observers this appeared impossible. The line would traverse nearly two thousand miles of largely unsettled country, much of it without local timber – poles would have to be hauled more than two hundred miles. The iron telegraph wire alone weighed three hundred fifty pounds per mile, and it would be conveyed along with tools, insulators, and batteries over roads that ranged from marginal to nonexistent.[44] Even if the line could be built, the Indians might destroy it, or the vast herds of bison roaming the plains might sweep it away.[45] And if maintaining a working line on the plains posed a challenge, the mountains were even worse. Experiments with building lines in the Sierras had already proved that alpine weather did not suit the telegraph. "When it snows in the Sierras, *it does snow*," a California telegrapher reported after a storm felled his lines in the winter of 1860. "It is a splendid route to build a telegraph line over in the summer, providing you leave it alone in the winter."[46]

Undaunted, Sibley formed an independent company to construct the line, and he submitted a bid for the maximum of $40,000 in guaranteed government business. Three lower bidders withdrew their offers for unknown reasons, though Sibley may well have been involved.[47] In September 1860, with the nation heading for an election that would spur a sectional civil war, Sibley entered a new round of negotiations with his

---

[42] Elwood to Sibley, 2 November 1860, Sibley Papers (Addition).

[43] Craig to Sibley, 23 October 1860, Sibley Papers (Addition); Sibley to Jeptha Wade, 25 October 1860, Wade Papers. Interestingly, this is precisely the mistake that was made with Jay Gould in 1878.

[44] Electron, "The Pacific Telegraph," 31 October 1864, *The Telegrapher*, 14.

[45] Thompson, *Wiring a Continent*, 356.

[46] Frederick MacCrellish to Charles Stebbins, 27 December 1860, Sibley Papers (Addition).

[47] Thompson, *Wiring a Continent*, 357.

partners in the Association for the patent rights in the Western territories collectively held by the cartel.[48] Skeptics cautioned that Sibley would not be able to finish the line in time to win the government subsidy, while in the meantime he would lock up the patent rights and prevent the confederation from forming a better agreement with another builder.[49] In the end, however, only the American Telegraph Company objected to granting Sibley the patent rights.

Sibley dispatched Western Union director Jeptha Wade to California with the daunting assignment of uniting the four feuding California telegraph companies and contracting for construction from San Francisco to Salt Lake. Upon his arrival in San Francisco, Wade found the California companies competing with each other "with their bristles up" and arguing over patent claims, much as the Association's members had been a decade before.[50] "Each thinks his line is best, in the best place, and the only one we ought to have anything to do with," Wade complained.[51] Wade made progress negotiating with each company separately, but when he assembled the company presidents, "good sense" gave way to the festering anger and bluster of "years of ruinous rivalry." Wade's description was reminiscent of the meetings of the rival Eastern telegraphers in the early days, but for one distinctly Western detail: in the California negotiations, Wade reported he had twice seen "pistols displayed." Wade concluded that such behavior inspired "disgust" in the "sensible capitalist."[52]

In March 1861, as the nation teetered on the edge of war, Wade declared success in "the most tedious and perplexing job" he had ever undertaken.[53] The California State Telegraph Company absorbed three other California companies and signed a contract to build the Pacific line from San Francisco to Salt Lake via Sacramento.[54] California State Telegraph formed a new company, the Overland Telegraph, to construct

[48] Sibley to J. D. Caton, 6 December 1860, Caton Papers.

[49] Thomas Bassnett to Caton, 18 December 1860, Caton Papers.

[50] The Morse magnetic relay patent was renewed in 1860, but Morse's original patent, covering his system of telegraphing, had already been renewed and was set to expire in June 1861. In the meantime, the California State Company was the only firm legally using the Morse patent, and litigation against its rivals was pending. See Robert J. Chandler, "The California News-Telegraph Monopoly, 1860–1870," *Southern California Quarterly* 58(1976): 467.

[51] Wade to Isaac Elwood, 1 January 1861, Sibley Papers (Addition).

[52] Jeptha Wade to Isaac Elwood, 24 January 1861, Sibley Papers (Addition).

[53] Wade to C. H. Stebbins, 6 February 1861, Wade Papers.

[54] California State Telegraph Company Board Meeting, 16 March 1861, WUC; Reid, *The Telegraph in America*, 501. The California State Telegraph was first incorporated in 1853.

the line, and California State Telegraph shareholders bought most of the $1.25 million in Overland stock.[55] For the Eastern portion of the transcontinental line, Sibley created a new company of his own, the Pacific Telegraph Company. Wade became the president of the new firm, incorporated in Nebraska with $1 million in capital subscribed by Western Union insiders. Sibley appointed Edward Creighton, who had surveyed several possible routes, to build the Eastern portion of the line from Omaha to Salt Lake. If one company reached Salt Lake City four months ahead of the other, the trailing company would have to pay a fifty-dollar fine for every additional day of construction.[56]

On July 4, 1861, as President Lincoln called Congress together to declare the Confederacy in rebellion, workers planted the first pole of the Pacific Telegraph, one of the greatest feats of construction in the nineteenth century. Without the benefit of the transcontinental railroad, which did not open until 1869, the project depended upon the motive force of seven hundred oxen and one hundred mules to carry men and material across the plains. Creighton's four hundred men were each outfitted with a rifle and navy revolver, and one hundred head of cattle – a self-propelled beef supply, accompanied the party. Separate teams of workers dug holes, raised cedar and pine poles, and pinioned three quarters of a million pounds of iron wire, unwinding a line across the country at a rate of three to ten miles per day.[57] The often-discussed threat from Indians saboteurs did not materialize – a combination of gift giving and promotion of the belief that the "Great Spirit" was in the line allegedly discouraged tampering.[58]

The Eastern expedition reached Salt Lake on October 24 and the Western crew arrived two days later. The formal announcement of the line's completion came on November 15 – four months and eleven days after the venture began and nearly eighteen months sooner than the most optimistic predictions.[59] With the Civil War worsening, the line across the continent became a potent symbol of national unity, and the first official messages it carried confirmed that the West remained part of the Union. When the line reached Salt Lake City, Brigham Young announced in the

---

[55] Ibid., 493.
[56] Ibid., 493–4.
[57] The single-day record for construction was sixteen miles. Lewis Coe, *The Telegraph: A History of Morse's Invention and Its Predecessors in the United States* (Jefferson, N.C.: McFarland, 1993), 40.
[58] Sibley, "Memories of Hiram Sibley," 134.
[59] "The Pacific Telegraph Line," *The New York Times*, 29 October 1861, 5.

inaugural message, "Utah has not seceded, but is firm for the Constitution and laws of our once happy country."[60] The first official dispatch from California carried a similar message to Abraham Lincoln from Stephen J. Field, the Chief Justice of California and brother of Cyrus Field.[61] "Time is annihilated," reported the *Chicago Tribune*, "indeed, more than annihilated to the Californians, since the difference is three hours in their favor."[62]

The press hardly exaggerated the eradication of the information lag between East and West. On the Pony Express, a short-lived, expensive, and undeniably romantic venture to transmit private mail via brave young mounted men dashing full-speed along a string of frontier outposts, a message took ten days to travel from Missouri to California. The Pacific Telegraph reached across the same distance in just minutes. Two hundred messages per day flew through the line even before it officially opened. A ten-word message from Washington to San Francisco cost $6, twice the three-dollar limit set by the Pacific Telegraph Act.[63] "The tariff is fixed by law," Representative Schuyler Colfax objected in a letter to the *Chicago Tribune*, but apparently to no avail.[64]

The Pacific line brought Western Union both profit and prestige and made it one of the world's most far-reaching enterprises.[65] It also proved a very lucrative investment for Sibley and his associates. The enterprise expended only $147,000 in building the eastern half of the line, but distributed $1 million in nominal capital stock to investors. This they later exchanged for Western Union stock on a generous basis, shortly before Western Union increased its capital. For their $147,000 in cash, investors received Western Union stock with a par value of $6 million. By 1866, even with Western Union's stock trading at half of par, one dollar invested in 1860 in Sibley's Pacific telegraph scheme yielded $20. The line itself, however, was not long-lived. In 1868, Western Union built new lines on the Transcontinental Railroad right-of-way, abandoning the original transcontinental telegraph. The millions in Western Union stock issued to insiders for the first Pacific telegraph line now represented little more than debris scattered on the plains.[66]

---

[60] "The Pacific Telegraph Line," *The New York Times*, 19 October 1861, 5.
[61] Thompson, *Wiring a Continent*, 368.
[62] "The Pacific Telegraph," *Chicago Tribune*, 26 October 1861, 1.
[63] Thompson, *Wiring a Continent*, 369.
[64] Schuyler Colfax, "Tolls on the Pacific Telegraph," *Chicago Tribune*, 11 November 1861, 1.
[65] Reid, *The Telegraph in America*, 496.
[66] Thompson, *Wiring a Continent*, 370; Reid, *The Telegraph in America*, 497.

When the Civil War began in April 1861, four major telegraph companies – all parties to the Treaty of the Six Nations – provided most of the
telegraph service in the United States. Only two of them, Western Union
and J. D. Caton's Illinois & Mississippi, lay entirely within the Union.
The other two, the American Telegraph Company and Norvin Green's
Southwestern, had lines both North and South. The Southwestern's territory ran from Louisville to New Orleans and west to the Mexican frontier. The American Telegraph Company's trunk ran from Newfoundland
to New York and Washington and then along the Southern seaboard to
Galveston.[67] Initially, these North–South connections proved a boon.
Telegraph activity spiked as sectional tensions heightened, bringing a
surge in profits to the lines that operated on both sides of what would
become the Confederate border. The American Telegraph Company paid
a handsome 12 percent dividend rate going into 1861.[68] In November
1860, Green reported that his Southwestern Telegraph's New Orleans
lines were full of business dispatches thanks to the economic instabil-
ity generated by what Green called the "revolutionary agitations of the
South."[69] But the advantage was short lived; the war cut the North–
South telegraph networks in two. The Southwestern carried on business
between Louisville and secessionist New Orleans until the summer of
1861, when a Confederate army seized the company's Southern wires.[70]
On April 18, the day after Virginia seceded, Confederate troops captured
Harpers Ferry and cut off one of the American Telegraph Company's two
Washington trunk lines.

Forward-looking leaders on both sides immediately recognized that the
telegraph was a military asset. The Union government, however, moved
slowly to secure the lines. Despite the imminent danger of a Confederate
raid on the capital, the manager of the American Telegraph Company's
Washington office recalled, the telegraph was "left open to everybody, for
any business whatever, treason or otherwise." The Confederate raid on
Harpers Ferry spurred executives to take action on the Union's behalf.
After consulting with federal officials, Edward S. Sanford, the president

---

[67] Reid, *The Telegraph in America*, 519.
[68] Meeting of the Board of Directors of the American Telegraph Company, 28 February
1861, WUC. At the May 1861 board meeting, the dividend was cut to 1.5 percent. The
American Telegraph Company did not increase its capital, did not issue significant debt,
and did not allow its lines to deteriorate, so it is reasonable to assume that its dividends
reflected genuine profits.
[69] Norvin Green to Susa Green, 28 November 1860, Green Papers (U.K.).
[70] Norvin Green to Henry Bingham, 6 June 1890, WUC; Edward Rosewater testimony,
"Postal Telegraph Facilities," 51st Congress, WUC.

of the American Telegraph Company, issued secret censorship orders to "arrest and detain" any dispatch in a cipher code or not clearly relating to "regular business." In a vague directive that placed great discretionary power in the hands of the company's office managers, Sanford also ordered a halt to messages "in any way injurious to the interest of the Government."[71] On April 19, news that a mob had harassed federal soldiers in Baltimore led the American Telegraph Company's Washington manager – on his own authority – to cut communication with Richmond. But a closer collaboration with the government soon developed. Federal militia guarded the American Telegraph Company's Washington office, and the following day the War Department sent a representative to serve as a censor.[72] In late April Secretary of War Simon Cameron asked Thomas Scott, the president of the Pennsylvania Railroad, to supervise the railroad and telegraph.[73] Scott appointed his own deputies to the task, but without any materials, equipment, or funding for a military telegraph, Scott's men depended upon Sanford and the American Telegraph Company.[74]

The actual situation, however, was more complicated than Sanford's secret patriotic directives made it appear. The American Telegraph Company was already cooperating with the Confederate government as well. In February 1861, with seven states already seceded, Sanford had answered a summons to discuss telegraph matters in Montgomery, the first Confederate capital.[75] The American Telegraph Company was vulnerable to accusations of Northern sympathies; despite its extensive

---

[71] Alfred B. Talcott, Testimony, House Judiciary Committee Hearings on Telegraph Censorship, 37th Congress, 24 January 1862, National Archives (37) HJ-T.1–29. Talcott recalled seizing "a great many messages, private and public." Richard B. Kielbowicz has noted that this censorship was extraordinary both in its precedence and in the discretion it gave to a private company with only the vaguest guidelines. See Richard B. Kielbowicz, "The Telegraph, Censorship, and Politics at the Outset of the Civil War," *Civil War History* 40, no. 2 (1994): 98. There is a possibility that some ad hoc censorship of telegrams preceded these actions. Amos Kendall complained to Caton in mid-March that the U.S. government had stopped some messages. Kendall to Caton, 14 March 1861, Caton Papers.

[72] Talcott, Testimony.

[73] Experience with modern industrial warfare makes it difficult to imagine that the U.S. military did not immediately recognize the strategic value of the railroad and telegraph, but Robert Angevine has argued that even the army's aid to railroads before the war did "not increase its appreciation of the railroads' military value or its ability to incorporate them into practice." The telegraph appears to have been similarly ignored. Angevine, *The Railroad and the State*, xv.

[74] Benjamin Sidney Michael Schwantes, "Fallible Guardian: The Social Construction of Railroad Telegraphy in 19th-Century America" (University of Delaware, 2008), 119.

[75] Hiram Sibley to Isaac Elwood, 4 February 1861, Sibley Papers (Addition).

Southern business, the American Telegraph Company had only a single director from the South, Dr. William Morris. On May 11 the Confederate Congress authorized President Jefferson Davis to take control of telegraph lines in the Confederacy. The next day Sanford and Morris held an emergency meeting in Washington and Morris assumed the presidency of a provisional "Southern Telegraph Company" consisting of the American Telegraph Company's lines from Virginia to New Orleans. Morris left immediately for Montgomery to provide the Confederate government with "guarantees for security to all southern interest."[76] Under guidelines from the Confederate Postmaster General, Southern Telegraph Company operators took an oath of loyalty to the Confederacy. The "new" company assumed some responsibility for procuring materials for military telegraphy and constructing field telegraphs for the Confederate armies, beginning a close association between the private firm and the Confederate war effort that grew still closer as the conflict dragged on.[77] In July 1861, Southern American Telegraph Company shareholders met in Richmond and formally resolved to manage the American's Southern lines, for their exclusive benefit, as the Southern Telegraph Company.[78]

In the Western Confederacy, the Southwestern Company similarly split in two. John Van Horne, a Southwestern superintendent, opened a Southern headquarters in Nashville and carried on the company's business in the Confederacy, leaving only a few lines in Norvin Green's control in Kentucky. Communication between the Union and Confederate sections of the company effectively ceased for the duration of the war. Green's decision to remain in Kentucky, however, nearly proved disastrous for the

---

[76] J.R. Dowell to H. D. Plant, 12 May 1861, Southern Telegraph Company Papers.

[77] William Morris to Postmaster General John Reagan, 21 May 1861, Southern Telegraph Company Papers; John Reagan to William Morris, 23 May 1861, Southern Telegraph Company Papers; John Reagan to "Gentlemen," 24 May 1861, Southern Telegraph Company Papers. According to legend, representatives from the two firms met on the Long Bridge outside Washington a final time on May 21. There is no evidence to support this story. See William R. Plum, *The Military Telegraph During the Civil War in the United States*, 2 vols., vol. 1 (Chicago: Jansen, McClurg & Company, 1882), 69.

[78] C. P. Culver, *The Southern Telegraph* (Confederate Imprints, University of Georgia Library, 1863). This solution enraged Culver, whose family owned many shares of the Washington & New Orleans line, which the American Telegraph Company had recently leased. Except for this lease, the American Telegraph Company probably owned none of the lines in the South. The shareholders in the Washington & New Orleans received a 6 percent rent, but none of the large dividends that the Southern Telegraph Company generated. Culver claimed that of the thousands of shares in the American Telegraph Company, only six hundred were held by the Richmond parties that controlled the Southern Telegraph Company.

Southwestern's Southern operations. In 1862 the Confederate government took over the lines, citing the "confusion" sown in the Southwest by Green's decision to take "refuge in the enemy's lines."[79] An alliance between Southwestern managers and military authorities in the region repelled the Confederate takeover. A few months later the government appointed the Southern Telegraph Company's Morris as supervisor over all telegraph lines in the Confederacy.[80]

For the telegraph companies entirely within the Union, the Civil War was an unmixed blessing. The war created a steadily growing rush of government, business, and press traffic. For the military, the telegraph became an indispensable tool for mobilizing men and materiel. The War Department's procurement practices created a "mixed military economy," wherein the powerful Quartermaster's Department used both private contractors and "public enterprises" to obtain the goods and services it required.[81] In a relationship similar to that enjoyed by the railroads, a combination of civilian and military leaders managed the telegraph. Their overlapping responsibilities to both the War Department and the private firms blurred the boundaries between public and private interest until they were almost indistinguishable. Under the regulations of the Quartermaster's Department, the formal contracting process was too cumbersome for railroads and telegraphs, while the complexity and celerity of railroad and telegraph operations encouraged the War Department to allow civilian managers to remain in charge and even negotiate their own rate schedules.[82] Western Union and the American Telegraph Company encouraged the perception that they served the Union in a spirit of patriotic voluntarism. In reality the two companies' managers, serving as government officials while overseeing their own firms, managed to turn the government into the client, protector, and builder of the private telegraph companies.

[79] John Reagan to Thomas L. Carter, 16 September 1862, Southern Telegraph Company Papers.

[80] Dowell to William Morris, 1 June 1862, Southern Telegraph Company; John Reagan to Thomas L. Carter, 16 September 1862, Southern Telegraph Company Papers; William Morris to Dowell, 17 September 1862, Southern Telegraph Company.

[81] Mark R. Wilson, *The Business of Civil War: Military Mobilization and the State, 1861–1865* (Baltimore: The Johns Hopkins University Press, 2006).

[82] Paul A. C. Koistinen, *Beating Plowshares into Swords: The Political Economy of American Warfare, 1606–1865* (Lawrence, Kans.: University Press of Kansas, 1996), 156; Wilson, *The Business of Civil War*, 135; John E. Clark, *Railroads in the Civil War: The Impact of Management on Victory and Defeat* (Baton Rouge: Louisiana State University Press, 2001), 23–4, 62.

When the war began, the American Telegraph Company's lines in and around Washington were of critical value to the federal government. For seven months the American Telegraph Company served as an ad hoc military telegraph, with Sanford directing his company to pay for all the operators and equipment that the government required. A telegrapher in Washington recalled this was a "generous and patriotic act on the part of Sanford," though Congress later reimbursed the American Telegraph Company, which Sanford had surely anticipated.[83] Henry O'Rielly, of course, saw the situation in a different light. He complained in May 1861 that though Secretary Cameron understood the necessity of a military telegraph, Sanford had seized the opportunity out of self-interest. "The American Telegraph Company use their power as such large companies and rich people usually do, to have a large finger in the pie," O'Rielly wrote.[84]

Western Union played an even greater part in military telegraphy. To secure Ohio's border with Virginia, Governor William Dennison invited Western Union's general manager, Anson Stager, to devise a cipher system for communication between regional governors. When George B. McClellan assumed control of the federal troops in the Department of the Ohio, he appointed Stager the superintendent of military telegraphs for the entire Department, giving him authority over all the telegraph lines in the region.[85] McClellan explained the appointment as a necessity, since "so large a portion of the lines" in his territory belonged to Western Union.[86] "So large a portion," but not all – Stager's appointment gave him control over lines owned by rivals to his own corporation.[87] And though Stager's military responsibilities steadily increased, he remained Western Union's general manager.

The Union military built more than 1,100 miles of telegraph lines in the first seven months of the war and employed more than a thousand operators. The lines advanced with the Union armies at a rate of eight to twelve miles per day, providing what McClellan called an "indispensable auxiliary" to the military.[88] The loose organization of military telegraphy

---

[83] David Homer Bates, *Lincoln in the Telegraph Office: Recollections of the United States Military Telegraph Corps during the Civil War* (New York: The Century Co., 1907), 35–6.
[84] Henry O'Reilly to J. J. Speed, 11 May 1861, O'Reilly Papers (RHS).
[85] Plum, *The Military Telegraph*, 44, 92–3.
[86] George McClellan to Governor Gates, 13 May 1861, Caton Papers.
[87] Plum, *The Military Telegraph*, 93–4.
[88] Ibid., 125–6.

placed several different telegraph organizations in the field in competition for operators and resources. Major Albert J. Myer, the army's only commissioned signal officer at the outset of the war, attempted to incorporate the telegraph in the Army Signal Corps and take it out of the hands of the private companies and the civilian Stager.[89] But Secretary of War Cameron preferred Stager's leadership, and in October 1861 he asked Stager to submit a comprehensive plan for a military telegraph service.

With President Lincoln's approval, Stager assumed control of the new United States Military Telegraph Corps. Stager had envisioned the corps as a purely civilian unit, but the Union Quartermaster would release supplies only to commissioned officers, and civilian leaders would be personally responsible for government funds advanced to the corps – a potential liability for Stager and his men. The War Department thus decided to commission Stager and a dozen of his managers, giving them the authority of rank while their subordinates remained out of uniform. This compromise placed the military operators in a difficult position. They "braved nearly all the dangers incident to the service," but "without rank, name or position."[90] Even the pay of the military telegrapher was a concession – at a maximum of $60 per month in 1861, he earned considerably more than the $13 paid to a private soldier, but less than the more than $100 per month earned by a first-class commercial telegrapher who worked fewer hours in greater comfort.[91]

In February 1862, Congress expanded the scope of Stager's Corps. At the beginning of the year, Congress had authorized President Lincoln to "take possession of any or all the telegraph lines in the United States, their offices and appurtenances" and place them under military control.[92] The administration had no intention of doing so, and instead increased the power of the private managers. The new secretary of war, Edwin Stanton, made Stager the supervisor of all the telegraph lines in the United States with the American Telegraph Company's Sanford serving as "military supervisor of telegraphic messages" – the Union's official censor. In practice, though Stanton understood the importance of controlling the wires

---

[89] Paul J. Scheips, "Union Signal Communications: Innovation and Conflict," *Civil War History* IX, no. 4 (1963): 399–401.

[90] Ibid., 131.

[91] Ibid., 106; ibid., 107.

[92] Statutes at Large, 37th Congress, 2d Session, Chapter XV, 334. The Railroad Act of January 1, 1862 similarly authorized the government to seize, regulate and control the Northern railroads. Angevine, *The Railroad and the State*, 134.

far better than his predecessor and earned a reputation as a "notorious" censor of the press, he did not need to seize uncooperative lines.[93] Gaps remained in what was really a "hit or miss censorship." Stanton's own orders suggested that military supervision should not "interfere" with "private business."[94] Except for a couple of isolated incidents, no Northern telegraph company resisted Stager's supervision.[95]

Under the direct oversight of the secretary of war, Stager had authority over the construction and organization of military lines, the purchase of materials, and the appointment and removal of officers and operators, who served in an independent chain of command. Even generals in the field could not move or close telegraph posts without Stager's approval. The Military Telegraph Corps connected to commercial lines on which military messages had priority over all other messages, and nonmilitary messages could be excluded when necessary.[96] It is impossible to know to what degree Stager conducted his military duties with his responsibility to Western Union in mind. In April 1862, he told his associate Jeptha Wade that he looked forward to relief from his military commission, but would remain until it could "be given up without detriment to the Telegraph interests of the country."[97] Stager's definition of "Telegraph interests" may have included all of the North American Telegraph Association, but probably not any "outside" company. A senior manager at the Illinois & Mississippi Telegraph believed Western Union deliberately used its "immense" political influence to win the government's cooperation with the civilian companies and then to commission Stager with their "general supervision." Stager, it seemed, believed "the interests of the Government, of the Western Union Company and of Anson Stager" were "identical."[98]

Secretary Stanton kept the Military Telegraph Corps in what a senior officer in the rival Army Signal Corps described as his "iron grasp,"

---

[93] David Mindich, "Edwin M. Stanton, the Inverted Pyramid, and Information Control," in *The Civil War and the Press*, ed. David B. Sachsman, S. Kittreell Rushing, and Debra Reddin van Tuyll (New Brunswick, N.J.: Transaction Publishers, 2000), 190.

[94] "Telegraph Censorship," Senate Report No. 64. J. Cutler Andrews, *The North Reports the Civil War* (Pittsburgh: University of Pittsburgh Press, 1955), 641.

[95] Plum, *The Military Telegraph*, 93.

[96] Major General Halleck, Special Field Order No. 151, Clowry Papers; Major General Halleck to Major General Grant, 5 December 1862, Clowry Papers; R. C. Clowry to R. W. Crampton, 28 January 1865, Clowry Papers.

[97] Anson Stager to Jeptha Wade, 16 April 1862, Wade Papers.

[98] Thomas Bassnett to J. D. Caton, 15 December 1861, Caton Papers.

observing that Stanton always consulted with the "corporation representatives who dominated the War Department."[99] Ulysses S. Grant recalled that Stanton so strictly controlled the Military Telegraph that an operator once refused to allow Grant to enter a telegraph office or use the cipher because Stanton had issued an order not to admit the "commanding general or any one else."[100] Because military commanders had a tendency to misplace their cipher books, Stanton placed military cipher communications entirely in the hands of the civilian operators of the Military Telegraph Corps.[101]

A. J. Myer, who headed the all-military Signal Corps, resented collusion between the civilian Military Telegraph Corps and the telegraph companies. He condemned the "powerful and despotic sway of the corporations" and the "gigantic arm of monopoly ... stretched out in greed to clutch" the military telegraph.[102] Hoping to acquire greater control of field telegraphy, Myer challenged Stager's authority again in 1863. Stanton, like Cameron before him, sided with Stager. He dismissed Myer, and placed the entire responsibility for military telegraphy in Stager's corps of "practical Telegraphers."[103]

In both the North and South, the boundaries between the private companies and military lines blurred beyond recognition as the conflict escalated. William Morris served simultaneously as the president of the Southern Telegraph Company and overseer of the Confederate military lines, which were an adjunct to the commercial lines rather than an independent entity. The Southern Telegraph Company routinely built new lines according to specific requests by Confederate military commanders.[104] In the North, the line between military and commercial lines was

[99] A. W. Greely, "The Military Telegraph Service," in *The Photographic History of the Civil War*, ed. Francis Trevelyan Miller (New York: The Review of Reviews Co., 1911), 344.

[100] Ulysses S. Grant, *Memoirs and Selected Letters: Personal Memoirs of U.S. Grant, Selected Letters 1839–1865* (New York: The Library of America, 1990), 460–1.

[101] "Order of the Secretary of War," 1 January 1864, Clowry Papers. Clowry's small collection of papers include two reports of lost cipher books in the Department of the Missouri alone. William W. Whessy to George H. Smith, 15 November 1863, Clowry Papers; J. W. Davison, 30 November 1863, Clowry Papers.

[102] Myer is quoted in Scheips, "Union Signal Communications," 412; Rebecca Robbins Raines, *Getting the Message Through: A Branch History of the U.S. Army Signal Corps*, Army History Series (Washington, D.C.: Center of Military History U.S. Army, 1996), 412.

[103] Anson Stager, "Circular to the Headquarters of the U.S. Military Telegraph," 23 February 1864, Clowry Papers.

[104] References to a variety of such orders may be found in the Southern Telegraph Company Papers.

more clearly delineated, but military and commercial management was even more tightly intertwined. Anson Stager made it his policy never to build government lines when private companies could do the business cheaper. When the Military Telegraph Corps did build lines in Union territory, Stager assured the private companies that the government would sell them the lines at the end of the war rather than maintaining them as a government telegraph.[105] Stager claimed in 1862 that government communications provided "comparatively small revenue" for the private companies but "greatly depressed" commercial business.[106] Yet there is no evidence that the private companies lost money at the hands of the government. Stager simultaneously served as chief of the military lines *and* bill collector for the companies. Sanford also pulled double duty, acting as the Telegraph Association's negotiator for government payments for the use of the Morse relay while continuing to serve as the government's chief censor.[107]

As in the private companies, operators were the military telegraph services' most valuable asset. More than a thousand military operators served in the Union's Corps, securing their offices and codebooks, sleeping beside their keys, and demanding military commanders not interfere with their lines while depending upon them for protection and logistical support.[108] Operators often came under enemy fire, particularly when building improvised field lines on stakes or strung from tree to tree. In a pinch, a skilled operator on the front could forego his sounder and receive messages by holding a live wire to his tongue.[109] Service in the Confederate military telegraph often required working "night and day." Operators protested that their pay did not keep up with rampant inflation in the Southern states. Despite appeals for salary increases, wages remained low and the Confederate telegraph corps ran perpetually short of operators and clerks.[110] North and South, military telegraphy exacted

---

[105] J. J. Wilson to J. D. Caton, 14 December 1861, Caton Papers.
[106] Stager's 1862 annual report is reprinted in full in Plum, *The Military Telegraph*, 361–2.
[107] Proceedings of the Seventh Annual Meeting of the North American Telegraph Association, 17 August 1864, Caton Papers.
[108] Theodore Hall to R. C. Clowry, 10 June 1865, Clowry Papers; John Severing to General True, 1 April [year unknown], Clowry Papers.
[109] This particular trick was observed by General William Sherman. W. J. Johnston, *Telegraphic Tales and Telegraphic History: A Popular Account of the Electric Telegraph – Its Uses, Extent and Outgrowths* (New York: W. J. Johnston, 1880), 76–7.
[110] William Morris to John Reagan, 29 May 1863, Southern Telegraph Company Papers; John F. Miller, 20 October 1863, Southern Telegraph Company Papers; Dowell to William Morris, 25 February 1864, Southern Telegraph Company Papers.

a heavy toll from operators: an estimated one in twelve was killed, wounded, captured, or otherwise died in service.[111]

In both sections, military telegraph operators resisted low wages and onerous working conditions by organizing and threatening to strike. In many industries in the North, workers overburdened by inflation, taxation, and the draft joined "turnouts." Workers in essential war-related industries found their indispensability cut both ways – combined labor action was a potent weapon met with accusations of conspiracy, disloyalty, and even treason.[112] United States Military Telegraph Corps operators, civilians in a military service, could not just resign their posts. Some had been drafted into the military and given special leave to serve in the Telegraph Corps, and resigning from the Corps meant returning to active military duty. Others who switched to commercial jobs were drafted and then detailed to the Telegraph Corps at lower military pay.[113] The Telegraph Corps shared a "black list" with the commercial companies to ensure that incompetent or troublesome operators who left the military service could not find private work.[114] When a group of eighteen operators demanded a raise and threatened to strike, Stager announced that operators attempting to "quit the service in combined bodies" faced military arrest and trial as "conspirators." Not surprisingly, most of the operators recanted.[115]

Southern operators were better organized and formed a union, the Southern Telegraph Association. Few details about the union or its membership have survived, but employers accused the Association of "extorting pay" and trying to prevent newcomers from learning the telegraph trade.[116] The Association never launched a strike, but posed a threat, and in 1864 Morris preemptively dismissed enough Association

---

[111] Plum, *The Military Telegraph*, 337, 352.

[112] Grace Palladino, *Another Civil War: Labor, Capital and the State in the Anthracite Regions of Pennsylvania, 1840–1868* (Urbana and Chicago: University of Illinois Press, 1990), 122–3.

[113] R. C. Clowry to Secretary Stanton, 28 October 1863; R. C. Clowry to Anson Stager, 4 November 1864, Clowry Papers. Plum, *The Military Telegraph*, 106–7.

[114] R. C. Clowry to Anson Stager, 20 June 1865, Clowry Papers.

[115] Plum, *The Military Telegraph*, 113–17. For letters from the "conspirators," see the Gross Papers. Stager's approach to strikers during the war was consistent with the response of other Union generals who helped to thwart strikes in industries engaged in war production. See Philip S. Foner, *History of the Labor Movement in the United States: From Colonial Times to the Founding of the American Federation of Labor* (New York: International Publishers, 1947), 328.

[116] Undated Minutes of the Executive Committee of the Southern Telegraph Company, Southern Telegraph Company Papers.

members to create disruptions and delays in service. Morris reported the names of the discharged operators to draft authorities. Contrite offenders were detailed back to the telegraph service as conscripts; the rest were mustered into regular military service.[117] Northern industries similarly used draft agents to undermine labor organizing – provost marshals practically served as capital's enforcement arm.[118]

During the Civil War, Northern businesses enjoyed record profits due largely to inflation caused by the printing of paper currency not backed by gold or silver. By 1864 the value of the greenback had fallen to thirty-five cents relative to the value of a dollar in gold, pushing down the real value of wages, rents, and interest and boosting business profits.[119] Western Union prospered to an unprecedented extent.[120] It began paying dividends in 1857, and by 1862 the annual payout, despite Stager's protests of poverty, had risen to 9 percent. However, even these generous cash payments were dwarfed by a flood of Western Union "stock dividends," a financial tool that served both to enrich existing shareholders, and, somewhat misguidedly, as a weapon against emerging competitors. The government, it seemed, was not the only institution that could print paper.

To buy telegraph stock in the early 1860s, an investor could not simply ask a broker to place an order. Major exchanges such as the New

---

[117] Secretary of War Seddons to William Morris, 2 March 1864, Southern Telegraph Company Papers; William Morris to Secretary Seddons, 3 March 1864, Southern Telegraph Company Papers.

[118] Palladino, *Another Civil War*, 140–1.

[119] Wesley Clair Mitchell, *A History of the Greenbacks* (Chicago: The University of Chicago Press, 1903), 382; Mark Thornton and Robert B. Ekelund Jr., *Tariffs, Blockades, and Inflation: The Economics of the Civil War* (Wilmington, Del.: Scholarly Resources, Inc., 2004), 68.

[120] Roger Ransom reviewed the scholarly debate on the economic effect of the war and concluded that on balance, scholars now agree that the war did not propel the industrial economy forward. See Roger Ransom, *Conflict and Compromise: The Political Economy of Slavery, Emancipation, and the American Civil War* (New York: Cambridge University Press, 1989), 258, 264. Heather Cox Richardson presented the now widely accepted consensus that the American economy was institutionally transformed by the Civil War. In contrast to the antebellum period, businesses "had begun to operate on a national scale." Richardson, *The Greatest Nation of the Earth*, 1. Ransom has recently argued that the question is not whether the Civil War accelerated economic growth, it did not, but whether growth could have continued at a similarly rapid pace without the transformations that took place as a result of the North's victory. See Roger Ransom, "War and Cliometrics: Adventures in Economic History," *The Journal of Economic History* 66, no. 2 (2005): 271–282.

York Stock Exchange listed only a handful of stocks – mostly railroads, no telegraph companies. Instead, brokerage houses sold telegraph stocks at auction, and Western Union stock was in such high demand that it was not only dear in price, but also practically very difficult to obtain.[121] New shares emerged through the issue of "stock dividends." A stock dividend was similar to what today is called a "stock split," whereby new shares are given to existing investors according to a ratio, such as two shares for one. A modern stock split increases the number of shares but does not reflect any change in a company's intrinsic value, which is measured by the company's earning potential rather than capital assets. In the explanation of an infamous stock operator, a split is like re-pricing a $1 per-pound package that was "hard to move" at a more "easily vendible" price of twenty-five cents per quarter pound.[122] On the other hand, nineteenth-century law required a "stock dividend" to reflect an increase in a company's capital assets, usually in the form of retained earnings invested in new lines, equipment, and patents. If investors believed the new stock reflected real value, the price per share would remain unchanged even though the number of shares had increased. New shares that did not reflect such an increase in asset value were considered "watered stock," and the company that issued it "overcapitalized."[123]

Western Union issued a series of stock dividends in the 1860s.[124] In 1862, the company announced a 27 percent stock dividend, bringing its total capital to just under $3 million – about the same as the American Telegraph Company, its primary rival. In March 1863, Western Union issued another 9 percent cash dividend and a *100 percent* stock dividend,

---

[121] Though the New York Stock Exchange did not list telegraph stocks, newspapers such as *The New York Times* published classified advertisements for telegraph stock available for auction. Western Union did not list on the New York Stock Exchange until the fall of 1865. Executive Committee Minutes, 19 January 1865, WUC.

[122] Edwin Lefevre, *Reminiscences of a Stock Operator* (Greenville, S.C.: Traders Press, 1923), 306.

[123] Post–Civil War investors began the shift from asset pricing to earnings pricing in the stock market. Though "no-par" stock was still two decades away, in 1904 Thorsten Veblen dismissed the notion that a modern corporation's common stock could be "watered." Thorstein Veblen, *The Theory of Business Enterprise* (New York: Charles Scribner's Sons, 1904), 117–18.

[124] Western Union also issued new stock in the 1850s. J. D. Reid gives an account of these stock bonuses and Thompson reprints them, but the math is completely wrong. The discrepancy is probably explained by typographical errors by Reid, a lack of accounting for new stock issued in mergers, and Thompson's failure to check Reid's calculations. See James D. Reid, *The Telegraph in America and Morse Memorial*, 2d ed. (New York: John Polhemus, 1884).

doubling its nominal capital, followed by another 33 percent stock dividend in December. Despite the dramatic increase in shares, Western
Union's stock price climbed as well, tracking the wartime surge of railroad stocks, which doubled in price in two years.[125] In 1864, demand for
Western Union stock became so frenzied that buyers in the company's
hometown of Rochester converted "pianos, guitars, furniture of various
kinds, mortgages and homesteads" into cash to buy the stock. Shares sold
for $225, more than twice the "par value" that was supposed to represent
the value of company assets. The Springfield *Republican* declared a pan-
demic of "telegraph fever." Western Union reportedly rose "with every
smile on Sibley's face."[126] In May 1864 the company issued yet another
100 percent stock dividend, making for a "red-letter day in Rochester."[127]
A share of Western Union with the par value of $100 in 1860 thus had a
par value of $678 in May 1864 – and was worth nearly $1,500 at market
prices.[128] A shareholder who bought stock in 1860 and held until 1864
would have seen his annual cash dividend payment grow nearly seven
times larger, while inflation had increased consumer prices in the North
by only 75 percent during the same period.[129]

Western Union was not the only telegraph company that thrived. The
American Telegraph Company had lost the Southern portion of its network and slashed its quarterly dividend in the spring of 1861. However,
its Northern holdings, with government cooperation, made up the difference. Demand for telegraph service was so great that the American
Telegraph Company could barely keep up with new construction, and
the company so badly needed skilled operators that it paid the $300
exemption to retain operators drafted by the military.[130] Soon after
the war began, the American Telegraph Company was back to paying

[125] Emerson David Fite, *Social and Industrial Conditions in the North during the Civil War* (New York: The Macmillan Company, 1910), 45.
[126] Parker, "How the Men of Rochester Saved the Telegraph," 132; Fite, *Social and Industrial Conditions in the North During the Civil War*, 157; Thompson, *Wiring a Continent*, 398–400.
[127] Reid, *Telegraph in America*, 537.
[128] In May 1864, the stock traded at more than $200 per share. "Western Union Telegraph Official Statement of Its Business," *Rochester Democrat*, 25 November 1865.
[129] Wilson, *The Business of Civil War*, 228.
[130] Meeting of the Board of Directors of the American Telegraph Company, 27 August 1863, WUC Collection. Thompson overstates the degree to which the American Telegraph Company suffered in the war. Although it is true that the Washington to New Orleans portion of the line was cut off, this section had been acquired by lease and was appar-ently not such a significant portion of the total business that the company was doomed without it. See Thompson, *Wiring a Continent*, 373–5.

an 8 percent dividend.[131] The Southwestern Company, which had initially lost more than two-thirds of its property in the Confederacy, also rebounded.[132] By late 1864, its dividends were larger than they had ever been, despite guerrillas frequently cutting Southwestern lines in Kentucky and Tennessee.[133]

The windfall profits enjoyed by the members of the North American Telegraph Association depended in large part on the lack of competition in telegraphy, an advantage in danger of disappearing when the Morse patent expired in June 1861, six years ahead of the recently renewed patent on the telegraph receiving magnet. In a petition most likely drafted by the now-experienced lobbyists of the Telegraph Association, Morse begged the Senate Committee on Patents to issue a special extension, arguing that competitors using the patent-free Morse telegraph would try to circumvent the active patent on the Morse magnetic relay, its "Siamese twin." After twenty years of litigating to defend his patent claims, Morse hoped Congress would grant him "the small boon" of a special renewal.[134] The Committee favorably reported a bill to extend the Morse telegraph patent to April 1867 when the receiving magnetic patent would expire. But with the start of the war, the bill fell by the wayside.[135]

The prosperity of the telegraph during the war and the expiration of the Morse patent made new competition inevitable. The North American Telegraph Association maintained exclusive control over the Morse relay, however, putting competitors at a technical disadvantage.[136] In 1862 the Independent Telegraph Company challenged the American Telegraph Company between Boston and New York, connecting to Washington soon thereafter. The Independent, as its name implied, was excluded from the telegraph cartel and its cozy relationship with the War Department. Therefore messages over the Independent's lines were not subject to

---

[131] Meeting of the Board of Directors of the American Telegraph Company, 23 May 1861 and 22 August 1861, WUC Collection. At most board meetings, Wilson Hunt was the lone dissenter calling for a lower dividend.

[132] Thompson, *Wiring a Continent*, 375.

[133] Norvin Green to Pinckney Green, 28 October 1864, Green Papers (U.K.); Norvin Green to Pinckney Green, 8 September 1864, Uncataloged Green Papers (FHS).

[134] Senate Report 310, 36th Congress, 2 March 1861.

[135] "A Bill to extend a patent heretofore granted to Samuel F. B. Morse," S. 575, 36th Congress, 2nd Session, 2 March 1861.

[136] Without the patent for the Morse relay magnet, the new lines were unable to work long circuits without repeating by hand, a process that was slow, expensive and liable to error. On the other hand, they did not have to pay half their capital stock to Morse, as the early Morse companies had been required to do. See Hiram Sibley to A. B. Smith, 25 March 1863, Sibley Papers (Addition).

government "supervision," but the Independent also carried none of the government correspondence for which the American Telegraph Company and Western Union were well paid.[137]

The Telegraph Association divided on how to respond to new competition. American Telegraph Company managers judged the Independent a legitimate threat. President Edward Sanford believed his company should "strike home," crushing the upstarts with deep rate cuts rather than buying them out and encouraging other invaders "to try the same game." Sibley, on the other hand, believed such "opposition" companies had little hope of success against the Six Nations anyway. Cartel rules prevented opposition companies from connecting to cartel lines in the United States or Canada, and cartel companies had locked up the railroad rights-of-way between New York, Chicago, Pittsburgh, and St. Louis, leaving the opposition to build "poor lines" through trees along highways.[138]

Sanford turned out to be correct. The Independent and two other new firms – the Inland and the United States Extension – merged in 1864 to overcome the hurdles erected by the Six Nations cartel. The combined United States Telegraph Company was backed by investors whom manager J. D. Reid described as "men of enterprise and large wealth," though in fact none had notable fortunes.[139] The new firm had a nominal capital of $6 million – $2 million for the shareholders of the merging lines and $4 million to sell to "country" investors who might catch the "telegraph fever."[140] The aggressive new enterprise already boasted ten thousand miles of interurban lines competing directly with Western Union and the American Telegraph Company.[141] To overcome the Six

---

[137] This situation persisted until May 1864, when the Independent's New York and Washington offices were briefly seized by the military during the "Bogus Proclamation" scandal. The lines were restored two days later, and the Independent was granted the option to connect directly to the War Department and carry government messages in exchange for government supervision. It is not clear if this offer ever was accepted. See Bates, *Lincoln in the Telegraph Office*, 235–40; Blondheim, "'Public Sentiment Is Everything'."

[138] Hiram Sibley to A. B. Smith, 25 March 1863, Sibley Papers (Addition).

[139] Little is known about the men in Reid's list of twenty original directors. Those who have left a record were bankers, brokers or entrepreneurs who were publicly respected but apparently not particularly powerful. One notable exception is Freeman Clarke, who became a Republican Congressman and had been one of the founders of Western Union. See Reid, *Telegraph in America*, 530.

[140] O. H. Palmer to Hiram Sibley, 4 May 1864, Sibley Family Papers (Addition).

[141] Reid, *The Telegraph in America*, 521; Abram P. Eastlake, "The Great Monopoly," *Lippincott's Magazine of Literature, Science and Education* (1870): 365. James McKaye, "The United States Telegraph Company," *Telegrapher*, 24 September 1865, 162.

Nations' advantages in rights-of-way between major cities, the United States Company sought alternate access to railroads or resorted to tricks, such as planting poles just beyond a railroad's fence line.[142] In New York, the company worked "like Beavers" to get a footing, opening an office on Wall Street and purchasing property on Broadway for a grand headquarters to rival that of the American Telegraph Company. To build up its staff, it poached operators and managers from the other companies, offering higher salaries and stock bonuses.[143] The new company publicly attacked the Six Nations with an antimonopoly campaign. United States Company president James McKaye accused the North American Telegraph Association of being an egregious monopoly. The success of the United States Company, he argued, provided "conclusive evidence" that the people had "no love for overgrown corporations" or "exclusiveness" and would support a new company that promised to assert independence and "the right of competition."[144]

The ambition of United States Telegraph was most evident in its challenge to one of the Telegraph Association's most valuable assets: the telegraph line to the Pacific. Borrowing Sibley's own strategy, the United States Company formed an independent subsidiary and issued new stock to fund a transcontinental line. McKaye sought from Congress the same generous right-of-way provisions that Sibley had secured in the Pacific Telegraph Act of 1860, and he found supporters at the Capitol. In the view of many Congressmen, Western Union had flagrantly flaunted the rate limits set in the Pacific Telegraph Act. Western Union insisted the hazard and expense of the line, which allegedly remained unprofitable, required steep prices.[145] In 1864, Republican Senator Samuel C. Pomeroy of Kansas sponsored a bill to grant the United States Company the use of public land and resources for a line to the Pacific with branches into the Idaho Territory. The "Idaho Act" passed both houses of Congress virtually without debate, though an amendment eliminated a guarantee of $20,000 per year in government business (Western Union's Pacific line was guaranteed $40,000) when the line was completed.[146]

---

[142] Thompson, *Wiring a Continent*, 402–3.

[143] John Horner to Hiram Sibley, 25 December 1864, Sibley Papers.

[144] James McKaye, "The United States Telegraph Company," *Telegrapher*, 24 September 1865, 162. Reprinted from the *New York Tribune*.

[145] "Memorial of the Pacific Telegraph Company, against the withdrawal of the telegraph subsidy, and reducing the rates of telegraphing," 37th Congress, 3rd Session, Misc. Doc. No. 20.

[146] S. 290, 38th Congress, 1st Session; Statutes at Large, Chapter 220, 38th Congress, 1st Session.

The support the United States Company most badly needed was continuous subscriptions to its stock – critics charged this was in fact the firm's chief source of operating funds. Western Union, in inflating the telegraph stock bubble with its stock dividends, had inadvertently created a market for United States Telegraph stock. But Western Union's managers concluded that the pendulum could swing both ways. They believed that if the bubble burst, United States Company stock would not sell "for 50 cents on the dollar," taking the upstart down with it.[147] Thus in May 1864, Western Union directors *doubled* the company's capital, adding $11 million in new stock – an industry insider described it as "clear and unmixed water" – to let the air out of the telegraph stock balloon.[148] The strategy backfired.

With the United States Company rapidly adding territory, Western Union's leaders expressed renewed interest in consolidating the North American Telegraph Association. In January 1864, Sibley tried to buy a majority stake in Green's Southwestern Company, but Green and his Kentucky partners wanted no part of volatile Western Union stock.[149] Green believed "one grand telegraph interest" should ultimately "cover the whole continent," but Western Union's capital expansion had gone too far. How many times, Green asked Sibley, could Western Union multiply its capital shares and still pay a dividend?[150] The final doubling of Western Union's stock had been, Green wrote, a "stupendous blunder."[151]

Other companies were less reluctant, however. When the North American Telegraph Association met in New York in August 1864, the cartel had dwindled from seven companies at the previous meeting to five – Western Union swallowed the New York, Albany & Buffalo in December 1863 and the Atlantic & Ohio in April 1864.[152] By the end of the year, rumors spread that the American Telegraph Company would merge with Western Union. Reports of a trip by Western Union managers from Rochester to New York – home to the headquarters of the American Telegraph Company – led to merger speculation that pushed up the

[147] O. H. Palmer to Hiram Sibley, 4 May 1864, Sibley Papers (Addition).
[148] Reid, *Telegraph in America*, 485.
[149] Norvin Green to Hiram Sibley, 31 January 1864, Sibley Papers (Addition); Thomas Rutherford to George Douglass, 23 June 1864, George Douglass Papers.
[150] Norvin Green to Hiram Sibley, 29 February 1864, Sibley Papers (Addition).
[151] Norvin Green to Pinckney Green, 29 October 1865, Uncataloged Green Papers (FHS).
[152] Seventh Annual Meeting of the North American Telegraph Association, 17 August 1864, Caton Papers.

American Telegraph Company's stock price by 35 percent.[153] The rumor-mongers were onto something.[154] The "Consolidation Egg" seemed ready to hatch. Beginning in January 1865, committees from both companies met several times in an attempt to negotiate a consolidation.[155] The deal failed and the bubble burst, but perhaps the grand merger would have gone through had Hiram Sibley, the industry's great unifier, been present to shepherd the negotiations. Instead, Sibley had gone to Russia to promote an audacious plan for a telegraph line to Europe.

When the Atlantic Cable sputtered and failed in the summer of 1858, the prospects for telegraph communication between Europe and America dimmed. Some experts feared the cable's failure proved that long-distance submarine transmission was impossible, and a few contemplated another route to Europe that would not require a long cable. Hiram Sibley envisioned a telegraph line that would span the United States, sweep north through British Columbia and the Russian territory of Alaska, cross the Bering Strait with a short submarine cable, and then continue west all the way to St. Petersburg and Europe.[156] Even before winning federal support for the Pacific telegraph, Sibley and his California partners planned an extension through Oregon to Alaska. Sibley insisted in 1860 that Western Union must get the "inside track" on the great enterprise.[157]

Sibley found an equally enthusiastic partner in Perry McDonough Collins, an adventurer and friend of Senator William Gwin, Western Union's ally in California. Like Gwin, Collins was a determined promoter of extending American trade and influence across the Pacific. With a commission from President Franklin Pierce, Collins traveled across northern Asia in 1856 as a commercial agent for the United States government and explored a potential telegraph route.[158] Collins planned a

---

[153] E. D. L. Sweet to J. D. Caton, 28 November 1864, Caton Papers.

[154] John Horner to Hiram Sibley, 25 December 1864, Sibley Papers.

[155] Meeting of the Board of Directors of the American Telegraph Company, 25 January 1865, WUC; Western Union Executive Committee Minutes, 30 January 1865, WUC; Meeting of the Board of Directors of the American Telegraph Company, 23 February 1865, WUC.

[156] In later years, Henry O'Reilly insisted that it was *he* who first suggested this "overland" route to Europe in 1852, but it was not until Sibley embraced the project that its prospects brightened. The unsigned article for which O'Reilly claimed credit appeared in a telegraph journal in 1852. Henry O'Reilly, "Memorial to the Russian Imperial Academy," n.d. 1861(?), O'Reilly Papers (RHS); "Telegraphic Connection Between Old World and New," *American Telegraph Magazine*, October 1862, 26.

[157] Hiram Sibley to Isaac R. Elwood, 26 January 1860, Sibley Papers (Addition).

[158] Rosemary Neering, *Continental Dash: The Russian-American Telegraph* (Ganges, BC: Horisdal & Schubart, 1989), 12.

line through five thousand miles of unsettled territory from Oregon to the mouth of the Amur River on the Siberian frontier between China and Russia. A proposed Russian line would connect at the Amur and traverse the seven thousand miles to St. Petersburg. North America would link to Europe by a mere fifty miles of submarine cable across the Bering Strait.[159] As the transcontinental line neared completion in 1861, Sibley told Collins his men were "pressing hard" to continue on to Alaska. Having already crossed the daunting Rocky Mountains, Sibley thought the expedition could be completed in two years – perhaps even in one.[160]

However, to build what came to be known as the "Collins' Overland Line" or the "Russian Extension" demanded more than just entrepreneurial enthusiasm. The enterprise required the cooperation of the American, British, and Russian governments and substantial financial backing, all at a time when the nation's attention was focused on the Civil War. Still the Union government eagerly supported the adventure. Secretary of State William Henry Seward, who later proposed purchasing Alaska in part because of the reports sent from the telegraph expedition, threw his support behind the Overland Line and urged Congress to make concessions to the project.[161] In July 1864, President Lincoln signed legislation granting right-of-way and access to materials on public lands for the Collins' Overland Line, following similar concessions made by the British and Russian governments.[162]

With the Pacific Telegraph Sibley had proved to investors that he could execute even the most ambitious scheme on schedule and provide enviable returns. More than two-thirds of Western Union shareholders leapt at an exclusive offering of $10 million in Russian Extension Company stock. Only $5 had to be paid upfront for each $100 subscribed, with further assessments to follow as needed (the offering suggested they would not exceed $20 per share). On the open market, the stock commanded a premium 30 to 60 percent above the price paid by insiders.[163]

---

[159] Senate Report No. 13, 37th Congress, 2d Session, 17 February 1862; George F. Kennan, *Tent Life in Siberia* (New York: Putnam, 1871), 1–2.

[160] Sibley to Collins, 16 October 1861, Sibley Papers (Addition).

[161] John B. Dwyer, *To Wire the World: Perry M. Collins and the North Pacific Telegraph Expedition* (Westport, Conn.: Praeger, 2001), 114.

[162] "Statement of the Origin, Organization and Progress of the Russian-American Telegraph, Western Union Extension, Collins' Overland Line," May 1866, O'Reilly Papers (RHS), 7–10, 61, 69.

[163] "Statement of the Origin, Organization and Progress of the Russian-American Telegraph, Western Union Extension, Collins' Overland Line," May 1866, O'Reilly Papers (RHS), 64; Thompson, *Wiring a Continent*, 428.

In the summer of 1864, Hiram Sibley sailed for St. Petersburg to promote the Russian Extension, in what would prove to be his last undertaking on Western Union's behalf. Poor health had forced him to give up the
presidency of Western Union, and he never again played a decisive role in
the company's management. The more cautious Jeptha Wade took Sibley's
place as president, and he worried that Western Union should attend to
"important matters nearer to home" rather than enlarging a business
already too large to "do well," but the Russian expedition already had
momentum.[164] Despite the ongoing war, the United States Navy contributed a vessel to Western Union's convoy – eight ships loaded with a
small army of three hundred laborers, telegraphic engineers, draftsmen,
topographers, and other assorted experts.[165] The Union Army furloughed
Charles S. Bulkley, an officer in the Military Telegraph Corps, to oversee
construction.[166] By the end of 1865, more than one thousand men worked
at various points along the line from British Columbia to Siberia. Reports
of the advancement of the Russian Extension fueled the "telegraph fever"
for Western Union's stock. It may have been Sibley's final undertaking,
but it was also perhaps his most audacious. If the line succeeded, it would
give Western Union the great advantage that the American Telegraph
Company had almost secured a decade earlier: a monopoly on telegraph
communication to Europe and Asia.

By the end of the Civil War in April 1865, the United States Military
Telegraph Corps had constructed more than fifteen thousand miles of
telegraph line at a cost exceeding $2.5 million. By one estimate, military
lines carried 6.5 million messages in five years.[167] With this feat accomplished, and Reconstruction beginning, the question became how to dis-
pose of the Confederate and Union military lines and reestablish private
telegraphy.

The Southern companies might have presented a particularly thorny
problem. The Southern Telegraph Company and Southwestern Company
had made, beyond all doubt, "a solid contribution to the Confederate
war effort."[168] As the Confederacy crumbled, the Southern Telegraph

---

[164] Wade to Sibley, 15 November 1863, Sibley Family Papers (Addition).
[165] "Collins' Overland Telegraph," 31 October 1864, *The Telegrapher*, 9.
[166] Plum, *The Military Telegraph*, 208.
[167] Ibid., 337, 352.
[168] J. Cutler Andrews, "The Southern Telegraph Company, 1861–1865: A Chapter in
the History of Wartime Communication," *The Journal of Southern History* 30, no. 3
(1964): 343.

Company's superintendent insisted that energetically transmitting military messages was a duty of "patriotism" and even advocated sharing business with the competing Southwestern Company to advance the Confederate cause.[169] Moreover, both firms realized significant profits throughout the war. The Southern Telegraph Company paid regular dividends to its Confederate shareholders until January 1865. In the first nine months of 1863, one of the only periods for which financial records exist, the Southern Company reported nearly a 35 percent profit.[170]

In congressional testimony decades later, Edward Rosewater testified to Congress that the Southern private lines should have been seized as "contraband of war" because they had been used against the federal government with "more effect than battalions and brigades of soldiers."[171] Such a confiscation would have struck a blow to the Northern stockholders of the American and the Southwestern Telegraph Companies. Louisville businessmen and Northern patent holders such as Amos Kendall and Samuel Morse owned the stock of the Southwestern. Norvin Green claimed in his response to Rosewater's accusations that "no charge or intimation of disloyalty" had ever been leveled at the stockholders in Louisville.[172] Green suggested that the *Southern* portion of the Southwestern had been disloyal, but not the company as a whole, which was true in only a narrow sense. Green had personally placed Van Horne, his best manager, in charge of the Southern lines, and evidently charged Van Horne to earn a profit in the South for the Louisville shareholders.[173] Because Confederate money had no value in the North, Van Horne used Southern profits to purchase cotton, which he tried – without success – to smuggle north to Southwestern shareholders in Louisville.[174]

The Confiscation Act of 1862 authorized the seizure of Confederate property for many purposes, but it offered no guidelines for returning property. This posed an acute problem for both railroads and telegraphs, two industries vital to the Confederate military. In the War Department differing opinions on the return of railroad property led to a patchwork

[169] J. B. Tree to William Morris, 19 November 1864, Southern Telegraph Company Papers.
[170] Andrews, "The Southern Telegraph Company," 327–8, 343. Southern Telegraph Statement, 1 October 1863, Southern Telegraph Company Papers.
[171] Edward Rosewater, Statement before the Committee on Post-Offices and Post Roads, 18 March 1890, WUC, 3.
[172] Norvin Green to Henry H. Bingham, 6 June 1890, WUC.
[173] Thomas Rutherford to George Douglass, 23 June 1864, George Douglass Papers.
[174] M. A. Green to Pinckney Green, 16 July 1865, Uncataloged Green Papers (FHS). Green was apparently unaware of this attempt until after the war.

of policies.[175] However, the telegraph escaped such controversy, probably because of the influence of Northern investors in the War Department. The Southwestern Company simply assumed control of the Southern portion of its lines after the war. The shareholders of the Southern Telegraph Company returned their lines to the American Telegraph Company. Though there is a hint in the records of the American Telegraph Company that the government confiscated some of the Southern Telegraph's stock, the American Telegraph Company determined to "pay the costs and expenses" in confiscation proceedings to secure settlements that would be "best for the interest of the Company."[176] In sum, the record suggests that the Northern companies turned their lines over to Southern managers for use in the Confederate war effort, and then, at the war's end, the Northern companies quietly took their property back.

The disposition of the lines under the control of the United States Military Telegraph Corps also presented a complex problem of ownership. Of the more than fifteen thousand miles of line built by the Corps, only one thousand were "field lines" constructed for the invading Union armies. Most of the lines the Corps put up were reconstructions of commercial lines damaged or destroyed in the fighting, including thousands of miles in the South whose ownership was murky at best.[177] On November 30, 1865, Stager ordered the Military Telegraph Corps to release the lines owned by the commercial companies and discharge nonessential operators.[178] Cipher clerks and censors who temporarily remained with the Military Telegraph Corps often occupied commercial offices and their orders entitled them to accept payment for commercial telegraphing on the side.[179]

The scant remaining evidence indicates that the intertwined interests of the major telegraph companies and the War Department extended to the rebuilding of the telegraph in the ruined South. Norvin Green negotiated directly with Captain William Gross, the Military Telegraph officer in command of the Southwestern's region, in the hope of averting the need to "besiege the War Department for months, perhaps years" to take possession of former military lines.[180] However, negotiation gave way

---

[175] Angevine, *The Railroad and the State*, 154.

[176] Meeting of the Board of Directors of the American Telegraph Company, 23 November 1865, WUC.

[177] Plum, *The Military Telegraph*, 349.

[178] William L. Gross, Circular, 30 November 1865, Gross Papers.

[179] William L. Gross, Circular, 3 November 1865, Gross Papers.

[180] Norvin Green to William Gross, 31 July 1865, Gross Papers.

to bribery. On July 31, 1865, Green offered to buy some Southwestern stock for Gross, and two months later Gross received shares with a nominal value of $2,000, the sale backdated to the most recent payment of dividends. No stock in the booming Southwestern could be found on the market for less than $120 per share, but Green sold Gross shares at $100, letting him use the certificates as collateral, and allowing him to pay at his convenience. With no money down, Gross received a choice investment worth $2,400 plus substantial dividends, with an obligation to eventually repay only $2,000. Thus a low-level telegraph officer received his own slice of the spoils of war.

Two weeks later, Green scolded Gross for providing too much detail in a report to Stager. The Southwestern wanted a line built by the Confederate military with supplies stolen from the Union Military Telegraph. Gross's request for instructions from Stager would "elicit inquiries and cause postponements," and Green insisted Stager had agreed to give the line to the Southwestern outright. However, the order had to come from Gross, the regional commander, because an order from Stager would "become matter of official record" and require approval from the War Department. Gross could get the line for the Southwestern without official "trouble or comment." Stager helpfully quashed Gross's indiscreet report by declaring it a "private letter" rather than an "official document."[181] Though no further correspondence on the subject has survived, Green later helped Gross get an industry job, suggesting Gross performed to Green's satisfaction.[182]

We can speculate that few transactions such as the one between Green and Gross left such a clear record, and exceedingly few such records are likely to have survived to the present; yet this one example of influence and casual corruption speaks volumes about how the leading telegraph companies divvied up the spoils of the war. For the Military Telegraph Corps, the final reckoning came in February 1866, when the federal government released the military lines in every state south of the Ohio to the control of the private companies. Less than six months later, just one of those companies towered above them all.

---

[181] Norvin Green to William Gross, 13 November 1865, Gross Papers; R. C. Clowry to William Gross, 2 August 1865, Gross Papers.

[182] Norvin Green to William Gross, 27 July 1866, Gross Papers. Stager also probably assisted his superintendents in finding work. R. C. Clowry, who would one day become the president of Western Union, appealed to Stager for a job after the war and recommended that Stager forward a copy of the Military Telegraph's "blacklist" to Western Union to keep undesirable operators out of the service. R. C. Clowry to Stager, 1 January 1865 and 20 June 1865, Clowry Papers.

3

"An Entering Wedge" against Monopoly

In December 1865, Massachusetts Republican John B. Alley, chairman of the House Committee on the Post Office and Post Roads, introduced a resolution calling for an inquiry into the "expedience" of creating a national telegraph system operated exclusively by the Post Office Department.[1] A government telegraph had not been on the House agenda for a generation, and Congress faced more pressing concerns, including reunifying the nation and reconstructing the South. The official historian of the Thirty-Ninth Congress judged Alley's Post Office committee to be of such little importance that he excluded it entirely from his chronicle.[2] Nonetheless, Alley's resolution marked the first tentative but significant steps toward introducing federal regulation to the burgeoning telecommunications industry, which teetered on the brink of a private monopoly.

The North American Telegraph Association had long aspired to monopolize the telegraph as a cartel, but in a postwar rush its members abandoned their policies of tense cooperation for whole-scale consolidation. Internal strife had been the norm since the cartel's creation, but now the ambitions of Western Union, which had built the transcontinental telegraph and recently absorbed two cartel partners, threatened the association's stability. Western Union's major rivals exhibited a similar zeal for growth. From inside the cartel the American Telegraph Company eyed major acquisitions, while the United States Telegraph Company

---

[1] Congressional Globe, 39th Congress, 1st Session, 1865, 115.
[2] William H. Barnes, *History of the Thirty-Ninth Congress* (New York: Harper & Brothers, 1868), i, 22–32.

continued to threaten from the outside, destroying the cartel's monopoly in the East and beginning construction on a transcontinental line to threaten its monopoly in the West.

The seven months beginning with the introduction of John Alley's House resolution in December 1865 proved to be one of the most pivotal periods in telecommunications history. In Washington, Alley's resolution culminated in the Telegraph Act of 1866, the first federal law regulating telecommunications. And in the marketplace, Western Union took control of its two largest competitors, creating a functional, if not quite absolute, monopoly on telegraphy.

Though the Civil War's "plunder and trophies of victory" had accrued to nearly all the companies in the North American Telegraph Association, Western Union had risen above the rest during the war years.[3] This came as no surprise to other members of the cartel. After the December 1861 meeting of the "Six Nations," a manager from the Illinois & Mississippi Telegraph warned that Western Union's Rochester managers had a hidden agenda, "a grand and far reaching policy calculated in time to swallow up or make tributary all other organizations."[4] At the time the accusation had seemed farfetched. More than three years of rancorous negotiations had been required to create a cartel out of the competing Morse and House telegraph companies, with hurdles and pitfalls so numerous that further consolidation hardly appeared imminent. Uniting the entire American telegraph system under a single management would create a more complex and geographically widespread corporation than any the nation had ever seen – if this was Western Union's course, it was into uncharted territory.

Rochester's fledgling monopolists soon realized that the reunited federal government was almost certain to play a new role in the industry, and, once realizing it, they spared no effort or expense in influencing the outcome. For a generation, Americans had almost universally accepted that though the telegraph had a public purpose, construction and management of the lines was a private enterprise. The emergence of a private monopoly launched a new debate about the obligation of the federal government to protect the public interest from the power of big business. John Alley had fired the first salvo in what became a thirty-year policy war with Western Union.[5]

[3] Ibid., 4.
[4] Thomas Bassnett to J. D. Caton, 15 December 1861, Caton Papers.
[5] Alley's motives unfortunately remain obscure. However, a letter the following August from E. H. Bebe to J. D. Caton suggested that the Postmaster General's investigation of a

In the winter of 1865 the telegraph reached across the United States and was slowly extending up the Pacific coast toward Russian America. Cyrus Field and his English backers prepared a third attempt to lay a submarine cable from Europe to North America. Even the war-shattered South was once again connected by wire to the rest of the nation thanks to new lines the Military Telegraph Corps had built as the Union Army advanced. By the end of 1866, more than 80,000 miles of telegraph wire webbed the nation, about twice as many miles as the railroads.[6]

Though the American telegraph network had vast geographic breadth, ownership of the network was exceedingly narrow. Of the six original members of the North American Telegraph Association, only four remained. In the East, the American Telegraph Company operated from Newfoundland all the way down the Eastern Seaboard to the Gulf of Mexico. Western Union carried traffic from New York to the Old Northwest and across the continent over the only working line to California. Norvin Green's Southwestern Company connected Louisville to New Orleans and ran lines into Texas. J. D. Caton's Illinois & Mississippi controlled much of the Midwest.

The independent United States Telegraph Company had meanwhile expanded rapidly into the territories of both Western Union and the American Telegraph Company and commenced building a line to California. But despite generous financial backing from enthusiastic telegraph speculators, the company's "dash and wealth" had led – perhaps inevitably – to overreaching into profitless territory where demand was weak.[7] Outside observers believed gross mismanagement and extravagant spending were among the company's chief problems, and without cash infusions from the gullible stock buyers of the war boom, the firm

government telegraph was intended to be the "entering wedge of a determined effort to break up the Monopoly." Bebe, however, was referring to B. Gratz Brown's Senate resolution, not to Alley's earlier House resolution (see page 89). Whether the two are related is unknown. E. H. Bebe to J. D. Caton, 20 August 1866, Caton Papers.
[6] Computing both track mileage and wire mileage for this period is an inexact science. According to the U. S. Bureau of the Census, railroad mileage was 8,336 in 1851 and 44,614 in 1871. Given a swift rate of construction, it is probable that in 1866, there was less than 40,000 miles of railroad. The Bureau of the Census relied on Western Union for its telegraph data. At the end of 1866, Western Union controlled 76,000 miles of wire, which was probably more than 90 percent of the total miles in the United States. See U.S. Bureau of the Census, *Historical Statistics of the United States: Colonial Times to 1957* (Washington, D.C.: U.S. Government Printing Office, 1960), 423 and 484.
[7] James D. Reid, *The Telegraph in America: Its Founders, Promoters, and Noted Men*, 1st ed. (New York: Derby Brothers, 1879), 521.

would collapse.[8] As the deteriorating financial condition of the company became apparent, President James McKaye resigned.[9]

To take over the management of their troubled firm, the United States Company's directors selected a young government bureaucrat named William Orton. The appointment proved auspicious – over the next twelve years, no individual played a greater role in shaping the telegraph industry. A "self-made man" from Cuba, New York, Orton had worked as a printer's assistant, a schoolteacher, and a bookseller. He succeeded briefly as the proprietor of a publishing house on New York's Park Row before the Panic of 1857 ruined his business. He studied law and became an influential member of New York's emerging Republican Party. In 1862 he accepted the onerous post of collector in the new, disorganized Bureau of Internal Revenue. Orton impressed Treasury Secretary Salmon P. Chase with his effectiveness and judgment, and in July 1865 President Andrew Johnson appointed Orton to the highest job in the bureau, Commissioner of Internal Revenue. Four months later Orton resigned the post to take charge of the United States Telegraph Company.[10]

The thirty-nine-year-old Orton had neither worked for nor invested in any telegraph company, a lack of experience that actually suited him for his new job because he had played no role in the past twenty tumultuous years of telegraph patent litigation, personal betrayals, and fortunes made and lost. His probity, ardor, and steely clarity were unusual in an industry marked by the wild ambition and frequent perfidy of its pioneers. A senior Western Union manager praised Orton for refusing to employ "subterfuges and tricks" in the conduct of even the most "bitter business warfare."[11]

When he assumed the presidency of United States Telegraph, Orton erroneously believed the firm was in a "highly prosperous condition." The company had twice paid dividends, giving its stock what Orton later realized was "fictitious value" that raised false expectations, and investors were beginning to catch on.[12] Some publicly accused Orton's predecessor of attempting to enrich a "ring" of insiders by boosting the

---

[8] Robert Luther Thompson, *Wiring a Continent: The History of the Telegraph Industry in the United States, 1832–1866* (Princeton, N.J.: Princeton University Press, 1947), 404–5.
[9] Reid, *The Telegraph in America*, 522.
[10] According to Reid, tax attorney Grosvenor Lowrey had worked with Orton on a case and recommend him to the United States Board. Ibid., 524. "William Orton: Sudden Termination of a Busy and Useful Life," *Journal of the Telegraph*, 1 May 1878, 129–31.
[11] Special Meeting of the Board of Directors, 23 April 1878, WUC.
[12] William E. Orton to B. E. Bates, 24 September 1866, WUC.

stock price with dividends paid out of stock sales, rather than net earnings. In an embarrassing letter published in the *New York Tribune*, an irate stockholder criticized the company for returning to investors a "portion of their own subscriptions" under the fraudulent name of dividends.[13] Orton recognized that he "had become the captain of a foundering ship."[14] In the last quarter of 1865, the United States Company earned record revenues but spent far more. During a reckless expansion spree the company had built shoddy lines in poor locations, installed inferior equipment, and opened many "nonpaying" offices.[15] There never had been profits to justify the dividends paid. Orton cut expenses, halted expansion, and proposed maximizing existing lines by adding extra wires between major cities to increase valuable through business. By selling the property intended for a grand headquarters on Broadway and completing a line to California, Orton believed his firm could challenge overcapitalized Western Union on "about equal" footing and perhaps "outlive its present embarrassments."[16]

The competitive principles upon which the United States Company had been founded – independence and competition – became lesser priorities than sheer survival. Despite his company's exclusion from the Telegraph Association, Orton matched the cartel's rates, sold space for Western Union wires on some United States Company poles, and proposed a cooperative scheme in which one company would abandon territory in which two competing companies were losing money.[17] Such anticompetitive measures would infuriate the public, but public service was neither Orton's concern nor his duty. The interest of stockholders was "paramount to those of the public," and he would endorse any anticompetitive steps that would "make or save many" even though "outsiders" complained that the telegraph companies were "coalescing."[18]

Early in 1866 telegraph traffic suddenly slowed, but Orton saw opportunity in the downturn. Western Union was saddled with $4 million in

---

[13] Reprinted in *The Telegrapher*, 16 October 1865, 173.

[14] Reid, *The Telegraph in America*, 523.

[15] "The United States Telegraph Company," *The Telegrapher*, 1 June 1867, 242.

[16] William Orton to George Davis. 8 January 1866, WUC. In this letter Orton compared Western Union's value per mile, which he estimated at $600 per mile (which he reached by dividing Western Union's 44,000 miles of wire by $22 million in capital plus $4 million in debt), to the United States' lines per mile cost of $400. But, he noted, "The true test of value is after all – earnings and ability to pay dividends."

[17] William Orton to J. W. Kirk, 13 January 1866, WUC, William Orton to O. H. Palmer, 21 December 1865, WUC.

[18] William Orton to George Davis, 15 January 1866, WUC.

bonded debt and the enormous dividend obligation created by more than quadrupling its capital during the war.[19] Orton concluded that if he could cut expenses, the United States Company could leap ahead of its overburdened rival. Demanding his subordinates "stop every dollar of expense possible," Orton led the way by slashing the pay of his chief deputy and threatening the salaries of other employees.[20] The move proved another overreach. As monthly losses continued to grow, Orton contemplated the desperate measure of commencing a rate war that would likely see his company "die fighting manfully" rather than being "quietly leeched to death."[21]

Consolidation with the American Telegraph Company or Western Union appeared the best remaining option. Orton denied rampant rumors that his company had commenced surrender negotiations. But privately he speculated that if the three companies consolidated and limited their combined capital to $25 million, the united company could easily pay a 10 percent dividend – the American Telegraph Company and Western Union paid only 5 per cent presently and the United States Company paid zero.[22] Consolidation was a fate "far better" than carrying on a competition that left the stockholders nothing. Whatever the public's objections, Orton believed a united company could provide satisfactory service "if management was in proper hands."[23]

While Orton struggled to find a way to reward his stockholders, in Congress the conversation about the telegraph moved in a very different direction. In early 1866, Missouri Republican B. Gratz Brown proposed a resolution in the Senate – parallel to Alley's in the House – asking the Postmaster General to study the feasibility of a public telegraph. In the previous two Congresses, Brown had promoted the Radical Republican agenda, but lately he had moderated his stance on Reconstruction and had turned to promoting a transcontinental railroad and telegraph line that would pass through Missouri.[24] The existing telegraph system, Brown told the Senate, inspired "very great" public objection to the

[19] William Orton to J. W. Kirk, 13 January 1866, WUC.
[20] William Orton to J. W. Kirk, 29 December 1866, WUC, William Orton to J. W. Kirk, 13 January 1866, WUC.
[21] William Orton to George Davis, 15 January 1866, WUC.
[22] William Orton to George Davis, 17 January 1866, WUC. Emphases in the original.
[23] William Orton to George Davis, 15 January 1866, WUC. The emphasis on "new" is Orton's own.
[24] Norma Lois Peterson, *Freedom and Franchise: The Political Career of B. Gratz Brown* (Columbia: University of Missouri Press, 1965), 144–55.

"sinister combinations" that controlled the wires and to the "negligence" that made service so bad in the remote sections of the country that messages were "almost unintelligible."[25]

Brown's proposed to address the public outrage against the industry by creating a government telegraph system. In Brown's view, a government telegraph offered two great advantages. First, it would create competition in wire news – presently monopolized by the Associated Press – improving both the quality and quantity of commercial and political reports. This was particularly urgent in the West, where a single line to California created a telegraph bottleneck easily exploited by the AP.[26] Second, Brown believed a government telegraph would be more democratic than the existing commercial system. The "extortion" practiced by the cartel limited public demand for the telegraph. A government telegraph could build lines on "poorer routes," and shorter lines would subsidize longer ones with a uniform national rate – a policy of the Post Office for nearly twenty years. A government telegraph would harmonize "the great modern method of transmitting intelligence" with the "public interest." Instead of "high rates for limited business," the public telegraph would offer widely available "cheap" service. In sum, as Morse had dreamed decades before, the telegraph would be a faster version of the democratic postal mail.[27]

Brown anticipated objections that a government telegraph would destroy private property and free enterprise. But he insisted the government would not harm property rights if it fairly compensated telegraph investors. As for free enterprise, Brown charged that because the telegraph industry was already under the control of only two great concerns, Western Union and the American Telegraph Company, it was not a free market anyway. "There is no benefit of competition here," he argued. "It is sealed against [competition] as much as Brigham Young's heaven is against a rebellious wife."[28]

Brown also rejected the notion that private industry could more cheaply and efficiently manage the telegraph than the Post Office Department. He offered a long disquisition on the cost of telegraphy. Citing statistics

---

[25] Congressional Globe, 39th Congress, 1st session, 494.
[26] For a detailed discussion of the California news associations, see Robert J. Chandler, "The California News-Telegraph Monopoly, 1860–1870," *Southern California Quarterly* 58 (1976).
[27] Congressional Globe, 39th Congress, 1st Session, 979–80.
[28] Congressional Globe, 39th Congress, 1st Session, 980.

compiled in an 1860 monograph by telegraph engineer George Bartlett Prescott,[29] Brown estimated that at $63 per mile all the telegraph lines in the United States were worth about $2 million, though their nominal capital was more than twenty times as much. Prescott's figures suggested that the national average cost per word transmitted was only one-twentieth of a cent, or three cents for sixty words – the same as it cost to mail a letter. Surely the government could do the business more cheaply, at no cost to the treasury, and for the betterment of the people's welfare.[30]

Meanwhile, Orton had decided on a way out of his conundrum: rather than fight Western Union, he would join it. Though Orton had little hope that Western Union would offer generous terms for consolidation, he knew his company had to make a move if shareholders were ever to see a return on their investment. The calculus of profit and loss was inescapable: the United States Telegraph Company had never made a dollar of profit; the further its lines extended, the greater its losses. The company's stock stood at a weak $40 per share, but Orton privately admitted that if shareholders had "known the facts," the stock would have sold for $25 or less."[31]

In February, Western Union President Jeptha Wade traveled to New York and met with Orton at the Fifth Avenue Hotel. Western Union was the obvious choice for Orton. Not only had it been empowered by the war and its close connection with the Union effort, but its monopolistic tendencies were also well known and feared among its competitors. Western Union had also, under Sibley, floated the idea of buying the United States Company in the past. Orton refused Wade's initial offer to merge the two companies on the basis of their relative capital – he believed Western Union's stock had been "watered" even compared to the exaggerated capital of the United States Company – and proposed consolidation on the basis of relative revenues instead.[32] Western Union's directors approved the merger and flirted with calling the consolidated company "The Union Telegraph Company" – a name widely reported

---

[29] George B. Prescott, *History, Theory, and Practice of the Electric Telegraph* (Boston: Ticknor and Fields, 1860).
[30] *Congressional Globe*, 39th Congress, 1st Session, 980.
[31] William Orton to Joisah King, 12 March 1866, WUC.
[32] The proposed capital merger was at proportion of 87.5 percent Western Union, 12.5 percent United States Telegraph, while the proportion of relative revenues was 80 percent to 20 percent. Reid, *The Telegraph in America*, 523–5.

in the press.[33] However, at the behest of a manager from California, the company retained "Western" as a permanent part of its brand.[34]

With the unanimous approval of its directors, the United States Telegraph Company joined Western Union on March 1. Orton immediately came under attack from angry shareholders, leading him to issue a circular defending the merger.[35] The public preferred competition, Orton admitted, but "the necessity for retrenchment" after the boom years of the Civil War demanded consolidation. He promised the merger would save half a million dollars in the first year and perhaps twice as much as efficiency improved.[36] Orton's circular included previously unpublished data on the relative revenues of the two companies. Shareholders concluded that the largely redundant lines of the United States Telegraph Company had little value, and thus neither did the corresponding increase in Western Union's capital. Western Union stock plummeted.[37] Under attack from a committee of angry former board members, Orton insisted that he had given the directors reliable information, whereas his predecessor had misled them to approve paying dividends that were "never earned."[38]

The sudden demise of the United States Telegraph Company alarmed many telegraph operators, particularly the members of the fledgling National Telegraphic Union (NTU). Formed in New York in 1863 as part of the larger movement toward telegrapher organization on both sides during the war, the NTU was more a mutual benefit society than a trade union, providing medical and funeral benefits for its members but never agitating for improvements in wages. Reflecting a classic Whig-Republican faith in the concordance of interests between labor and capital, the NTU sought to improve the overall standing of the profession of telegraph operator while "promoting and maintaining" a "just,

---

[33] This was reported in several places, and it is recorded as Cornell's suggestion in "Meeting of the Board of Directors of the Western Union Telegraph Company," 1 March 1866, WUC.

[34] "Meeting of the Board of Directors of the Western Union Telegraph Company, 7 March 1866, WUC.

[35] William Orton to O. H. Palmer, 5 March 1866, WUC.

[36] William Orton, Circular from the United States Telegraph Company, *The Telegrapher*, 16 April 1866.

[37] This came as a shock to Western Union – Jeptha Wade told his son that the merger was expected to drive up the price of Western Union stock. Wade to Randall Wade, 24 February 1866, Wade Papers.

[38] William Orton to George T. Davis, 6 April 1866, WUC.

equitable, and harmonious" relationship with employers.[39] Telegraphers thought of themselves as special and above ordinary working men, and in a sense they were – they were the most costly and essential element in operating the telegraph and could be replaced only by other skilled operators.

Telegraphy was a "genteel" profession; both in terms of skill and salary, operators were members of what was later called an "aristocracy of labor."[40] In 1870 the *New York World* described telegraph operators as "a more intelligent class than so-called workingmen."[41] "First-class operators" were usually male, and most often young and unmarried. Many believed telegraphy to be a stepping-stone to something greater, an "upwardly mobile" occupation. Operating rooms traditionally employed a "hierarchy of skill and status," with office managers at the top and novice operators at the bottom. With the approval of managers, an ambitious operator could work his way up through the ranks through improvements in skill and technical expertise.[42] Telegraphers were one of the first "technological elites" and perhaps "the very first mass white-collar employees," at the forefront of what a labor historian described as a "lower middle class in the making."[43]

Industry consolidation appeared to threaten the special status of the telegrapher's profession and the telegraphing public more generally. *The Telegrapher*, the NTU's biweekly newspaper, condemned the Western Union–United States Telegraph merger as good for stockholders but "an injury" to the public and "death for telegraphers." Presciently, though the American Telegraph Company and several dozen small opposition firms remained in the field, *The Telegrapher* decried the blossoming of a "great monopoly" that would decrease operators' salaries "as surely and naturally as water runs down hill." The United States Telegraph Company

---

[39] Edwin Gabler, *The American Telegrapher: A Social History, 1860–1900*, Class and Culture (New Brunswick, N.J.: Rutgers University Press, 1988), 146–7. The NTU mission statement is also quoted in Gabler. Eric Foner, *Free Soil, Free Labor, Free Men: The Ideology of the Republican Party before the Civil War* (New York: Oxford University Press, 1970), 19–20.

[40] Edwin Gabler, *The American Telegrapher: A Social History, 1860–1900* (New Brunswick, N.J.: Rutgers University Press, 1988), 57; Bruce Laurie, *Artisans into Workers: Labor in Nineteenth-Century America* (New York: Hill and Wang, 1989), 128.

[41] "The Telegraph Operator's Strike," *Journal of the Telegraph*, 1 February 1870, 54.

[42] Paul Israel, *From Machine Shop to Industrial Laboratory: Telegraphy and the Changing Context of American Invention, 1830–1920* (Baltimore: Johns Hopkins University Press, 1992), 65.

[43] Thomas C. Jepsen, *My Sisters Telegraphic: Women in the Telegraph Office, 1846–1950* (Athens, Ohio: Ohio University Press, 2000), 38–9; Gabler, *The American Telegrapher*.

offices would close and Western Union's workforce would be one-third less than the two companies operating separately. Western Union had become "so vast in its proportions" that renewed competition was unlikely, especially given that the American Telegraph Company was negotiating to buy from Western Union the pieces of the United States Telegraph Company that competed in the American Telegraph Company's territory. "*Sic transit Gloria* opposition," concluded *The Telegrapher*.[44]

However, not all the operators in the union shared *The Telegrapher's* critical view of consolidation. The New York chapter of the NTU issued a resolution condemning the newspaper. "The employees of a company are supposed to be friendly to its interest and jealous of its good name," complained the New Yorkers.[45] A writer from the Harrisburg chapter praised the "gentlemen" who "officered and controlled" the two remaining telegraph giants and reminded readers that a telegrapher should commit himself to the success of his company rather than the general prosperity of operators, and he should not want "the opposition lines to prosper."[46] Even outright support for a monopoly was not unheard of among operators. In an unsigned commentary about the affairs of the American Telegraph Company, a writer in *The Telegrapher* called for a policy which would "diminish, rather than increase, opposition ... so that there may be a union again, and telegraphing become, as it ought to be, a *unit* on this continent."[47]

Samuel Morse himself shared the belief that the passing of the United States Company would "result for the mutual benefit of all concerned." At last the telegraph was organized the way he wished from the beginning, not "cut up in O'Rielly fashion into irresponsible parts," but in "one great whole" like the Post Office. He admitted to his former business partner Amos Kendall that the telegraph was "becoming doubtless a *monopoly*," but such unity would be a "public advantage" if Western Union were properly managed by "upright and responsible men" who conducted the business "with fairness, and with liberality."[48]

Henry O'Rielly was not yet a spent force. Though oft defeated in his public battles with Western Union and the Telegraph Association, O'Rielly had never given up on creating a transcontinental telegraph collective

[44] "Telegraph Miscellanea," *The Telegrapher*, 15 March 1866.
[45] "District Proceedings," *The Telegrapher*, 1 May 1866.
[46] W. B. W., "The Other Side," *The Telegrapher*, 1 June 1866.
[47] "American Telegraph Company," *The Telegrapher*, 1 March 1866.
[48] Samuel Morse to Amos Kendall, 19 March 1866, Morse Papers.

of small independent companies that he called the "Atlantic & Pacific Range." In March 1866 his latest scheme failed when his contractor and several subscribers abandoned him to join a competing venture. In a circular, O'Rielly proclaimed that a nefarious "ring" had stolen his subscribers under "false and fraudulent" pretenses, but he assured the public that he nonetheless would soon provide the people with "lines built for *moderate rates.*"[49] Sensing that the time was right to win government backing for "free enterprise in telegraphing *on an honorable basis,*" O'Rielly announced his plans for the National Telegraph Company, an enterprise designed to resist absorption by "the dominant monopoly."[50] As in all O'Rielly projects, National Telegraph would be democratic, with its $10 million capital held by "many times more" shareholders than existing companies. Over two decades the Post Office Department had shown that lower postage rates led to higher volume. Using the same "cheap postage" model, National Telegraph would undermine the telegraph companies that sought "to monopolize the business at exorbitant rates, and thus benefit the few at the expense of the many."

O'Rielly's prospectus for the National Telegraph Company called for federal sponsorship in the form of legislation promising "privileges and a grant of certain facilities."[51] His efforts met with quick success in the Republican dominated Congress. A bill sponsored by Ohio Republican Senator John Sherman, the brother of Union General William Tecumseh Sherman and later known as the sponsor of the 1890 Sherman Antitrust Act, would give the National Telegraph Company the right to build lines on any land in the public domain, on military and post roads, and "over, under, and across the navigable streams or waters of the United States." Furthermore, the company could take materials from public land for the "needful uses in construction, maintenance, and operation" of its lines, and preempt public land for its stations. These privileges were less substantial than they might appear. The land grant was for stations only, unlike grants offered to the transcontinental railroads, which received land for profitable development.[52] The right to cut poles from public land

---

[49] Henry O'Reilly, "Atlantic and Pacific Telegraph," *The Telegrapher,* 1 May 1866.

[50] O'Reilly quote is from Henry O'Reilly, "Atlantic and Pacific Telegraph," *The Telegrapher,* 1 May 1866.

[51] "Prospectus of the National Telegraph Company," n.d. 1866, O'Reilly Papers (RHS).

[52] Public land preemption was limited to one-quarter section per station – a convenience rather than a reward. See Lloyd J. Mercer, *Railroads and Land Grant Policy: A Study in Government Intervention* (New York: Academic Press, 1982), 8–19. H. R. 575, 39th Congress, 1st Session, 1866.

was of little use where trees were of insufficient size and quality for telegraph poles. Many states already granted rights-of-way on post roads, and road rights-of-way were not nearly as valuable as railroad rights-of-way. Whether "post roads" included railroads – which by this time carried most of the mail – was not specified, an ambiguity that would later become the subject of numerous legal battles.

The bill's most unusual features were in what it required *from* the telegraph company. The Postmaster General would have the power to set rates on government messages with priority of transmission. An antimonopoly stipulation prevented the National Telegraph Company from merging with another company or selling its franchise without Congressional approval. Most importantly, after two years the government could purchase the company's lines "for postal, military, or other purposes" at a price determined by a committee of "disinterested persons" selected by the company and the Postmaster General.[53]

The purchase clause would create an unprecedented relationship between the federal government and a private telegraph company. Under the common law tradition of police power and the constitutional principle of eminent domain, the government retained a virtually unlimited right to seize property for the public interest.[54] But the federal government lacked the political will to exercise eminent domain for regulatory purposes, and no one argued in 1866 that federal or state governments had the right to create a public telegraph by condemning existing telegraph companies without their consent. The Pacific Railroad and Telegraph Act of 1862, which made substantial public grants to private railroad corporations, included a forfeiture clause that would turn the railroad over to the government, but only if it was not completed on time or did not fulfill requirements enumerated in the bill.[55] In fact, the debate over whether the government should support the transcontinental railroad emphasized the Republican preference for promoting economic expansion without allowing the government to replace private enterprise – public ownership of the transcontinental railroad never received serious consideration.[56]

---

[53] H. R. 575, 39th Congress, 1st Session. The two-year provision was changed to five years in the final bill.

[54] William R. Brock, *Investigation and Responsibility: Public Responsibility in the United States, 1865–1900* (New York: Cambridge University Press, 1984), 58–61.

[55] Revised Statutes Chapter 120, 37th Congress, 2nd Session.

[56] Heather Cox Richardson details these arguments in her chapter on railroad development. Richardson, *The Greatest Nation of the Earth*, Chapter 6.

The purchase clause in the proposed National Telegraph Company bill could be interpreted in two very different ways. The government could exercise the purchase provision for regulatory purposes – that is, if the National Telegraph Company failed to provide acceptable prices and quality of service, it was threatened with extinction as a private venture. Or the purchase provision could be exercised if a future Congress determined it was preferable that the telegraph be operated by the Post Office rather than as a private venture. In this interpretation, the National Telegraph Company invited a federal Trojan horse into the telegraph industry.

While committees in both houses pondered the National Telegraph Company bill, the question remained whether a publicly operated telegraph was feasible or desirable; neither Congress nor the Postmaster General had considered the question since Postmaster General Cave Johnson issued a report favoring a public telegraph in 1845.[57] Representative Alley and Senator Brown requested a report from the current Postmaster General, the likely overseer of nationalized lines. With some help from the telegraph industry, Postmaster General William Dennison issued his report on June 2, 1866. Dennison projected a 22,000-mile telegraph system along the "principal mail routes," at a price of $300 per mile for three-wire lines. He concluded that the total cost of a government network would be $6.8 million plus maintenance and depreciation. Dennison did not estimate gross receipts, as he could not predict the effect of private competition or how the government line would fare with "the public confidence." His conclusion, however, suffered from no ambiguity: it would not be "wise" for the government to sponsor a postal telegraph, not only because of poor financial prospects, but also because he doubted its "feasibility" in the "American political system."[58] The sources of Dennison's report undoubtedly had significant influence on his conclusion. Dennison had conveyed his "interrogatories" to two telegraph experts and the presidents of the American, United States, and Western Union Telegraph Companies, who were deeply interested in the report's findings.

The telegraph company presidents offered a rich assortment of arguments against government interference in the telegraph industry, ranging

[57] For discussion of this report, see Chapter 1.
[58] "Letter from the Postmaster General," Ex. Doc. No. 49, 39th Congress, 1st Session, 1866.

from technical and practical constraints to financial necessities and appeals to preserve free enterprise. Their primary argument attempted to dispel the similarities between the telegraph and the postal mail by suggesting that there were few economies of scale in telegraphy. A sack of mail could be delivered as easily as a single letter, but a telegram demanded "a calm, unoccupied brain, and a steady hand to manipulate its contents, letter by letter, in a language of monotones." A "slip of the finger" or a "truant thought" could entirely change its meaning. Unlike a letter, which required "but the toss of a practiced hand to change its route and put it under the cover of a new bag," a telegram had to be manually received and resent along its course, all along requiring "a whole wire" for its "solitary passage." Every single addition to the telegraph business – lines, wires, offices, increased volume of messages – thus multiplied the need for "care and responsibility" in a "ratio unknown to other enterprises."[59] Furthermore, postmasters were patronage appointees and could not serve as telegraphers – skilled operators must be young "men of the truest character and nicest honor" who would "devote their time and mind" to telegraphy.[60]

The telegraph business was notoriously unsteady and uneven, the presidents argued. Virtually any form of meteorological disturbance, in addition to trees, rust, "stupidity," and "deviltry," could render the fragile wires useless. Significant breaks could result from unanticipated causes – sharpshooters practicing their skills by shooting insulators off telegraph poles, or "the tail of a boy's kite" shorting the wires.[61] Major news or financial excitement created spikes in usage and traffic delays that took days to resolve. Though the telegraph business had made them rich, the presidents advised that the government had best stay out of it, for its own good.

The most surprising claim the company presidents made was that even with high rates, skilled operators, and no government interference, telegraph companies *still* earned nothing after expenses. Though the companies had paid dividends, the executives argued that if they had properly invested their surpluses in maintenance and replacement of aging lines, "no profits could have been shown at all." Thus, the presidents argued,

---

[59] "Letter from the Postmaster General," Ex. Doc. No. 49, 39th Congress, 1st Session, 10.
[60] "Letter from the Postmaster General," Ex. Doc. No. 49, 39th Congress, 1st Session, 19.
[61] "Letter from the Postmaster General," Ex. Doc. No. 49, 39th Congress, 1st Session, 24 and 26. The kite claim appears to be one that preoccupied Orton, who complained of the "petty annoyance of kite tails" in an 1877 memorandum as well. William Orton, "Memoranda for Dr. Green," 14 November 1877, WUC.

telegraph consolidation was not a luxury but a necessity, and lower rates would be catastrophic. The collapse of the United States Telegraph Company provided a case in point. Created to challenge the Six Nation cartel, the company had lost so much money that it had been "glad to consolidate" with Western Union for "mutual safety" from expenses and competition. If, as Brown claimed, the cartel charged extortionate rates, then the United States Company could have succeeded by reducing rates to undercut its competitors. But the "instinct of self-preservation" prevented the firm from taking a course that would only "secure it a speedier decease."[62] Two companies, competing "legitimately and honestly" on the same route simply could not operate profitably. The United States Company's merger with Western Union, to which detractors now attached "the opprobrium of 'monopoly,'" was the result, "not of power, but of the pressure of mutual necessity." Even without competition, Western Union could eke out only enough return to stockholders to give the stock "a fair value as an investment," and the American Telegraph Company's profits would disappear if rates were significantly reduced.[63] High rates were not extortion, but a necessity given the rising cost of stationery, wire, and labor.[64]

A public telegraph company, the chiefs of the private companies argued, would destroy private property to no public benefit, and, potentially, to public harm. A postal telegraph in competition with the private companies could lower prices only by using the public purse to cover its losses, thereby undercutting and destroying the private property invested in the telegraph. The private companies, their presidents explained, "never proposed to the public to be eleemosynary institutions. They were built to make money." They had spent "vast sums" for that purpose and never "dreamed that a government, established by the people for the purpose of protecting their common interests" would become a competitor.[65] Dennison's conclusion, based on the industry's self-assessment, was that the best path for the government – indeed, the only path it could justly pursue – was to leave the telegraph in private hands, allowing it to be

---

[62] "Letter from the Postmaster General," Ex. Doc. No. 49, 39th Congress, 1st Session, 16.
[63] "Letter from the Postmaster General," Ex. Doc. No. 49, 39th Congress, 1st Session, 10–12.
[64] "Letter from the Postmaster General," Ex. Doc. No. 49, 39th Congress, 1st Session, 17. The consolidation of the Magnetic Telegraph Company with the American Telegraph Company led to an immediate rate increase to which the other members of the Six-Party Contract objected. See Chapter 1.
[65] "Letter from the Postmaster General," Ex. Doc. No. 49, 39th Congress, 1st Session, 14.

served by "that spirit of self support which gives sinew to the national character, and vigor and manhood to the citizen."[66] The Dennison report so pleased Western Union executives that they ordered four thousand copies to distribute as propaganda.[67]

However useful for the private companies' purposes, the Dennison report had the disadvantage of being untrue. The Southwestern, American, and Western Union Telegraph Companies had all generated tremendous profits. Western Union's dividend appeared small only because the company had more than *quadrupled* the nominal capital on which it was paid.[68] Corporations often watered their stock for precisely this purpose – to hide "excessive or exceptional profits" from the public and deflect criticism of high prices.[69] Contemporary critics observed that the telegraph suffered not from competition or a lack of profits, but from mismanagement and grossly diluted capital. The financier Jay Cooke, who was rumored to have an interest in the National Telegraph Company, rejected the conclusions of the Dennison report. He explained to Senator John Sherman that terrible management caused high rates and poor service. The companies had "*fleeced*" the public and there was no good reason why the telegraph should not connect the major post offices. "The Companies themselves don't have one dispatch on their lines where they could have twenty if the price was *cheapened*," he wrote.[70] An operator with seventeen years' experience also wrote to Sherman to explain that "incompetent, extravagant and reckless management" caused the United States Company to collapse, rather than excessive competition. He rejected the claim that the telegraph was not profitable. "*All* prominent telegraphers are now very rich," he wrote. "They were universally poor when they embarked in this enterprise."[71] Shareholders had been richly rewarded with dividends

---

[66] "Letter from the Postmaster General," Ex. Doc. No. 49, 39th Congress, 1st Session, 12.

[67] William Orton to Jonathan D. Defrees, 8 June 1866, WUC; William Orton to John D. Defrees, 13 June 1866, WUC.

[68] For example, Norvin Green reported shortly before merging with the American Telegraph Company that the Southwestern had produced profits equal to 15 percent of *capital* – not merely revenue – and that had the company not overpaid for recent acquisitions, the net profit returned on capital would be 50 percent for 1865. Norvin Green to Pinckney Green, 29 October 1865, Uncatalogued Green Papers (FHS).

[69] David L. Dodd, *Stock Watering: The Judicial Valuation of Property for Stock-Issue Purposes* (New York: Columbia University Press, 1930), 12.

[70] Jay Cooke to John Sherman, 22 June 1866, Sherman Papers. Emphasis in the original.

[71] W. W. Kelchner to John Sherman, 28 June 1866, Sherman Papers. Charles W. Noble, one of the National Telegraph Company's incorporators, told Sherman the same thing. The major telegraph stockholders in the last ten years had "not only *made money*"

and the doubling and trebling of their capital stock. The telegraph executives had not denied this in their letter to Dennison, but argued that the "wealth of a few men" was only incidental.[72]

Leaders at Western Union and the American Telegraph Company proved eager to practice the anticompetitive gospel they preached in the Dennison report. Though the American Telegraph Company had been split in two during the war, its Northern profits had swelled, and it had absorbed a dozen smaller companies to buttress its control of the East.[73] In 1865, American Telegraph Company began courting Southwestern, which Western Union had also targeted. Morse and his business agent Amos Kendall, who still owned substantial shares in both American and Southwestern Telegraph Companies, encouraged the consolidation. A united firm promised earnings as great as Western Union's, but with only a quarter of the capital stock.[74] Investors agreed, and in January 1866, American Telegraph Company purchased Southwestern for $1 million in stock. Rumors swirled that this was only the first conquest in American Telegraph Company's campaign, that the company would soon announce plans for a submarine cable to Cuba and Central America, and a transcontinental line from San Antonio to San Francisco.[75]

Western Union's merger with United States Telegraph encouraged further consolidation because many United States lines lay within the "sovereign" territory of the other "Six Nation" telegraph firms, including American Telegraph Company. Western Union offered to sell the competing lines to the cartel members but operated them in the meantime in violation of the cartel agreement. The partners in the cartel feared Western Union would use the competing United States lines to force them to concede and join the "grand monopoly."[76] Since the cartel's creation,

but "grown *enormously wealthy*. See Wade, Cornell, Sibley, Amos Kendall and every telegraph man in the U.S." Noble to Sherman, 20 June 1866, Sherman Papers.

[72] "Letter from the Postmaster General," Ex. Doc. No. 49, 39th Congress, 1st Session, 17.

[73] Abram P. Eastlake, "The Great Monopoly," *Lippincott's Magazine of Literature, Science and Education* (1870): 364.

[74] Norvin Green to Pinckney Green, 4 February 1865, Green Papers (U.K.). This does not necessarily mean Green believed Western Union's stock was not watered. Watered stocks had a nominal capital much greater than the actual value of the invested capital, a condition that could exist even if the watered company was able to make its dividend payments.

[75] John C. Van Duzen to William L. Gross, 5 February 1866, Gross Papers

[76] The American Telegraph Company paid Western Union $1 million for the United States lines in American Telegraph Company territory. William Orton to Unknown, 26 June

members had feared that it lacked the strength to police its own members, that the Association was but "a rope of sand."[77] But when the cartel failed, it was not because the companies undercut each other on price (which did not occur), nor because the Association did not have the power to enforce its own sanctions (though it did not). The Six-Party Contract was intended to provide security for investments and exclude competition. Western Union's leaders believed that a single firm monopoly could best deliver on that promise by absorbing its partners. The cartel ultimately collapsed for the very same reasons that it had been created.

The profitable American Telegraph Company was the juiciest plum in the cartel, paying dividends even after the downturn in telegraph business forced its rivals to suspend theirs.[78] The American Telegraph Company paid three times as much in dividends per dollar of capital as Western Union, and its lines were prosperous and growing, including a line to California that spelled trouble for Western Union's transcontinental monopoly.[79] But, as usual, it was the interests of American Telegraph Company's investors, not its business prospects, that drove it into Western Union's net.

On June 12, 1866, Western Union merged with the American Telegraph Company on a basis of three shares for one. The official agreement declared the merger would both "facilitate and expedite" the transmission of messages and "advance the interests of stockholders."[80] The latter reason was probably foremost in the minds of the American Telegraph Company's directors. Buying the United States Company and its poor quality, redundant lines had hardly made Western Union an irresistible juggernaut.[81] Managers of the Illinois & Mississippi Telegraph had called Western

---

1866, WUC; J. J. Speed to J. J. Wilson, 23 March 1866, John Dean Caton Papers; Edward Bebe to J. H. Wade, 9 May 1866, John Dean Caton Papers.

[77] Hiram Sibley to J. D. Caton, 11 March 1860, Caton Papers.

[78] "Letter from the Postmaster General," Ex. Doc. No. 49, 39th Congress, 1st Session, 18.

[79] S. Churchill to J. D. Caton, 22 March 1865, Caton Papers, William Orton to O. H. Palmer, 17 May 1866, WUC.

[80] "Meeting of the Board of Directors of the Western Union Telegraph Company," 14 June 1866, WUC.

[81] The economist Gerald W. Brock, for example, argued that since Western Union acquired United States Company lines in the American Telegraph Company's territory, Western Union no longer required connections with the American Telegraph Company, while the American still required connections with Western Union. This is wrong for two reasons. First, Western Union was negotiating to sell those lines to the American Telegraph Company, as required by the Six-Party Contract. Second, the lines in question were of poor quality and on poor rights-of-way. There is no reason to believe that Western Union could work them any more profitably than the United States had, and if it is simply a

Union's merger with the United States Company "a great mistake" and a *"calamity."*[82] Former United States Company manager J. D. Reid later claimed that American Telegraph Company's listless leaders lacked the determination to fight and saw "the value of combination."[83] Listless or not, consolidation enriched American Telegraph Company shareholders, for whom monopoly promised freedom from the tempest of competition. With American Telegraph Company gone, its shareholders and profitable lines absorbed, only the federal government could hope to take on Western Union. As matters stood, Western Union was unquestionably "in the ascendant, sole possessors of the field."[84]

Western Union promptly dismantled its former rival. Managers determined that much of American Telegraph Company's workforce could be "dispensed with, without detriment to the interests of the consolidated company," and promptly dismissed its officers as well. In August, Western Union's own executives decamped from Rochester and established their new headquarters in American Telegraph Company's former offices at 145 Broadway, just north of Wall Street, in New York City.[85]

Soon after the American Telegraph Company disappeared into Western Union, debate began in the Senate on Sherman and O'Rielly's National Telegraph Company. Sherman explained to the Senate that three options lay open to "expedite or facilitate" the construction of telegraphs. The government could build lines "to compete with existing lines," but Postmaster General Dennison and the Senate Post Office committee agreed that this was too expensive and required the Post Office to take on a duty for which it was not prepared. The second option was for Congress to incorporate a private company to build a competing telegraph. The committee dismissed this course as certain to draw "objection from its very novelty."[86] Except for the defunct Bank of the United States and the recently incorporated

question of whether Western Union was willing to void the Six-Party Contract, advance into the American Telegraph Company's territory, and possibly operate at a loss, then it could have done so whether it bought the United States lines or not. See Gerald W. Brock, *The Telecommunications Industry: The Dynamics of Market Structure* (Cambridge, Mass.: Harvard University Press, 1981), 83.

[82] Thomas Caitlin to J. D. Caton, 26 March 1866, Caton Papers. Emphasis in the original.

[83] Reid, *The Telegraph in America*, 525–6.

[84] Congressional Globe, 39th Congress, 1st Session, 3077.

[85] Meeting of the Board of Directors of the Western Union Telegraph Company, 15 June 1866, WUC.

[86] Congressional Globe, 39th Congress, 1st session, 3076. The Committee considered a bill, S. 249, along the lines of option two. S. 249 was apparently never printed, but it

Pacific railroads, Congress had no precedent for empowering a corporation formed in the District of Columbia to conduct business in the states, and no national incorporation law existed for this purpose.[87] Sherman embraced a third option: a federal grant of privileges to a private company incorporated in the state of New York. To an extent, this was not a novel idea. The privileges proposed were the same – as Sherman noted – as those granted to Western Union in the 1860 Pacific Telegraph Act.[88] However, the grant to the National Telegraph Company was notably different in two ways. First, the privileges would be granted to a telegraph company with no existing lines – the National Telegraph Company had been formed only in April by O'Rielly and a group of incorporators that included Charles T. Sherman, Senator Sherman's eldest brother.[89] Second, although the early drafts of the Pacific Telegraph Act granted privileges to a specific company, the final version required competitive bids. Sherman argued that Western Union's dominance demanded urgent action and justified a special grant to a private corporation. "The present monopoly that now controls all the telegraph wires of this great country is in the hands of a single corporation," he told his colleagues in the Senate, "and the only question is, whether we shall leave them in the ascendant, sole possessors of the field, or whether we shall, if we can, create competition."[90]

Western Union executives kept a wary eye on the Sherman bill and its growing list of supporters. In May, rumors reached Orton, now Western Union's vice president, that financier Jay Cooke was considering backing the National Telegraph Company because of his dissatisfaction with Western Union's rates.[91] Orton wrote to Cooke to try to dissuade him

was presumably similar if not identical to H. R. 575, which appears to deal with the same issue in the same particulars.

[87] Morton Keller, *Affairs of State: Public Life in Late Nineteenth Century America* (Cambridge, Mass.: Belknap Press of Harvard University Press, 1977), 173. Naomi Lamoreaux has identified the lack of a national corporation law as one of the most significant obstacles in creating a federal antitrust regime. Naomi R. Lamoreaux, *The Great Merger Movement in American Business, 1895–1904* (New York: Cambridge University Press, 1985), 164.

[88] Congressional Globe, 39th Congress, 1st Session, 3076. Western Union won privileges by successfully bidding on the contract for the Pacific Telegraph and was not specifically named in the 1860 law. It is interesting to note that without Congressional authorization no private company could cross the Ohio.

[89] The Incorporators are listed in H. R. 575, 39th Congress, 1st Session.

[90] Congressional Globe, 39th Congress, 1st Session, 3077.

[91] Cooke had a warm association with Sherman, particularly involving Treasury matters. The two were close enough that Cooke invited Sherman to Gibraltar, his summer home on an island in Lake Erie. Cooke to Sherman, 1 June 1866, Sherman Papers.

and prevent his "money, influence or business" from boosting the opposition. However, Cooke had a close connection to Sherman and probably to the Ohio men behind the National Telegraph Company.[92] After
the Committee on the Post Office and Post Roads positively reported
Sherman's bill, Western Union lobbied to have the legislation modified.
Orton wrote to New York's Senator Edwin D. Morgan, recently the chair
of the Republican National Committee, and urged him to "scrutinize"
the proposed bill. Orton helpfully offered Morgan a list of amendments
to attach to the bill to prevent the Senate from "gratuitously" bestowing
valuable privileges that Western Union had acquired by "years of effort,
and at vast expense."[93] Western Union opposed *any* new telegraph law,
Orton wrote, since "no public necessity" required Congress to interfere in
the industry. The inequitable Sherman bill granted privileges to *only* the
National Telegraph Company, a speculative venture dependent upon government favors and "as certain to be a failure as the sun is to rise." If the
government insisted on granting privileges, Orton wondered, "Then why
not pass a *general* [telegraph] law?"[94] Morgan "cheerfully" submitted a
series of amendments proposed by Western Union in his own name.

The proposed measures reflected Orton's intent to write the first federal telegraph regulations in the way that best served Western Union.[95]
One amendment limited the right to access post roads to federal territories, forcing any new company to pay for the right-of-way privileges
that Western Union had acquired in some states. Another amendment
required that companies accept and resend messages from other companies without prejudice or suffer a $100 fine per message. Western Union
would have opposed such a provision when the Six Nations cartel ruled
the industry with exclusive connections, but now that Western Union
had merged with its partners, this provision would prevent a group of
small competitors from challenging their outsized rival by forming an
exclusive cartel of their own. To the provision granting the National
Telegraph Company the government's telegraph business, an amendment
instead proposed that the Postmaster accept competitive bids. Orton and
Morgan also introduced two new sections to the bill. One would make it
illegal for any company to build wires within twenty-five feet of an existing company's lines, a ploy obviously intended to block companies from

[92] William Orton to O. H. Palmer, 18 May 1866, WUC. For friendly correspondence
between Cooke and Sherman, see John Sherman Papers.
[93] William Orton to Edwin D. Morgan, 8 June 1866, WUC.
[94] William Orton to Edwin D. Morgan, 12 June 1866, WUC. Emphasis is mine.
[95] Edwin Morgan to William Orton, 9 June 1866, Edwin D. Morgan Papers.

building on the railroad rights-of-way Western Union already occupied. The second new section contained the most significant proposed change: that the privileges granted to the National Telegraph Company would also go to "*every other* incorporated company or association engaged in the business of telegraphing within the United States."[96]

When the telegraph bill came before the Senate on June 27, Republicans James Grimes of Iowa and John Conness of California argued that sponsors intended the unamended bill to enhance the value of National Telegraph stock and a general telegraph law should be passed instead. Sherman sharply disagreed. Western Union offered such "powerful competition" that challengers required special assistance and a guarantee that they would not sell out to the monopoly as had the American and United States Telegraph Companies. A general telegraph law would extend the included privileges to Western Union, a company "seeking to monopolize the whole business," when it was manifestly in the interest of the government to "build up new rivals." B. Gratz Brown agreed that Western Union had made "competition an impossibility," but he embraced the concept of a general telegraph law as an invitation to all companies to "break the force of monopoly." Although Brown believed the proposed bill fell "far short of the of the true remedy for the evil," he hoped it might prove "an entering wedge" leading to government control of the telegraph and making it "open to all as cheaply and extensively" as the Post Office.[97]

Sherman acquiesced to the pressure for a general telegraph law, removing the National Telegraph Company and opening the bill's provisions to any telegraph company.[98] This change did not silence the bill's detractors. Nevada Republican James Nye, the sharpest of several critics, dismissed the government's attempt to create competition as a farce. As new companies appeared, Nye surmised with more than a little prescience, Western Union would buy them up and pass the cost on to the telegraphing public. This would only "enlarge and swell the powers" of Western Union, which would become even "more monopolizing." The National Telegraph Company, Nye charged, had never built any lines and would

---

[96] "Amendments," S.R. 357, 39th Congress, 1st session, 13 June 1866. Emphasis is mine. Notably absent from the printed Morgan amendments was any change to the section of the bill that granted Congress the right to purchase the National Telegraph Company.

[97] Congressional Globe, 39th Congress, 1st Session, 3427–8.

[98] It is interesting to note that O'Rielly himself apparently soured on the bill favoring the National Company specifically. O'Rielly later claimed he had wanted a general law and had asked Sherman to remove his name from the bill "chartering a *special* company" and instead "went for *general and equal laws* on all such matters." Henry O'Rielly, "The National Telegraph Law," manuscript notes, n.d. 1872, O'Reilly Papers (RHS).

surely sell its franchise to Western Union at the first opportunity, making the scheme's wealthy backers even wealthier without creating new competition.[99] The provision requiring Congress to approve a consolidation between National Telegraph and any other company provided scant reassurance. "Tell me what cannot be done by the consent of Congress, and I will show you a white blackbird," Nye pronounced to laughter from his colleagues.[100]

The Senate debate also acknowledged limits to federal power. Nye suggested that the object of telegraph legislation should be to regulate rates, but Sherman admitted that even on the Pacific Overland Telegraph, created by permission of the federal Telegraph Act of 1860, Congress did not have the effective authority to set rates.[101] Indiana Democrat Thomas Hendricks complained that the Sherman bill granted a corporation in one state the power to exercise its franchise in another state without permission, a violation of the state right to exclude "foreign" corporations, and, in the absence of a national incorporation law, an inappropriate assumption of federal power.[102] Hendricks charged that the "post road" clause in the bill was another illegitimate excuse to create federal authority where none existed. The federal government's attempt to create competition would contribute instead to an unequaled "system of speculation."[103]

Sherman's telegraph bill passed the Senate by a three-vote margin despite bipartisan opposition from several Republicans and all six Senate Democrats.[104] Orton and Morgan's amendment making it a "general" telegraph law had passed, but their other proposed amendments failed.[105] When the Senate bill reached the House in July, Western Union lobbyists again tried to halt its progress. On the House floor John Alley fought off amendments that would send the bill back to the Senate, where it would

---

[99] Congressional Globe, 39th Congress, 1st Session, 3481–2.

[100] Congressional Globe, 39th Congress, 1st Session, 3483.

[101] This was a curious assertion, since the Telegraph Act of 1860 did contain rate limits. However Western Union had by and large ignored the rate requirements, or construed them in such a narrow way that a large number of messages were able to circumvent rate limits. See Chapter 2.

[102] Herbert Hovenkamp, *Enterprise and American Law, 1836–1937* (Cambridge, Mass.: Harvard University Press, 1991), 259.

[103] Congressional Globe, 39th Congress, 1st Session, 3488–9.

[104] I am grateful to Richard John for sharing his roll call data. There were only six Democratic senators in the session.

[105] Morgan offered only a single amendment requiring a competitive bid for government telegraph business instead of allowing the Postmaster General to set the rates. The amendment met with heavy resistance and was defeated by a tie vote. Congressional Globe, 39th Congress, 1st Session, 3489.

"sleep the sleep of death." According to Alley, "influences of an extraordinary character" had been brought to bear on the bill in both houses of Congress.[106] Orton personally represented Western Union at the Capitol, though he denied allegations that he called "Members from their seats" to give them orders. Having so recently held a senior office in the Treasury Department, however, his influence must have been strongly felt.[107]

No pressure from Western Union could hide the fact that consolidations in the telegraph industry had eliminated most competition. Fears of a telegraph monopoly were well founded and not easily allayed. "The bill is important to the interest of the American people," Alley told the House, and more urgent now that the major telegraph firms had been "consolidated into one." Western Union, Alley charged, had become "the most gigantic monopoly in this country, if not the world."[108] E. B. Washburne of Illinois, who later became one of Western Union's most tenacious foes, claimed that shortcomings in the bill were irrelevant – the "combining, confederating, and consolidating" of the telegraph companies was "taxing the people to a most enormous extent." He concluded, "If this bill will in any way tend to break down that monopoly, I am for it."[109] After several futile attempts by Western Union's allies to prevent a vote, the House approved the bill. President Johnson signed it into law on July 24.

The Telegraph Act of 1866 reflected the ideological evolution of the Republican Party. Prior to the Civil War, the Republican faith in economic progress included a wariness toward corporations and economic concentration.[110] The lingering effects of this distrust were evident in the Republican argument in Congress that Western Union's dominance of the telegraph, itself a vital instrument of economic progress, threatened the public interest. The Republican tenet that government enterprises tended to corrupt the natural harmony of the economy was also reflected in the amendment to the telegraph bill that prevented it from granting special favor to any particular company. But the demands of governing during the war had expanded the Republican view of the government's role in the economy to embrace the active promotion of economic development rather than merely protecting the harmony of the free market.

---

[106] Congressional Globe, 39th Congress, 1st Session, 3744.
[107] It was felt beyond all doubt in the New York delegation to the House, which voted against the bill by a margin of 12–2 among Republicans, and 4–0 among Democrats. Journal of the House of Representatives, 11 July 1866, 1004.
[108] Congressional Globe, 39th Congress, 1st Session, 3744.
[109] Congressional Globe, 39th Congress, 1st Session, 3746.
[110] Foner, *Free Soil, Free Labor, Free Men*, 22–3.

Republican support for the Telegraph Act – with the notable exception of much of the Western Union-friendly New York delegation – reflected the belief that a prosperous free market required competition in telegraphy. The evolution of the Telegraph Act from the incorporation of a specific firm to a general law intended to encourage competition reflected both evolving Republican policy and what one historian calls a persistent core "vision of universal harmony and a determination to foster economic progress."[111]

As enacted, the Telegraph Act of 1866 did not even mention the National Telegraph Company.[112] Instead, the privileges granted in the law were open to any company that accepted the law's requirements, including the provision granting the government the right after five years to purchase the lines of any company that accepted the act's privileges.[113] This particular clause, though it later proved to be enormously important, received scarcely a mention in the Congressional debate. However, it was probably the hidden motive for the pursuit of a special charter for the National Telegraph Company in the first place. Legislators who argued that the National Telegraph Company was a speculation apparently believed that Western Union would buy it up. But another possibility existed: that the builders of the lines intended to sell them not to Western Union, but to the federal government. The editors of *The Telegrapher* reported in July that they had learned the object of the National Telegraph Company was to turn the lines over to the government, "to be worked in conjunction with the Post-office."[114]

Curiously Western Union did not seek to cut the purchase provision in the amendments Orton asked Senator Morgan to promote, perhaps because the buyout provision was advantageous. In two years the capital of the company had ballooned from $11 million to over $40 million, while its stock traded at half of its par value. Orton had suggested before the wave of consolidations began that a united company with $25 million in total capital could provide a reasonable return for shareholders. But could the company meet its dividend obligations on a capital 60 percent greater than that? Might Western Union's managers have perceived an

---

[111] Richardson, *The Greatest Nation of the Earth*, 6. Richardson also notes, "There was seldom a direct line from theory to legislation: rather, a variety of factors usually affected the final version of Republican policy." This is certainly evident in the patching together of the Telegraph Act.

[112] U.S. Statutes at Large 14 (1866): 221–2.

[113] In early versions of the bill, this provision had been two years.

[114] "Government Telegraphs," *The Telegrapher*, 2 July 1866.

arbitrated government buyout as serving the best interests of its share-holders? Over the next decade critics often accused Western Union of seeking to foist its watered stock on the federal government in a buyout.

John Sherman, the Telegraph Act's author, apparently thought so little of the bill that he failed to even mention it in his memoirs.[115] Perhaps this was because his "authorship" was limited. O'Rielly later claimed he had written the bill after Sherman requested his advice on telegraph matters.[116] The language granting rights-of-way and public land and resources was copied from the Pacific Telegraph Act of 1860. Aside from the provision allowing for government purchase of the lines, the bill's only novel aspect was its stated aim to spark competition.[117] It is certainly conceivable that Sherman had a financial interest in the National Telegraph Company as well – the incorporators included his brother and several of his Ohio associates.[118] Sherman received updates on the effort to organize capital for the company, and some of his own money might have been at stake.[119] Certainly Sherman was more interested in creating a competitor for Western Union than his House counterpart John Alley, who arranged with Orton to buy $9,000 in Western Union stock just five months after railing against the "monopoly" in the House.[120]

Despite Sherman's later disregard for it, the Telegraph Act of 1866 was an important piece of legislation with far-reaching consequences. In creating a mechanism by which the federal government could nationalize the telegraph industry, Congress made a firm and lasting claim to regulatory power over the telegraph. Perhaps the best indications of the law's significance were the vigorous efforts Western Union made to defeat and then ignore it. Indeed, Western Union did not formally accept its provisions

---

[115] John Sherman, *John Sherman's Recollections of Forty Years in the House, Senate and Cabinet: An Autobiography* (Chicago: Werner, 1895).

[116] Henry O'Reilly, "The 'National Telegraph Law,'" manuscript notes, n.d. 1878, O'Reilly Papers (RHS).

[117] O'Reilly later claimed that he had $4 million subscribed for the company, which was "defeated by treachery." Henry O'Reilly, "The 'National Telegraph Law,'" n.d. 1872, O'Reilly Papers (RHS).

[118] John Sherman and Charles T. Sherman appear to have had some financial interests in common. See, for example, Charles E. Sherman to John Sherman, 7 June 1866, Sherman Papers. Sherman also appears to have influenced the Ohio House delegation, which voted overwhelmingly in favor of the bill.

[119] Sherman received at least two updates from National Telegraph Company incorporator Charles W. Noble, and there is also surviving correspondence from Rush Sloan, another incorporator. See Sherman Papers.

[120] William Orton to John B. Alley, 26 December 1866, WUC.

until June 1867.[121] The decision to submit to the Telegraph Act of 1866 did not reflect a change of heart by managers opposed to regulation, but was wholly practical: the law gave the telegraph company free access to rights-of-way – on both roads and railroads – in territory under federal control, which in 1867 included both the Southern military districts and much of the West.[122] Still, Western Union managers feared the bill would work as intended and encourage new competition, and after a costly series of consolidations, Western Union could not afford new competitors. Given the telegraph's limited capital requirements, especially after the Morse patents expired, rights-of-way posed the most substantial barrier to entry for new competitors, and the Telegraph Act of 1866 granted free rights-of-way to all comers on every post road in the country.

Western Union's officers may also have opposed the legislation for the simple reason that *any* government involvement in the telegraph business presented a threat. To be sure, the purchase clause created an unwieldy, all-or-nothing, regulatory regime. None of the Telegraph Act's supporters publicly argued that the regulatory reach of Congress included more subtle measures such as setting rates. But however cumbersome and impractical the purchase clause might have been, it defined a federal responsibility to ensure that the telegraph industry served the public interest. Since the Telegraph Act may be justly claimed as the first federal law to regulate telecommunications, it is not surprising the industry's dominant firm did not welcome the intrusion.[123] Popular political opposition to monopolies and the meddlesome hand of regulation posed grave risks. Orton, in a letter to an ally in Congress, perfectly illustrated the appeal of laissez-faire to an officer of one of the nation's first great corporations at a moment in history when the national government was displaying ever greater potency: "I have read somewhere this sentence which conveys a truth more patent in this country at this time than of any other at any former period: 'the World is Governed too much.'" Orton feared government

[121] Debate over accepting the act began a full year earlier. Meeting of the Board of Directors of the Western Union Telegraph Company, 25 July 1866, WUC; Meeting of the Board of Directors of the Western Union Telegraph Company, 5 June 1867, WUC.

[122] Various claims made by critics and managers in later Congressional testimony on this point are probably incorrect. Norvin Green advocated for accepting the act in July 1866 and reported the reason for Western Union's acceptance in July 1867 – this is almost certainly the correct account. Norvin Green to George Douglass, 5 July 1867, George Douglass Papers.

[123] James M. Herring and Gerald C. Gross, *Telecommunications: Economics and Regulation* (New York: McGraw Hill Book Company, 1936), 210.

interference in "private affairs" – by which he meant business, despite the fact that Western Union had grown well beyond any historic definition of a "private" interest. "The legislation of money out of your pocket and into mine is a dangerous and unwarranted assumption of power," he concluded.[124]

Even as Western Union absorbed its two greatest competitors, smaller opponents endured and new competitors entered the field. The Atlantic & Pacific Telegraph Company steadily crept west from New York City, headed for Buffalo via Albany, destined to reach Cleveland and then Chicago. In July 1866 investors chartered the Pacific & Atlantic Telegraph Company, also with the intention of connecting New York and Chicago. As the two companies' nonsensically similar names implied, both companies aspired to transcontinental networks, and of the diminutive firms that persisted – there were perhaps forty or more – these two ultimately posed the greatest challenges for Western Union.[125] An 1866 editorial in the *Telegrapher* reviewed the new arrivals in the field and aptly captured both the zeal with which investors committed their funds to new ventures and the prospects for their success: "Great amounts of money" would "be spent and wasted," but "telegraphers generally, if not the stock-holders," would "have their share of the spoils."[126]

---

[124] William Orton to Robert S. Hale, 18 July 1866, WUC.
[125] No reliable statistics exist, but there were probably three or four dozen small firms and estimates range as high as fifty. Emerson David Fite, *Social and Industrial Conditions in the North During the Civil War* (New York: The Macmillan Company, 1910), 158.
[126] "New Enterprises," *The Telegrapher*, 15 June 1866.

4

"A Very Big Thing"

In 1867 the ice did not recede from Siberia's Gulf of Geezhega until late May. George Kennan and five other men waited on the shore for the arrival of a supply ship carrying critical equipment and provisions for the "Collins' Overland" expedition, Western Union's costly, improbable attempt to build a twelve-thousand-mile telegraph line from North America to Europe via Asia. More than seven months had passed since the last ship from California reached Siberia, and the most recent news from home was already a year old. On June 1, Kennan spotted a whaler that had sailed from San Francisco on the first day of March. The ship carried bitter news: an Atlantic submarine cable had been finished in the summer of 1866 and worked successfully ever since. A three-month-old edition of the *San Francisco Bulletin* reported Western Union's announcement that work on the Collins Overland Line had ceased and the enterprise "abandoned." For most of a year, Kennan and his men had been working on a project that had already expired.[1] In a world made smaller by faster communication, some news still traveled too slowly.

After a reversal in 1858, when the Atlantic telegraph cable appeared to work for a few days and then sputtered out, and a calamity in 1865, when a new cable snapped and sank after 1,200 miles had been laid, conventional wisdom held that long submarine cables were impractical. But in 1866 Cyrus Field, the indefatigable promoter of the Atlantic telegraph, met with success at last. His expedition not only laid a functioning cable, but also recovered, spliced, and successfully worked the cable that had been lost in 1865 – Field later described it as a "jewel at the bottom of

[1] George F. Kennan, *Tent Life in Siberia* (New York: Putnam, 1871), 421–2.

the ocean two and a half miles deep."[2] To the surprise of many investors, the capacity of the two working cables exceeded demand. Even if Western Union's Russian Extension could be finished, it could not hope to compete with the working submarine cables. The race to link the Old World with the New was over. Western Union President William Orton offered to continue building the Russian line with federal funding for the "sake of national pride,"[3] but Secretary of State William Henry Seward declined, acknowledging that telegraphs could not be built "without capital," and capital required the promise of speedy revenues.[4]

The Russian Extension reveals an odd truth about Gilded Age investing: there was often a great deal of money to be made in failure.[5] Some $3 million had been expended on the project, but it wasn't Western Union's money. The Extension had its own capital stock, which Western Union shareholders subscribed to separately. For several months, Western Union allowed these insiders to exchange their worthless Russian Extension stock, at a rate of nine for ten, for Western Union bonds that paid 7 percent per year. Had the Extension succeeded, the inside investors would have claimed the spoils. Now that it had failed, the shareholders at large shared the burden. After a "fortunate few" swapped $2.5 million in valueless Extension stock for more than $3 million in Western Union bonds, the company announced the suspension of the project.[6]

The failure of the Russian project proved no great disaster for Western Union, in large part because the Atlantic cable contributed to the company coffers. The English-backed cable connected in Newfoundland to the American Telegraph Company's feeder lines. Six weeks before the cable opened, the American Telegraph Company had merged into Western

---

[2] Cyrus Field, *The Atlantic Telegraph* (New York: J. W. Amerman, 1866), 28; ibid.
[3] William Orton to William Henry Seward, 25 March 1867, WUC.
[4] "The Russo-American Telegraph," *The New York Times*, 2 April 1867, 1.
[5] This idea was introduced to me with great clarity in a keynote address by Richard White. As White explained, the trick was to swap non-negotiable securities for negotiable securities before the venture disappeared – precisely the technique employed by investors in the Russian Extension. Richard White, Keynote, Harvard University History of Capitalism in North America Conference, 26 October 2006.
[6] The windfall for investors in the Extension stock was substantial. Western Union gave $1 in bonds for every ninety cents paid in assessments on Russian Extension stock, plus an additional 8 percent as interest. Only $2.5 million of the $10 million in stock had been assessed, but $3,170,292 in bonds was issued, paying 7 percent until due in 1875. Orton later admitted that this was an "injustice" to shareholders and the bonds had been issued over his objections. William Orton to G. D. Rosengarten, 21 July 1868, WUC; Robert Luther Thompson, *Wiring a Continent: The History of the Telegraph Industry in the United States, 1832–1866* (Princeton, N.J.: Princeton University Press, 1947), 435.

Union. Thus every dispatch to or from the cable passed over Western Union feeder lines on land. For all practical purposes, the Atlantic cable terminated not at Heart's Content in Newfoundland, but in Western Union's office on lower Broadway.[7]

After consolidating with the American Telegraph Company and the United States Telegraph Company in 1866, Western Union operated a network with more than two thousand offices and 37,380 miles of telegraph line, reaching across the entire North American continent.[8] A Louisiana newspaper concluded that the consolidated company was thus "a very big thing."[9] The unified management had created what one historian claims was the largest corporation in the country.[10] Western Union's capitalization of $40 million, though "watered," was nearly twice the storied New York Central Railroad's capitalization of $24.4 million in 1866.[11] Its scale was unmatched by any single organization except perhaps the federal post office. Despite this great "success," however, Western Union managers found they faced two significant challenges.

The first challenge was how to manage such a far-flung empire effectively. Despite offering business communication as its chief product, Western Union lacked the administrative capacity to operate its vast network as a unified whole. A colleague had warned Hiram Sibley, the leading proponent of consolidation for more than a decade, that a merger with the American Telegraph Company alone would create "too large a concern for one management," even if a dozen "Sibley's" were in charge.[12]

Telegraph manager and historian J. D. Reid described the late 1860s as the dawn of a new period in telegraph history: "the era of administration." The system-builders and consolidators were replaced by the "administrative talent" required to bring "unity, coherence, and control" to the telegraph.[13] This development, however, was at first more aspirational than operational. Western Union displayed little such coherence. Consolidation aggregated the telegraph firms but did not truly unify them. The "discordant elements" of several companies – each with its

[7] "The General Telegraph Office of the Western Union Telegraph Company in New-York City," *The Telegrapher*, 15 July 1867, 249.

[8] Annual Report of the Western Union Telegraph Company, 30 June 1891, WUC.

[9] Baton Rouge *Weekly Gazette and Comet*, 30 June 1866, Wade Papers.

[10] Thompson, *Wiring a Continent*, 442.

[11] New York (State). State Engineer and Surveyor, *Annual Report on the Railroads of the State of New York* (Albany: Weed, Parsons & Co., 1866), 67.

[12] Bliss to Sibley, 7 February 1865, Sibley Papers.

[13] James D. Reid, *The Telegraph in America: Its Founders, Promoters, and Noted Men*, 1st ed. (New York: Derby Brothers, 1879), 530.

own equipment, methods, rules, and rates – created administrative chaos beyond the control of the managers in New York City.[14]

The second challenge was the opposition that Western Union's dominance of the telegraph generated on several fronts. Some observers had praised the 1866 wave of mergers as meeting public demand "for prompt and uninterrupted transmission of messages" and ending "delays in checking and booking from one line to another."[15] But even though dozens of small firms still vied for shares of the growing telegraph business, the term "monopoly" attached to Western Union with growing frequency. A writer in *Lippincott's Magazine* noted in 1870 that Western Union's "enemies" called the company the "Great Monopoly," which Western Union managers accepted as an "apt designation."[16] In becoming such "a very big thing," Western Union had also become a threat. Unification of the telegraph forced Western Union to confront the demands of telegraph users, the challenges of new competitors, and the frustration of its own employees, many of whom, like Kennan's team stranded in Eastern Siberia, felt increasingly ill used. In becoming one of the first ubiquitous corporations in American history, Western Union had also become a lightning rod.

Among the nation's private businesses, only the railroads matched the size and complexity of Western Union. Although the intricacy of rail operations was greater, the telegraph's speed and volume required exceptional coordination and "tight internal control." Historians who have perceived a "managerial revolution" taking shape in American business in the decades after the Civil War have assumed that the administrative requirements of the telegraph made it a good candidate for monopoly. However, this assumption takes the effect for the cause.[17] The promise of the Great Monopoly was the end of competition and a larger and more certain return on capital. The plodding reorganization of Western Union after it merged with its partners testifies to the fact that creating a strong centralized command of the business was a secondary concern. The managerial revolution as it unfolded at Western Union was at best a

---

[14] Ibid., 535.

[15] "Telegraph Consolidation," *The New York Times*, 15 June 1866, 4.

[16] Abram P. Eastlake, "The Great Monopoly," *Lippincott's Magazine of Literature, Science and Education* (1870): 372.

[17] See, for example, Alfred D. Chandler, *The Visible Hand: The Managerial Revolution in American Business* (Cambridge, Mass.: Belknap Press of Harvard University Press, 1977), 80, 89.

trial-and-error affair.[18] Market dominance proved a generous substitute for efficient operations.[19]

Though Western Union had nearly eliminated external competition, the company roiled with internal strife. The "Rochester men" who built Western Union now had to contend with prominent investors from the firms merged in 1866. The "New York interest" from the former American Telegraph Company demanded a greater share of the management. At a "stormy" board meeting in January 1867, the New Yorkers ousted several Rochester directors and named eight new members. An observer on the board characterized the new directors as "the strongest and best men to be found in New York" who would boost "public confidence" in the management.[20]

With Hiram Sibley and acting president Jeptha Wade retired, William Orton assumed command. Orton exemplified an accelerating trend in American business in the postwar years: the separation of ownership from operational management. Orton may have won the job in part because he had no affiliation with either the Rochester or New York factions, having only a year of experience in the industry as the president of the United States Telegraph Company.[21] Orton had threatened to resign from Western Union because the Rochester-dominated board opposed large salaries. Western Union's managers had generally been investors in the company and derived their wealth from dividends and frequent

---

[18] Walter Licht differs from Chandler in his view of the development of railroad bureaucracies, arguing that they developed in stages and through a process of trial and error. Telegraph management appears to have developed more in this manner. See Walter Licht, *Working for the Railroad: The Organization of Work in the Nineteenth Century* (Princeton, N.J.: Princeton University Press, 1983), 19.

[19] I am using the term "centralized" here to refer to the degree to which decisions were initiated at headquarters or required the approval thereof. Relative to the later development of the multidivisional "decentralized" corporation, Western Union was definitely "centralized." Nonetheless, officers at headquarters projected authority in only a limited way in the 1860s. Glenn Porter noted in his introduction to Yates that "except in extreme circumstances, it appears that firms could function for long periods in relatively inefficient ways." Such extreme circumstances did not really affect Western Union until after the 1860s. See Alfred D. Chandler, *Strategy and Structure: Chapters in the History of the Industrial Enterprise* (Cambridge, Mass.: The M.I.T. Press, 1962); JoAnne Yates, *Control through Communication: The Rise of System in American Management* (Baltimore: The Johns Hopkins University Press, 1989), xi.

[20] Norvin Green to Martha Green, 7 January 1866, Green Papers (U.K.). T. T. Eckert, Anson Stager, P. McD. Collins, and H. P. Selden.

[21] The conflict in the board continued at least into the summer of 1867, when John Dean Caton was kept off the board because it could not be agreed upon whether he would replace a New York man or a Rochester man. Norvin Green to J. D. Caton, 11 June 1867, Caton Papers.

issues of new stock. Orton, however, had no personal wealth and owned no telegraph stock. He demanded and eventually received a cash salary of $10,000 a year.[22]

Orton's new command consisted of three "grand divisions" roughly corresponding to the territory controlled by the individual companies before the consolidation of 1866. Each of the division superintendents had previously managed telegraph companies in their respective regions, and they enjoyed significant autonomy.[23] Superintendents received guidelines and "general orders" but made their own decisions about construction, staffing, supplies, and even legal issues. Historians have noted the similarity of both railroad and telegraph organizations to military commands, but at Western Union the military metaphor was largely rhetorical – the chain of command did not reach many offices.[24] When the *Journal of Commerce* blasted the company for its "errors, blunders, mischiefs, and general neglect of the public interest," Orton admitted that it was "exceedingly difficult to preserve proper discipline over an army of operators" in far-flung offices that were rarely under the direct supervision of even mid-level managers.[25] Orton launched a company newspaper, *The Journal of the Telegraph*, to transmit essential news, orders, and policies and unite the "previously independent elements" of his command. Though in-house publications became an industrial commonplace in the twentieth century, in 1867 *The Journal of the Telegraph* was a novelty.[26] Orton hoped the *Journal* would "educate all parts of the service alike," spreading "the best mode of conducting any branch of the business" across the network – what in modern business is called dissemination of "best practices."[27]

---

[22] Norvin Green to Pinckney Green, 30 July 1866, Uncatalogued Green Papers (FHS).

[23] The Central Division's Anson Stager had been Western Union's general superintendent, the Eastern Division's Thomas T. Eckert had been Stager's subordinate and rival in the United States Military Telegraph Corps, and the Southern Division's John Van Horne had been Norvin Green's Southern superintendent during the war.

[24] Gabler makes a case for the influence of the military on Western Union's hierarchy and takes issue with Chandler's suggestion that military influence on management was minimal. I agree with Gabler that the rhetoric of the military is present in Western Union's management structure, but beyond familiar wording, there is little evidence to suggest that local managers were compelled to observe a strict chain of command. See Edwin Gabler, *The American Telegrapher: A Social History, 1860–1900* (New Brunswick, N.J.: Rutgers University Press, 1988), 46, 219n; Chandler, *The Visible Hand*, 95, 205.

[25] William Orton to David Stone, 23 July 1869, WUC.

[26] Western Union was ahead of its time in this respect. In-house magazines were an early-twentieth century phenomenon intended to "humanize the workplace for workers and managers." Yates, *Control through Communication*, 17.

[27] William Orton to Anson Stager, 22 May 1873, WUC.

The flow of information upstream to Orton's office in New York was limited. Until 1873, Western Union lacked even a system for inspecting branch offices.[28] Orton read the operators' union newspaper, *The Telegrapher*, to keep abreast of employee concerns. When, for example, Orton read that a local manager had docked the wages of an operator who had attended her father's funeral, he ordered the wages paid and also demanded an end to docking operators for absence due to illness.[29] Despite such occasional interventions, authority over personnel remained highly dispersed, with no central policies on salaries, seniority, or grievances, and many decisions left to the judgment – or caprice – of local managers.[30] Even the condition of the company's lines was something of a mystery to central managers in 1866. Despite paying lip service to the "science" of telegraphy, managers lacked any systematic information about the quality of their lines and the requirements for their improvement. Orton hired a respected British electrician, Cromwell Fleetwood Varley, to survey the state of Western Union's wires and equipment. Varley returned a "marvelously minute and exhaustive" report on the embarrassing condition of Western Union's network. Even the best wire in service had a greater resistance than the European standard, a widely used relay magnet had a resistance equivalent to one hundred miles of wire, and fully half the wires in the system were so poor in quality or condition that they were "practically unavailable" for standard use. In response, Orton launched a long-term overhaul of the entire Western Union system, a project that took years to complete.[31]

No issue more clearly demonstrated the difficulties of central managerial control in Western Union's early days as a consolidated firm than the confusing array of telegraph rates. In late 1867, Orton put Colonel William Gross, an officer from the United States Military Telegraph Corps, in charge of a newly created "Tariff Bureau." The bureau's mission was both exceedingly simple and extraordinarily complex: collect rate information from every office in the network, compare the rates, and create a new rational system. At the time, every one of Western Union's nearly three thousand offices maintained a unique list of local rates with minimal oversight. Divisional superintendents lacked comprehensive rate

---

[28] Orton to Stager, 14 May 1873, WUC.
[29] William Orton to J. G. Hinchman, 25 March 1872, WUC.
[30] Paul Israel, *From Machine Shop to Industrial Laboratory: Telegraphy and the Changing Context of American Invention, 1830–1920* (Baltimore: Johns Hopkins University Press, 1992), 72.
[31] Reid, *The Telegraph in America*, 534–5.

information for the offices within their own divisions. The result was an irrational patchwork of rates that lacked practical mechanisms for making adjustments and limited the price-setting power of central managers to "reconciling differences and regulating discrepancies."

Charged with completely overhauling the dysfunctional rate "system," Gross began with the logical step of asking every office for a current list of rates. He met with fierce resistance. Central Division Superintendent Anson Stager declared that the requested list required his managers to write out three or four thousand place names and rates, and they would not "cheerfully comply." However, this recalcitrance proved a relatively minor problem; the larger difficulty Gross discovered was that only *three* offices in the entire network had complete lists of rates, ten had nearly complete lists, and most offices had, at best, a list of local rates plus a few major cities. The tariff list in most offices consisted of old rates used by other companies before their merger, with occasional additions or subtractions. As Stager explained, "Most of the offices themselves cannot tell with certainty whether the rate they are using is correct, how it came to be what it is, or why they have no rate."[32]

Stager's objections to Gross's mission were not entirely practical; he found Gross disrespectful and eventually refused to communicate with him entirely.[33] Orton attempted to reconcile them, reminding Gross that "General Stager" – formerly the superintendent of the U.S. Military Telegraph – was superior to "Colonel Gross" in rank, age, and seniority, but to no avail.[34] Gross deemed it a matter of honor not to apologize to Stager and resigned his office with his work incomplete, returning home to Omaha at his own expense because Stager refused to give him a Western Union railroad pass.[35] The rate problem, though critical to the company, had been subordinated to the idiosyncrasies of the senior managers. The "indescribable muddle" of rates endured.[36]

---

[32] Stager to Gross, 9 December 1867, Gross Papers; Stager to Gross, 11 December 1867, Gross Papers.

[33] Gross had inadvertently run afoul of Stager's competition with Gross's friend Eckert, whom Stager believed had attempted to supplant him at the War Department when they were both senior officers in the United States Military Telegraph Corps. Green explained to Gross, "[Stager] cannot afford to quarrel with Eckert without a more laudable cause; but thought he saw that Eckert was using you to his prejudice."[1] Green to Gross, 18 March 1868, Gross Papers.

[34] Orton to Gross, 11 January 1868, WUC.

[35] Orton to Gross, 11 January 1868, WUC; Gross to Orton, 13 February 1868, Gross Papers; Orton to Gross, 11 April 1868, Gross Papers.

[36] W. W. Chandler to A. B. Chandler, 13 February 1868, Gross Papers.

What is striking about the early days of the "era of administration" is how much Western Union remained scarcely more integrated than the North American Telegraph cartel it had led before consolidating its partners. The functional requirements of the "unified" telegraph exceeded the technical and bureaucratic capabilities of Western Union's management. Yet the true aim of the mergers was already accomplished. Despite decrepit lines, a patchwork rate structure, and limited central control, the united Western Union was enormously profitable. For the first two years after unification, Western Union's profit margin was just under 40 percent.[37] The high profit margin allowed the company to reconstruct its lines with retained earnings rather than raising additional capital or taking on debt. Without competition or other downward pressure on rates and despite managerial defects, the telegraph at last promised to be the profit producer that its promoters had long insisted it should be.

In a sense, Western Union was not the only "telegraph monopoly." Though actually a customer of Western Union, the Associated Press (AP) aspired to its own monopoly, not of the wires themselves but the news that flowed over them. In the 1860s the AP became, in effect, a bilateral monopoly: the AP provided content and Western Union provided the platform in a testy union of message and medium. Before the advent of the telegraph, federal postal policies promoted a robust and democratic press, allowing editors to exchange newspapers by mail for a pittance.[38] As transportation speeds accelerated and expanding markets increased the demand for commercial news, the value of timely intelligence spurred competition in the news business. The number of daily newspapers in the United States swelled from twenty in 1800 to more than 250 by 1850.[39] The complexity and expense of gathering continuous news from distant points by telegraph exceeded the limited financial resources and small staffs of most newspapers, so editors formed combinations to gather news, share

---

[37] Monthly earnings and expenses were published in the *Journal of the Telegraph* from July 1866 through October 1870.

[38] After Congress passed the Postal Act of 1792, editors could exchange newspapers for a nominal fee of one cent for distances under one hundred miles, and only one and a half cents for distances over one hundred miles. The volume of exchange was large – between one-third and one-half of the total weight of the post in the 1820s. By the 1840s, the average newspaper received 4,300 other newspapers per year. Richard R. John, *Spreading the News: The American Postal System from Franklin to Morse* (Cambridge, Mass.: Harvard University Press, 1995), 36–7.

[39] Charles Sellers, *The Market Revolution: Jacksonian America, 1815–1846* (New York: Oxford University Press, 1991), 370.

expenses, and monopolize telegraph lines to block competitors.[40] In 1846 New York newsmen had formed the AP to collect European news from ships arriving in Boston and telegraph it to New York, which soon became the nation's "nerve center." The AP collected news from around the country, repackaged it into dispatches, and distributed it far and wide.[41]

Because news dispatches on the wires could be "dropped" at many stations at little expense per station, the telegraph news business offered virtually unlimited economies of scale. Profits increased every time the telegraph reached a new AP customer, adding revenue at very little additional cost. Lacking a competing news service, AP customers had little choice but to accept whatever fees the AP charged, and increased fees produced pure profit for the AP. In sum, the AP had overwhelming incentives to monopolize the wire news business.[42]

Without the cooperation of the telegraph companies, however, the AP monopoly would have been impossible. The fierce telegraph rivalry in the 1850s troubled the AP because opposing lines competed for press business and encouraged the AP's challengers.[43] The AP countered this threat by contracting with competing telegraph companies and paying whatever rate the companies asked with a stipulation that no other press agency could use the lines at a lower rate.[44] When the Six-Party Contract stabilized the telegraph industry, the AP chose a new tack, committing all of its Eastern business to the American Telegraph Company which it had helped foster and all of its Western business to Western Union. After the 1866 telegraph consolidation, the near-monopoly in telegraphy buttressed the monopoly in wire news, creating a mutually reinforcing "bilateral monopoly."[45] At the core of this cooperation was a simple but commanding regulation for AP newspapers: they could accept no wire news dispatches except those produced by the AP and carried by Western Union.

---

[40] Menahem Blondheim, *News over the Wires: The Telegraph and the Flow of Public Information in America, 1844–1897* (Cambridge, Mass.: Harvard University Press, 1994), 59–60.

[41] Ibid., 55.

[42] As Blondheim notes, this is an ideal recipe for a "natural monopoly." Ibid., 99–100.

[43] Ibid., 102–3.

[44] Ibid., 104. This amounted to bribing the telegraph companies not to carry competing news reports.

[45] Richard B. Du Boff, "The Telegraph in Nineteenth-Century America: Technology and Monopoly," *Comparative Studies in Society and History* 26, no. 4 (1984): 579. Du Boff claims that such collusion led to "steeper and discriminatory telegraph rates," with the burden passed on to the public.

This partnership with the AP was not the easy source of profit for Western Union that it appeared. The bilateral monopoly focused public outrage on the telegraph giant but brought it limited gains. Prior to the 1866 consolidation, the "independent" telegraph companies used resentment toward the AP monopoly to embarrass the North American Telegraph Association. The AP's general agent, D. H. Craig, complained that AP competitors filled newspapers across the nation with complaints about "the 'monopoly' of the Associated Press, the 'dictation' of its managers and the 'extortion' of the old Telegraph Companies."[46] In the Congressional debate leading to the Telegraph Act of 1866, Senator B. Gratz Brown pointed to the telegraph–press combination as a crucial reason for the government to encourage telegraph competition and prevent the concentration of the nation's news "in the hands of a few journals" in New York.[47]

Western Union managers claimed that without press combinations, rates for news transmission would be substantially higher and service reduced, giving a substantial advantage to the richest presses.[48] Indeed it was true that the AP's economies of scale had the *potential* to make news reports less expensive. But like all monopolies, the AP had a strong incentive to charge premium prices.

Newspapers priced out of the market or simply excluded from the syndicate justly protested. In 1862, Western editors angry about the high rates, poor quality, and limited relevance of the AP's dispatches formed the Western Associated Press. When the Civil War ended, the Western AP challenged the New York AP in "the Press Association War of 1866–1867,"[49] a conflict reminiscent of the infighting that plagued the telegraph industry in the 1850s. Newspapers excluded from the cartel threatened to form cartels of their own, while the New York AP's own members cheated and undercut each other. A new cartel appealed to editors "most anxious to escape from the position of *servitude*" inflicted upon them by "the city monopolists."[50] The AP ejected the *New York World*, a leader of the syndicate, for cooperating with the enemy and forming a united front with the rival Western AP. The *World*'s editor vowed that he and

---

[46] Daniel H. Craig to F. Hudson and S. H. Gay, 1 January 1866, Manton Marble Papers.

[47] Congressional Globe, 39th Congress, 1st Session, 979–80.

[48] "Letter from the Postmaster General," 39th Congress, 2nd Session, Report No. 49, 33.

[49] Knight took the title from the headline in a Cincinnati newspaper at the conclusion of the "war." Peter R. Knight, *The Press Association War of 1866–1867*, Journalism Monographs (Austin, Tex.: The Association for Education in Journalism, 1967).

[50] D. H. Craig to the Gentlemen of the N.Y. State Press, 6 December 1866, Marble Papers.

his allies would spend "any amount of money" to battle the New York AP by uniting all the newspapers the cartel had excluded.[51] Recognizing the dangers of a protracted competition, the editors of the New York AP agreed to peace negotiations in January 1867 and inked a new deal with Western Union.[52]

Western Union and the New York AP remained uneasy partners. Western Union accused the AP of "packing" Atlantic cable press reports with personal messages, obliging the telegraphers to send private messages at reduced press rates.[53] Orton complained that AP employees were "very lukewarm" if not "secretly hostile" to the telegraph company in their joint commercial news business.[54] Above all, Western Union insisted on upholding the AP's contractual obligation not to "in any way encourage or support any opposition or competing telegraph company."[55] Under this provision the AP could not sell news to any paper that did not receive *all* its news from Western Union wires. Noncompliant editors were cut off from further dispatches. Western Union could easily spot violations, because the offending paper would print the news "specials" taken off competing telegraph lines.[56]

The most substantial drawback of Western Union's partnership with the AP was that it created bitter enemies for Western Union – every newspaper excluded from the syndicate took aim at the dual monopoly. Western Union's contract with the AP officially permitted it to make deals with "outside" newspapers, but only if it charged "precisely equal rates" on a per "drop" basis. If an association of ten papers in a city paid $100 to transmit a report, the agreement required Western Union to charge a single "outside" newspaper in that city the same rate for its report – ten times as much as the ten-newspaper syndicate paid per paper.[57] Western Union did not actually refuse the business of non-AP papers, but the technicality was small consolation to newspapers that could not afford the AP's rates, much less pay Western Union's full price for transmission.

This problem was especially pronounced in the West. A "first class paper" could not survive without receiving the same Eastern telegraph

[51] Manton Marble to J. Medill, 4 January 1867, Marble Papers.
[52] Knight, *The Press Association War of 1866–1867*, 55–6; Blondheim, *News over the Wires: The Telegraph and the Flow of Public Information in America, 1844–1897*.
[53] William Orton to David M. Stone, 9 October 1867, WUC.
[54] William Orton to David M. Stone, 12 October 1867, WUC.
[55] Contract cited in Blondheim, *News over the Wires: The Telegraph and the Flow of Public Information in America, 1844–1897*, 151.
[56] William Orton to David M. Stone, 11 October 1867, WUC.
[57] William Orton to Samuel Bowles, 30 January 1869, WUC.

news as its rivals, and Western Union alone controlled all the wires to the Pacific states.[58] Rather than submit, editors excluded from the Associated Press turned to elaborate schemes to "steal" the news. Henry George, who later won renown as a radical and author of *Progress and Poverty*, clashed with the dual monopoly in 1868. As a representative of the San Francisco *Herald*, George tried to buy news from the New York AP, which rejected the *Herald* at the request of its California competitors. George made "private arrangements" instead.[59] For $20 per week, a newspaper in Harrisburg sold him AP dispatches before they went to press. For another $5, a clerk at the newspaper clipped stories of interest to California readers and slipped them under the door of a telegraph company – a Western Union competitor – with an office in the same building. The "stolen" news flashed back to Philadelphia over the empty evening wires and then traveled via Western Union to California.[60] The complex path of George's dispatch prevented AP General Agent James Simonton from determining the source – George gleefully reported that Simonton went "completely off the track" with frustration. Simonton laid "traps" – such as a false report that Illinois had ceded Chicago to Indiana – to trace the *Herald*'s news to its source, but George remained certain that he would not be found out.[61]

Western Union had a contract with the *Herald* to transmit five hundred words per day to San Francisco and acceded to George's scheme despite pressure from Simonton.[62] In April 1869 Simonton negotiated a new contract with Western Union for press rates to California, and under the new fee structure, the price George paid for his daily dispatch more than doubled.[63] George, in turn, raged against Western Union, printing

---

[58] Henry George, "The Western Union Telegraph Company and the California Press, *New York Herald*, 25 April 1869, 10.

[59] Henry George to James Nugent, 12 January 1869, Henry George Papers; Henry George to James Nugent, 14 January 1869, Henry George Papers.

[60] Henry George to John Nugent, 23 January 1869, Henry George Papers..

[61] Henry George to John Nugent, 27 January 1869, Henry George Papers. The Indiana report is discussed in Henry George to John Nugent, 6 February 1869, Henry George Papers.

[62] Henry George to John Nugent, 6 February 1869, Henry George Papers; Henry George to John Nugent, 23 February 1869, Henry George Papers.

[63] George, "The Western Union Telegraph Company and the California Press." Under the new contract, the four established newspapers each paid $833 each per month for 2500 words, while the *Herald* would pay $2,000 per month for only five hundred words. The contract included a provision to grant any paper outside the association five hundred words at $1,000 per month, but George claimed this proviso merely added "insult to injury" since it would be "'rare old news' that the opposition would get for its share."

six thousand copies of a circular haranguing the company for ruining California's only Democratic paper and turning the state over to the AP, a "most odious and oppressive monopoly."[64] In a letter enclosed in a circular he sent to Rhode Island Senator William Sprague, George exhibited the gift for radical rhetoric that later made him such a famous opponent of land monopolies. The effort to squelch the *Herald*, wrote George, exemplified "the heartless, conscienceless tyranny of the monopolies," a "tyranny worse in every respect than the feudalism of the middle ages." Could "anything be more infamous, any exercise of arbitrary power more dangerous?"[65]

George found an ally in James Gordon Bennett, editor of the influential *New York Herald*, which became Western Union's most tenacious opponent in the press. The *Herald* was a formidable opponent; as early as the 1840s it had established itself as the circulation leader in New York and by the Civil War had become the most popular daily newspaper in the nation.[66] The Democratic Bennett sympathized with George's claims that the press cartel sought to eliminate California's only Democratic paper, and he printed George's circular with a favorable editorial comment. Though the *Herald* was a member of the New York AP, Bennett's course often diverged from his partners. In 1867 the *Herald* briefly withdrew from the AP, and Western Union supported the *Herald*'s New York opponents in trying to prevent the renegade *Herald* from returning to the cartel.[67]

In early 1868 Bennett struck back at both parts of the bilateral monopoly. The emergence of opposition telegraph lines in New England and along the Atlantic seaboard gave Bennett a way to transmit the *Herald*'s news "specials" to newspapers throughout the East – a blatant violation of his exclusive contract with the AP and Western Union. Orton insisted that the AP cut off any newspaper receiving the *Herald*'s specials from opposition lines.[68] In response, the *Herald* "opened its broadsides"

---

[64] George, "The Western Union Telegraph Company and the California Press."

[65] Henry George to William Sprague, 26 April 1869, Henry George Papers.

[66] George H Douglas, *The Golden Age of the Newspaper* (Westport, Conn: Greenwood Press, 1999), 33, 76.

[67] This episode is vaguely explained in Blondheim, *News over the Wires: The Telegraph and the Flow of Public Information in America, 1844–1897*, 153. Orton alluded in November 1867 to the close relations with the press, writing to Anson Stager, "I think it will be our own fault if we do not maintain our present intimate and satisfactory relations with the papers embraced in the press associations east and west." William Orton to Anson Stager, 18 November 1867, WUC.

[68] William Orton to Samuel Bowles, 25 January 1868, WUC.

on Western Union, issuing daily editorials attacking the telegraph monopoly and Western Union managers.[69]

The heart of the *Herald's* attack was a claim that "parties in the interest of the Western Union Telegraph Company" were trying to sell the company to the federal government for $60 million, half again the size of its nominal capital and $50 million more than what "disinterested parties" believed the whole concern was worth.[70] In successive editorials, the *Herald* railed against the fantastic scheme as "the highest point of rascally impudence." Western Union would bribe Congress to buy its lines and give it a "happy and timely escape" from new competition at the public expense.[71] Western Union's managers denied the *Herald's* claims as "wholly false and slanderous" and asked the AP to include a Western Union disclaimer in press reports sent across the country – free of charge, of course.[72] Over the next several weeks, *Herald* editorials accused Western Union of trying to control the press through the AP.[73] Orton denied that Western Union had any power over the press, but he also penned an angry letter to the AP implying that AP's editors should repudiate the *Herald* and render "ample justice" in their newspapers.[74] Orton had reason to be worried. The *Herald's* attack had an acute effect on Western Union's stock price. Since 1866, Western Union's stock had declined from $60 to $36, for which the *Herald* blamed the "blundering and incompetent management of the current officers."[75] The attacks drove the price still lower, prompting Orton to meet with a "committee from Wall Street" to rebut the *Herald's* calumnies, which he feared were "killing" Western Union.[76]

One way Western Union could stop the *Herald* was to order the AP not to serve newspapers that attacked the telegraph company. In the middle of the 1868 *Herald* attack, the AP's contract with Western Union neared its expiration, and Orton informed the AP that he expected the syndicate

---

[69] William Orton to Norvin Green, 5 February 1868, WUC.
[70] "The Western Union Telegraph Company in the Market," *New York Herald*, 6 February 1868, 5.
[71] "The Western Union Telegraph Company's Job," *New York Herald*, 7 February 1868, 4.
[72] William Orton to Wilson G. Hunt, 6 February 1868, WUC; William Orton to J. W. Simonton, 8 February 1868, WUC.
[73] "The Telegraph and the Press," *New York Herald*, 12 February 1868, 8; "The Press and the Telegraph," *New York Herald*, 14 February 1868, 4.
[74] William Orton to the New York Associated Press, 13 February 1868, WUC.
[75] "The Press and the Telegraph," *New York Herald*, 14 February 1868, 4.
[76] William Orton to J. W. Simonton, 17 February 1868, WUC, William Orton to G. P. Lowry, 13 March 1868, WUC.

to respond to the *Herald*'s criticism of Western Union, which other AP newspapers frequently reprinted.[77] Though no official stipulation prevented any AP newspaper from attacking Western Union, "being only human," it would be "very natural" for Orton to remember such hostility during contract negotiations.[78] When negotiations began, Western Union rejected any contract that included the *Herald* as retaliation for the *Herald*'s "grave and utterly unfounded charges" against the character of Western Union managers.[79] The impasse dragged on for months.

The way out proved to be yet another threat. Orton believed the principal New York papers – except for the *Herald* – offered only "earnest support" for Western Union because they feared Western Union would ally with "disaffected outside journals" and create a "most powerful competitor." As a final negotiating ploy, he threatened to create just such a competitor himself. An in-house Western Union news service could contract with all the nation's newspapers without prejudice, bring the strife to an end, and remove the AP's "rod over the telegraph." Orton believed Western Union could increase the price for transmission by 10 percent and still provide service comparable to the AP for less than the AP charged. This threat proved credible enough, and soon the New York AP reached a new agreement with Western Union that was amenable to the Great Monopoly. It did little, however, to dampen the public's concerns regarding the dueling monopolies, and the *New York Herald* remained the company's chief antagonist in the press.[80]

Western Union managers employed a contradictory narrative about monopoly. Publicly, they insisted that their company was not a monopoly, but privately they promised stockholders that competitors had no chance. They often claimed that the nature of the telegraph business dictated that only one company could operate profitably, and thus competition was at best unsustainable and at worst a fraud that fed upon investors' appetite for speculation. By 1869 the half-dozen competing telegraph firms combined for a paltry 9,000 miles of wire – less than one-twelfth of Western Union's 121,000 miles. In three years, Orton boasted to stockholders, Western Union had constructed 2,000 more miles of new lines than all of the opposition companies *combined*. According to Orton, the "separate

---

[77] William Orton to J. W. Simonton, 17 February 1868, WUC.
[78] William Orton to J. W. Simonton, 24 March 1868, WUC.
[79] William Orton to David M. Stone, 12 November 1868, WUC.
[80] Blondheim, *News over the Wires: The Telegraph and the Flow of Public Information in America, 1844–1897*, 157.

and irresponsible" opposition lines merely served to impair "the progress of legitimate telegraphy" and "the general unity of the system." Rather than presenting a credible alternative to Western Union, these lines fed on enthusiasm for speculation, Orton argued. Speculators endeavored to "fleece a credulous public" by attracting investors to lines that were certain to fail after they had paid off the contractors who built them, contractors who were, themselves, the prime movers in the companies' creation. "People will subscribe for stock in a projected telegraph line to the moon," Orton chided a commercial newspaper calling for greater investment in opposition lines.[81]

Orton painted a bleak but not inaccurate picture of the opposition telegraph companies. One such rival firm, the Franklin Telegraph Company, operated between Washington, New York, and Boston. In 1866, Western Union declined an offer to buy the Franklin for a meager sum, declaring the company was worth no more than the salvage value of the wire and poles.[82] The Franklin's meager profits went to pay the interest on the debt owed to the contractor who built the lines. The investors would never see a return, while the once penniless contractor now enjoyed his fortune by riding about town in a "carriage and four." Orton thought it an important lesson: anyone seeking to invest in "mushroom telegraph companies" should first ascertain if the promoters already kept a carriage.[83] Nonetheless the Franklin persisted, moving its headquarters from Boston to New York, hiring new managers, and despite its precarious state, encroaching on Western Union's New England business.[84]

Orton identified the Atlantic & Pacific Telegraph (A&P) as another contractors' swindle. The A&P planned to build 3,000 miles of line from New York to Chicago and eventually California. Rather than contract with railroads, the company took advantage of the free rights-of-way granted in the Telegraph Act of 1866 and built along highways. The contractors took between $600 and $1,600 in stock for every mile they built, though the cost of construction was not more than $200 per mile. The contractors profited by selling their stock at fifteen cents on the dollar or more, "depending mainly on the credulity of the customer."[85] They

[81] William Orton to Charles T. Wood, 22 August 1868, WUC.
[82] William Orton to George P. Hale, 29 September 1869, WUC.
[83] William Orton to Anson Stager, 30 June 1868, WUC.
[84] William Orton to Anson Stager, 26 May 1869, WUC.
[85] Annual Report of the President of the Western Union Telegraph Company, 13 July 1869, WUC.

never intended the unprofitable company they bequeathed to shareholders to be a "permanent enterprise," but it would nonetheless grow until the contractors had built all the shoddy, overpriced lines the public would pay for.[86]

Not surprisingly, the A&P claimed to be a legitimate venture. The A&P planned to connect only to high-volume urban centers – "paying points" – and concentrate on lucrative "through" business. Promoters bragged that the Atlantic & Pacific could pay a 7 percent dividend with the same sum that Western Union required simply to service its debt.[87] The A&P purported to chart a cautious course. To win customers through the sheer growth in demand for service, rather than by competitive rates, the A&P matched Western Union's rates and kept costs down.[88] However, reports from informants convinced Orton that the A&P had expenses more than twice revenues and funded construction with the sale of worthless stock.[89] If so, the A&P took in more than simply foolish speculators. Tycoon Andrew Carnegie, a former telegrapher, believed that the Atlantic & Pacific threatened Western Union. Orton concluded this merely indicated that the A&P had managed to fool Carnegie, who should have been "too shrewd to be caught."[90]

Another rising competitor, the Pacific & Atlantic Company (P&A), had more in common with the Atlantic & Pacific Company than just a reflective name. In 1866, the small, profitable, Pennsylvania-based P&A began to expand aggressively, unveiling plans to raise $3 million in capital to build a Pittsburgh-centered network connecting points between New York and Chicago.[91] The company's contractor collected $550 per mile of line – so far above the true cost of construction that one observer noted the enterprise had a "philanthropic character."[92] To raise the capital required to keep the scheme alive, boosters promoted the P&A as a regional alternative to the despised Western Union. They allocated shares

---

[86] William Orton to Anson Stager, 4 April 1868, WUC.
[87] *To Business Men, Capitalists and All Seeking Investments* (New York: Van Kleeck, Clark & Co., Stationers and Printers, 1868), 14. Western Union paid approximately $350,000 in interest on its bonds in fiscal 1869, making the Atlantic & Pacific's claim not that outlandish. *Journal of the Telegraph*, 1 July 1869.
[88] Atlantic and Pacific Telegraph Company Executive Committee Meeting Minutes, 16 November 1867, WUC; Atlantic and Pacific Telegraph Company Executive Committee Meeting Minutes, 7 January 1868, WUC.
[89] William Orton to Delos DeWolfe, 23 December 1867, WUC.
[90] William Orton to Gaither, 20 December 1867, WUC.
[91] The P&A went to Chicago through Pittsburgh. The A&P went via Albany and Buffalo.
[92] Reid, *The Telegraph in America*, 443–4.

of stock to the Western communities that the P&A intended to connect, vowing that ownership would remain "outside the stock corruptions of New York" and exclusively in the hands of the "business men of the West." This strategy had ample precedent: many of the early telegraph companies depended upon capital from local businessmen who hoped to profit both by owning *and* using the telegraph.[93] The P&A required three-fourths of the stockholders to approve any consolidation, thus guarding against the mergers which had "swept out of existence" most other independent companies. "Take a share in this only cure of a monopoly," proclaimed a P&A circular as though advertising patent medicine.[94] Orton described the stock sales as a fraud perpetuated by sales agents wandering "from town to town" canvassing for subscriptions, exchanging shares to cover their hotel bills, employing every possible means to float "the bubble" by selling more worthless subscriptions.[95] Of course, Western Union had almost as fragrantly defrauded shareholders this way in the failed Russian Extension.

Despite their questionable viability, the Great Monopoly's new competitors did prove to be a serious irritation. The Telegraph Act of 1866 provided a new opening for competitors to get access to railroad rights-of-way. Opposition companies made "persistent efforts" to convince the railroads that because they carried the mail, their roads were post roads and under federal law open to any telegraph company.[96] Railroads seeking a better deal on telegraph service than Western Union offered were all too willing to share in this interpretation of the Telegraph Act.[97]

Railroads also contested the ownership of the telegraph lines on their rights-of-way. Western Union and the railroad both contributed to construction, and once the lines were up, neither party could "assert exclusive jurisdiction" with certainty.[98] The Pacific & Atlantic Company tested this ambiguity in 1867 by adding cross arms to the Pennsylvania Railroad's telegraph poles, often just below the arms bearing Western Union wires.

---

[93] Gerald W. Brock, *The Telecommunications Industry: The Dynamics of Market Structure* (Cambridge, Mass.: Harvard University Press, 1981), 63.

[94] "The Pacific and Atlantic Telegraph Company of the United States, Desire to Make the Following Statements for Your Consideration," Private Circular, Undated [1869?], WUC.

[95] "Annual Report of the President of the Western Union Telegraph Company," WUC.

[96] William Orton to F. A. Comley, 18 September 1868, WUC.

[97] Carnegie is quoted in Joseph Frazier Wall, *Andrew Carnegie* (New York: Oxford University Press, 1970), 216.

[98] William Orton to Benjamin Harris Brewster, 9 December 1868, WUC.

The Pennsylvania Railroad's contract with Western Union was not exclusive, and except for a few miles of line built by Western Union, the road had installed most of the poles.[99] The P&A had paid a steep price to the railroad for this new right-of-way: Andrew Carnegie, recently a superintendent of the Pennsylvania Railroad, founded the Keystone Telegraph Company and negotiated an inside deal with his former bosses for a right-of-way across Pennsylvania. Just two weeks later Carnegie sold the Keystone – which had neither lines nor any assets beyond its right-of-way – to the P&A for three times its capital value.[100]

Orton railed against the installation of P&A wires on Western Union poles as an "indignity" and "injustice."[101] If the Pennsylvania Railroad's managers – "sneak thieves" – would not voluntarily remove the wires, Western Union would remove them by force rather than "be quietly smothered by an uninvited guest."[102] Western Union's men tore down the P&A wires on the poles jointly owned with the Pennsylvania Railroad poles and won an injunction against their restoration.[103] The P&A tried the same trick on the Chicago, Columbus & Indiana Central Railroad, where Western Union had had exclusive contracts since 1862.[104] When the P&A started stringing wires on new crossbars three feet below Western Union's, Western Union promptly sent crews to rip them down. The P&A obtained an injunction and had the Western Union men arrested. Both subsequently filed a flurry of requests for injunctions, turning the courts into a theater for their commercial war.

Settling private business disputes became one of the principal responsibilities of state courts in the postbellum period, and the injunction was one of the most popular weapons.[105] Orton ordered managers to "introduce

---

[99] Harold C. Livesay, *Andrew Carnegie and the Rise of Big Business*, 3rd ed. (New York: Pearson Education, 2007), 69.

[100] Wall, *Andrew Carnegie*, 214; James A. Ward, *J. Edgar Thomson: Master of the Pennsylvania* (Westport, Conn.: Greenwood Press, 1980), 185. Wall claimed that the Keystone's franchise on the Pennsylvania Railroad was exclusive, but Western Union already had lines on the road. In fact, Western Union had used the road in 1856 to outflank the Atlantic & Ohio Telegraph Company's Pennsylvania operation. Western Union bought the Pennsylvania Telegraph Company, which the railroad had granted the right to put wires on the railroad's poles. The Atlantic & Ohio bought Pennsylvania Telegraph in 1857, giving Western Union control over the Atlantic & Ohio, which it formally absorbed in 1864. Thompson, *Wiring a Continent*, 296.

[101] William Orton to J. Edgar Thompson, 3 December 1867, WUC.

[102] William Orton to Anson Stager, 6 January 1868, WUC.

[103] Orton to Benjamin Harris Brewster, 9 December 1868, WUC.

[104] William Orton to B. E. Smith, 7 August 1868, WUC.

[105] William Orton to William Dennison, 7 August 1868, WUC; "Injunction of the Pacific and Atlantic Telegraph Company against the Western Union Telegraph Company; State

every species of litigation" that would "harass and delay."[106] Western Union would not submit to the "humiliation" of allowing "unprincipled speculators" to compete using the company's own property.[107]

After Western Union won its suit in the Illinois Supreme Court, the P&A took the case to federal court. The Circuit Court judge would not enforce Western Union's contractual monopoly of the right-of-way, but deemed the question at hand to be not whether the P&A could put up its own line of poles, but whether it could put its wires on Western Union's poles without causing irreparable harm – the legal standard for an injunction. Fifteen Western Union witnesses testified that additional wires on the poles caused all manner of harm: the line could be shorted by broken wires, poor insulation, static charge, accidental connection by kite strings, or even "a sort of web, thought by some to be a spider's web"; messages might be routed to the wrong company; and the overburdened poles might collapse altogether! The judge determined such risks were greatly exaggerated and certainly not irreparable and thus rejected the injunction.[108] Nonetheless the legal tug-of-war over rights-of-way continued on railroads and in courtrooms throughout the country.

Western Union's other significant rival, Atlantic & Pacific Telegraph, challenged the Great Monopoly on the nearly completed transcontinental railroad. The 1862 federal act that launched the road's construction required the railroad companies to build telegraph lines unless Western Union's Pacific line moved to the railroad right-of-way.[109] An 1864 law authorized the United States Telegraph Company to build lines on the transcontinental right-of-way as well.[110]

of Illinois, County of Cook," 4 August 1868, Caton Papers. Morton Keller noted that during this period state courts were used extensively for disputes between private parties, and the injunction became the principle weapon in the legal arsenal. See Morton Keller, *Affairs of State: Public Life in Late Nineteenth Century America* (Cambridge, Mass.: Belknap Press of Harvard University Press, 1977), 354–61.

[106] William Orton to Anson Stager, 6 August 1868, WUC.

[107] William Orton to J. D. Caton, 20 August 1868, Caton Papers.

[108] "The Pacific & Atlantic Telegraph Co. of the United States versus The Western Union Telegraph Co.," printed decision, WUC.

[109] This condition was indeed so prominent that it was reflected in the title of the bill. "An Act to Aid in the Construction of a Railroad and Telegraph Line from the Missouri River to the Pacific Ocean," Misc. Doc. No. 108, 37th Congress, 2nd Session.

[110] Whether the intent of Congress had been to encourage telegraph competition or to protect the telegraph industry from railroad competitors became the subject of a legal debate in the 1880s.
Chapter 220, *Statutes at Large*, 2 July 1864, 373–4.

Western Union's transcontinental telegraph line had been costly both in treasure and in lives. Managing the employees on the line was difficult. In an apology for messages lost and garbled on the way to California, Orton admitted that the men willing "to live remote from civilization, and take the risk of hostile Indians" could not easily be kept under the "strict discipline" of the telegraph business.[111] As late as 1868, hostile Indians killed or wounded nearly a dozen operators per year. Some of the more remote stations became so hazardous that Western Union abandoned them.[112]

Even before the transcontinental railroad opened in 1869, Western Union moved its line to the new road and concluded an agreement with Union Pacific to add a wire for railroad business. Union Pacific retained the right to build its own lines and transmit commercial messages, but with no other wires east of Omaha, it could not compete with Western Union. However, in 1870, both the Union Pacific and Central Pacific sealed an alliance with Atlantic & Pacific Telegraph, which agreed to extend its New York and Chicago line to Omaha to connect to the railroad lines.[113] Once the A&P line reached Omaha, Western Union would lose its monopoly on comunication to the Pacific coast.

Western Union's strategy to monopolize the telegraph required policies that would bankrupt rivals at the "smallest possible loss."[114] Within the company, managers disagreed about what that strategy entailed. Experience showed that rate wars were a dangerous business. Orton often claimed that to earn a dollar, Western Union had to spend seventy cents – a margin that eroded quickly when rates fell.[115] But Western Union's size allowed it to sustain heavy losses to damage competitors or prevent them from using low rates to attract business. Hiram Sibley called this strategy "burning the district" and used it to great effect in the 1850s.[116] Orton also believed that Western Union should use low rates to compel challengers "to lose at every point and every day."[117]

However, disagreement prevailed in the 1860s about whether high rates restricted demand, and if cutting tariffs would increase revenue

[111] William Orton to Charles Dana, 30 April 1868, WUC.
[112] "Annual Report of the President of the Western Union Telegraph Company, 13 July 1869, WUC.
[113] Western Union Executive Committee Minutes, 5 April 1870, WUC.
[114] William Orton to J. W. Kirk, 23 June 1868, WUC.
[115] See, for example, William Orton to A. A. Balcombe, 11 November 1867, WUC.
[116] Norvin Green to Jeptha Wade, 16 December 1878, WUC.
[117] William Orton to Anson Stager, 10 January 1868, WUC.

enough to offset the decrease in profitability. The opposition companies publicly argued that demand increased dramatically at lower rates. The A&P told potential investors that experience in other industries addressing a "general want" had shown that lower prices created "more than sufficient business."[118] *The Telegrapher* offered the same assessment, claiming in 1868 that a "reasonable reduction" in Western Union rates had "not reduced the receipts" at points of competition.[119] Orton was also surprised to discover that low rates did not damage Western Union's profits as much as he anticipated. In many cases in which rates had been reduced, "the increase of business" enabled Western Union "to make as good a show" as before the cuts.[120] The opposition companies, stinging from their losses, appealed to Western Union for a mutual rate hike, but Orton refused to raise rates and even proposed to keep them low after the competition had been defeated. He urged his subordinates to consider "making further reductions of what appear to be exorbitant rates, as rapidly as possible."[121] Orton still insisted that Western Union should reduce only where competition demanded it or an increase of messages would offset the decline in margin, and close monitoring revealed that in some cases lower rates ultimately led to lower revenue.[122] However, Western Union managers gradually began to see reducing rates as a sound policy.

Yet tension remained between cutting rates and paying dividends. Critics charged that Western Union's nominal capital value of $41 million drastically overstated the true value of the lines, and the expectation of dividends on this watered stock required Western Union to charge outrageous rates. The *New York Herald* identified Western Union's inflated capital as the "radical evil at the foundation of all the trouble."[123] The "par value" of a company's stock was supposed to reflect the real value of the physical plant, patents, and franchises of a company. However, on the stock market, shares traded at fractions or multiples of par, reflecting the market's assessment of the profit-producing potential of those assets and the margin of dividends. Prosperous industrial corporations in the 1860s might pay a 10 percent dividend, whereas Western Union paid only 4

---

[118] *To Business Men, Capitalists and All Seeking Investments*, 12.

[119] "Effects of Telegraphic Competition," *The Telegrapher*, 21 May 1868.

[120] Orton attributed this in part to "natural growth" as well as reduced rates. William Orton to J. W. Kirk, 23 June 1868, WUC.

[121] William Orton to Charles T. Wood, 22 August 1868, WUC.

[122] William Orton to J. L. Bedlow, 24 September 1868, WUC. For a case in which lower tariffs lowered revenues, see Orton's discussion of rates between Chicago and Milwaukee, William Orton to George B. Prescott, 30 November 1868, WUC.

[123] "The Western Union Telegraph Company – Business Character of Its Management," *New York Herald*, 21 February 1868, 1.

percent. However, Wall Street priced Western Union shares at a steep discount to about one-third of par value. The 4 percent dividend paid on a nominal capital of $41 million was the same as a 10 percent dividend on the market-assessed capital of $16 million. Orton argued that Western Union thus paid only as much in dividends as would be expected of any other industrial enterprise – not an inflated amount at all.[124] Regardless, between 1866 and 1869 Western Union paid out just over 19 percent of its revenue in dividends, almost double the percentage paid by the New York Central Railroad.[125]

Orton believed that speed and quality of service, not price, drove competition in telegraphy.[126] Western Union's priority should therefore be to expand capacity and improve line quality. A year of building new facilities would allow the company to "secure a volume of business at a considerable reduction in rates which would pay handsome profits, satisfy the public, and make it impossible for competing lines." Retained earnings would pay for the improvements, but only if stockholders agreed to postpone increasing the dividend, or better still, forego dividends for a year.[127] The dividend obligation prevented Western Union from making improvements to support a higher volume at lower prices. Cutting rates remained a competitive tool, but not a general policy.

Western Union's hefty dividend obligation and the poor condition of its lines did not escape the notice of its employees, who much like their employer were learning about the new norms of postbellum capitalism as they went along. In the late 1860s, the National Telegraphic Union's newspaper, *The Telegrapher*, frequently linked dividend payments to Western Union's other problems. The creation of the Great Monopoly, *The Telegrapher* argued, lowered operating expenses, but the gains went entirely to shareholders as dividends – an assessment that Orton largely shared.[128] Telegraphers also believed that their wages and working conditions suffered for the sake of dividends. Lower salaries, longer hours, denial of "customary vacations" – according to *The Telegrapher*, all were

---

[124] William Orton to Henry Bentley, 15 February 1869, WUC. The critic referred to is Gardiner Greene Hubbard.
[125] Data derived from Western Union Telegraph, *Journal of the Telegraph*, vols. 1–2 (Western Union Telegraph Company, 1867), 242. and State Engineer and Surveyor, *Annual Report on the Railroads of the State of New York* (Albany: Weed, Parsons & Co., 1866), 176.
[126] William Orton to Jeptha Wade, 30 November 1868, WUC.
[127] William Orton to Z. G. Simmons, 8 February 1869, WUC.
[128] "Competition and Co-Operation," *The Telegrapher*, 21 September 1867, 1.

intended "to swell the dividend of their employers."[129] Western Union demanded such an intense pace from its employees that some of them, *The Telegrapher* claimed, were dying of consumption from their exertions in poorly lit, badly ventilated offices.

American telegraphers in the late 1860s suffered from a grave – and legitimate – status anxiety. Broad trends in industrial labor and pressures specific to the telegraph threatened their elite standing as skilled, relatively high-wage workers. In the decades after the Civil War, industrial workers experienced a decline in leisure time and the loss of control over workplace conditions. Skilled artisans were converted into "semiskilled machine operatives," workers' job discretion disappeared, and industrial management replaced the "culture of the shop."[130] Most of these changes became noticeable during the long depression that began in 1873, but the tension workers experienced between the traditions of the preindustrial shop and the demands of the industrial factory was a constant concern from the 1840s through the 1890s.[131]

In telegraphy, these deleterious trends for skilled workers emerged with remarkable speed. Western Union was in the vanguard of the transition to an industrial economy, so it is not at all surprising that deteriorating working conditions occurred at Western Union years before similar trends became evident in other industries. The decline was particularly pronounced at Western Union for two important reasons. First, labor accounted for more than 60 percent of Western Union's operating expenses, making workers a target for improving efficiency and cutting costs. Second, Western Union's enormous size and scale demanded tight bureaucratic control.

In the early years of the telegraph, shoddy lines, poor insulation, and unreliable batteries made its operation not merely a skill, but a craft. Telegraphers who entered the industry in the 1850s learned their art by apprenticeship. Many were not only operators of the key but masters of the entire apparatus and process of electromagnetic telegraphy, which they modified and improved when opportunities arose. Operators pioneered the practice of receiving by sound rather than recording needle. It is no coincidence that Thomas Edison started his career as an inventor while working as a telegrapher.

---

[129] "Competition and Co-Operation," *The Telegrapher*, 21 September 1867, 1.
[130] Bruce Laurie, *Artisans into Workers: Labor in Nineteenth-Century America* (New York: Hill and Wang, 1989), 215–216.
[131] Herbert G. Gutman, *Work, Culture and Society in Industrializing America, 1815–1919* (New York: Vintage Books, 1976), 50.

When telegraph networks were small and line outages frequent, telegraphers enjoyed a great deal of autonomy in the workplace and even a fair amount of leisure time on the job. Offices were often quiet when traffic was slow or shut down completely when poor weather disrupted the lines. As networks expanded, line quality improved, and volume increased, the operator's task became less improvisational and more mechanistic. The value operators added to telegraphy shifted from creatively managing a complex process to serving as a dependable cog in a tightly coordinated machine. Telegraphers had once been maestros, but now they were more like metronomes. Consistency and speed became the most prized skills of first-class operators. The operators' room in large telegraph offices became less like a workshop and more like a factory floor.

Operators also faced shrinking wages and fewer opportunities for advancement. The war boom in telegraphy increased the demand for operators, but a postwar telegraph downturn and force reductions following Western Union's 1866 consolidations with its rivals tipped the telegraph labor market in favor of employers. Western Union adjusted for postwar economic deflation by filling vacancies at lower wages. Operators who transferred offices often received lower pay in their new jobs.[132]

The diary of an operator in Western Union's Cleveland office illustrates the operators' concerns during this period. William Andrew Manning began writing about his work in 1867. Early entries in his diary describe a relaxed workplace, with poor weather often silencing the lines and business slow enough that Manning found time at work to read Dickens novels he borrowed from the public library. Manning did not join the conservative National Telegraphic Union, but he did stand with his fellow operators in a small labor action in 1867 – a petition asking their supervisor for permission to smoke in the office. He granted their request – "nearly all the boys had their meerschaums out"[133] – and installed two tobacco machines.[134] Manning joined the Telegraphic Glee Club. Even on a busy Saturday, he still made time to read Shakespeare at his key. "Allowances must be made for *Saturday*," he recorded.[135]

By 1869, Manning's feelings about working for Western Union had taken a turn. The office managers required veterans to work one nightshift a week, leading to "great dissatisfaction." Soon afterward his supervisor

[132] Vidkunn Ulriksson, *The Telegraphers: Their Craft and Unions* (Washington, D.C.: Public Affairs Press, 1953), 21.
[133] William Andrew Manning, Diary 1867, 1 May 1867, Manning Papers.
[134] William Andrew Manning, Diary 1867, 29 June 1867, Manning Papers.
[135] William Andrew Manning, Diary 1868, 18 April 1868, Manning Papers.

issued an "imperial ukase" against looking out the window while on duty. Manning wrote that this left him sucking his thumbs while "gazing listlessly" at the "romantic looking battery box" all day.[136] Manning felt that Western Union had become "most remarkably stingy" in its consideration for employee "comfort." He concluded, "The only privilege we have is the privilege of resigning."[137]

The Telegrapher printed regular complaints that Western Union treated its operators as though they served at the mercy of the corporation.[138] The editors stressed that this necessarily resulted from "the business of a practical monopoly," in which "the interests of the employees must and will suffer."[139] The paternalism that had been common in the small firms that had employed most operators disappeared as Western Union became a "large, impersonal, and nationally powerful" company.[140] Operators and commentators in the press expressed nostalgia for the bygone American Telegraph Company, whose managers had "seemed to take pleasure in making the official relations between capital and labor mutually agreeable."[141]

Western Union managers gripped the reins ever tighter. Operating an enormous concern whose profit depended upon coordination, celerity, and volume required consistently enforced regulations. *The Telegrapher* complained that operators were "treated like boys" in schoolrooms, with watchful monitors enforcing the "many rules or general orders which fall from 'Headquarters'" with reprimands and fines.[142] Manning recorded in his diary that he worked so hard now that he could barely take notice of the weather outside. "It might have rained almost a deluge and I been ignorant of it – so much was I engrossed in the interests of the 'great monopoly' that would tomorrow discharge [me] for the least insignificant overt act," he complained.[143]

Many telegraphers saw unionism as the solution to labor's declining condition, but interest in the cautious National Telegraphic Union (NTU) had waned. In 1869, only three districts sent representatives to

136 William Andrew Manning, Diary 1869, 24 April 1869, Manning Papers.
137 William Andrew Manning, Diary 1867, 13 May 1869, Manning Papers.
138 For one such example, see G. J., "The Abuses and Sufferings of the Chicago Telegraphers," *The Telegrapher*, 23 October 1869, 1.
139 "Patent of the Late Professor Page," *The Telegrapher*, 20 June 1868, 1.
140 Gabler, *The American Telegrapher*, 147.
141 Eastlake, "The Great Monopoly," 365.
142 "A Few Words to the Grumblers," *The Telegrapher*, 15 April 1867, 182.
143 William Andrew Manning, Diary, 31 May 1869, Manning Papers.

the seventh – and final – NTU convention.[144] Despite complaints that Western Union was an impersonal and cold-hearted leviathan, the company sapped some support for the NTU by duplicating its limited services. Western Union's *Journal of the Telegraph* provided a company-friendly alternative to *The Telegrapher*, and the company-sponsored Telegraphers' Mutual Benefit Association competed with the NTU in providing death benefits.[145] While NTU leaders fretted about the decline of their organization, they continued to cling to a Republican free labor ideology that idealized the harmonious relationship between labor and capital. The founders of the NTU had been reluctant to use the word "union" in the name of their organization and preferred to promote "a mutual kindly feeling" between operators and employers. Wage increases were not an organizational goal, and the NTU disclaimed any action that would antagonize the telegraph companies, including strikes, which the union dismissed as a form of extortion.[146] Republican free labor ideology generally held that unhappy workers had the right to leave their jobs, but not to disrupt the workplace.[147] Even the Knights of Labor, which led many strikes in the 1880s, officially rejected strikes in its platform.[148]

The telegraph industry had changed a great deal even in the few years since the NTU declared in its constitution "that the interest of the employer and employee are identical."[149] The appeal to the individualism of the skilled laborer and the "harmony of interests" between master and mechanics was dubious when it was presented in opposition to artisan unions in the 1830s; in the postwar telegraph industry, it was entirely anachronistic.[150] After 1866, a first-class operator could sell his labor to essentially a single stable buyer – Western Union. Yet in even its most radical statements, the NTU offered only narrow criticism of Western Union. "As a corporation, simply, we bear it no ill-will," explained a *Telegrapher*

---

[144] "Proceedings of the Seventh Annual Convention of the National Telegraphic Union," *The Telegrapher*, 2 October 1869, 41–2.
[145] Gabler, *The American Telegrapher*, 196.
[146] "In Union is Strength," *The Telegrapher*, 29 February 1869, 220.
[147] Eric Foner, *Free Soil, Free Labor, Free Men: The Ideology of the Republican Party before the Civil War* (New York: Oxford University Press, 1970), 26–7.
[148] Philip S. Foner, *History of the Labor Movement in the United States: From Colonial Times to the Founding of the American Federation of Labor* (New York: International Publishers, 1947), 507.
[149] "Constitution of the National Telegraphic Union," *The Telegrapher*, 15 December 1866, 89–90.
[150] Sean Wilentz, *Chants Democratic: New York City & the Rise of the American Working Class, 1788–1850* (New York: Oxford University Press, 1984), 285.

editorial in 1867. Even as a "monopoly concern," Western Union's only fault was its "very illiberal policy toward employees."[151] By the end of 1867, *The Telegrapher* modified its stance slightly, insisting the union had "no personal hostility to the Western Union Company or its managers," but acknowledging that it was not in the best interest of telegraphers for Western Union to permanently monopolize the industry.[152] The NTU proposed creating competition with a cooperative telegraph company owned in part by operators, an idea undoubtedly inspired by the National Labor Union, which promoted cooperatives to turn workers into their own masters.[153] However, despite frequent announcements of the imminent launch of a telegraph cooperative, no such venture materialized.

Though a telegraph monopoly did not appeal to operators, telegraph competition had an undesirable side effect: rate wars. "Cut-throat competition" went hand in hand with reductions in wages and privileges.[154] As competing telegraph companies emerged in 1868 and 1869, *The Telegrapher* vowed that operators refused to be "taxed" to pay for rate cuts.[155] Western Union managers agreed that when "speculative opposition lines" instigated rate wars, "the laborer becomes the first to suffer."[156]

In October 1869, operators at the troubled Franklin Telegraph Company were particularly concerned about the pressure of competition on their wages. The Franklin, which operated from Boston to Washington with a headquarters in New York, had been in a precarious financial state. Operators accepted lower salaries while the company struggled, but as the Franklin's condition improved, they demanded a 25 percent wage increase. On October 26 most of the Franklin's operators went out on strike. Despite managers' claims that the strike had hardly interrupted business, nearly every Franklin office closed. Employees at competing companies pledged moral and material support for the strikers. Western Union operators urged the Franklin strikers to "stand firm" and "make the first telegraphers' strike a success." William Manning noted that employees in his office expressed the "deepest interest" and "were determined that as a precedent this strike should not be a failure."[157] Within

[151] "A Few Words to the Grumblers," *The Telegrapher*, 15 April 1867, 182

[152] "The Telegrapher and the W.U. Co.," *The Telegrapher*, 2 November 1867, 84.

[153] David Montgomery, *Beyond Equality: Labor and the Radical Republicans, 1862–1872* (Urbana, Ill.: University of Illinois Press, 1967), 179.

[154] "Competition on a Cheap Basis," *The Telegrapher*, 30 November 1867, 116.

[155] "Why Is It?" *The Telegrapher*, 25 December 1869, 140.

[156] *Journal of the Telegraph*, 1 November 1869, 270.

[157] William Andrew Manning, Diary, 28 October 1869, Manning Papers.

three days the Franklin surrendered, increased operator salaries by 21 percent, and reinstated all the striking workers.[158] The strike emboldened frustrated operators across the industry. *The Telegrapher* called the action a "complete success" and recounted several vital lessons learned: scabs proved ineffective, female telegraph operators refused to take the place of the striking men, and operators showed they had power "to compel justice" but were "disposed to be *reasonable* in their demands." One could be a striker, *The Telegrapher* seemed to say, without being a radical.[159]

In fact, the Franklin strike signaled that the conservative ideology of the NTU was waning. During the Civil War and over the following decade, labor unionism made the greatest advances since the Jacksonian era. Agitation for higher wages and a shorter workday increased dramatically in New York, where Western Union maintained its headquarters and largest office. In 1867, New York State's Radical Republicans pushed an eight-hour law through the legislature, and strikes multiplied in New York City.[160] Organizers formed the National Labor Union to centralize the union movement with national congresses – at its peak in the late 1860s, the NLU had as many as four hundred thousand members in both skilled and unskilled professions.[161] Telegraphy was one of only a handful of trades not represented in the NLU, perhaps because the National Telegraphers Union had nearly disappeared.[162]

In place of the failing NTU a new, more aggressive union emerged: the Telegraphers' Protective League (TPL). Organized in secret in 1868, the TPL was in many ways the opposite of the NTU.[163] While the NTU promoted the mutual interest of the corporation and its employees, the TPL's constitution called for "protection against the aggression of this powerful accumulation of capital" – Western Union.[164] As a "'pure and

[158] "The Franklin Telegraph Company in Trouble, A Strike All Along the Line," *The Telegrapher*, 30 October 1869, 76–7; "Strike of the Telegraphers," *The New York Times*, 28 October 1869, 8; "The End of the Franklin Strike, The Operators Victorious," *The Telegrapher*, 6 November 1869, 81.

[159] "The Telegraphers' Strike," *The Telegrapher*, 6 November 1869, 84.

[160] Sven Beckert, *The Monied Metropolis: New York City and the Consolidation of the American Bourgeoisie, 1850–1896* (New York: Cambridge University Press, 1993), 173.

[161] Keller, *Affairs of State*, 169.

[162] Montgomery, *Beyond Equality*, 177–81.

[163] Thomas C. Jepsen, *My Sisters Telegraphic: Women in the Telegraph Office, 1846–1950* (Athens, Ohio: Ohio University Press, 2000), 148–50. Jepsen suggests that the NTU was "more interested in promoting professional standards and providing benefits to members" than the "workplace issues like pay and working conditions" addressed by the TPL.

[164] The TPL constitution is quoted in Ulriksson, *The Telegraphers*, 20.

simple' trade union," the League proposed to protect the interests of telegraphers, not to dismantle the corporate structure of the telegraph industry.[165] However, even this recognition of divergent interests between operator and corporation was a significant departure from the NTU's appeals to harmony.

The TPL remained clandestine during the Franklin strike, but it was almost certainly the instigator. William Manning had secretly joined the Cleveland "circuit" of the League in May 1869. After the Franklin strike, he reported increasing enthusiasm for the League.[166] Western Union condemned the TPL's secrecy and the "cowardly and criminal" loyalty oath its members took upon induction – a gross violation of "freedom of contract," the foundation of free labor. A Western Union director told the *Times* that the "public interest" required that the telegraph be controlled "by responsible companies, and not by secret irresponsible leagues."[167] Western Union's *Journal of the Telegraph* portrayed the League as a powerful, shadowy faction, headed by a New York triumvirate "with the absolute right" to control the actions of two thousand workers whose labor was "indispensable to society." With but a word, the cabal could halt "the communications of a continent" and "arrest the chief arm of commerce."[168] In reality, like most national unions in the late 1860s, the League had little practical power and was loosely organized – perhaps too loosely, as subsequent events revealed.[169]

In January 1870, the TPL launched a nationwide strike against Western Union. Despite the company's claim that the League had planned a "secret conspiracy" as a "trial of strength,"[170] evidence suggests that the strike was an accident. A senior manager in California announced adjustments to salaries in the San Francisco office, modestly reducing two operators' salaries and significantly increasing one. The local circuit

---

[165] Gabler, *The American Telegrapher*, 148.

[166] William Andrew Manning, Diary, 31 October 1869 and 14 November 1869, Manning Papers.

[167] "The Telegraphers Protective League," 15 January 1870, *Journal of the Telegraph*, 37.

[168] "The Strike," *Journal of the Telegraph*, 15 January 1870, 44.

[169] Montgomery, *Beyond Equality*, 156.

[170] "The Strike," *Journal of the Telegraph*, 15 January 1870, 38. The descriptions of the 1870 strike in the *Journal of the Telegraph* and *The Telegrapher* run opposite each other, with each blaming the other side for instigating the crisis. However, I do not believe the claims made by the TPL that Western Union tested a new system-wide policy of salary cutting in California. Orton was opposed to cutting salaries (see Chapter 5), and if Western Union intended to instigate a fight with the League, it is unlikely that it would have done so in January 1870, when Orton was in Europe.

of the TPL negotiated an agreement to restore the reduced salaries. But after a recent consolidation with the only competing line in California, Western Union's San Francisco office was overstaffed, and in what was likely a deliberate choice, the manager fired two TPL leaders. After a protest in the Sacramento office, managers dismissed eight more operators.[171] An informant told managers that operators believed a rumor – communicated by union members via a secret cipher on Western Union's own wires – that their salaries would be cut by 20 percent, and a strike against the California offices was imminent.[172]

On Saturday, January 1, Western Union operators in San Francisco and Sacramento walked off their jobs. A winter storm had knocked down lines in the Midwest, so the news from California traveled slowly. On Monday morning word reached Cincinnati and Chicago, where operators vowed solidarity with their Western colleagues. In New York, leaders of the League voted to support the strike. R. W. Pope, the League's "Grand Chief Operator," issued a statement – over Western Union lines – declaring that the reductions in California were the beginning of nationwide salary cuts and Western Union was determined to "crush" the TPL. In an overt threat, Pope also announced that the TPL controlled "all the important telegraphic points in the United States."[173]

After three days, with the strike still confined to California, Western Union managers met with a committee from the TPL. The League promised to prevent a nationwide strike if Western Union restored the dismissed California operators, but managers insisted the union had no legitimate grievance. When the meeting adjourned without an agreement, the TPL sent a message over the wires calling for its members to abandon their keys. At Western Union headquarters in New York, some sixty workers "filed out in procession, leaving the hooks full of messages, and only one or two operators to attend them."[174] Similar scenes unfolded in telegraph offices across the country. "The strike is general," Manning wrote in his diary in Cleveland. "The boys are a unit in enthusiasm and determination."[175]

The telegraphers' strike of 1870 was the first labor action in history conducted by wire, and the first strike to afflict most of a single industry

[171] "The Strike on the Western Union Lines," *The Telegrapher*, 15 January 1870, 165; Ulriksson, *The Telegraphers*, 28.
[172] "Statement of James Gamble," *Journal of the Telegraph*, 15 February 1870, 72–3.
[173] "A General Strike on the Western Union Lines," *The Telegrapher*, 8 January 1870, 157.
[174] "A General Strike on the Western Union Lines," *The Telegrapher*, 8 January 1870, 157.
[175] William Andrew Manning, Diary, 5 January 1870, Manning Papers.

nationwide – a development made possible by Western Union's geographic reach and market share.[176] Despite the loose organization of the union, control of the keys allowed the League to coordinate workers scattered across the continent. "We cling like ivy to the wall, we will together stand or fall," promised a dispatch from Washington that League members received at perhaps hundreds of other offices at the outset of the strike.[177] At 3:47 p.m. on January 4, only a handful of workers were on strike while the rest waited for news from the negotiating committee. By 3:50 p.m., operators across Western Union's entire network had left their posts. Once outside their offices, the striking workers lost access to Western Union wires, but the Atlantic & Pacific Telegraph Company and other rivals – which the TPL did not strike – provided "every aid and comfort in their power to the strikers," including updates from around the country that sustained the diffuse protest.[178] Unfortunately for the League, Western Union had the same communications capability. Within hours the company had determined which of its offices the union had struck, reassigned workers from unaffected offices, and closed many satellite offices to concentrate on essential business such as AP dispatches.

The League succeeded in getting its members to join the strike, but its elitist nature – only male, first-class operators could join its secret circuits – left Western Union two untapped pools of operators from which to draw: women and railroad telegraphers.[179] The use of female operators to break the strike should have come as no surprise to the leaders of the TPL. The National Typesetters Union had excluded women from its ranks, and to break a ten-month strike against the New York *World* in 1868, managers brought in one hundred nonunion female typesetters.[180] Since

---

[176] The Iron Molders' Lockout of 1866 spread to New York, Indiana, Ohio, Kentucky, Virginia, and Ontario. Most other strikes in the period were confined to particular cities or regions. See James E. Wolfe, "Iron Molders' Lockout of 1866," in *Labor Conflict in the United States: An Encyclopedia*, ed. Ronald L. Filippelli (New York: Garland Press, 1990).

[177] "The Strike," *Journal of the Telegraph*, 15 January 1870, 40.

[178] Orton to Stager, 8 February 1870, WUC; "The Telegraphers' Strike," *The New York Times,*, 7 January 1870; William Andrew Manning, Diary, 9 January 1870, Manning Papers.

[179] It is unclear to what degree, if any, the TPL included railroad operators. Because railroad operators were not generally "first-class," they were probably not inducted into the organization. However, early in the strike the TPL threatened to call out its railroad members if the railroads provided Western Union with operators to fill vacated positions. "Telegraph Operators' Strike," *Chicago Tribune*, 4 January 1870, 4.

[180] Ellen Carol DuBois, *Feminism and Suffrage: The Emergence of an Independent Women's Movement in America, 1848–1869* (Ithaca, N.Y.: Cornell University Press, 1978), 131–2.

then, the Typesetters Union had admitted a chapter of women, but the TPL had not. Many women operators supported both the Franklin and Western Union strikes with surprising militancy given their exclusion.[181] But some, whether for personal reasons or from frustration at their exclusion from the union, remained at work. Railroad managers pressured and bullied their railroad telegraph operators (a lower caste than "first-class" operators) to accept reassignment to aid Western Union. Some refused to work as strikebreakers – often suffering dismissal – but in the end railroad operators represented the majority of Western Union's "plugs."[182]

The press covered the strike extensively, reporting daily on the status of Western Union's lines and the League's meetings. Only the *New York Herald* came to the strikers' defense. Western Union used its relationship with the AP to bludgeon the League. The AP's reports, the union claimed, were "gross misrepresentations" of the true number of strikers and the grievances of the union.[183] According to Manning, the press conducted frequent interviews with strikers and used "every opportunity to turn the information" against the union.[184] Western Union managers insisted in the press that the strike was neither widespread nor disruptive, and it verged on collapse. Newspapers dismissed the strikers as lacking any "real grievance" and criticized the secrecy of the League and the "conspiracy" of its action and the tyrannical "absolute control" that union leaders allegedly had over the strikers.[185] The League appropriated similar language, claiming that Western Union perpetrated a "most inexcusable and unjustifiable conspiracy" to reduce wages for "the sole purpose of competing with and monopolizing the business of other companies."[186]

On the eighth day of the strike, Manning worried that the situation looked "blue" for the operators.[187] Between 2,000 and 3,500 of Western Union's 6,000 employees joined the strike at the outset, but a steady trickle of workers returning to work increased as the strike wore on.[188]

---

[181] Jepsen, *My Sisters Telegraphic*, 151.

[182] "The Telegraphers' Revolt," *Chicago Tribune*, 5 January 1870, 4.

[183] "The Strike on the Western Union Lines," *The Telegrapher*, 15 January 1870, 165.

[184] William Andrew Manning, Diary, 7 January 1870, Manning Papers.

[185] Reprinted in "The Telegraph Operator's Strike," *Journal of the Telegraph*, 1 February 1870, 54.

[186] "Another Card from Operators," *The New York Times*, 11 January 1870, 5.

[187] William Andrew Manning, Diary, 11 January 1870, Manning Papers.

[188] Western Union usually claimed that only 2,000 workers went on strike. The estimate of 3,500 is from the *Chicago Tribune*, which was not antagonistic toward the strike but was certainly not sympathetic either. "End of the Telegraph Strike," *Chicago Tribune*, 19 January 1870, 2.

On the first two days the union had almost silenced Western Union's wires. But by the morning of the third day it appeared "the worst was past," and by the evening of the fourth day, managers genuinely believed the strike could be defeated.[189] On the fifth day, Western Union announced an amnesty for employees who immediately returned to work, reversing a policy against reinstatement. The strikers regarded the policy change as "an indication of weakness,"[190] but many accepted the amnesty and returned to their keys.

By January 10, the strike's seventh day, Western Union had reopened every office in the country, including several where managers had permanently dismissed the striking operators.[191] *The Telegrapher* claimed that stockholders were losing hundreds of thousands of dollars, but the strike inflicted even greater losses by damaging Western Union's "prestige" and transferring business to its rivals."[192] However, stockholders pledged their support for managers' opposition to the union, and bolstered by the railroads and the press, the company did not falter. Despite Manning's reports in his diary that the strikers were in "excellent spirits" and telling each other, "Stand firm – the monopoly totters," it was the union that tottered.[193] On January 19, the Grand Chief Operator of the League issued a statement releasing the brethren from their oaths so that they could return to their offices and plead for their jobs. In a scene played out across the country, Manning's "circuit" met at the local A&P office and voted to dissolve.[194] The strike had lasted a total of two weeks. For operators, it had accomplished nothing.

"It was the most formidable strike ever made in this country," concluded the *Chicago Tribune* without much exaggeration. In terms of the sheer number of workers, there had been larger strikes, but the national scale of the telegraphers' strike was without precedent. It had seemed at first that Western Union's exclusive control over so much of the country's telegraphing would cause the strike to "so interfere with the business of the public that the company would have to yield."[195] But to challenge such a vast corporation with so many nodes of business, the TPL required a national strategy, and the strike was fatally without

---

[189] "The Strike," *Journal of the Telegraph*, 15 January 1870, 38.
[190] William Andrew Manning, Diary, 8 January 1870, Manning Papers.
[191] "The Situation," *Journal of the Telegraph*, 15 January 1870, 44.
[192] "The Telegraphers' Strike," *The Telegrapher*, 15 January 1870, 168.
[193] William Andrew Manning, Diary, 13 January 1870, Manning Papers.
[194] William Andrew Manning, Diary, 19 January 1870, Manning Papers.
[195] "End of the Telegraph Strike," *Chicago Tribune*, 19 January 1870.

design. Contrary to Western Union's claims that the League had plotted a vast conspiracy, the California TPL alone had launched the strike at one of the slowest times of the year for telegraphy, giving a significant advantage to Western Union. The League blundered by not including railroad telegraphers and women operators in the movement. The union lacked both organizational and financial strength to sustain the long strike that ensued.[196]

Contemporary critics stressed that the strike had no legitimate cause, but the cause is plain enough in the writing of critics and supporters alike: workers feared Western Union's monopoly power. *The New York Times* noted that telegraphers had little to say about their wages and "the outcry was raised that the strike was the result of a monopoly." The *Times* suggested some outside party with a motive to embarrass Western Union was behind the strike.[197] But no conspiracy is necessary to explain operators' fears about a monopoly in their trade. An operator told *The Telegrapher* the issue in the strike was not salaries, which were adequate, but the operators' wish "to be treated like rational beings and not like galley slaves."[198]

The strike's origin in California is telling. Western Union had only a single competitor in California, the Atlantic & Pacific States Company. In 1869, a rate war in California reduced prices below cost, forcing the Atlantic & Pacific States to merge with Western Union.[199] The reduction in force in Western Union's California office resulted from the elimination of competition. The lesson for operators was clear: the monopoly decreased telegraph employment opportunities. Operators disappointed by what they perceived as declining working conditions and an increasingly impersonal management could expect more of the same wherever Western Union achieved a monopoly. In a circular to the public, the TPL claimed that Western Union chose not to reduce "fat dividends" and instead "the scant pittance paid to their overworked operators is taxed to make up all deficiencies caused by this unjust, uncalled for, and dishonorable warfare upon the public and opposition lines."[200] Even if Western Union had no such salary reduction plan in place, had such a plan existed, what power did operators have against the monopoly?

[196] Gabler, *The American Telegrapher*, 150; Ulriksson, *The Telegraphers*, 20.
[197] "The Beginning and the End of the Telegraphers' Strike," 20 January 1870, 4.
[198] Justitia, "The Lessons of the Strike," *The Telegrapher*, 5 February 1870, 189.
[199] "The Telegraphic Fight," *The Telegrapher*, 18 December 1869, 132.
[200] W. W. Burnham, C. J. Ryan and J. M. Peters, "Circular to the Public," *The Telegrapher*, 15 January 1870, 166.

The failure of the TPL revealed that the "Great Monopoly" could turn the wires, the press, and the railroads against its workers and crush a strike. For critics who feared Western Union had concentrated too much power, the failed strike confirmed their suspicions. Moreover, the strike vindicated advocates of a national telegraph firm – Western Union had shown the network could be sustained under even the most trying circumstances. Striking workers could not choke off enough capacity or shut down enough nodes to bring down the network. They could slow the machine but not stop it. Once the strike became a battle of attrition, the poorly funded, disorganized union stood no chance against the corporate leviathan.

The destruction of the TPL left the strikers in a precarious position. Orton seized the opportunity to curtail the influence of the pro-labor *Telegrapher*, vowing that no operator who read it could satisfactorily "perform the duties of an employee."[201] *The Telegrapher* denounced Western Union for trying to give its "namby-pamby official organ," *The Journal of the Telegraph*, a monopoly on telegraph industry news and threatened to expose the censorship in Congressional hearings.[202] Orton, who read the workers' paper himself, stubbornly insisted he had not officially banned *The Telegrapher*, but he regarded its promoters as sympathetic to "the views and policy" of Western Union's "enemies."[203]

Orton left the fate of the operators who had joined the "causeless and unprovoked combination" against Western Union to individual superintendents to decide.[204] Company policy required only that any operator "who came to the rescue" during the strike not be dismissed or demoted in favor of a returning striker.[205] In one division, managers imposed "humiliating and distasteful" conditions on former strikers, while in another they received them kindly.[206] Managers singled out women operators for punishment. Because women had received unique training and employment opportunities at Western Union, managers judged their disloyalty worse than male operators. Though the union had excluded them, women who joined the strike in solidarity were not rehired.[207]

[201] William Orton to Anson Stager, John Van Horne, and Thomas T. Eckert, 9 February 1870, WUC.
[202] "Are the Western Union Employees Slaves?" *The Telegrapher*, 12 March 1870, 232.
[203] William Orton to J. W. Ashley, 2 March 1870, WUC.
[204] William Orton to George W. Lee, 18 February 1870, WUC.
[205] William Orton to A. J. Shepard, 4 November 1870, WUC.
[206] "The Right Spirit," *The Telegrapher*, 16 April 1870, 272.
[207] Jepsen, *My Sisters Telegraphic*, 152.

Telegrapher William Andrew Manning recorded in his diary that in the Cleveland office managers denied several good operators their former jobs. But Manning's boss reinstated him after he promised he would have "nothing further to do with Telegraph Leagues." For a time, he earned less than the "rats" who filled in during the strike, and he worked two nights per week while the "rats" worked only one. "My future prospects are not flattering, but I hope for the best and try to drive away the melancholy," he wrote. "The best days of the telegraph operator are evidently over."[208]

[208] William Andrew Manning, Diary, 29 January and 17 February 1870, Manning Papers.

5

No Middle Ground

A New Yorker strolling north from Wall Street in 1870 might have failed to notice the five-story building at 145 Broadway unless he gazed up toward the roof, where a swarm of one hundred wires streamed out of a cupola in all directions. This unmistakable visual cue announced 145 as the headquarters of Western Union, the nexus of the nation's telegraph network. One observer marveled at the "almost endless journey" the iron threads began on lower Broadway: to Newfoundland where they connected to the "slender electric cord that binds the Old World to the New"; to the West across "verdant prairies," "desert plains," and "over the snowy ranges of the Sierra Nevada, to the Golden City on the Pacific shore"; and then north, deep into British Columbia, where they reached past the last "outpost of civilization."[1] With the proper connection, the eighty operators at the corner of Broadway and Liberty Street could transmit to more than 4,500 offices in the Unites States over 54,000 miles of line. Western Union managers insisted time and again that their company was not a monopoly, and the presence of several other telegraph offices around Wall Street lent some credence to this claim. But control of nine-tenths of the nation's lines resided in the offices at 145 Broadway, and the Atlantic cable companies and the Associated Press (AP) shared the same address. One could be forgiven for assuming that the telegraph obeyed a single master.[2] The question, as Western Union matured into its

[1] "The General Telegraph Office of the Western Union Company in New-York City," *The Telegrapher*, 15 July 1867, 249.
[2] These statistics are for 1869. In 1865, Western Union had only forty-five thousand miles of wire and one thousand offices, but consolidation and growth rapidly expanded the system. See William Orton, "Annual Report of the President of the Western Union Telegraph

postbellum monopoly, was who would that master be? Would private capital continue to maintain its tight grip on the wires, or, instead, would the federal government heed the demands of public activists and extend its postal prerogative to include the telegraph?

The Telegraph Act of 1866 granted the government only two positive powers: the authority of the Postmaster General to set the rates for government messages, and the right to purchase the telegraph companies after 1871 at a price determined by a joint committee of government and industry representatives. There can be no dispute that the Act implied that the federal government had a legitimate interest in promoting telegraphic communication. But the extent of the federal mandate to regulate or to enter the market remained ambiguous. Western Union president William Orton told a Senate committee that he interpreted the purchase provision to give Western Union five years to extend new lines, increase capacity, and "improve the conduct" of business so that the public was "fairly served" at "reasonable rates."[3] To Orton, these were the only terms for legitimate government interference in the industry. Other parties, however, were more ambitious.

The limits on federal regulatory power over the telegraph fell squarely into a larger debate about the appropriate level of federal management of the Gilded Age economy. In the wake of the Civil War, the federal government was more expansive than at any previous point in American history. An "activist national state" emerged from the war, embodying a "reforming impulse," trumping state's rights and embracing greater authority and more extensive purpose.[4] Historians have disagreed about the source of government expansion, whether it was the creature of capital or demanded by labor and farmers – whether it was "regressive or progressive."[5] They have also disagreed about the practical strength of the federal government in the postbellum period, and whether it was truly capable of acting with the force of a modern liberal state.[6] However,

---

Company," 13 July 1869, WUC; "Annual Report of the President of the Western Union Telegraph Company, 1 October 1865, WUC; "The Annual Election," *Journal of the Telegraph*, 15 October 1870, III, no. 22, 266.

[3] Argument of William Orton on the Postal Telegraph Bill, (New York: 1874), 8–9.
[4] Eric Foner, *Reconstruction: America's Unfinished Revolution* (New York: Harper & Row, 1988), xxiv.
[5] Heather Cox Richardson, "North and West of Reconstruction: Studies in Political Economy," in *Reconstructions: New Perspectives on the Postbellum United States*, ed. Thomas J. Brown (New York: Oxford University Press, 2006), 78.
[6] Stephen Skowronek, *Building a New American State: The Expansion of National Administrative Capacities, 1877–1920* (New York: Cambridge University Press, 1982),

the postbellum federal government indisputably embraced an active role in the expanding industrial economy, and such state activism conflicted with both the laissez-faire tradition and Democratic hostility to central-ized government power. Opposition to concentrated economic power in private hands ran headlong into the belief that the government would cor-rupt the natural order of the economy if granted the authority necessary to exert regulatory control over private industry.[7] Republican principles held that the state should promote economic development without inter-fering in the economy, which was naturally beneficent and self-regulating if left unmolested.[8]

The near-monopoly of the telegraph thus epitomized a dilemma. Western Union, the "Great Monopoly," effectively controlled a vital industry and answered only to private shareholders. Reformers decried the danger of allowing a soulless corporation to provide a vital public ser-vice. Government was empowered, in theory, to respond. Yet the federal government had few established mechanisms for industrial regulation and no experience in creating them.[9] The solution for many reformers was a telegraph controlled by America's most extensive public institu-tion – the Post Office. From the creation of the Western Union monopoly in 1866 to the early 1890s, proposals for a government telegraph sys-tem persistently appeared in Congress – according to one tally, advocates introduced more than seventy bills to create a postal telegraph.[10] Though nothing ultimately came of the postal telegraph, this result was not inevi-table. In fact, only one thing was assured: throughout the debate Western Union maneuvered to make sure that regardless of the outcome, its share-holders would be the winners.

Supporters of the Telegraph Act of 1866 saw its potential as an "enter-ing wedge" against Western Union, implying more dramatic govern-ment action was in the offing. An insider at the Illinois & Mississippi

13, Richard Franklin Bensel, *Yankee Leviathan: The Origins of Central State Authority in America, 1859–1877* (New York: Cambridge University Press, 1990), 17.
7 Morton Keller, *Affairs of State: Public Life in Late Nineteenth Century America* (Cambridge, Mass.: Belknap Press of Harvard University Press, 1977), 185.
8 Heather Cox Richardson, *The Death of Reconstruction: Race, Labor, and Politics in the Post-Civil War North, 1865–1901* (Cambridge, Mass.: Harvard University Press, 2001), 7.
9 The closest the government came to operating a telegraph was the United States Military Telegraph Corps, which was managed by executives from the major telegraph compa-nies. Albert Myer's attempts to wrest the military telegraph from the corporations and move it into the Signal Corps were a singular failure. See Chapter 2.
10 Frank Parsons, *The Telegraph Monopoly* (Philadelphia: C. F. Taylor, 1899), 16.

Telegraph Company reported that the law was only the first move by a Congressional faction planning a "determined effort to break up the Monopoly." The next step, according to the insider, was legislation authorizing the Post Office Department to build and operate telegraph lines between Washington and New York. The efficient and profitable operation of the Washington–New York line would bolster a movement in Congress to build government lines "to every possible commercial city in the Union."[11] In December 1866, Illinois Republican Representative E. B. Washburne satisfied the first part of this prediction by introducing a bill to appropriate $50,000 for the construction of a Washington–New York line.[12] Washburne called it "somewhat of an experiment," but it was intended as a Trojan horse.[13] The profitable operation of the Washington–New York line would prove the Post Office was ready to take over the telegraph.[14]

Washburne threatened to be a formidable enemy to Western Union. In a period in which Congressional tenures were short and professional politicians were relatively rare – more than half of the members of the Thirty-Ninth Congress were freshmen – Washburne, nicknamed the "Father of the House," served for eighteen years. A leading Radical Republican from a prominent political family, Washburne chaired the House committee that impeached Andrew Johnson.[15] In May 1868, while Johnson's impeachment collapsed in the Senate, Washburne reissued his proposal for a government telegraph between Washington and New York.[16] In support of his bill, he issued an extensive report comparing the American telegraph to European systems. According to several pages of statistics detailing the use and efficiency of the telegraph in each country, the American telegraph was a relative failure. Washburne concluded that in the United States the telegraph had made "less progress

---

[11] E. H. Bebe to J. D. Caton, 20 August 1866, Caton Papers.

[12] H. R. 892, 39th Congress, 2nd Session.

[13] *Congressional Globe*, 14 December 1867, 39th Congress, 2nd Session, 133. Iowa Republican John Kasson introduced a similar, but even broader bill the same day, H. R. 891, 39th Congress, 2nd Session.

[14] Lester G. Lindley, *The Constitution Faces Technology: The Relationship of the National Government to the Telegraph, 1866–1884* (New York: Arno Press, 1975), 98.

[15] Three of Washburne's seven brothers were also successful politicians. Cadwallader served in the House and became governor of Wisconsin, Israel served in the House and became governor of Maine, and William served in the House and the Senate. All the brothers were born "Washburn," and only Elihu changed the spelling of his name to "Washburne." See Keller, *Affairs of State*, 61, Gaillard Hunt, *Israel, Elihu and Cadwallader Washburn: A Chapter in Biography* (New York: The Macmillan Company, 1925), 174.

[16] H. R. 1083, 40th Congress, 3rd Session.

toward perfection" and was "practically of less value to the masses of the people" than in "any other civilized country on the globe." Of all the world's "enlightened" states, only two – the United States and Great Britain – had left the telegraph in private hands. But Great Britain had seen the error of her ways, and "with singular unanimity" the English people now demanded a government telegraph.[17]

In England a two-firm oligopoly controlled most of the telegraph industry, and an increasingly popular view held that it did not provide adequate service. In the early 1860s, reformers proposed encouraging competition by granting rights-of-way on public highways to any telegraph company – a precursor, if not a forbearer, to the American Telegraph Act of 1866.[18] After the English companies doubled their uniform rate in 1865, demand for reform from the public, the press, and commercial interests converged. In 1866, Frank Ives Scudamore, a top official in the General Post Office, issued a study that compared the British telegraph system to its European neighbors and concluded that the private British system was entirely deficient.[19] The popularity of the English penny post and Scudamore's leadership in expanding postal services contributed to public confidence in telegraph nationalization. In an argument already familiar in the telegraph debate in the United States,

[17] The comparison between the European and American telegraphs became a standard feature in arguments on *both* sides of the postal telegraph debate for the next twenty-five years. It is tempting to argue that this is an early example of what Daniel Rodgers calls the "transnational borrowings and imitation" of the "transatlantic progressive movement." But the postal telegraph debate came earlier than the "Atlantic crossings" on which Rodgers focused. Richard Ely, an economist of great interest to Rodgers, was a strong postal telegraph advocate, but he came to the subject long after the arguments for the postal telegraph had been formulated and refined. See E. B. Washburne, "Union of the Telegraph and Postal System," Misc. Doc. No. 129, 40th Congress, 2nd Session, 1–3. Daniel T. Rodgers, *Atlantic Crossings: Social Politics in a Progressive Age* (Cambridge, Mass.: The Belknap Press of Harvard University Press, 1998), 97–102.

[18] The proposal of this similar reform in both countries may be entirely coincidental. When the English reform was under discussion, there was no telegraph reform movement in the United States, which was in the midst of Civil War. The American general telegraph law, as I have discussed in Chapter 3, did not follow a deliberate design. Although it is possible that Henry O'Rielly or other reformers were aware of English reform efforts, opening public highways was one of a small enough number of options that it is reasonable to assume the idea was formed independently in the United States.

[19] It is interesting that Scudamore did *not* use statistics from the United States' telegraph. He claimed the distances in the United States were too long for a fair comparison. Opponents of the postal telegraph in the United States usually made the inverse claim about European statistics – that is, that the comparison was inappropriate because the distances involved were too short. See Jeffrey L. Kieve, *The Electric Telegraph in the U.K.: A Social and Economic History* (New York: Barnes and Noble Books, 1973), 129.

English reformers described the telegraph as postal communication by another means. The public welfare required government control of such a vital disseminator of information.[20] Editorials praised Scudamore's plan and postal telegraph petitions flooded Parliament. With only mild opposition, Parliament passed the Telegraph of Bill of 1868, nationalizing the telegraph and eliminating private service.[21]

Reformers in the U.S. Congress sought to follow the British example. A new generation of telegraph activists replaced the likes of the dogged Henry O'Rielly. After Washburne, the most important of the new voices for reform was that of Gardiner Greene Hubbard, a prominent Boston attorney with a strong New England pedigree and a missionary zeal for public works.[22] Hubbard had retired from practicing law to devote his energies to education for the deaf and a variety of municipal business ventures, including a street railroad from Cambridge to Boston and the Cambridge Water and Gas Light Companies.[23] Like O'Rielly, Hubbard was ahead of his time – more in line with later Progressive Era reformers than his Gilded Age peers. Although he embraced typical principles of "good government" and "moral rejuvenation," his demand for a government telegraph was a departure from orthodox dedication to the "free market" typical of liberal reformers.

Hubbard proposed creating a postal telegraph by chartering a private company that would contract with the Post Office Department to provide telegraph service much the same way that the department contracted the private railroad companies to carry the mail. Because the Post Office

---

[20] David Hochfelder has compared the British and American postal telegraph movements, and I am indebted to him throughout my discussion of this issue for his succinct summary and lucid analysis. See David Paul Hochfelder, "A Comparison of the Postal Telegraph Movement in Great Britain and the United States, 1866–1900," *Enterprise and Society* 1 (2000).

[21] Kieve, *The Electric Telegraph in the U.K.*, Ira J. Cohen, "Toward a Theory of State Intervention: The Nationalization of the British Telegraphs," *Social Science History* 4, no. 2 (1980): 178–9.

[22] On liberal reform, see John G. Sproat, *"The Best Men": Liberal Reformers in the Gilded Age* (New York: Oxford University Press, 1968), 5–10.

[23] Hubbard's ancestors came to Massachusetts in 1635, his maternal grandfather was a prominent Boston merchant, and his father was Judge Samuel Hubbard, a member of the Massachusetts Supreme Court and a severely religious man who was a founder of the American Board of Commissioners and Foreign Missions, the American Temperance Union, and the American Tract Society. Hubbard launched his legal career in the 1840s as a partner to Benjamin R. Curtis, who left the practice for the United States Supreme Court. Alexander Graham Bell to Mabel Hubbard Bell, 4 April 1902, Hubbard Papers; Mabel Hubbard Bell, notes, Hubbard Papers; Edward Warren Day, *One Thousand Years of Hubbard History* (New York: Harlan Page Hubbard, 1895), 336.

had an established record of handling the mail with "celerity, certainty and secrecy in transmission, low and uniform rates, and ample facilities," it seemed well suited for telegraphy.[24] Using a statistical brew similar to Washburne's, Hubbard concluded that the volume of telegraph business could be much greater – including social messages, still a rarity on American telegraph lines – if expenses and rates were 30 and 50 percent lower respectively.[25] With Hubbard himself in command, the properly capitalized private firm would "realize a large profit on the investment" – certainly larger than bloated Western Union – the Post Office would earn "a small net revenue," and the American people would get inexpensive, accessible telegraph service.[26] Hubbard's proposal received a warm reception from Postmaster General Alexander Randall, a close associate of President Johnson.[27] Hubbard's father-in-law, Robert H. McCurdy, a prominent New York merchant and leading Republican, provided Hubbard with letters of introduction to members of the House of Representatives, and Hubbard set off for the capital to lobby for a postal telegraph.[28]

In the late 1860s, Washington was entering a notorious political era. The impeachment of Andrew Johnson failed amid rumors that his crooked administration had been saved only by the corruption – perhaps even the purchase – of the Republicans who broke ranks and voted to acquit him.[29] Hopes for a new era of good government accompanying Civil War hero Ulysses S. Grant's inauguration in 1869 were soon disappointed.[30] The ideologically driven politics of the Reconstruction era were gradually replaced with an organizational politics in which the parties were motivated primarily by the desire to stay in power – a "politics of complacency" in a system in which the first priority was the interests of politicians themselves.[31]

[24] Gardiner Greene Hubbard, *Letter to the Postmaster General on the European and American System of Telegraph, with Remedy for the Present High Rates* (Boston: Wright and Potter, 1868), 3–4.

[25] It is probably not a coincidence that this is the compromise Scudamore introduced in 1868 to make English nationalization of the telegraph palatable, although the 1869 settlement ultimately did create a government telegraph monopoly.

[26] Hubbard, Letter to the Postmaster General, 26–7.

[27] Dorothy Ganfield Fowler, *The Cabinet Politician: The Postmasters General, 1829–1909* (New York: AMS Press, 1967), 128–33.

[28] G. G. Hubbard to R. H. McCurdy (transcript), 1 July 1868, Hubbard Papers.

[29] Mark Wahlgren Summers, *The Era of Good Stealings* (New York: Oxford University Press, 1993), 41–5.

[30] Keller, *Affairs of State*, 259.

[31] Ray Ginger, *Age of Excess: The United States from 1877 to 1914* (New York: The Macmillan Company, 1965), 98, Mark Wahlgren Summers, *Party Games: Getting,*

The expanding power of the federal government created countless new opportunities for special interests. In the Forty-Third Congress members introduced nine hundred bills in the first *month* – an astonishing average of three each.[32] The federal government suddenly had an "amorphous and almost infinitely expandable sphere of 'discretionary' initiatives," and the boundaries of federal interest remained largely undelineated.[33] One historian famously dubbed this expansion of government "The Great Barbecue," a federal feast of "lands, tariffs, subsidies, favors of all sorts" distributed to "influential citizens" by "sympathetic politicians."[34] The executive was weak and Congress was overstretched and inexperienced. A gap yawned between the state's new obligations and its capacity to meet them; lobbyists and self-promoters leapt into the breach.[35]

Hubbard took up residence at Willard's Hotel, the nexus for Washington lobbyists, though he would have blanched at the suggestion that he represented a "special interest." Hubbard thought of himself as a promoter of the public welfare, a "facilitator of communication between citizens and the government."[36] According to an 1873 exposé of the Washington scene, legions of such men arrived with each session of Congress, and one could "hardly find a male resident of the Capital" who was not "firmly convinced" of his "influence" in some part of the federal government.[37] Hubbard secured his first significant ally in Minnesota Republican Alexander Ramsey, the chair of the Senate Committee on Post Offices and Post Roads. Ramsey introduced Hubbard to other potential supporters, including John Farnsworth, chair of the House Committee on Post Offices and Post Roads. The two legislators were invaluable allies

---

Keeping, and Using Power in Gilded Age Politics (Chapel Hill: The University of North Carolina Press, 2004), 17.

[32] Summers, *The Era of Good Stealings*, 108.

[33] Margaret Susan Thompson, *The 'Spider Web': Congress and Lobbying in the Age of Grant* (Ithaca, N.Y.: Cornell University Press, 1985), 45.

[34] Vernon Louis Parrington, *Main Currents in American Thought: An Interpretation of the American Literature from the Beginnings to 1920*, 3 vols., vol. 3 (New York: Harcourt, Brace and Company, 1930), 23.

[35] Ibid., 38. Elisabeth S. Clemens has also argued that an expansive state invited increased lobbying, though her interest is primarily in the period after 1890. See Elisabeth S. Clemens, *The People's Lobby: Organizational Innovation and the Rise of Interest Group Politics in the United States, 1890–1925* (Chicago: The University of Chicago Press, 1997), 29.

[36] Joel H. Silbey, *The American Political Nation, 1838–1893* (Stanford, Calif.: Stanford University Press, 1991), 61.

[37] Edward Winslow Martin, *Behind the Scenes in Washington* (Philadelphia: The Continental Publishing Company, 1873), 215.

because bills could not reach the floor without committee approval.[38] Hubbard reported enthusiasm for his postal telegraph proposal, claiming most Congressmen only wondered that "no one ever thought of it before."[39]

Ramsey introduced Hubbard's bill to the Senate in July 1868, and Farnsworth introduced an identical bill in the House.[40] By the standards of the Great Barbecue, Hubbard's proposal was modest. The bill bore a striking similarity to early drafts of the National Telegraph Act of 1866, which had attempted to create competition in the telegraph industry by chartering a firm to rival Western Union. Hubbard proposed to incorporate a new company in Washington, D.C., free from "any known and distinguished individuals" who might subvert his control of the enterprise.[41] Strict limits on capital expansion would prevent overcapitalization, Western Union's cardinal sin. The bill did not grant Hubbard's "Postal Telegraph Company" an exclusive franchise – the Postmaster General would accept bids from *any* telegraph company willing to provide service between every city of more than five thousand inhabitants at a rate of one cent per word for each five hundred miles, plus a postage stamp for delivery.[42] The lines of the contracting company would run into post offices, which would provide space for operators free of charge and deliver messages with the mail.[43]

Western Union was quick to reject Hubbard's proposal, and dismissive of its prospects. While "ostensibly in the public interest," Orton judged Hubbard's plan just another speculative scheme to enrich the incorporators by selling stock.[44] The threat of government interference in telegraphy was insubstantial, because the "visionary policies" that Hubbard promoted rested on "fallacious," easily refuted assumptions about the

---

[38] Thompson, *The 'Spider Web,'* 94. Thompson stresses that committees acted not only as filters but also as "cuegivers" on the floor, giving significant guidance to other members on how to vote. A bill without committee support was doomed.

[39] G. G. Hubbard to R. H. McCurdy (transcript), 10 July 1868, Hubbard Papers.

[40] "A Bill to Incorporate the United States Postal Telegraph Company, and to establish a postal telegraph system," S. 608, 40th Congress, 2nd Session. The House bill is H. R. 1415.

[41] G. G. Hubbard to R. H. McCurdy (transcript), 1 July 1868, Hubbard Papers.

[42] In the House Committee on Post Offices and Post Roads assessment of the bill, it was noted that as of the 1860 census there were only 313 towns with more than five thousand inhabitants, or approximately one-tenth the number of locations reached by Western Union in 1869. "Postal Telegraph," 24 February 1869, House Report No. 32, 40th Congress, 3rd Session, 15.

[43] S. 608, 40th Congress, 2nd Session.

[44] William Orton to George Walker, 18 November 1868, WUC.

industry.[45] Orton asked Western Union electrician George Prescott to prepare a response to the postal telegraph proposals, hoping to use the occasion to show "not only Members of Congress, but men of common sense" the errors of the "profoundly ignorant" reformers.[46]

According to Prescott's report, Washburne and Hubbard had imagined solutions that were much worse than the nonexistent problem they were designed to solve. Western Union already provided less expensive, more reliable, more extensive, and more efficient service than any other network in the world (a claim that could be verified only using Western Union's own statistics and an impossibly tenuous series of comparisons to telegraph rates, speeds, and volume in Europe, with its smaller, denser states, frequent national border crossings, censorship regimes, different methods for counting messages, and array of currencies).[47] Prescott's report argued the Post Office was incompetent, already in deficit, and without any experience in the "science" of telegraphy. The report insisted that Western Union was *not* a monopoly, but the alleged advantages of a unified government telegraph were "precisely the same" as those that had led to the creation of Western Union. Moreover, a government monopoly would be worse than a private monopoly because it would make the telegraph a political tool subject to abuse by the party in power.[48] An editorial in Western Union's *Journal of the Telegraph* concluded that Washburne intended to punish the "gigantic monopoly" he had "conjured up" by creating an even more "repulsive" monopoly that put the wires in the "hands of shysters and political runners."[49]

In the press, Hubbard's postal telegraph proposal received a warmer response than expected. The *New York Herald*, long Western Union's fiercest foe, began a new campaign against the "monster monopoly,"

[45] William Orton to Henry Bentley, 5 December 1868, WUC.
[46] William Orton to George B. Prescott, 30 November 1868, WUC.
[47] Western Union provided the only statistics on telegraphy in the United States and sculpted the information as needed. Accounting for all the geographic and statistical variations between the United States and Europe is still somewhat beside the point. While European government telegraphs were used as supporting evidence in arguments for a postal telegraph, I believe the question is ultimately not relative cost or rates, but whether the telegraph is a public service or a private investment.
[48] The Proposed Union of the Telegraph and Postal Systems: Statement of the Western Union Telegraph Company (Cambridge, Mass.: Welch, Bigelow, and Company, 1869), 22, 113–22, Richard Sutch and Susan B. Carter, *Historical Statistics of the United States: Earliest Times to the Present*, 5 vols., vol. 4 (New York: Cambridge University Press, 2006), 1039.
[49] "Government and the Telegraph," *Journal of the Telegraph*, 1 May 1868, 4; "The Bill to Construct a Telegraph Line from Washington to New York," *Journal of the Telegraph*, 22 May 1868, 4.

printing daily editorials demanding the government take over the telegraph.[50] Hubbard presumed he would get no support from the AP, which
he derided as "one of the greatest monopolies in the country."[51] But a
concurrent contract squabble with Western Union encouraged AP newspapers to criticize the company. The generally friendly *New York Times*,
the van of the critics, published Hubbard's Western Union critique and
commended the "'solid men of Boston' and other Eastern cities" who
sought to create "a great company to work with the Post Office."[52] Even
this moderate support for the postal telegraph came as a surprise, as AP
editors were doubly constrained against supporting the legislation. First,
the AP contracts with Western Union required that editors not "advocate measures hostile" to the telegraph company.[53] Second, newspapers
opposed a provision in Hubbard's bill requiring the press to pay regular
commercial rates rather than the reduced rates the AP negotiated. Editors
feared this would nearly quadruple the transmission costs for news, perhaps forcing many Western papers out of business.[54]

Though Hubbard saw his campaign for a postal telegraph as a great
public service, demand for reform was perhaps not as widespread as he
imagined. Western Union managers argued that only a small portion of
the public had any use for the telegraph, and though there are no reliable
statistics from the 1870s, in 1887 Western Union's president claimed only
2 percent of Americans used the telegraph in a given year.[55] However,
support for the postal telegraph was substantial enough that Western
Union shareholders grew increasingly "alarmed" with each "portentous
report" from Washington. Orton predicted that negative reports from
the Congressional committees reviewing the legislation would drive up
Western Union stock by 5 percent.[56] In addition to distributing Western
Union's own report against the postal telegraph, Orton ordered the
adjustment of inconsistent tariffs that Hubbard publicized as evidence
of Western Union's malfeasance, so there would be fewer "just causes for
complaint."[57]

[50] "The Government and the Telegraph," *New York Herald*, 21 December 1868, 4.
[51] Gardiner Green Hubbard to R. H. McCurdy, 18 January 1869, Hubbard Papers.
[52] "The Telegraph in America," *The New York Times*, 6 December 1868, 12.
[53] Horace White to E. B. Washburne, 4 June 1868, Washburne Papers. White apologized to
Washburne for this stricture, but admitted the *Chicago Tribune* was bound to observe the
contract.
[54] Joseph Medill to E. B. Washburne, 21 February 1869, Washburne Papers.
[55] Norvin Green to PMG William Villas, 17 November 1887, WUC.
[56] Orton to U. H. Painter, 24 December 1868, WUC.
[57] William Orton to Anson Stager, 18 December 1868, WUC.

Orton predicted there was no chance Congress would approve Hubbard's scheme, but just to be certain of his forecast he set himself and Western Union's lobbyists to work against Hubbard. As a prominent Republican and former Commissioner of Internal Revenue, Orton was a valuable broker in an era when political reputation and access were "negotiable commodities."[58] Because Congressional committees had no professional research staff, legislators relied on hearings and lobbyists for information. Virtually all the support for the postal telegraph came from the dominant Republican side of the aisle, where Orton's elite position in the party ensured that Western Union representatives or Orton himself were at all hearings on telegraph matters. Soon Orton and his lieutenants became familiar figures in the halls of the Capitol and at Willard's Hotel.

When a Chicago newspaper accused Orton and his associates of being "the most formidable lobby" in Washington, Orton declared that if the accusation were true, "the lobbying business must be sadly on the wane."[59] But in truth, Orton had developed an impressive operation with a large stable of informants in Washington. The manager of Western Union's Washington office served as Orton's public messenger and bird-dog. Orton also had an especially valuable inside man, Uriah Hunt Painter. Painter officially worked for *The Philadelphia Inquirer* and *The New York Sun* and was reputedly the man to see to get a story planted in the newspapers. But he was also foremost among a minority of Washington correspondents who sold their information and influence, working for both the Pacific railroads and Western Union.[60] In addition to discreetly providing intelligence, Painter doubled as the clerk for the House Committee on Post Offices and Post Roads, the committee posing the most immediate threat to Western Union. In a *Herald* story about Painter in 1870, a reporter claimed petitioners could get bills through the committee "'easy enough' if they 'fix Painter.'"[61] Orton considered Painter the "pivotal point" in Western Union's lobby.[62]

Western Union also had numerous "friends" in Congress. Some relationships were conducted too discreetly to appear in the company records, but even the known list of supporters is long. A few examples illuminate

[58] Thompson, *The 'Spider Web,'* 159.
[59] William Orton to Charles A. Tinker, 26 July 1869, WUC.
[60] Summers writes of Painter, "By no means were all or even most journalists as venal." See Mark Wahlgren Summers, *The Press Gang: Newspapers & Politics, 1865–1878* (Chapel Hill: University of North Carolina Press, 1994), 109–14.
[61] Summers, *The Press Gang*, 115.
[62] Orton to Painter, 6 January 1869, WUC.

the types of assistance rendered. Edwin D. Morgan, a Republican senator from New York, was a major Western Union stockholder and served
for years as a director. In addition to defending Western Union on the
floor of the Senate, Morgan took instructions from the company on
rewriting legislation and hand-delivered Orton's correspondence to other
Congressmen. Other federal politicians had less obvious but highly valuable connections to Western Union's interest. For example, William B.
Allison, an Iowa Republican in the House who became one of the most
powerful figures in the Senate, had been Orton's "warm personal friend"
since Orton's days in the revenue service. Orton reported that Allison
"rendered in a very quiet way, most valuable… indeed, invaluable services" to Western Union in the company's campaign to roll back a tax on
gross receipts and a protectionist tariff on imported telegraph wire.[63]

The company's most valuable "friends" were the Speakers of the House
of Representatives. With no formal seniority system and high turnover in
the House, the Speaker held the most powerful position on Capitol Hill.
He controlled debate, and even more importantly, he made appointments
to committees, where the power to determine policy resided.[64] Speaker
Schulyer Colfax was a friend to both Orton and Western Union – Orton
once promised that no manager would be "censured for undue liberality"
in providing favors to Colfax.[65] James G. Blaine, the Speaker from 1869
until 1875 and later a senator, proved an even more useful friend. Even
before Blaine ascended to the Speaker's desk, he advocated for Western
Union in a recurring dispute over the annual payment for government service on the transcontinental line, helping Western Union secure a "large
sum of money" and silencing "the clamors of reckless and unscrupulous
opponents." Orton noted that he would happily "go a little outside of the
ordinary courtesies" to show his appreciation for Blaine's "services."[66]

Western Union curried favor with legislators through the generous
distribution of "franks," stamps used to send free messages. "Free" business grew so rapidly that Orton created a special bureau to oversee it in
1868. The company made no secret of its dispersal of franks. Orton told
a Congressional committee the "judicious use of complimentary franks"
among national, state, and municipal authorities had saved the company

[63] William Orton to Anson Stager, 9 July 1870, WUC. Allison sought employment for his
nephew, and Orton told Stager that if the nephew "is not properly qualified now" for a
job, "try to put him in the way of becoming better qualified."
[64] Thompson, The 'Spider Web,' 179.
[65] William Orton to Anson Stager, 12 May 1868, WUC.
[66] William Orton to J. L. Bedlow; 8 July 1868, WUC.

"many times the money value of the free service."[67] Critics charged that free service constituted 2 percent of the total cost of business – a healthy dividend denied to shareholders.[68] However, Orton claimed in 1873 that complimentary business accounted for only $58,000 in business distributed to two thousand "distinguished men in politics, business, and literature." He insisted that this was hardly enough for "bribery and blackmail." Still, Orton once explained that distributing franks to unsympathetic officials made him feel like a disappointed boy who risked his life to save a drowning stranger and received nothing in return but a new pair of suspenders. The boy surely did not imagine he "had a 'mortgage' on the stranger, or desired to levy a 'black mail,'" but *some* return could fairly be expected.

Yet privately Orton expressed ambivalence about the unmistakable odor of corruption that franks gave off. When Western Union lobbied to defeat Washburne's bill, for example, the *New York World* reported that Western Union rewarded all the members of the Congressional committee for their cooperation with franks.[69] During the 1868 postal telegraph debate, Painter asked for 1,300 franks to distribute to Congress. Orton offered to provide a frank to any legislator who requested one, but he rejected Painter's broadcast approach, lest critics charge Western Union with trying "to influence the action of Members." Every frank sent to a member of Congress included an explanation that it was only a "courtesy" and not intended to place the recipient "under obligation,"[70] but it is difficult to take this disclaimer seriously. *The Telegrapher* charged that every legislator who used a frank knew it was "intended as a bribe to influence his official action."[71] However, the cash value of the franks, even to a legislator with a family at a great distance, was probably not enough to constitute an effective bribe for most Congressmen.[72] Franks

---

[67] Orton's testimony is quoted in Parsons, *The Telegraph Monopoly*, 92.
[68] Western Union distinguished between "free" business, which it transmitted in exchange for service provided by railroad, steamboat and express companies, and "complimentary" business, which was doled out to reward present or potential allies. See "The Dead-Head System," *The Telegrapher*, 17 September 1870, 28.
[69] *New York World*, 22 February 1867.
[70] William Orton to George A. Halsey, 11 January 1869, WUC.
[71] "The Dead-Head System," *The Telegrapher*, 17 September 1870, 28.
[72] There was, however, concern among Congressmen that salaries had not kept up with the cost of living in Washington. Congressmen were paid $5,000 per year in the early 1870s, while housing in Washington could cost as much as $300 per month. For Congressmen living a great distance from home, the relative value of free telegrams might have been reasonably large. See Summers, *The Era of Good Stealings*, 238.

were a way to spread goodwill, a sort of light corruption – not a system of quid pro quo, but a favor to encourage legislators to listen to their "friends" from Western Union.[73] Nor did Western Union generally need to buy friends. Congressmen "in the pocket" of Western Union or any other corporation were often following their own previously established and publicly disclosed loyalties.[74]

Western Union's "friendships" with government officials crossed party lines. The company appeared to have a Republican bias – many of its allies were national Republican leaders, perhaps because of Orton's long-standing political affiliations. Orton took pains to remind Washburne that they were friends and political allies who differed only on telegraph policy.[75] However, despite alliances with top Republicans, Orton insisted to friends and enemies alike, "You will not forget that our *corporation* has no politics."[76] Western Union's top executives were almost evenly divided among high-placed Democrats and Republicans.[77] In 1872, for example, Western Union board member E. D. Morgan chaired the Republican National Convention, while company vice president Augustus Schell chaired the Democratic National Convention. Orton explained to a Congressman that the partisan "days of Amos Kendall," when postmasters would "rifle the mails" to remove newspapers offensive to Southern Democrats had passed. Western Union's managers could not afford to use the company for political purposes. No business dependent upon "public patronage" could afford any "offensive display of political partisanship."[78]

Managers promoted what might be called "corporate nonpartisanship." Western Union was committed to no party and to only one political cause – the success of Western Union. As a company often buffeted by political winds, Orton rigged Western Union to sail in any weather.

Gardiner Greene Hubbard developed a lobby of his own. He moved into a Washington boarding house in a room just upstairs from his friend Iowa Senator Francis Palmer, and, like his competition, he took his meals

---

[73] Mark Wahlgren Summers notes that "personal favors" were often much more useful to lobbyists than bribes, and trivial gifts were common. A soap manufacturer lobbying for a lower tariff on materials put a bar of soap on every desk in Congress. Ibid., 110.

[74] Thompson, *The 'Spider Web,'* 156.

[75] William Orton to E. B. Washburne, 19 December 1868, Washburne Papers.

[76] William Orton to James G. Blaine, 6 July 1868, WUC. Emphasis in the original.

[77] O. H. Palmer and Orton were Republican; Norvin Green, Augustus Schell, and Wilson Hunt were Democrats.

[78] William Orton to James M. Beck, 3 February 1872, WUC.

at Willard's Hotel.[79] He printed fifteen hundred copies of his postal telegraph pamphlet, and though he doubted that politicians would read it, he hoped the newspapers would reprint excerpts – a tall order given the AP's fealty to Western Union.[80] Hubbard cultivated friendships with several leading Republicans and won Washburne's tentative support. Republicans generally favored his plan, but Democrats opposed it – as did the New York delegation from both parties.[81] Hubbard found an unexpected ally in E. D. L. Sweet, a Chicago Western Union manager who had resigned his position because he "could not defend" Western Union's policies.[82] With nearly twenty years of telegraph experience, Sweet provided Hubbard with an insider's perspective and proved a valuable witness before Congressional committees. Orton accused Sweet of selling out the "private affairs" of Western Union.[83]

Hubbard lobbied with zeal befitting his conviction that the postal telegraph was "a great public benefit" and creating it his patriotic duty.[84] However, he also believed the postal telegraph would be "very profitable" and "make a fortune for all connected with it."[85] Orton claimed the profit-hungry Hubbard represented "no one but himself and associates,"[86] yet he carried on an active and genteel correspondence with his adversary, apparently hoping to dispel some of his more radical claims, or perhaps to convince Hubbard to advocate for a cause more favorable to Western Union: a government *buyout,* rather than a government-sponsored *competitor.*

Western Union managers argued that the Telegraph Act of 1866 prevented the government from creating a postal telegraph that would compete with private firms and destroy the value of their property. A government-sponsored company would have a host of advantages, including the backing of the federal treasury, free office space in post offices, and the power to condemn rights-of-way as needed. Because no

[79] Gardiner G. Hubbard to G. M. Hubbard, 8 December 1870, Hubbard Papers.
[80] Gardiner G. Hubbard to G. M. Hubbard, 13 January 1869, Hubbard Papers.
[81] Hubbard's allies included Senator Francis Palmer of Iowa, Senator Willard Warner of Alabama, and House leader Henry Dawes of Massachusetts. Gardiner G. Hubbard to [unknown] (transcribed), 22 December 1871, Hubbard Papers.
[82] "Superintendent E. D. L. Sweet," *Journal of the Telegraph,* 15 June 1868, 4; William Orton to Anson Stager, 8 May 1868, WUC; Gardiner G. Hubbard to G. M. Hubbard, 14 January 1869, Hubbard Papers.
[83] William Orton to Anson Stager, 8 February 1869, WUC.
[84] Gardiner G. Hubbard to G. M. Hubbard, 22 January 1869, Hubbard Papers.
[85] Gardiner G. Hubbard to G. M. Hubbard, 14 January 1869, Hubbard Papers.
[86] William Orton to Senator E. D. Morgan, 11 February 1869, WUC.

private corporation could compete against such advantages, the postal telegraph amounted to the destruction of private telegraphy without the "just compensation" promised by the Telegraph Act. However, "just compensation" could be lucrative for telegraph investors. The formula used when the English government bought out private telegraph lines to create a public monopoly would pay Western Union shareholders nearly triple the market value of their stock.[87] Not surprisingly, Western Union managers insisted that the buyout provision in the Telegraph Act was "all the legislation necessary" and proscribed any other course to a postal telegraph.[88]

Hubbard disagreed with the argument that government competition would unjustly destroy private property. He invoked the Supreme Court's ruling in *Charles River Bridge v. Warren Bridge*, which determined a competing public charter or franchise could be granted "if the interests of the public require it even if it destroys the value of the first and without the payment of any damages." If the state could grant a second franchise for the public benefit, then certainly it could execute such a franchise itself. Hubbard also claimed the English precedent for buying out telegraph companies on the basis of revenues did not apply to the United States. In England, competing firms had steadily reduced prices, but Western Union compelled "the public to pay high rates" and then demanded a buyout "at this exaggerated value."[89]

Orton was optimistic in late 1868 that Hubbard and Washburne could be defeated. In March 1869, Ulysses S. Grant, whom Orton thought to be hostile to a government telegraph, would take office and replace pro-Hubbard Postmaster General Randall. In the meantime, Hubbard and Orton waged a "bitter and determined" contest in the House and Senate Committees on Post Offices and Post Roads.[90] Western Union won a sound victory in the House committee, which declared in a unanimous report that the "supposed economy" of a postal telegraph was "in large measure delusive."[91] The report so pleased Orton that he prepared

---

[87] The English government paid the telegraph companies twenty years of net profit based on the year closing June 30, 1868. If the same treatment had been applied to Western Union in 1868, the purchase price would have been just over $52 million, when the market value of the stock was around $16 million. Western Union Annual Report, 30 June 1891, WUC; Kieve, *The Electric Telegraph in the U.K.*, 154–6.

[88] *U.S. Statutes at Large*, Chapter 231, 39th Congress, 1st Session.

[89] G. G. Hubbard to O. H. Palmer, 31 December 1868, Hubbard Papers.

[90] William Orton to Anson Stager, 8 January 1869, WUC.

[91] "Postal Telegraph," 24 February 1869, Report. No. 32, 40th Congress, 3rd Session, 14–15.

an extract for transmission to every newspaper in the country, free of charge, via the AP.[92] Hubbard's last-ditch effort to get his bill through the Senate against heavy opposition that he believed had been "bought" by Western Union fell short. The 40th Congress adjourned without telegraph reform.[93]

The prospect of another season of anti–Western Union agitation in Congress worried Western Union managers. Orton wrote privately that he feared the postal telegraph movement had grown "more formidable" than ever.[94] He determined to fight back, publicly. Western Union released an annual report to the public for the first time in three years, plainly calculated in tone and content to prove the value of the company's existing lines, stress organizational improvements, and reject government intervention. Orton also tried to lower Western Union's rates to limit public criticism and "lessen the probabilities of Congressional interference."[95] When a long-awaited new rate system debuted in 1869, Orton ordered managers at every office to visit their local newspapers and encourage stories announcing the rate reductions and granting Western Union "all the credit which is our due from the public."[96] The company also experimented with half-rate "night messages" sent over wires largely unoccupied after the close of the business day. First introduced on a limited basis in 1867, night messages would show the company had a "generous spirit" in response to public demands for "cheap telegraphic communication."[97] In 1870 Orton expanded half-price night messages to all points east of the Mississippi at precisely the same time that postal telegraph proposals rippled through Congress.[98] The reformers' agitation was beginning to have an appreciable effect.

In 1869 the English government completed the nationalization of the telegraph, a milestone that the American press greeted with signs of cautious support. A *New York Times* editorial applauded the new British

[92] William Orton to J. W. Simonton, 23 February 1869, WUC.
[93] Gardiner G. Hubbard to R. H. McCurdy (transcript), 23 February 1869, Hubbard Papers. The bill reported was S. 978, 27 February 1869, 40th Congress, 3rd Session. It differed from the first Hubbard bill only in that it allowed for "*any* telegraph company or companies" to contract with the Post Office Department.
[94] William Orton to George B. Prescott, 4 May 1869, WUC.
[95] William Orton to E. B. Grant, 12 May 1869, WUC.
[96] William Orton, "Circular No. 8," 9 August 1869, WUC.
[97] Meeting of the Board of Directors of the Western Union Telegraph Company, 21 February 1867, WUC.
[98] "Night Messages at Half Rates," *Journal of the Telegraph*, 15 August 1872.

system, concluding that the American private system was comparatively overpriced and unsatisfactory – no one could "pretend" that Western Union had made telegraphy "as efficient as it can be made."[99] Orton responded to *Times* publisher George Jones with his typical retort that the American postal telegraph was nothing but a speculator's scheme. But he also explicitly stated that he was willing to negotiate with the government for a sale "on equitable terms." If the government wanted to buy Western Union, Orton acknowledged, "We are ready to sell."[100]

Orton adopted a conciliatory tone in his correspondence with Hubbard, who had embarked on a national speaking tour to promote the postal telegraph. He urged Hubbard to consider "any practical plan" to avoid "further contests" in Congress.[101] Orton met with Hubbard's partner, E. D. L. Sweet, who had recently become the manager of the Atlantic & Pacific Telegraph Company, a Western Union competitor. Orton admitted to Sweet that the postal telegraph scheme could be "so modified as to make it very desirable" for Western Union.

Hubbard embraced Orton's attempt at conciliation, promising Orton that his postal telegraph scheme could be "enlarged" to include Western Union, greatly enriching its shareholders while helping to "build up the finest telegraph system in the world."[102]

Hubbard was so pleased with Orton's apparent new spirit of cooperation that he made it public almost immediately in a speech before the Philadelphia Board of Trade. Hubbard allowed Orton to review an early draft, and Orton criticized passages that might "excite hostility" against Western Union "on account of alleged mismanagements in the past."[103] But in the final draft, perhaps recognizing the opportunity that Orton's purported willingness to sell to the government represented, Hubbard cut everything "at all offensive" to Western Union.[104] He not only praised Western Union's managers as "men of ability, integrity, and experience in business," but he also even adopted one of Orton's favorite arguments: that

---

99 "Governments and the Telegraphs," 14 August 1869, *The New York Times*, 4.

100 William Orton to George Jones, 16 August 1869, WUC. Oddly Orton nearly reversed himself completely in a letter to the *Philadelphia Ledger* the following day. William Orton to George W. Childs, 17 August 1869, WUC.

101 William Orton to Gardiner G. Hubbard, 20 August 1869, WUC, William Orton to Gardiner G. Hubbard, 15 November 1869, WUC.

102 William Orton to Anson Stager, 20 November 1869, WUC. This meeting and its spirit are confirmed in Gardiner G. Hubbard to R. H. McCurdy (transcription), 20 November 1869, Hubbard Papers.

103 William Orton to Gardiner G. Hubbard, 23 November 1869, WUC.

104 William Orton to Anson Stager, 27 November 1869, WUC.

competition played a *negative* role in the industry, reducing receipts and increasing expenses unnecessarily.

Yet Hubbard maintained that Western Union's overinflated capital led to high rates that strangled demand for the telegraph. Hubbard invoked a metaphor that Josiah Quincy, the president of the American Cheap Transportation Association, employed to describe the railroads: to pay their dividends, corporations acted like "feudal barons on the Rhine," extorting money from all who traversed their domains.[105] Extortionate high rates would continue until telegraph stock reflected the "fair cost of the property" and the telegraph united with the post office. Hubbard promised that his more efficient system would reward investors with up to 10 percent dividends on the *real* value of the lines.[106] The telegraph would be a cheap, accessible, public monopoly – essentially what would later be known as a public utility.

In late 1869 Orton agreed to a modified version of Hubbard's plan that pegged the value of Western Union's lines at $25 million, significantly higher than the $15 million market value of Western Union's stock.[107] Orton insisted that their cooperation remain a secret,[108] though Hubbard received assurances that Speaker of the House Blaine, a Western Union ally, would give him a "strong [select] committee" and Orton would be "a tower of strength" in his campaign.[109] But Hubbard's reform movement lost its way in Congress. In January 1870, the Senate Committee on Post Offices and Post Roads – chaired by Hubbard ally Alexander Ramsey – released the first positive Congressional report on the postal telegraph since the days of Kendall and Morse. Ramsey condemned the private American telegraph system for its inflated capital, high rates, and limited use by the general public and recommended a scheme similar to Hubbard's. However, the House Select Committee on Postal Telegraph, led by C. C. Washburn (who took up telegraph reform after his brother Elihu left Congress), proposed instead to follow the English example by

---

[105] Gardiner Greene Hubbard, *The Postal Telegraph: The Only Means by Which the Telegraph Can Be Made the Ordinary Method of Communication* (Boston: Press of Rand, Avery, & Frye, 1869), 7, 16.

[106] Ibid., 13, 18.

[107] William Orton to Anson Stager, 27 November 1869, WUC; William Orton to Anson Stager, 7 December 1869, WUC.

[108] Gardiner G. Hubbard to R. H. McCurdy (transcription), 23 December 1869, Hubbard Papers.

[109] Gardiner G. Hubbard to R. H. McCurdy (transcription), 20 January, 1870, Hubbard Papers; Gardiner G. Hubbard to R. H. McCurdy (transcription), 28 January 1870, Hubbard Papers.

buying out the telegraph companies and prohibiting private telegraphy. Ramsey's committee rejected the Washburn scheme as too costly and sure to create "an annual tax upon the whole people for the benefit of the small number who use the telegraph."[110] Washburn's proposal was a boon for Western Union: a buyout would cost so much that Congress was unlikely to ever approve it, but the presence of Washburn's bill undermined the momentum of Hubbard's more practical approach.[111]

With the reform effort in disarray, Orton used a two-day appearance before the House Select Committee on the Postal Telegraph in May 1870 to attack both Hubbard and Washburn. Apparently not recognizing that Orton had turned on him, Hubbard defended the notion that telegraph competition was not in the public interest and argued that reduced rates led inevitably to mergers, swelling the capital and dividend obligations of the telegraph companies. Orton concurred and dismissed "monopoly" as a mere "catch-word" unjustly fastened to Western Union. "The mere fact of a monopoly proves nothing," he argued. The question was only whether Western Union administered the telegraph "properly and in the interest, first, of the owners of the property, and second, of the public." He insisted that claims of "flagrant abuses" by Western Union were illegitimate.[112] Washburn accused Western Union of holding that "no earthly power" could regulate telegraph rates, but Orton responded that only *Congress* lacked regulatory power. If Western Union gouged the public with extortionate rates, Orton argued, "a few thousand dollars" was enough to create a competitor that would, "like the gimlet hole in the hogshead," drain away business until Western Union offered lower rates. This ease of competition made the telegraph more secure "against oppressive exactions" than any other business in the United States.[113]

What came next, however, was a blistering attack on the proponents of the public telegraph. Orton charged that the postal telegraph scheme would enrich Hubbard and his associates "who never owned a rod of telegraph in the world," by more than a million dollars. Because Western Union controlled 90 percent of the lines to be "stocked in" to Hubbard's new company, Western Union would inevitably take control.

[110] "Report to Accompany Bill S. No. 422," Senate Committee on Post Offices and Post Roads, 41st Congress, 2nd Session, Report No. 18, 1–2.
[111] William Orton to Hugh Allan, 10 March 1870, WUC.
[112] Government Telegraphs: Argument of William Orton, President of the Western Union Telegraph Company, on the Bill to Establish Postal Telegraph Lines (New York: Russells' American Steam Printing House, 1870), 9, 13.
[113] Ibid., 31.

"If the Western Union Company is such a tyrant and monster, with a competition existing over a large portion of the territory, what would it be with that competition extinguished, and under the protection of the Government and in partnership with it?" Orton asked.[114] In a peculiar reversal of roles, Orton argued that Hubbard's plan would enrich telegraph shareholders and provide no public benefit. Standing as "a citizen claiming a little patriotism" rather than a shareholder hoping to reap a windfall, Orton demanded that the government stay out of the telegraph industry or else "take the whole business" in a general buyout. "In my judgment," he concluded, "there is no middle ground."[115]

Without Orton's cooperation, neither Hubbard nor Washburn had the momentum to get their bills through either house of Congress.[116] However, Hubbard, like O'Rielly before him, refused to surrender, making appearances before Congressional committees with such regularity that Orton suggested he might "by and by be looked upon as part of the Congressional clock-work."[117] Iowa Republican Francis Palmer of the House Select Committee on Postal Telegraph issued a report strongly favoring Hubbard's proposal on the grounds that Western Union intended "to monopolize the telegraphic business of the country." The present management had improved the system, but "new men" could take charge at any annual meeting – as occurred just a few months later – and "use its immense power for speculative or political purposes." Though there were worse monopolies than Western Union, none had "greater power" and the potential "to cause as great injury to the public."[118] But Palmer failed to win over the other members of his committee, and Washburn issued a competing report critical of Hubbard's plan.[119] Hubbard pressed on, but he admitted to his wife that sometimes he wished that the postal telegraph "were buried in the ocean beyond resurrection."[120]

[114] Hubbard admitted in earlier Congressional testimony that he and his colleagues could profit substantially from his bill. William Orton to George Walker, 28 February 1870, WUC.

[115] Argument of William Orton, 46–7.

[116] For a critique of Washburn's effort, see Lindley, *The Constitution Faces Technology*, 140–50.

[117] Orton to Painter, 25 May 1870, WUC.

[118] "Postal Telegraph System," 41st Congress, 2nd Session, Report No. 115.

[119] "Postal Telegraph in the United States, 41st Congress, 2nd Session, Report No. 114.

[120] Hubbard's skill as a lobbyist attracted him several new clients: Harper's Publishing Company, Cunard Steamers, and Tom Scott of the Pennsylvania Railroad paid him to promote legislation on their behalf. Scott provided substantial financial support and promised to back Hubbard's postal telegraph scheme. Hubbard to Gertrude Hubbard, 27 May 1870, Hubbard Papers. Lindley, *The Constitution Faces Technology*, 179–81.

Orton's neutralization of Hubbard, however, was about to be challenged from within. Though there was little doubt that Western Union still controlled the American telegraph, who controlled Western Union was less certain. The company's $41 million in nominal stock represented a remarkable concentration of capital, but command of the stock was diffuse. Western Union had traded on the New York Stock Exchange since 1865, and as shares changed hands, so did ownership of the company – often obscurely.[121] Patent holders and local entrepreneurs – usually merchants and small industrialists seeking to benefit from both their investment and a telegraph connection to their region – had jointly owned the first telegraph companies.[122] These early investors had grown as wealthy as the New York "heavy capitalists" they had once set themselves against. Western Union had grown into a position of unquestioned national dominance, but early investors owned only small portions of Western Union. The largest holders, the Cornell family, controlled less than 5 percent of the stock, and Hiram Sibley, who had mortgaged everything to invest in Western Union, owned less than 2 percent. As late as 1867, hundreds of Rochester "country holders" still owned perhaps 20 percent.[123] The rest, including the controlling interest, was quickly finding its way into very different hands.

In the industrial boom following the Civil War, corporate capitalists took the place of the proprietary merchants and small industrialists who had ruled the American economy in the antebellum period.[124] Financiers and industrialists who commanded large pools of aggregated capital became the dominant figures in American enterprise. Western Union

[121] Western Union Executive Committee Meeting, 19 January 1865, WUC.

[122] Gerald W. Brock, *The Telecommunications Industry: The Dynamics of Market Structure* (Cambridge, Mass.: Harvard University Press, 1981), 61–3.

[123] These finding are based on two lists of shareholders found in the Sibley Papers. The list of Rochester holders is dated 1867, and the list of larger holders, based on the attached officer names, is probably from 1867 or 1868, and may have been made up at the same time. Both lists may be found in the Sibley Family Papers, Box 1.
Together, the lists account for only $23 million of Western Union's $40 million in capital, and I presume that the lists do *not* include Western Union shareholders who received stock in exchange for American, United States, and Southwestern Telegraph stock. The Board of Directors from 1869, however, suggests that there were only a few large holders in that category, including Norvin Green, Wilson Hunt, Francis Morris, Cambridge Livingston, and John Dean Caton. Morse and Kendall owned substantial shares in both the American and Southwestern Telegraph Companies and presumably retained some Western Union shares. If there were any other large holders of Western Union stock as late as 1869, they were not represented on the Board of Directors.

[124] Martin J. Sklar, *The Corporate Reconstruction of American Capitalism, 1890–1916: The Market, the Law, and Politics* (New York: Cambridge University Press, 1988).

exemplified this change, and by greatly accelerating the speed of communication, helped make it possible. Proprietary capitalists of an earlier era founded Western Union, but in the late 1860s the company's stock became attractive to a different breed of investor – ambitious financiers interested in more than one firm and even more than one industry, seeking to maximize on an investment portfolio rather than to serve the interest of a particular firm. These investors had little of the sense of ownership that had driven Sibley and his Rochester cohort – indeed, many of them made money not by investing in Western Union, but investing against it as "short sellers." For this new breed of investor, the dividend and the market performance of a company's stock were far more important than the productivity or long-term fate of the firm.[125]

By 1870, one of the greatest investor entrepreneurs of the era, Cornelius Vanderbilt, had quietly acquired a controlling stake in Western Union. "Commodore" Vanderbilt had made a fortune in steam shipping and then turned his entrepreneurial energy to the railroads. In 1869, he merged two of his roads to create the New York Central and Hudson River Railroad, one of the nation's largest corporations. At the October 1870 meeting of the Western Union board of directors, the first signs appeared that Vanderbilt – or at least his close associates – had added Western Union to his growing empire. In an abrupt change of leadership, thirteen of Western Union's twenty-nine directors left the board, including several current managers and former telegraph industry leaders. Among the new members, five stood out: Augustus Schell, Horace Clark, John Steward, Daniel Torrance, and James Banker were all railroad investors connected to Vanderbilt.[126] Schell was a prominent New York Democrat and a close friend and business associate of Vanderbilt – one of the "captains" of the "Vanderbilt combination."[127] Clark and Torrance, the

---

[125] Thomas Childs Cochran, *Railroad Leaders, 1845–1890* (Cambridge, Mass.: Harvard University Press, 1953), 10–11.

[126] Division Superintendent George Mumford and Treasurer O. H. Palmer, both from Rochester, left the board, as did District Superintendent Edward Creighton. Early telegraph investors John Dean Caton, Jeptha Wade, and Francis Morris also resigned. Interestingly, Moses Taylor and William E. Dodge, both merchants and leading members of New York's merchant-centered Chamber of Commerce – and both in the process of converting from traditional merchants to investors in the new industrial economy – also departed from the board. See "The Annual Election," *Journal of the Telegraph*, 266. Thomas Kessner, *Capital City: New York City and the Men Behind America's Rise to Economic Dominance, 1860–1900* (New York: Simon & Schuster, 2003), 25–30, 124–5.

[127] "Schell, Augustus," in *Dictionary of American Biography*, ed. Dumas Malone (New York: Scribner's Sons, 1935), 424, T. J. Stiles, *The First Tycoon: The Epic Life of*

Commodore's sons-in-law, were both active in Vanderbilt's businesses, and Clark was rumored to be a potential successor to Vanderbilt.[128] Schell, Banker, Steward, and Clark served together as directors on Vanderbilt's railroads.[129] The new Western Union directorate elected Schell and Clark to the Executive Committee, the subset of the board that actively managed the company, and Schell became one of the company's three vice presidents.

Vanderbilt had apparently staged a coup.[130] The industry's labor newspaper, *The Telegrapher*, hailed the change on the board as a sign that a "decidedly old-fogeyish" management was at last on its way out.[131] Curiously, the editors made no reference for several weeks to the fact that the new board belonged to Vanderbilt, but by December they referred frequently to the "Vanderbilt management."[132] Commodore Vanderbilt himself admitted to no such influence. Three years after his associates took control of the company and just months before he installed himself and his son William H. Vanderbilt on the Western Union board, the cagey Vanderbilt denied to a *Times* reporter that he had any interest in the telegraph. "If I had the Western Union Telegraph Line, I wouldn't want to be bothered with it," he insisted.[133]

Despite such denials, Western Union had the hallmarks of a Vanderbilt target: a corporation with "immense strengths," a weak stock price, and need of managerial reform.[134] The news of Vanderbilt's associates taking over Western Union's board drove the troubled stock up 10 percent overnight. According to one investor, the "*boys*" in the "cautious and close-mouthed" Vanderbilt management were the best financial operators on the continent, and they had "only begun" to drive up the stock.[135] Within five months of the Vanderbilt coup, Western Union stock had

Cornelius Vanderbilt (New York: Alfred A. Knopf, 2009), 397. "Schell, Augustus," in *National Cyclopaedia of American Biography* (New York: James T. White & Company, 1893), 463.

[128] Cochran, Railroad Leaders, 1845–1890, 26.

[129] Charles Edgar Ames, *Pioneering the Union Pacific: A Reappraisal of the Builders of the Railroad* (New York: Appleton-Century-Crofts, 1969), 424.

[130] Gardiner G. Hubbard to Gertrude Hubbard (transcription), 17 November 1870, Hubbard Papers.

[131] "The Western Union Telegraph Company – New Management and New Policy," *The Telegrapher*, 22 October 1870, 68.

[132] Capitol, "Congress and the Telegraph," *The Telegrapher*, 114.

[133] Quoted in Wheaton J. Lane, *Commodore Vanderbilt: An Epic of the Steam Age* (New York: Alfred A. Knopf, 1942), 272.

[134] Stiles, *The First Tycoon*, 510.

[135] John Connor to Hiram Sibley, 25 February, 1871, Sibley Papers (Addition).

doubled in value, and *The Telegrapher* claimed that the "Vanderbilt party" could manipulate the price at will.[136] Rumors surfaced that Vanderbilt intended not to reform Western Union, but to run up the stock and then sell the company to the government.[137] The *New York Herald* reported in January 1871 that Vanderbilt had dispatched Horace Greeley to Washington to negotiate with the Postmaster General and President Grant to sell Western Union to the government for $30 million.[138] The eccentric reform newspaper *Woodhull & Claflin's Weekly* condemned the rumored sale as "an infamous scheme" for the holders of Western Union's "bubble stock" to "unload" their investment at the expense of the "working people of the country."[139] Though unsubstantiated, the story was not implausible, and its placement in *Woodhull & Claflin's Weekly* lent it credence. Sisters Victoria Woodhull and Tennessee Claflin were popularly believed to be intimate friends of the Commodore, and market commentary in the *Weekly* was often believed to reflect Vanderbilt's views (though a recent Vanderbilt biographer has credibly argued that Vanderbilt's link to Woodhull and Claflin has been greatly overstated).[140] Recent history was on the side of the rumor mongers: Morse and Kendall had launched the telegraph itself in a similar government-sale "scheme" just two decades before. It is little wonder, then, that a brilliant operator like Vanderbilt might plan for the federal treasury to guarantee his investment.

Whatever the source or credibility of the rumors, the Telegraph Act of 1866 empowered the federal government to purchase Western Union. Political pressure on the "monopoly" had hardly waned since the passage of that legislation, though much of the debate now centered on the creation – by purchase, contract, or charter – of a "postal telegraph." The postal telegraph debate appeared to be a contest between the corporation and the state, as some members of Congress sought to use federal power to protect the public interest by freeing the telegraph from Western

[136] "No Telegraphic Monopoly," *The Telegrapher*, 25 March 1871, 244.
[137] Capitol, "Congress and the Telegraph," *The Telegrapher*, 3 December 1870, VII, no. 15, 114.
[138] "The Hatchet Buried – Horace Greeley at the White House," *New York Herald*, 4 January 1871, 7.
[139] "A Last Effort of the Western Union Telegraph Company," *Woodhull & Claflin's Weekly*, 14 January 1871, 8.
[140] Lois Beachy Underhill, *The Woman Who Ran for President: The Many Lives of Victoria Woodhull* (Bridgehampton, New York: Bridge Works Publishing Co., 1995), 87, Stiles, *The First Tycoon*, 501–4.

Union's grasp. But as in the Civil War, the state/private dichotomy could be misleading when it came to Western Union. Western Union's influential lobby and substantial government contract gave it a powerful – some would say "corrupting" – presence *in* the state. The two had long worked hand in glove. In 1869's "A Chapter of Erie," Charles Francis Adams wrote that corporations depended upon "the public corruption" for their political power, casting business influence in government as a moral problem.[141] However Western Union's political agenda did not require explicit moral corruption. Rather, Western Union's lobby deftly defined the interest of one of the largest and most powerful corporations in the nation as merely private property deserving of state protection, effective "monopoly" or no. This assertion framed Western Union's holdings as part of the coalition between the state and private property that was already at the heart of postbellum political ideology. Thus even the most drastic measure against Western Union – the nationalization of the telegraph – properly conceived, was less a threat than another opportunity for profit.

The Vanderbilt clique's November 1870 takeover reinvigorated Hubbard's efforts. Orton, in the midst of reported "difficulties" with the Vanderbilt executive committee, once again moderated his tone toward Hubbard.[142] Orton informed Hubbard he would cooperate with a buyout if given the opportunity to prove Western Union's value "before competent, impartial, and untrammeled arbitrators."[143] Hubbard met Horace Clark, Vanderbilt's son-in-law and lieutenant, and believed he had convinced Clark to back his plan. Orton brought Hubbard before the executive committee, and, Hubbard reported, told the committee he "entirely approved and endorsed" Hubbard's plan.[144] A month later came newspaper reports that Vanderbilt had sent an emissary to Washington to negotiate the sale of Western Union to the government – though the proposed "sale" was more likely a transfer of stock into Hubbard's postal telegraph company. Hubbard lined up key Republican supporters in the Senate, several state legislatures passed resolutions in favor of a postal telegraph,

---

[141] Charles Francis Adams Jr. and Henry Adams, *Chapters of Erie* (Ithaca, N.Y.: Great Seal Books, 1956), 97.
[142] Whitlaw Reid to Charles Boynton, 22 December 1870, William Henry Smith Papers (OHS).
[143] Orton to Hubbard, 19 November 1870, WUC.
[144] Hubbard to Gertrude Hubbard, 16 December 1870, Hubbard Papers.

and in December 1871, President Grant endorsed the postal telegraph in his State of the Union Address. The telegraph promoted what Grant called the "groundwork of republican institutions": commerce, trade, and (through "speedy" news gathering) education. A postal telegraph, he suggested, would reduce rates and improve service.[145] Grant's Postmaster General, John Creswell, attacked Western Union as a destructive monopoly and urged the immediate creation of a government system. "There are now but two parties in the controversy over the postal telegraph," he wrote in his 1873 annual report, "on one side the people, on the other the Western Union Telegraph Company."[146]

Despite Hubbard's fervent efforts and the Vanderbilt clique's avowed support, the postal telegraph made little progress. Hubbard won favorable reports from the Senate Committee on Post Offices and Post Roads in 1870, 1872, and 1874 and the Senate Committee on Commerce in 1872, but the relatively low prestige of the Post Office Committees in both houses of Congress gave the bill little chance of reaching the floor.[147] In the House, John Farnsworth, a Western Union supporter, chaired the Post Office Committee and employed U. H. Painter, Western Union's top lobbyist, as his clerk. High turnover among the mostly junior committee members gave Farnsworth and Painter an unusually high degree of influence. In the Senate, Hubbard's ally Ramsey headed the Post Office Committee, but the committee's primary concern was management of the huge postal bureaucracy, and Ramsey lacked the clout to advance Hubbard's proposal.

In three years Ramsey secured the Senate floor for debate on the postal telegraph bill only once, at a poorly attended evening session in April 1872. Republican James Nye of Nevada, formerly an opponent of the Telegraph Act of 1866, complained that Hubbard's bill was so long and complicated that it made him "giddy to read it." Hubbard apparently believed there was "nothing left to be done on the face of God's earth" that could not be delegated to the Postmaster General.[148] Roscoe

---

[145] *A Compilation of the Messages and Papers of the Presidents*, vol. IX (New York: Bureau of National Literature, 1897), 4104.

[146] Report of the Postmaster-General and of the Attorney General of the United States, (Washington, D.C.: U.S. Government Printing Office, 1873), 35.

[147] Senate Report 18, 41st Congress, 2d Session; Senate Report 20, 42nd Congress, 2nd Session; Senate Report 242, 43rd Congress, 1st Session.; Senate Report 223, 42nd Congress, 2nd Session.

[148] The bill as debated was S. 341, 42d Congress, 2nd Session.

Conkling, a Western Union supporter, argued two hours was too little debate for a bill that required a week's worth of discussion.[149] But the bill never returned to the Senate floor.

With Congresses retreating from Reconstruction and the expansion of federal power, Hubbard could get little traction against the high-placed "friends" of Western Union. Orton's lobby needed only to convince legislators of the wisdom of *inaction*, which became easier as Congress turned away from a spate of postwar activism. Hubbard's plan for the government to charter a special company for him bore the unmistakable taint of special privilege. The alternative, an expensive purchase of Western Union's lines, became less likely as retrenchment increased after 1870. The economist David Ames Wells, a good friend of Orton, published a Western Union–sponsored pamphlet in opposition to the postal telegraph in 1872. Wells demanded a return to laissez-faire. "A measure like the one contemplated, of absorbing and operating the telegraph by the Government, is a step away from republicanism and toward imperialism," he wrote. This enlargement of federal power posed the greatest threat to democratic institutions.[150] In 1874 the Democrats – staunch opponents of the postal telegraph – took control of the House of Representatives, dimming Hubbard's prospects further.

Reports on the British postal telegraph, the would-be model for nationalization, discouraged a similar course in the United States. Frank Scudamore aggressively expanded the British Post Office to fulfill his promise of a public telegraph as effective as the private system. Rates fell as promised, but Scudamore repeatedly asked Parliament for additional funds. By 1873 he had overrun his allocations by more than eight hundred thousand pounds and misappropriated funds to cover expenses.[151] The scandal bolstered the American argument that the postal telegraph cost too much and the government could not effectively manage such a venture. Perhaps, speculated Western Union's *Journal of the Telegraph*, Hubbard and his allies would use the news from England "to intensify their patriotic appeals for the privilege of putting public money into private pockets."[152]

[149] Lindley, The Constitution Faces Technology, 183–7.
[150] David A. Wells, *The Relation of the Government to the Telegraph* (New York: Western Union Telegraph Company, 1873), 42.
[151] C. R. Perry, *The Victorian Post Office: The Growth of a Bureaucracy* (Rochester, N.Y.: The Boydell Press, 1992), 121–6.
[152] "How the British Postal Telegraph Service Is Made to Show a Profit," *Journal of the Telegraph*, 15 April 1873, 152.

While the prospects for a government buyout remained dim, Western Union managers set out to make money for shareholders in the traditional way. In the early 1870s Western Union undeniably made substantial improvements in the quality, scale, and price of its service. Circumstantial evidence suggests that the "Vanderbilt management" gave Orton the free hand he required to put his sprawling and ramshackle corporate house in order. Cornelius Vanderbilt boasted that he could run a railroad cheaper than anyone else, and he undoubtedly found a like-minded collaborator in Orton, who already subscribed to his own "ritual of economy."[153] Extravagant spending had destroyed the United States Telegraph Company, Orton's first telegraph firm, and Orton was convinced that Western Union's expenses were increasing at a dangerous rate. Despite the deflation in the American economy in the six years after the Civil War,[154] Western Union's annual expenditures continued to grow, driven largely by a huge increase in the size of the network and message volume. Orton pursued a strategy of cutting rates even as gross expenditures rose. Rate reductions served several purposes: lower rates took ammunition away from Congressional critics, pleased the public, and ruined small competing firms. Orton believed that given the "courage to reduce rates," Western Union could "control the business of the country."[155] Between 1866 and 1872, Western Union's average rate per message fell by 50 percent, increasing volume but eroding the profit margin.[156] In 1868, Western Union earned nearly forty cents of profit for every dollar of revenue, but by 1874 that margin had fallen to twenty-eight cents.[157] Western Union earned $2.6 million in profits in 1867 by transmitting 5.8 million messages. Five years later, the company transmitted 12.4 million messages but accumulated only $2.8 million in profits.[158] Adjusted for deflation,

---

[153] Cochran, Railroad Leaders, 1845–1890, 88.
[154] Richard Sutch and Susan B. Carter, *Historical Statistics of the United States: Earliest Times to the Present*, 5 vols., vol. 3 (New York: Cambridge University Press, 2006), 158, 82. This is a difficult discrepancy to explain. However it is conceivable that Orton was comparing prices of telegraph supplies and labor to prewar levels, which were all lower than prices in 1872. Nonetheless, he should have noted a steady lessening of this problem from 1866 to 1872.
[155] William Orton to E. B. Grant, 12 May 1869, WUC.
[156] William Orton to George H. Thurston, 19 August 1872, WUC.
[157] After 1874, margins climbed again to $0.34 and reached a high of almost $0.36 in 1878 before beginning another long decline. See "Western Union Annual Report for the Year Ending June 30, 1891," WUC.
[158] "Western Union Annual Report for the Year Ending June 30, 1891," WUC.

profits rose about 20 percent, but from Orton's point of view, Western Union had made little progress.[159]

Western Union managers demanded greater economy. Orton squeezed all the pennies he could from expenditures, upbraiding employees for failing to do their "duty" to eliminate every dollar of spending "not necessary to enable another dollar to be earned."[160] The cost of maintaining and operating existing lines and adding new lines to meet demand kept climbing – poles, wire, instruments, batteries, "and almost every item of property" the company consumed cost more by 1872 than ever.[161] Leaving no stone unturned in the search for savings, Orton launched a campaign against the runaway cost of office supplies. Though Orton created a corporate supply department in 1867, many superintendents purchased their own office supplies, often buying too much and occasionally profiting personally in their choice of suppliers. Orton condemned the "useless waste of material and postage" and declared war on the brazen use of fancy stationery with "special printed headings."[162] A manager could meet with Orton's wrath for attaching an unnecessary coversheet to a report or using a whole sheet of paper when a half-sheet would do.[163] When Orton first encountered a "pencil holder," he ordered that the wonderful invention should henceforth be distributed with every pencil, its general use tending to "reduce the consumption of lead pencils one half."[164]

But labor, not pencils, represented Western Union's greatest cost – sixty cents of every dollar spent. Telegraphy engaged two skilled operators in the transmission of every message. Greater volume always required a greater number of operators, and short-distance messages cost nearly as much to transmit as long-distance messages, since they consumed the same labor.[165] Several months after the failed operators strike of 1870,

---

[159] William Orton to George H. Thurston, 19 August 1872, WUC; deflation computed using Economic History Net's "How Much Is That?" calculators. Retrieved from: http://eh.net/hmit/ (Accessed 26 April 2008).

[160] William Orton to James Gamble, 17 March 1876, WUC.

[161] William Orton to Joseph Kinsey, 28 August 1872, WUC.

[162] William Orton to Anson Stager, 7 September 1876, WUC.

[163] William Orton to Anson Stager, 13 February 1877, WUC.

[164] William Orton to William Hunter, 4 December 1875, WUC.

[165] William Orton to Howard M. Jenkins, 30 November 1870, WUC. A short message "consumes as much time at each end, as much stationary, and costs as much for delivery – the only difference being that the investment in a short line of telegraph is less than a long one, and the cost of repairs and maintenance is in proportion to the length."

The Telegrapher described "a great telegraphic calm" and declared that all Western Union's operators were "now provided for" as well as before – in some cases better.[166] According to *The Telegrapher*, Orton – who had been in Europe during the strike – was "friendly" to operators and held in their highest esteem.[167] Internal communications are consistent with this view of Orton's desire for harmony, but wages represented such a significant cost that reducing labor expenditures was necessarily a constant consideration.

One method to lower the cost of labor was to employ women in place of men. In most nineteenth-century workplaces, the sexual division of labor kept women out of "men's" jobs. In a few unusual cases, such as telegraphy and typesetting, women performed men's work, but employers deemed them unworthy of an equal wage and reduced the price of labor wherever they employed them.[168] Orton claimed he did not share the common belief that a woman was entitled to "less compensation for the same service than a man," but he nonetheless hoped women would keep wages down by increasing the total supply of operators.[169] Craft unions often tried to keep women out of skilled trades for precisely this reason. Because operators traditionally learned telegraphy by apprenticeship, veteran male operators blocked women from the industry by refusing to teach them. Orton circumvented this obstacle by helping industrial magnate Peter Cooper start a free telegraph school for women in New York in 1869. There is little doubt that women subsequently reduced the labor cost of telegraphy. Critics claimed Western Union paid women only 50 or 60 percent as much as men, most likely because managers considered them unsuited for the "heavy" circuits and assigned them to posts that they judged beneath first-class male operators – hotel, intraurban,

---

[166] "A Great Telegraphic Calm," *The Telegrapher*, 19 November 1870, 100.

[167] "Return of President Orton," *The Telegrapher*, 12 February 1870, 200.

[168] Ellen DuBois's discussion of the conflict between women suffragists and the National Typographical Union reveals many similarities between women typesetters and women telegraphers. Both were considered useful but inferior, neither were allowed to work outside of the very narrow definitions of their jobs, both were shut out of unions and apprenticeship programs, and last but certainly not least, both were justifiably feared as a source of labor for breaking strikes. See Ellen Carol DuBois, *Feminism and Suffrage: The Emergence of an Independent Women's Movement in America, 1848–1869* (Ithaca, N.Y.: Cornell University Press, 1978), 129–42.

[169] However, this claim only goes so far, since women were not often allowed to perform the "same service." The highest paying, most prestigious telegraph jobs remained largely closed to them, in part because of the forced segregation of the sexes. William Orton to J. W. Phelps, 12 February 1869, WUC.

and small rural offices where traffic was light and salaries low.[170] The value of low-cost women operators to the telegraph industry is evident in their increasing employment. In the thirty years after 1870, the number of women operators rose from approximately 350 to more than 7,000.[171]

In the early 1870s, however, the demand for first-class male operators challenged managers to reduce labor costs despite a limited supply of suitably skilled workers. Managers occasionally poached workers from other divisions of their own company by advancing wages to induce operators to transfer, a practice Orton tried to stop by creating a unified wage policy.[172] In the tight market, Orton rejected demands from the executive committee to reduce labor costs by slashing wages, arguing that it was "better to pay good men fairly and even liberally, and then require them to perform their work faithfully, than to risk producing discontent by a reduction of pay."[173] However, this did not preclude managers from filling vacant positions at significantly lower salaries than those earned by departing employees, a regular practice.[174]

Orton claimed he could protect employee salaries from cuts only by getting more work from his operators.[175] Tardiness, absenteeism, and the tendency among operators at poorly disciplined offices "to be indolent and shiftless" forced Western Union to pay higher labor costs than necessary.[176] Perhaps, Orton once suggested, operators' "efficiency" had been impaired by Western Union's high salaries, which gave them "money to spend on cigars and in other extravagances" that made them unfit for work."[177] Yet still he opposed cutting wages, even for his workers' putative good. Orton had no sympathy for the longstanding employee grievance against Sabbath labor, because "the necessities of the public" demanded

---

[170] "The Pay of Women Telegraphers," *The Telegrapher*, 8 April 1871.
[171] Melodie Andrews, "What Girls Can Do: The Debate over the Employment of Women in the Early American Telegraph Industry," *Essays in Economic and Business History* 8 (1990): 110–12.
[172] William Orton to Stager, Van Horne, Eckert and Gamble, 11 October 1873, WUC. It appears that such a policy was never instituted.
[173] William Orton to Anson Stager, 16 July 1873, WUC.
[174] The *Telegrapher* charged that this tactic lowered morale and by reducing the quality of operators actually cost Western Union more money than it saved. See "A Few Practical Suggestions to Telegraphers," *The Telegrapher*, 3 September 1870, 12. Gabler documents several cases of this practice at work. See Edwin Gabler, *The American Telegrapher: A Social History, 1860–1900*, Class and Culture (New Brunswick, N.J.: Rutgers University Press, 1988), 72.
[175] William Orton to T. T. Eckert, 27 January 1874, WUC.
[176] William Orton to Anson Stager, 20 March 1874, WUC.
[177] William Orton to T. T. Eckert, 25 July 1874, WUC.

Sunday telegraphy – noncompliant operators faced dismissal.[178] He similarly resisted limits on the number of hours worked by salaried operators, arguing that an eight-hour day would destroy profits.[179] For health reasons superintendents often limited their employees to nine-hour day shifts and seven-hour night shifts, but operators would work more than seven hours a night for overtime pay. This health risk appeared to apply only when operators performed additional work without additional compensation, and Orton wryly observed that "the seeds of disease are entirely eradicated by fifty cents an hour!"[180]

Orton held himself to an even higher standard than his operators, and his fierce dedication to his office contributed to his chronic ill health. For years he suffered from "ague" that he attributed to malaria, though the vague descriptions of his periodic "attacks" make it difficult to diagnosis the "insidious enemy" that plagued him.[181] Orton's colleagues often worried that he overburdened himself.[182] "Labor is undoubtedly a joy and a glory, but it may be made an executioner," Western Union's newspaper warned during one of Orton's "spells."[183] Even days spent confined to a train car on trips to far-flung points in Western Union's empire provided Orton with no respite. Rather than resting or occupying himself with conversation in the club car, he would peer out the window at the Western Union lines along the tracks, jotting down notes and keeping a vigilant watch on the lines until at last it grew too dark to see.[184]

Improving Western Union's value also required Orton to address the millstone around the company neck: Western Union's bloated capital. Orton was determined to wring the "water" out of the stock. Since the 1850s, Western Union had grown by acquiring competitors with newly minted

---

[178] William Orton to F. A. Sturman, 11 April 1873, WUC. Orton expressed his frustration with Sturman's Sabbath complaints in a note to Sturman's supervisor as well. "He is probably ignorant of the old law maxim *qui facit per alia facit per se* which being freely rendered means that what one does by another, he does himself, and that to hire a substitute to break the Sabbath as he expresses a willingness to do, is as much an infraction of the divine law, as if he did the same work himself," Orton wrote. William Orton to R. C. Clowry, 22 April 1873, WUC.

[179] William Orton to Henry L. Dawes, 18 January 1872, WUC.

[180] William Orton to T. T. Eckert, 27 January 1874, WUC.

[181] William Orton to Anson Stager, 30 December 1875, WUC; William Orton to Anson Stager, 15 August 1876, WUC.

[182] James D. Reid, *The Telegraph in America and Morse Memorial*, 2d ed. (New York: John Polhemus, 1884), 575.

[183] "Work," *Journal of the Telegraph*, 1 October 1871, 254.

[184] William Orton to Anson Stager, 16 July 1873, WUC.

stock and had paid out huge stock bonuses to shareholders. The company increased its capital by fourfold during the Civil War, and then, according to critics, grossly overpaid for the American and United States Telegraph Companies in the 1866 mergers. Privately even Hiram Sibley regretted buying off the United States Company, which he admitted should have been destroyed instead.[185]

The problem of watered stock went well beyond Western Union and was most often associated with the railroad companies, including those owned by Vanderbilt, a notorious waterer.[186] Railroad developers, like their telegraph-building peers, used diluted stock to fund construction without taking on the obligations of bonded debt. The evil attributed to watered stock lay in its potential to dupe investors into backing overvalued enterprises, which ultimately drove up prices, reduced the quality of goods and services, and inefficiently allocated capital.[187] In twenty-first-century terms, the whole concept of "watered stock" is obsolete – capital value is equal to the market value of a stock, which reflects investors' collective assessment of its earnings potential, rather than its capital assets.

However, the size of Western Union's capital remained important for two reasons. First, dividends were paid on the basis of nominal capital. When Western Union's shares traded at one-third of par, it still paid a dividend on $41 million in nominal capital. The common perception, with some justification, was that a "watered" stock required managers to go to great lengths to meet investors' expectations for dividends – widely perceived to be the central source of value in a stock. For instance, while Western Union's nominal dividend of 3 percent for 1866–1869 was relatively low compared to its railroad peers, it paid out an astonishing 19 percent of revenue in dividends compared to the New York Central Railroad's rate of 11 percent.[188] Second, critics charged that Western

---

[185] T. R. Walker to Hiram Sibley, 2 February 1867, Sibley Papers.

[186] The legend of the term's origin held that financier Daniel Drew allegedly over-watered his cattle just before bringing them to market, thus selling heavier "watered stock." Henry Clews recorded this story and I have not seen a better one, though this story seems curiously literal. Henry Clews, *Twenty-Eight Years in Wall Street* (New York: Irving Publishing Co., 1888), 121.

[187] For a discussion of these problems and an assessment of their legitimacy see David L. Dodd, *Stock Watering: The Judicial Valuation of Property for Stock-Issue Purposes* (New York: Columbia University Press, 1930), 17–27.

[188] Data derived from Western Union Telegraph, *Journal of the Telegraph*, vols. 1–2 (Western Union Telegraph Company, 1867), 242 and Surveyor, *Annual Report on the Railroads of the State of New York*, 176.

Union had inflated its capital as part of a grand scheme to enrich an inside ring of investors and keep competitors out of the market by grossly exaggerating the cost of telegraphy, a tactic arguably on display throughout the dueling statistical presentations to Congress during the postal telegraph debate. "The process of watering disguises profits," *The New York Times* charged in an 1873 editorial. "It enables a company to do everything for its stockholders and nothing for the public. It gives a cover for rich and powerful capitalists, under which they can fleece the community and fill their own pockets."[189]

That watered stock represented a "real" problem is evident in Orton's determination to deflate Western Union's capital. A less diluted stock would reduce the burden of the dividend, increase the price of the stock, and deprive critics of one of their favorite barbs. After the Vanderbilt clique took over in the fall of 1870, Orton began to decrease Western Union's nominal capital to $30 million, a sum not far above the $25 million that he had considered the legitimate combined value of the American, United States, and Western Union Companies in 1866.[190] Orton used retained earnings and bonded debt to buy Western Union shares and hold them in the company's treasury, a process similar to modern stock buy-backs, taking $7 million in stock off the market by the end of 1872.[191]

Orton expressed grave doubts about Western Union's dividend as well. He believed that a revolution in communications was underway, and to capitalize on it his company should aggressively expand its network *ahead* of demand.[192] Western Union could match competitors wire for wire at every point they reached and leave no territory open for the opposition.[193] Orton's strategy suggests that he intuitively grasped that additional nodes increased the network's value exponentially, rather than linearly. A successful network, however costly, must also be ubiquitous. Moreover public pressure required Western Union to reach as many points as possible. Orton feared that withdrawing from unprofitable territory would spark public outrage. He complained that if Western Union closed struggling offices, "the next morning's *Herald*" would report that "a large delegation of indignant citizens" was on its way to testify to Congress

---

[189] "Stock-Watering," *The New York Times*, 9 September 1873, 4.
[190] William Orton to E. B. Grant, 12 May 1869, WUC.
[191] William Orton to Henry S. Potter, 23 October 1872, WUC.
[192] William Orton to Samuel Kepler, 23 February 1870, WUC.
[193] William Orton to John Van Horne, 3 July 1871, WUC.

"to urge upon it the necessity of the Government's taking charge of the telegraph."[194]

However visionary Orton's strategy might have been, shareholders expected earnings to be paid to them as dividends rather than retained for construction. Orton, however, advocated a different approach. He sought to improve Western Union's network, put the competition out of reach, and ultimately bring Western Union's actual value in line with its nominal value. Lower rates, more reliable service, less competition, and greater profits – in Orton's view all depended upon investing in new lines with the funds that dividend payments drained from the company coffers.[195] In the first nine years after the grand consolidation of 1866, Western Union spent $5.4 million on building new lines – a sum equivalent to only two years of dividend payments. Orton tried to convince major shareholders that Western Union would be worth *more* if the board reduced or suspended the dividend.[196] By the end of 1869, surplus funds were in such short supply that it appeared the company might borrow to pay the January dividend.[197] Instead, the board voted to suspend the dividend, giving Orton his way at last. They passed the dividend again in June 1870, and after the Vanderbilt coup in October, the new board upheld the policy of retaining earnings for building new lines and reducing outstanding stock. For the subsequent four years, the company paid no dividends.[198] Western Union's policies of reducing capital and suspending the dividend have often been attributed to Vanderbilt's influence, but Orton had proposed this program long before Vanderbilt's men appeared on Western Union's board.[199] The 1870 Vanderbilt coup freed Orton to pursue the policies that he been unable to as long as Western Union's directors refused to forego dividends.

Despite Orton's internal reform campaign, Western Union still antagonized much of the American public. The "Great Monopoly" bolstered the

---

[194] In this testimony, Orton was referring specifically to offices that were unprofitable because of local taxation, but it reflects his general sensitivity to criticism for closing offices. *Argument of William Orton*, 32.

[195] William Orton to Henry Bentley, 27 February 1869, WUC.

[196] William Orton to E. B. Grant, 12 May 1869, WUC.

[197] William Orton to Anson Stager, 16 November 1869, WUC.

[198] Dividends for 1875 were $2.7 million. Construction from 1866 to 1875 cost $5.37 million. *Journal of the Telegraph*, 15 October 1875.

[199] Maury Klein, *The Life and Legend of Jay Gould* (Baltimore: Johns Hopkins University Press, 1986), 196.

AP's dominance of the nation's news. Rates remained so high that only a small part of the population could afford to use the telegraph. The high price of telegraphy gave a communications advantage to large firms over small, to high-traffic urban centers over poorly connected small towns and rural regions. Even with the reconstruction and expansion of Western Union's lines, the network remained fragile and its performance inconsistent. In August 1873, Orton took a train to Irvington to join his family at their summer home. He wired ahead to have his carriage meet him on the 9:00 P.M. express, but the Irvington operator never received the dispatch. Thus the president of the greatest and, by his own frequent testimony to Congress, most reliable telegraph network in the world found himself "obliged to walk home on a very hot night, carrying an overcoat and a traveling bag."[200]

[200] Orton to T. T. Eckert, 7 August 1873, WUC.

6

The Specter of Competition

In the years following the Civil War, a building boom in crowded lower Manhattan pushed New York City's skyline to new heights. Except for a few church steeples, an invisible ceiling hovered over the city around five stories, the point at which commercial tenants refused to climb any more stairs. In 1870, the Equitable Life Insurance Building at 120 Broadway became the first office building to employ a passenger elevator, breaking the practical five-story limit with a lucrative sixth floor tucked under a mansard roof.[1] For decades New York's commercial architecture had been limited primarily to rookeries – undistinguished four-story "functional boxes."[2] In the 1870s, a shift toward a grander, taller commercial architecture began. "A liberal expenditure in architecture is a good investment," the New York *Daily Graphic* suggested in a report on new buildings reaching "up to the clouds."[3] The commercial district below Chambers Street teemed with the businesses essential to booming American industry – banks, exchanges, credit agencies, law firms, insurance, and express companies, all requiring proximity to one another and space for their growing ranks of employees.[4]

The "Great Monopoly," which connected New York's business community with the outside world, had outgrown its home. Western Union's

---

[1] Winston Weisman, "New York and the Problem of the First Skyscraper," *The Journal of the Society of Architectural Historians* 12, no. 1 (1953): 15.
[2] Lee E. Gray, "Type and Building Type: Newspaper/Office Buildings in Nineteenth-Century New York," in *The American Skyscraper: Cultural Histories*, ed. Roberta Maudry (New York: Cambridge University Press, 2005), 86.
[3] "A Telegraph Palace," *New York Daily Graphic*, 3 June 1873.
[4] Edwin G. Burrows and Mike Wallace, *Gotham: A History of New York City to 1898* (New York: Oxford University Press, 1999), 940.

headquarters at 145 Broadway was suitably close to New York's commercial and financial center, but the building could not accommodate the
new wires that seemed to sprout almost daily from its upper floors, nor
the growing army of operators who tended them. A year before the Panic
of 1873 brought the building boom to an end, Western Union announced
plans for a stately new headquarters at the corner of Broadway and Dey
Street, "one of the most valuable pieces of real estate in the city" – Western
Union paid nearly a million dollars for it.[5] The plot was catty-cornered
from Park Row, the hub of the newspaper business, and just blocks north
of Wall Street. Even the nearby New York Post Office, a hulking Second
Empire building four blocks around and nicknamed "the whale,"[6] was
half the proposed height of Western Union's headquarters, one of the
world's first skyscrapers.[7]

In July 1872, Western Union's directors selected the relatively inexperienced architect George Post to design their new headquarters. President
William Orton had called for an eight-story building – then a dazzling
height – to house a business that had more than doubled in message
volume in the preceding six years.[8] But Post, whom architect Daniel
Burnham later called "the father of the tall building in New York," proposed a ten-story design. At 230 feet the building would be four times
taller than the typical commercial rookery and second only to Trinity
Church – though by some accounts the weather vane actually topped
Trinity's spire.[9]

[5] William Orton to James Park, 20 March 1872, WUC.
[6] Lawrence Wodehouse, "Alfred B. Mullett and His French Style Government Buildings,"
    The Journal of the Society of Architectural Historians 31, no. 1 (1972): 33; Wallace,
    Gotham: A History of New York City to 1898, 942.
[7] Thomas Bender and William R. Taylor have described an "aesthetic tension" in the devel-
    opment of vertical New York, discovering a distinction between "civic horizontalism"
    and "corporate verticality." The Post Office and Western Union building are suggestive of
    this counterpoint, though it is worth adding that critics of the Post Office building were
    angry about the way in which it overshadowed City Hall – a monument to the primacy
    of federal government over municipal government. See Thomas Bender and William R.
    Taylor, "Culture and Architecture: Some Aesthetic Tensions in the Shaping of the Modern
    New York City," in *Visions of the Modern City: Essays in History, Art and Literature*, ed.
    William Sharpe and Leonard Wallock (Baltimore: The Johns Hopkins University Press,
    1987), 216. The question of which is the world's first true skyscraper cannot be answered
    because "skyscraper" has a variable definition, but Winston Weisman made a strong case
    for the Western Union building in his review of the problem. Weisman, "Problem of the
    First Skyscraper."
[8] William Orton, Memo, 10 April 1872, WUC.
[9] Sarah Bradford Landau, *George B. Post, Architect: Picturesque Designer and Determined
    Realist* (New York, N.Y.: Monacelli Press, 1998), 15, 31; Winston Weisman, "The

The Western Union building testified to the company's sense of its place at the center of the nation's commerce, and set a new standard for commercial architecture. The brick and granite façade rose to an ornate iron-railed balcony above the seventh floor; grand arcaded windows at the eighth floor; a lofty, dormered mansard roof on the ninth and tenth floors; and a clock tower and flagpole that soared skyward. Many of the apparently ornamental flourishes served telegraphic functions. The iron balcony railing anchored the hundreds of wires that fed into the operators' room. The huge eighth-floor windows provided natural light for the telegraphers. Iron trusses supported the mansard roof, leaving the operating room free from columns to create a vast attic for the employees' dining room and, most importantly, providing space for the batteries that gave life to the telegraph. The building had three elevators, steam heat, and a novel fire-fighting system with dedicated wells. Post designed the entire structure to be "fireproof."[10]

It was an imposing edifice for the "Great Monopoly," but although the enormous building evinced invulnerability (one critical historian called it a "bomb-proof citadel"), it concealed several significant problems.[11] Construction had been plagued with delays and minor disasters, many resulting from the building's massive size. The Rhode Island quarry providing most of the stone could not keep up with the order, and Post accused the firm of using the sheds intended for the Western Union job to cut stone for the State, War and Navy Building (known today as the Old Executive Office Building) in Washington instead.[12] The Western Union building's three-ton doorway lintel stone broke its tackle and sank the boat on which it was being loaded, and the nine-ton cornice piece was so enormous that it could not be shipped by regular steamer.[13] Mounting costs exhausted the building budget and the banking panic of 1873 nearly stopped construction altogether.[14] The press harped on the cost

Commercial Architecture of George B. Post," *The Journal of the Society of Architectural Historians* 31, no. 3 (1972): 181. *Journal of the Telegraph*, 15 February 1875.

[10] George Post to Alonzo Cornell, 8 April 1874, George Post Papers; Sarah Bradford Landau and Carl W. Condit, *Rise of the New York Skyscraper, 1865–1913* (New Haven, Conn.: Yale University Press, 1996), 79–81.

[11] Matthew Josephson, *The Robber Barons; the Great American Capitalists, 1861–1901* (New York,: Harcourt Brace and Company, 1934), 207.

[12] The building is today the Old Executive Office Building and was designed by Alfred B. Mullett, who was Supervising Architect for the federal government. Andrews to F. Merry, 26 May 1873, George Post Papers.

[13] Andrews to George Post, 13 May 1873, George Post Papers; Andrews to George Post, 20 June 1873, George Post Papers.

[14] Orton to Post, 27 October 1873, George Post Papers.

overruns to Post's great embarrassment. Western Union's lease on 145 Broadway expired early in 1874, and for more than a year the company faced eviction as construction dragged on. The "grand Hegira" to 195 Broadway – a move that required rewiring every telegraph pole in Lower Manhattan – did not begin until February 1875.[15] Even once occupied, the building lacked several finishing touches.[16] Granite piers above the portico intended for bronze statues of Benjamin Franklin and Samuel Morse remained empty.[17] The iron flagstaff atop the tower swayed so much in the wind that Post feared it would "not hold the Vane, much less a flag" [18] More than three years later, the building's great clock remained unfinished.[19] Yet the New York *Tribune* dubbed the Western Union building the "telegraphic heart of America."[20]

Within a short walk of Western Union's monument to its own dominance, at least half a dozen companies vied for a share of the American telegraph market. The "monopoly" label clung stubbornly to Western Union, and the company struggled with what had become its essential contradiction. On the one hand, Western Union managers insisted that the company controlled *only* 90 percent of the nation's telegraph system, an active opposition competed in an open market, and any abuse or gouging of the public would only hasten competition. On the other hand, they argued that the public would be better served if Western Union *were* a monopoly, that only a single telegraph company could efficiently and profitably perform the nation's business. Orton believed that low rates and quality service would "sugar coat" such a monopoly. The

---

[15] "Removal of the Western Union Office to the New Building," *The Telegrapher*, 30 January 1875, 29.

[16] Post to Orton, 18 March 1875, George Post Papers.

[17] Landau reports the statues were installed, but he apparently bases his assertion on a print produced by Western Union. *The Journal of the Telegraph* published the same image in February 1875 and noted that despite the artist's inclusion of the statues, their erection was a matter of "contemplation" and alternatives were under consideration. Following Orton's death in 1878 a proposal for Morse and Orton statues for "the niches in front" of the headquarters was suggested and declined. See *Journal of the Telegraph*, 15 February 1875; Meeting of the Executive Committee, 29 May 1878; WUC; Landau and Condit, *Rise of the New York Skyscraper, 1865–1913*, 81; Diana Balmori, "George B. Post: The Process of Design and the New American Architectural Office (1886–1913)," *The Journal of the Society of Architectural Historians* 46, no. 4 (1987): 343.

[18] J. B. Cornell to George B. Post, 31 October 1874, George Post Papers.

[19] Meeting of the Executive Committee, 20 November 1878, WUC. Despite the problems with the building, it launched George Post's career as a commercial architect, and Balmori notes, won him several major commissions from Vanderbilt and members of Western Union's board of directors. See Balmori, "George B. Post," 355.

[20] "The New Telegraphic Heart of America," *New York Tribune*, 1 February 1875, 12.

public would not "be frightened" and would accept monopoly without "wincing" if Western Union did the work better and more cheaply than competitors.[21] Persistent competition, Western Union managers insisted, was only so much waste.

In the abstract, there *could* have been legitimate competition in telegraphy in the 1870s. The actual state of competition, however, was less rosy. Through the construction of barriers to entry and the liberal use of predatory pricing, Western Union created conditions that made genuine competition virtually impossible. In the end, this strategy rebounded against the "Great Monopoly" in an unexpected way. Legitimate competitors were unlikely to prove a mortal threat to a company with such a commanding market position. Illegitimate competitors, however, created solely as mechanisms to extract wealth from investors and Western Union itself, were less predictable and ultimately more dangerous. Preventing such illegitimate competitors from fomenting "an indefinite state of warfare" proved beyond even Western Union's power.[22] It was this warfare, warfare waged not through the simple push and pull of supply and demand for telegraph service but with the mechanisms of the market itself, that nearly ruined Western Union.

None of the competing telegraph companies in the early 1870s could challenge Western Union individually, so the operators' advocacy newspaper *The Telegrapher* proposed the same solution that Western Union and its rivals embraced in the 1850s – cartelization. "Common Sense at Last," *The Telegrapher* declared in response to an 1871 agreement between Western Union opponents, the Pacific & Atlantic, Franklin, and Bankers' & Brokers' Companies, to consolidate their interests. Western Union would have a "more serious antagonist" than when each company was "fighting on its own hook."[23] But *The Telegrapher* also acknowledged that the opposition lines had thus far been mostly fraudulent ventures run by speculators and contractors who, "relying upon the known antagonism of the public to a telegraphic monopoly," repeatedly "reaped the harvest" of foolhardy investors.[24] The "common

---

[21] William Orton to George B. Prescott, 21 September 1876, WUC.

[22] Schumpeter argued that oligopolistic industries can only achieve equilibrium with great difficulty and are more likely to inspire perpetual warfare and struggles for control that generate "social waste." See Joseph A. Schumpeter, *Capitalism, Socialism and Democracy* (New York: Harper & Brothers, 1942), 79–80.

[23] "Common Sense at Last," editorial, *The Telegrapher*, 7 January 1871, 156.

[24] "The Policy of the Competing Telegraph Companies," editorial, *The Telegrapher*, 29 April 1871, 281.

sense" combination of opposition firms proved short lived. Tariffs in areas of competition remained perilously low because Western Union imposed ruinous "starvation rates."[25] Publicly Orton denied predatory pricing, but he admitted that when competitors attacked with lower rates, Western Union responded with even deeper cuts.[26] Deprived of "fair remuneration for service," the united competitors burned through their cash and piled up debt.[27] Less than a year after joining the opposition cartel, bankruptcy forced the Bankers' & Brokers' to lease its property to Western Union.[28]

The Atlantic & Pacific (A&P) and Pacific & Atlantic (P&A) presented a more substantial threat.[29] To discourage its rivals from consolidating and to avert a costly rate war, Western Union offered a "cessation of hostilities" and resumption of "fair rates"[30] and managers considered buying one or both firms. However, the Union Pacific owned a controlling stake in the A&P and Orton feared the railroad would coerce Western Union into overpaying.[31] Here Western Union's connection with the Vanderbilt clique proved useful. The ascension of Horace Clark, Vanderbilt's son-in-law and a Western Union director, to the presidency of the Union Pacific promised to smooth relations between the Union Pacific and Western Union until the "time was ripe" for consolidation.[32]

The P&A presented a more attractive takeover target. Orton publicly denied he had any interest in buying the P&A, but privately he advised friendly investors that P&A stock was "a fair risk to take."[33] In fact, the fix was already in. Orton and Horace Clark had cultivated a party of P&A shareholders who exchanged their stock for shares in Western Union.[34] Andrew Carnegie, an empire builder to rival Vanderbilt, led the

---

[25] "Fifth Annual Report of the Pacific and Atlantic Telegraph Co.," 2 May 1871, WUC.

[26] *Argument of William Orton*, 31.

[27] "Sixth Annual Report of the Pacific and Atlantic Telegraph Co.," 7 May 1872, WUC, William Orton to D. C. Littlejohn, 22 December 1871, WUC.

[28] "Failure of the Combination of Telegraph Companies, 7 October 1871, *The Telegrapher*, 52.

[29] Atlantic and Pacific Telegraph Company Executive Committee Minutes, 22 March 1871, WUC.

[30] "Sixth Annual Report of the Pacific and Atlantic Telegraph Co.," 7 May 1872, WUC.

[31] William Orton to Anson Stager, 7 February 1872, WUC.

[32] William Orton to Anson Stager, 15 June 1872, WUC.

[33] William Orton to R. C. Clowry, 10 October 1872, WUC; William Orton to Luther L. Kauffman, 29 April 1873, WUC.

[34] Thurston testified in Congress that P&A shares were not on the general market. "Proceedings of the Committee on Appropriations," 28 January 1873, 42nd Congress, 3rd Session, Misc. Doc. No. 73, 6.

inside party. He cashed in his own shares along with those of Pennsylvania Railroad principals J. Edgar Thomson and Tom Scott. Nearly worthless P&A stock was thus "transmogrified" into valuable Western Union shares in a deal that a Carnegie biographer called "crony capitalism at its most basic."[35] By the spring of 1873, the conspirators controlled enough of the P&A to appoint new officers and turn the company over to Western Union, "demoralizing" the rest of the opposition and denying the A&P a valuable partner.[36] In short order Orton had contained or subverted all of Western Union's legitimate competition.

But the plan was almost immediately complicated by events. Orton's co-conspirator Horace Clark died suddenly, and Orton learned that the P&A's condition was far worse – in terms of both debt and the quality of its lines – than insiders had led him to believe. The P&A's officers had meanwhile skimmed $80,000 in commissions from the sale of their stock to Western Union, and infuriated shareholders excluded from the ring's bargain with Western Union demanded the same deal. Carnegie raised the stakes from cronyism to extortion, warning Orton that if Western Union did not extend the offer to exchange the stock of all of the P&A's directors at a still higher price, the P&A would scuttle the deal by watering its stock with a million new shares and cutting rates by 25 percent. Western Union's board of directors learned of the conspiracy and halted the exchange of P&A stock for Western Union shares. Orton called Carnegie's bluff by offering only a 5 percent lease for outstanding P&A shares. Carnegie folded, turning the P&A over to Western Union.[37]

Carnegie's stalling proved costly for P&A shareholders not on the "inside." The Panic of 1873 struck financial markets in September, and Orton decreed that since "the shares of the most reliable corporations in the country" were "so greatly depressed," his company would lease the P&A for 20 percent less than previously offered, with all rental payments going first to pay the P&A's substantial debt.[38] The P&A's officers appealed to

---

[35] See Chapter 4 for discussion of how Carnegie built the Pacific & Atlantic with virtually none of his own capital. See David Nasaw, *Andrew Carnegie* (New York: The Penguin Press, 2006), 107–8.

[36] William Orton to Anson Stager, 3 May 1873, WUC; Western Union Executive Committee Minutes, 10 September 1873, WUC.

[37] Andrew Carnegie to William Orton, 19 June 1873, WUC; William Orton to Andrew Carnegie, 7 August 1873, WUC; Andrew Carnegie to William Orton, 10 August 1873, WUC.

[38] William Orton to W. G. Johnston, 12 November 1873, WUC; Western Union Annual Report, 14 October 1874, WUC.

shareholders to assent to the deal, admitting that the company had never been profitable and stock sales had been used to pay dividends. Because debt liens would otherwise render their property worthless, shareholders approved the lease.[39] Orton closed the P&A's unprofitable offices, and though Western Union retained many of the company's operators, at least some were laid off,[40] including a relative of South Carolina's U.S. Senator John J. Patterson – an error that Orton promised the senator he would correct with the "first suitable vacancy."[41]

The P&A's angry minority shareholders could not stop the merger. The rules of corporate governance gave no power to minority shareholders, and the courts set a high bar for shareholder claims that their property had been fraudulently expropriated.[42] Their last hope was that the state of Pennsylvania, where the P&A had its charter, would intercede against the merger. The new Pennsylvania constitution, one of a wave of state constitutions rewritten after the Civil War, included an antimonopoly provision that prohibited any telegraph company from merging or leasing its property to any other telegraph company.[43] Orton dismissed this clause as an absurd overreaching of state power akin to a constitutional repeal of "the laws of gravitation." Children would keep falling down stairs and failing telegraph companies would keep consolidating – "constitution and laws to the contrary notwithstanding." Despite a shareholder suit intended to delay, the P&A lease took effect before the state ratified the new constitution, averting a test of the law.[44]

Even on such advantageous terms, the P&A was a "bad bargain" for Western Union. The P&A's lines were almost entirely redundant and were in poor condition besides. The true aim for taking in such a weak competitor was to deprive the more threatening Atlantic & Pacific of "feeders"

[39] William G. Johnston, "To the Stockholders of the Pacific and Atlantic Telegraph Company," 1 December 1873, WUC.
[40] William Orton to David McCargo, 25 July 1873, WUC.
[41] William Orton to Senator John J. Patterson, 26 February 1874, WUC.
[42] Naomi Lamoreaux and Jean-Laurent Rosenthal have written about the "plight of minority shareholders." Under corporate governance rules, minority shareholders could do little to prevent their property from expropriation; courts set a very high bar for minority shareholders to prove they had been defrauded. See Naomi R. Lamoreaux and Jean-Laurent Rosenthal, "Corporate Governance and the Plight of Minority Shareholders in the United States before the Great Depression," in *Corruption and Reform: Lessons from America's Economic History*, ed. Edward L. Glaeser and Claudia Goldin (Chicago: University of Chicago Press, 2006).
[43] Morton Keller, *Affairs of State: Public Life in Late Nineteenth Century America* (Cambridge, Mass.: Belknap Press of Harvard University Press, 1977), 111.
[44] William Orton to W. G. Johnston, 5 December 1873, WUC.

beyond its meager territory. "Cutting off" potential allies prevented the A&P from creating a cooperative rival to Western Union's own extensive network, forcing the A&P to provide only limited service or else invest in building lines in new territory.[45] Economic conditions increased Western Union's advantage over struggling rivals. The Panic of 1873 marked the beginning of a depression that lasted until 1879 – the longest in the nation's history to date. In what was called the "Great Depression" (until the greater depression of the 1930s), thirty thousand firms failed in the first four years.[46] For a firm like the Atlantic & Pacific Telegraph, raising funds for expansion by selling stock became significantly more challenging. The failure of the P&A and the hard bargain Western Union drove for its shareholders made speculative telegraph stock still less attractive. The A&P placed its stock on the market only by offering it at a cut-rate price of fifteen cents on the dollar.[47]

By late 1874 Western Union once again verged on a complete monopoly of the telegraph industry. In June the company restored its semi-annual dividend – suspended since 1870 – despite rising costs and the deepening depression. Cornelius Vanderbilt, who had denied that he owned Western Union, placed himself and his son William on the Board of Directors, and the Commodore joined the Executive Committee in place of his deceased son-in-law, Horace Clark. Western Union had become undeniably a Vanderbilt enterprise. At the same time, the Atlantic & Pacific Telegraph Company passed into the hands of another industrial titan, Vanderbilt rival Jay Gould. Just when competition in the telegraph industry appeared to be doomed, Gould pressed the contest in new directions in an "antimonopoly" crusade that forced Western Union to defend its business from a far more complex attack than traditional rate wars.

Western Union's strategy of isolating and starving competitors by cutting off their connections to other networks required the "Great Monopoly" to dominate more than simple person-to-person telegraphy. In growth areas

---

[45] William Orton to Edward Jay Allen, 7 March 1874, WUC; William Orton to Anson Stager, 27 November 1869, WUC; William Orton to Anson Stager, 20 August 1869, WUC; William Orton to J. D. Caton, 17 October 1872, WUC; Joseph Frazier Wall, *Andrew Carnegie* (New York: Oxford University Press, 1970), 221.

[46] Jerry Markham, *A Financial History of the United States: From Christopher Columbus to the Robber Barons, 1492–1900*, 2 vols., vol. 1 (Armonk, N.Y.: M. E. Sharpe, 200), 296.

[47] William Orton to Anson Stager, 13 December 1873, WUC.

such as ocean cables, commercial news, and urban telegraphy Western Union sought not only to increase receipts, but also to keep potential competitors from gaining a foothold. In the business warfare of the first great tech boom, the threat of competition came not only from direct contests between existing technologies, but also from new technologies that advanced and disrupted the state of the art.

Commercial ocean cables had been in almost continuous operation since the opening of the Atlantic cable in 1866. Western Union did not own ocean cables, opting instead to control the cables' domestic feeder lines. This arrangement gave Western Union a practical monopoly on European telegraphic communication until 1869, when the French Cable Company landed a new cable in Duxbury, Massachusetts.[48] In deference to its partner, the Anglo-American Cable Company, Western Union declined to contract with the competing French Company, which forged an agreement with the Franklin Company instead. Like all the ocean lines, the French Company's single gutta-percha cable was finicky and subject to regular outages. Its domestic connection to the rickety Franklin likewise appeared certain to fail on "the first wet day." The French government added an intolerable delay by detaining all messages for official review, cutting the cable's effective volume in half.[49] Despite the drawbacks of the French cable, Western Union managers feared a cable rate war loomed, threatening the share Western Union took for the domestic transfer of cable dispatches. Orton proposed a cartel, now the universal solution for protecting telegraph investments. The Anglo-American and French Cable Companies would cooperate, divide their receipts, and hand *all* domestic cable traffic to Western Union.[50] The "practical consolidation" of the two cable companies restored high cable rates and Western Union's exclusive connection to the cartel "exerted a depressing influence" on domestic competitors.[51]

Yet the cable business remained a risky enterprise. Frequent outages offset the benefits of high rates. The French cable developed a fault at its Eastern end that reduced transmissions to a trickle. When one English cable failed in late 1870, the steamer sent to grapple for the damaged cable accidentally snagged the working cable and broke it, leaving the

---

[48] F. L. P., "The General Telegraph Office of the Western Union Company in New-York City," *The Telegrapher*, 15 July 1867, 249.

[49] William Orton to Anson Stager, 26 July 1869, WUC.

[50] William Orton to Hugh Allan, 10 November 1869, WUC.

[51] William Orton to Z. G. Simmons, 16 February 1870, WUC; William Orton to Peter Cooper, 16 March 1870, WUC; William Orton to Anson Stager, 20 November 1869, WUC.

continents without any telegraph communication for several days.[52] Two of the three cables failed again in 1873, just as the French Cable Company completed a fourth cable that immediately joined the consortium.[53] No competitor emerged to challenge the Atlantic cable cartel until the United States Direct Cable Company opened its long-delayed "independent" line between England and America in the summer of 1875.[54]

The opening of the Direct Cable illustrated how the cable consortium, for all the advantages the monopoly gave Western Union, also posed a certain danger. Ocean telegraph cables were widely perceived as hallmarks of civilization's progress serving the greater good of humanity, fragile threads knitting together Old World and New. Western Union acknowledged the cable's special purpose in appealing to the federal government for a variety of tariff exemptions, arguing that governments had "a larger interest in the maintenance of telegraphic communication than that of the parties who provide the capital."[55] However, such appeals to the greater good cut both ways. Critics charged the cable monopoly with exacting excessive rates and linked Western Union to the extortion, though Western Union had no direct control over cable rates.[56]

The London-based Anglo-American Telegraph Company felt none of the pressure that the American press and elected officials applied to Western Union. Shortly after the competing Direct Cable opened in 1875 and forced cable rates down from fifty cents per word to twenty-five, a technical failure knocked it out of operation. The Anglo-American Telegraph Company seized the advantage by quadrupling its rate to one dollar per word, and the American press howled at the "extortionate and oppressive rate." The Chicago *Tribune* went so far as to suggest that British government officials, "skilled in telegraphic affairs," should nationalize the ocean wires as they had their domestic telegraph.[57] Commercial exchanges and boards of trade held meetings to plot against the cable monopoly, and Orton feared a backlash that would "inevitably hit and hurt Western Union."[58] Orton demanded the Anglo-American Telegraph Company offer a lower rate and consolidate with the Direct

[52] William Orton to Anson Stager et al, 30 November 1870, WUC.
[53] William Orton to Henry Weaver, 20 January 1873, WUC.
[54] William Orton to Henry Weaver, 16 July 1875, WUC.
[55] William Orton to W. A. Richardson, 21 April 1873, WUC.
[56] William Orton to Hamilton Fish, 21 June 1873, WUC.
[57] "First Fruits of the Cable Monopoly," *Chicago Daily Tribune*, 2 October 1875, 8.
[58] William Orton to Henry Weaver, 1 October 1875, WUC.

Cable, but the battle between the cable companies dragged on for two more years and only telegraph consolidation in the New World finally forced a settlement.

In addition to the Atlantic, Western Union also dominated telegraph access to Cuba and the West Indies, and through them to South America. The International Ocean Telegraph Company landed a Cuba cable in Key West and established an exclusive connection with Western Union. A message from Havana to London initially cost $50, gradually declining to below $20 by the 1870s.[59] The two companies maintained a loose alliance until 1871, when the International Ocean was rumored to be planning an Atlantic cable from Spain to North America, competing with the Anglo-American consortium. Orton warned that competition in the telegraph business "invariably" led to "loss to all"[60] and convinced managers of International Ocean to a join the monopoly and move their offices into the Western Union building. By 1873 Western Union had purchased enough International Ocean stock to control the company and negotiate a pooling arrangement with its chief competitor in the West Indies, the Cuba Submarine Telegraph Company. In place of potentially costly competition, Western Union had once again established an "intimate, cordial, and satisfactory" combination.[61]

The celerity of the telegraph was useful to any two parties exchanging messages, but market news was by far the most valuable and time-sensitive information on the wires. In the postal telegraph debate before Congress, Orton dismissed "social messaging" as an insignificant duty for the telegraph. "The fact is, the telegraph lives upon commerce," Orton claimed. "It is the nervous system of the commercial system."[62] This was not an idle boast.[63] U.S. Chief Justice Morris Remnick Waite noted in an 1877 opinion that the telegraph had "changed the habits of business, and become one of the necessities of commerce."[64] The "necessity"

---

[59] William Orton to W. T. Smith, 12 March 1869, WUC.
[60] William Orton to W. T. Smith, 20 May 1871, WUC.
[61] William Orton to Thomas Hughes, 26 November 1873, WUC.
[62] *Argument of William Orton*, 24.
[63] In a pair of articles, Richard DuBoff argued that the telegraph contributed significantly to the centralization of markets and encouraged the development of oligopolies. See Richard B. DuBoff, "The Telegraph and the Structure of Markets in the United States, 1845–1890," *Research in Economic History* 8 (1983); Richard B. DuBoff, "The Telegraph in Nineteenth-Century America: Technology and Monopoly," *Comparative Studies in Society and History* 26, no. 4 (1984).
[64] *Pensacola Tel. Co. v. Western Union Tel. Co.*, 96 U.S. 1 (1877), 9.

of commercial telegraphy was partially self-fulfilling – once one firm employed the telegraph, its competitors had little choice but to follow suit.[65] But the telegraph had a profound effect on business by centralizing markets and control, evenly distributing price data, and altering the work flow in several industries, particularly those in which time-sensitive information about assets and inventories had great value, such as meatpacking. The seven major commodities exchanges in the United States sprang up after the invention of the telegraph and were wholly dependent upon the technology.[66]

The new "necessity" of telegraph market news made such business very lucrative. The commercial market bore high rates because current market information had a value much greater than the tariffs charged. Commercial news also generated return traffic in the form of market orders.[67] The Associated Press (AP) leapt into the commercial news business, filling approximately half of its daily digest to the West with Eastern market reports and price quotations.[68] Western Union formed its own Commercial News Department for gathering and disseminating market reports, though this proved a risky endeavor. Routine errors in telegraph transmission could cost the recipient thousands of dollars if the mistake involved price data or a transaction order, and no legal standard protected the telegraph company from liability for the entire loss. In the absence of any "successful defense" against proven damages, Orton even contemplated shutting down the company's Commercial News Department.[69]

Commercial news generated such bumper profits that many independent sellers entered the business, only to find themselves muscled out by Western Union.[70] With exclusive access to the Atlantic cable, Western Union controlled the release of European market news in the United

[65] Alexander Field has pointed out that this created a paradox: "Beyond a certain point, the social value of more rapid access to data at a distance from exchanges may not have matched the private value individuals attached to it." See Alexander James Field, "The Magnetic Telegraph, Price and Quantity Data, and the New Management of Capital," *The Journal of Economic History* 52, no. 2 (1992): 404.
[66] DuBoff, "Technology and Monopoly," 574; Field, 410.
[67] Gregory J. Downey, *Telegraph Messenger Boys: Labor, Communication and Technology, 1850–1950* (New York: Routledge, 2002), 85.
[68] Menahem Blondheim, *News over the Wires: The Telegraph and the Flow of Public Information in America, 1844–1897* (Cambridge, Mass.: Harvard University Press, 1994), 173.
[69] William Orton to John Van Horne, 26 November 1869, WUC.
[70] James D. Reid, *The Telegraph in America: Its Founders, Promoters, and Noted Men*, 1st ed. (New York: Derby Brothers, 1879), 610.

States. As a matter of protocol, the company began transmitting to all its commercial subscribers in the United States one or two minutes *before* releasing the same information in New York. Any potential competitor hoping to sell European market news in Chicago would thus receive it in New York at about the same time that Western Union customers were already receiving it in Chicago. Orton bragged that with such a system, no one could "expect to compete successfully."[71] Though critics accused Western Union of conspiring to "keep back" competing commercial dispatches, there was no conspiracy – Western Union's dispatch, sent first and with priority, won the race to market every time.

Defeated competitors railed against the commercial news monopoly, but Western Union's system probably reduced fraud. Before Western Union drove private providers out of business, its lines carried dozens of redundant reports filed by private correspondents. Because the value of reports depended upon their timeliness, correspondents sought to place their reports first at all costs. This contest created another kind of market: agents competed to bribe or conspire with operators "to put their messages ahead, and thus give one an advantage over another." Managers found such employee corruption exceedingly difficult to curtail. The possibilities for selling privileged information seemed endless: accepting bribes to send dispatches in an order favorable to a particular party, selling private commercial reports to third parties, various types of "eavesdropping," bribing delivery boys, even transmitting deliberately bogus reports. Although managers diligently investigated accusations and employed Allan Pinkerton and his detectives on several cases, enforcement could not solve the problem. Instead, the Commercial News Department eliminated the incentive to steal by replacing private reports with a monopoly Western Union report. This great "bugbear," as Orton insisted, instead of "endangering the public interests," was really "a means for their protection."[72]

Competing with Western Union in commercial news by conventional means was impossible, so the great value of commercial news encouraged competitors to innovate and challenge the monopoly indirectly with new technology. In 1867, the Gold & Stock Telegraph Company began transmitting stock quotations and gold prices from the New York Stock Exchange and the Gold Exchange. The Gold & Stock had no capacity to reach beyond New York, but its intraurban business thrived, and it

---

[71] William Orton to Anson Stager, 2 April 1868, WUC.
[72] *Argument of William Orton*, 13–14.

controlled several patents on an efficient "printing" telegraph, better known as a "stock ticker." The ticker used a pair of wheels – one for abbreviated names and one for prices – to print quotes on a spooled tape. Stock and gold prices were automatically available in any office in New York that purchased a subscription. By 1871 Gold & Stock had more than seven hundred subscribers and threatened to expand its business to other commercial centers, or worse, to join the arsenal of an opposition company.[73]

Orton believed that the transmission of stock and gold prices by automatic instruments was potentially the most lucrative franchise in all telegraphy.[74] In 1870, he forged a tentative agreement with the Gold & Stock to assist in its expansion to Chicago, where businessmen clamored for automatic quotations. He hoped to control Gold & Stock and pool its patents with Western Union's without consolidating the two companies. If the government implemented one of the postal telegraph schemes, Western Union could stay in the business of "private telegraphing" for manufacturers, counting rooms, offices, and exchanges.[75] The potential profitability of a joint monopoly on price tickers, combined with Western Union's interurban reach, led Gold & Stock's directors to sell enough stock to give Western Union control of their company. Gold & Stock continued transmitting stock quotations and took over the provision of private telegraph lines from Western Union. After a decade of partial ownership, Western Union absorbed Gold & Stock in 1881 with a lease that rewarded Gold & Stock's compliant shareholders just as its patents – its principal asset – began to expire.[76]

Western Union also developed interests in intraurban "automatic" telegraphy. The technology for sending and receiving messages without the aid of an operator was in its infancy, but automatic systems requiring only limited or one-way communication came into use in the 1870s in police and fire alarms and messenger call systems. "Call boxes" installed anywhere in a city could transmit simple, automated messages to a central office, identifying by code the location from which the message had been sent and the service required by the sender. For example, a messenger boy could be dispatched to the site of a call box to pick up a message

---

[73] Joel A. Tarr, "The City and the Telegraph: Urban Telecommunications in the Pre-Telephone Era," *Journal of Urban History* 14, no. 1 (1987): 44; Reid, *The Telegraph in America*, 611.
[74] William Orton to Anson Stager, 12 November 1870, WUC.
[75] William Orton to Anson Stager, 24 January 1871, WUC.
[76] Norvin Green to George W. Nash, 8 December 1881, WUC.

for transfer to the telegraph office. Call boxes did not allow discourse between sender and recipient, but they had great commercial promise for simple purposes. The entrepreneurs who founded the Gold & Stock Company formed the American District Telegraph and opened a call box system in New York in 1872. Western Union affiliated with A.D.T. for its messenger service, and the business grew to 4,500 subscribers by 1878. By 1885, district messenger companies in New York, including both A.D.T. and its competitors, had nearly 30,000 subscribers.[77]

No part of Western Union's business demanded more diligent protection from competition than railroad telegraphy. Railroad telegraph lines were both a logistical necessity and a bulwark against rivals. Railroad companies constructed and maintained telegraph lines along their rights-of-way, provided Western Union with free office space and, at thousands of points with low message volume, employed station agents who doubled as telegraph operators. By the 1880s, 90 percent of Western Union's lines were on railroad routes, and the railroads maintained 10,000 telegraph offices in exchange for free service on Western Union's network. Railroad relationships created the possibility for ubiquity at a reasonable price – Western Union paid salaries and rent at fewer than a quarter of its offices.[78]

Even more important than sharing costs, railroad partnerships blocked competitors from accessing interurban rights-of-way. Western Union usually required railroads to agree to exclusive contracts, an undisguised method of monopolizing important routes. However, Orton feared that the exclusive clause could not stand up against state laws – whenever a state authorized a general law for condemning railroad rights-of-way to encourage competition, Western Union's exclusive was likely doomed. By 1874, a few states had enacted such laws, though Orton believed "little benefit" had accrued to competitors. In a few cases, Orton planned to fill the side of the track opposite Western Union's lines with extra short lines that would block condemnation by a competitor. Competitors challenged the legality of Western Union's "closed" railroad contracts. Though the Telegraph Act of 1866 gave any telegraph company the right to build on any "post road," the meaning of that clause was not clearly defined

---

[77] James D. Reid, *The Telegraph in America: Its Founders, Promoters, and Noted Men* (New York: Arno Press, 1974), 635. Tarr, "Urban Telegraph," 50.
[78] James D. Reid, *The Telegraph in America and Morse Memorial*, 2d ed. (New York: John Polhemus, 1884), 748.

until federal postal legislation in 1872 defined "all railways and *parts* of railways" as post roads.[79] Nonetheless, declaring railroad rights-of-way to be post roads did not determine whether the right of telegraph companies to use post roads required the railroads' consent – a subject the Act did not address.[80]

Orton hoped that the Telegraph Act of 1866 could work to Western Union's advantage by giving the company access to every railroad in the country without consent or payment, forever eliminating "the obligation" to pay "an enormous sum of free telegraphing" in exchange for rights-of-way.[81] Western Union could instead maintain its competitive advantage by forging less expensive exclusive transportation and construction agreements with the railroads.[82] Rather than require exclusive access to the right-of-way, Western Union demanded the exclusive right to occupy railroad depots and receive special rates for transportation of poles, wires, and other materials. The simplest and least expensive method for constructing a durable telegraph line of cedar poles was for the railroad to run a special slow train and toss the poles from a freight car at marked positions. Keeping competitors off the trains effectively precluded them from constructing lines even if they had a right-of-way. To further discourage railroad companies from cooperating with the opposition, Western Union often inserted an extra clause allowing it to cease providing free telegraph service to the railroad once a competitor was established on the line.[83]

Yet exclusive construction agreements could not prevent the railroad companies themselves from trying to enter the telegraph business, a grave competitive risk. As early as the 1850s, Western Union managers feared that railroads could operate their own telegraph lines, but the relatively limited extent of most roads in the 1870s kept individual railroads from performing extensive commercial telegraph service.[84] Railroads were

---

[79] Statutes at Large, 17 Stat. 308, sect. 201; Revised Statues, sect. 3694. Approved June 8, 1872. Emphasis added.

[80] Anonymous note, *Michigan Law Review* 3, no. 6 (April 1905), 467–8.

[81] William Orton to U. H. Painter, 26 January 1872, WUC.

[82] The consent-free right-of-way remained a sort of Holy Grail for Western Union, but it would never be attained. In the 1905 decision *Western Union Co. v. Pennsylvania Railroad Co.* (25 Sup. Ct. Rep 133) the court determined finally that telegraph companies had no right to operate on railroads without their consent, tilting the balance of power in the relationship between railroads and telegraphs strongly in favor of railroads.

[83] William Orton to H. P. Dwight, 23 February 1874, WUC.

[84] Hiram Sibley to John Dean Caton, 8 January 1860, Caton Papers; Chandler, *The Visible Hand*, Chapter 5.

also restricted by the legal principle of "ultra vires," which limited corporations to perform only the business explicitly authorized by corporate charter – a limitation that gradually disappeared by the end of the nineteenth century.[85] Cornelius Vanderbilt's apparent interest in Western Union invited other railroad leaders to try to forge relationships with competing telegraph firms or challenge *ultra vires* restrictions by launching their own telegraph operations and ousting Western Union from their roads.

One such threat came from John W. Garrett, the president of the Baltimore & Ohio Railroad (B&O). The B&O built a telegraph line in the 1850s, and leased it to the American Telegraph Company, which merged with Western Union. Twenty years later a morass of obsolete contracts created more than a little ambiguity about who owned the line.[86] A rumor in 1873 that the B&O intended to allow another telegraph company to string wires on poles claimed by Western Union knocked 4 percent off Western Union's stock price overnight.[87] Orton convinced Garrett to reject the overtures from opposition companies seeking to build on the B&O, but the B&O's relationship with Western Union remained strained. Orton claimed the B&O abused the free service that Western Union performed by contract and chided B&O managers for sending long, unabbreviated telegrams. "In some instances the interests of your Company would have been better promoted by using the mails," Orton insisted.[88] Despite repeated attempts to renegotiate the ambiguous contracts, Orton could not coax Garrett to the table. In 1875 Garrett claimed the telegraph company's "derelictions of duty" nullified B&O's obligations, once again threatening to break with Western Union and strike a deal with the opposition.[89]

Trouble for Western Union also brewed on the Pacific railroads. The Congressional acts that chartered the Union Pacific and Central Pacific obligated them to build telegraph lines or contract with a telegraph company. In 1869 Union Pacific sold its telegraph line to the Atlantic & Pacific Telegraph in exchange for 24,000 nearly worthless A&P shares. The A&P soon after made a service contract with Central Pacific as well.[90] Western

[85] Morton J. Horwitz, *The Transformation of American Law, 1870–1960: The Crisis of Legal Orthodoxy* (New York: Oxford University Press, 1992), 77–8.
[86] William Orton to Cornelius Vanderbilt, 19 November 1875, WUC.
[87] William Orton to J. B. Stearns, 2 December 1874, WUC.
[88] William Orton to John W. Garrett, 13 December 1873, WUC.
[89] William Orton to Anson Stager, 30 November 1875, WUC.
[90] Julius Grodinsky, *Jay Gould, His Business Career, 1867–1892* (Philadelphia: University of Pennsylvania Press, 1957), 149.

Union had built its own lines on the Pacific railroads' rights-of-way and depended upon railroad transportation to maintain them. The Central Pacific instituted a punitive freight rate for transporting telegraph poles, charging two or three times the normal rate for sawed scantling of the same size and weight. Union Pacific charged Western Union's repairmen 50 percent more per more mile than other passengers.[91]

Orton believed the railroads intended to force a more favorable arrangement on Western Union.[92] However, it soon became apparent that a more sophisticated, indirect strategy was at work, one that proved much more dangerous to Western Union than punitive rates. That strategy was the work of Jay Gould. As it became evident that Gould had taken a controlling interest in the A&P, the possibility emerged that Gould, the most aggressive financier in an age dominated by them, intended to undermine Western Union's strategic partnership with the railroads in a back door raid on Western Union's telegraph monopoly.

From the newspapers that besmirched him as the most hated man in America to generations of historians who characterized him as the "Mephistopheles of Wall Street," Jay Gould has never suffered from a want of colorful description. Joseph Pulitzer described him as "one of the most sinister figures that have ever flitted bat-like across the vision of the American people." Other contemporaries condemned him as treacherous, false, impudent, "a despicable worm," and in Henry Adams's portrayal, "small and slight in person, dark, sallow, reticent and stealthy, with a trace of Jewish origin."[93] Gustavus Myers' 1909 *History of the Great American Fortunes* described Gould as "a pitiless human carnivore, glutting on the blood of his numberless victims; a gambler destitute of the usual gambler's code of fairness in abiding by the rules; an incarnate fiend of a Machiavelli." (Though in fairness, Myers added, Gould differed in degree but not in kind from the thieving Vanderbilt.)[94] A more recent biographer has tried to rescue Gould from the sea of calumny in which history has drowned him, suggesting that Gould was

---

[91] William Orton to Abram S. Hewitt, 18 July 1876, WUC.

[92] William Orton to Anson Stager, 14 July 1870, WUC; William Orton to Anson Stager, 8 November 1872, WUC.

[93] These quotes were compiled in Maury Klein, "In Search of Jay Gould," *Business History Review* 52, no. 2 (1978): 167–8. Klein has pointed out that anti-Semitic slurs were often attached to Gould, who was not Jewish.

[94] Gustavus Myers, *History of the Great American Fortunes*, III vols., vol. III (Chicago: Charles H. Kerr & Company, 1909), 286–7.

not a heartless demon, but a "man ahead of his time" who won the enmity of his rivals by beating them at their own game, while enjoying the intense loyalty of steadfast friends and partners.[95] The truth may split the difference.

Gould's reputation as a business titan blossomed in a series of high-profile contests. In 1868 Cornelius Vanderbilt clashed with Gould in a battle to control the Erie Railroad, which threatened Vanderbilt's New York Central. Gould won the fight, which required not only manipulation of the company's stock price, but also extensive litigation, Gould's flight to New Jersey to evade contempt charges, and, supposedly, Gould's purchase of the New York state legislature with half a million dollars carried to Albany in a suitcase.[96] Vanderbilt allegedly pronounced that the "Erie war" taught him "that it never pays to kick a skunk."[97]

By 1870, Gould had cemented his standing as a Wall Street renegade.[98] He also revealed a penchant for manipulating the institutions most likely to spawn opposition. He put William Marcy Tweed, the boss of New York's Tammany Hall political machine, on the Erie board of directors in exchange for favors from Tammany, and he "spent freely" to put friendly candidates into office.[99] He was dogged by rumors that he tried to control the press. In 1879 he bought the New York *World* from another railroad mogul, Tom Scott.[100] He also briefly controlled the New York *Tribune,* and popular belief held that editor Whitlaw Reid and his staff were nothing but "stool-pigeons" for Gould.[101] Gould never took direct editorial

---

[95] Maury Klein, "Jay Gould: A Revisionist Interpretation," *Business and Economic History* 15(1986): 67. In Klein's assessment of the terrible failures of historians to adequately assess Gould's legacy, he gives Josephson the most credit for obscuring the real Jay Gould, and Julius Grodinsky wins some praise for being the only historian to examine Gould's business career in a remotely objective way. See Grodinsky, *Jay Gould, His Business Career, 1867–1892.*

[96] Estimates of Gould's bribes range from $300,000 to $1 million. Even Klein has only a half-hearted defense of Gould. "If the rumors that flew and the stories told about the amounts exchanged are even half true, they are enough to satisfy any connoisseur of avarice," he writes. See Maury Klein, *The Life and Legend of Jay Gould* (Baltimore: Johns Hopkins University Press, 1986), 84.

[97] Josephson, *The Robber Barons; the Great American Capitalists, 1861–1901,* 133.

[98] Klein, *The Life and Legend of Jay Gould,* 128–9.

[99] Ibid., 97.

[100] Frank Luther Mott, *American Journalism: A History of the Newspapers in the United States through 250 Years, 1690–1940,* II vols., vol. II (New York: The Macmillan Company, 1941), 434.

[101] "The New York Tribune: A Page of Secret History Made Public by the New York Sun," 12 January 1876, *Chicago Tribune,* 7. Further corroborating details are offered by William Croffut in William A. Croffut, *An American Procession, 1866–1914, a Personal*

control of the *Tribune*, but attacks on him suspiciously disappeared from its pages.[102]

By the early 1870s, Gould had been ousted from the Erie Railroad – he exited with great profits – and had begun to develop new interests in other roads. The Union Pacific offered a prime target, with a factionalized ownership – including Vanderbilt and his partners – mired in litigation over construction contracts.[103] When the Union Pacific fell into a mortal rate war with the Pacific Mail steamship company and bankruptcy threatened the railroad, Gould swooped in, buying a large stake in Union Pacific and a controlling interest in the Pacific Mail Company. He ended the competition, raised rates, restored the Union Pacific's credit, and paid robust dividends. With his powerful influence in the Union Pacific, Gould realized he could invade the telegraph industry through the railroad's struggling minion, the Atlantic & Pacific Telegraph Company. Gould created a syndicate with members of the Union Pacific board and bought the railroad's A&P shares. Then he set out on a "vigorously aggressive" course, canceling the Union Pacific's contracts with Western Union and negotiating agreements with the Franklin Telegraph Company and the newly formed Direct Cable Company to challenge Western Union's dominance of transatlantic messages.[104]

In a bold step to bring the weak A&P into competition with Western Union, Gould also acquired one of Western Union's most senior managers, General Thomas T. Eckert. Eckert had served as Superintendent of the Military Telegraphs during the war, earning a brevet general's commission, an appointment as Assistant Secretary of War, and the enmity of Anson Stager, his superior officer and rival.[105] After the war, Stager headed Western Union's Central Division and became one of Orton's most trusted advisors; Eckert became Superintendent of the Eastern Division. Colleagues alternately lauded Eckert for his strength and self-reliance and criticized him as stubborn and autocratic – Orton tactfully described him as a "strict disciplinarian."[106]

Chronicle of Famous Men (Freeport, N.Y.: Books for Libraries Press, 1931; reprint, 1968), 198.

[102] Klein, *The Life and Legend of Jay Gould*, 135.

[103] Ibid., 138.

[104] Grodinsky, *Jay Gould, His Business Career, 1867–1892*, 148–9; Reid, *The Telegraph in America*, 580.

[105] Norvin Green to William Gross, 18 March 1868, Gross Papers.

[106] William Orton to David M. Stone, 26 July 1869, WUC; Reid, *The Telegraph in America*, 582.

Gould convinced Eckert to become the A&P's new president, winning Eckert's confidence by his "directness and frankness." Eckert later recalled that Gould had a great "breadth of view" of the telegraphy industry despite the fact that the subject was "almost entirely new" to him.[107] Gould also promised Eckert $15,000 per year – the same as Orton's salary at Western Union – and two thousand shares of A&P stock.[108] Eckert's resignation took Orton by surprise, and he charged Eckert with "secretly carrying on negotiations with [Western Union's] enemies."[109] The extent of Eckert's treachery, though, would likely have shocked even Orton. He and Gould had been working together for weeks, planning a devastating raid on two of Western Union's most precious competitive assets.

The demand for greater speed and lower costs spurred innovation in telegraph technology. Limited economies of scale in telegraph operations made even incremental improvements in efficiency and capacity especially valuable. To decrease plant and labor costs through advances in the state of the telegraphic art, Orton created a permanent research division headed by telegraph engineering expert George Prescott.[110] Orton never exhibited much faith in technological panaceas, however, believing instead that the surest way to improve speed and efficiency was to put up additional lines when existing lines grew crowded, hire the best operators to work them, and spell operators when they tired.

Orton's dim assessment of many technological "advances" was colored by his focus on the practical relationship between technology and profit. Any advance that did not contribute to the bottom line was not an advance at all. When Orton grew frustrated with the poor performance of intraurban wires used to transfer messages from Western Union's headquarters to other points in New York City, he considered abandoning the telegraph and relying entirely on messenger boys.[111] He criticized a proposed system of pneumatic tubes to connect Western Union's

---

[107] Norvin Green to H. P. Dwight, 29 March 1892, WUC; Thomas T. Eckert to Helen Gould Shepard, 16 May 1893, Helen Gould Shepard Papers.

[108] Meeting of the Western Union Executive Committee, 19 June 1879, WUC; Atlantic and Pacific Telegraph Co. Executive Committee Meeting, 26 November 1877, WUC. With the A&P in a precarious condition through much of Eckert's tenure, Eckert voluntarily drew only a small portion of his promised salary.

[109] William Orton to T. T. Eckert, 12 January 1875, WUC.

[110] Paul Israel, *From Machine Shop to Industrial Laboratory: Telegraphy and the Changing Context of American Invention, 1830–1920* (Baltimore: Johns Hopkins University Press, 1992), 129.

[111] William Orton to T. T. Eckert, 25 October 1872, WUC.

Chicago office to the Board of Trade, suggesting instead a system used at one time to communicate between Western Union's New York office and the AP: a cord suspended over the street between the two offices, with a wheel and a hand crank and two tin cans to ferry messages. The cord-and-can method was quick, reliable, and, Orton boasted, cost "very much less than the tube."[112] After the pneumatic tubes proved a "grand success" in Chicago and later in an extensive network in New York, Orton noted that their value was not simply the fast movement of messages, but "the novelty and notoriety" of the system, which he stubbornly insisted might still be less "economical and advantageous" than something simpler.[113]

Two areas of telegraph improvement promised much more than novelty and were of such great potential value that virtually every telegraph firm sought their perfection: automatic and multiplex telegraphy. For decades most of the innovation in telegraphy improved wires, insulators and batteries in incremental advances that competitors could not use to overcome Western Union's advantage of a national network of largely exclusive railroad lines.[114] However, automatic and multiplex telegraphy promised such great reductions in labor and increases in line capacity that a firm with such technology would threaten even giant Western Union. The celebrated potential of these advances, however, ran far ahead of their practical value.

The technology for the ideal form of "automatic telegraph" – one that could both send and receive messages without a skilled operator – did not emerge until the early twentieth century. The state of the art in the 1870s generally required some form of preparation or conversion of messages into a medium that could be "read" and reproduced by the instrument. As the telegraph promised "the annihilation of time" entirely, Western Union aimed for "instant and constant communication." Any automatic system that interposed delays for translation was a "change for the worse."[115] Orton believed that automatic telegraphy would always require special coding or other intermediate, inefficient steps and would never "run itself."[116]

[112] William Orton to Anson Stager, 18 February 1869, WUC.
[113] Orton to Stager, 16 November 1869, WUC.
[114] Paul Israel has pointed out, however, that in intraurban telegraphy, where the scale was much smaller, technological advances could create a substantial advantage for attracting subscribers. See Israel, *From Machine Shop to Industrial Laboratory*, 121–2.
[115] Western Union Annual Report, 13 July 1869, WUC.
[116] William Orton to J. D. Reid, 21 September 1869, WUC.

Nonetheless, the potential blockbuster value of automatic telegraphy drove a race to overcome the technical hurdles. An automatic telegraph could reduce or eliminate the need for highly skilled operators and consequently diminish labor costs, which generally amounted to more than half the cost per message, while increasing the number of words transmitted per minute, an effective increase of line capacity. In a few specific circumstances – reporting price data in the gold and stock ticker business, or sending messages from points where business was too small to support a skilled operator – the limited capabilities of automatic telegraphs could be overlooked. Orton agreed to pay $20,000 for the patent for the Phelps printing telegraph,[117] which could "be worked by any person of ordinary intelligence" eliminating the need for "employing educated operators." Orton ordered several Phelps printers installed at the Chicago office in a front room "near the windows" to attract the attention of passers-by.[118] Orton also considered buying the patent for the Wheatstone automatic telegraph, which had been much improved since its introduction in 1858 and was widely used in England.[119] Orton thought the Wheatstone of no "actual use" to Western Union, but he feared competitors might use it to attract capital from a credulous public and to use the funds to compete with Western Union in the "ordinary way."[120]

"Multiplex" telegraphy was of more immediate interest. Multiplexing allowed more than one message to be sent on a single wire at the same time, thus increasing existing capacity and eliminating the need to construct and maintain additional wires. Since the 1850s, inventors had patented a variety of ineffective multiplex devices, but none compared to the prototype developed by J. B. Stearns, the president of the Franklin Telegraph Company, in 1868. After directors of the failing Franklin declined to support Stearns' experiments and dismissed him from office,[121] Stearns took his "Duplex" to Western Union. The usually skeptical Orton greeted the Duplex as "the most important invention" since the Morse Telegraph.[122] Stearns' Duplex could carry two messages in opposite directions simultaneously on a standard wire, potentially doubling carrying capacity per line. Orton told Stearns he would "cheerfully give a million dollars" for

[117] Israel, *From Machine Shop to Industrial Laboratory*, 126.
[118] Orton to Stager, 8 October 1870, WUC.
[119] George B. Prescott, *Electricity and the Electric Telegraph*, 8th ed., 2 vols., vol. 2 (New York: D. Appleton and Company, 1892), 702.
[120] William Orton to Henry Weaver, 12 September 1872, WUC.
[121] Prescott, *Electricity and the Electric Telegraph*, 768–92.
[122] William Orton to Nathan C. Ely, 27 November 1872, WUC.

the Duplex, and even the $50,000 Western Union ultimately paid was an impressive sum.[123] Stearns worked with Western Union to test and improve the Duplex, and by 1873 Western Union was installing them as fast as they could be produced.

Merely controlling the Stearns Duplex, however, did not guarantee a competitive advantage. If there was one lesson that the first generation of telegraph entrepreneurs learned well, it was that patenting a device did not stop competitors from seeking to patent an alternate device to achieve the same result. Western Union's managers recognized that leading in innovation required retaining the top legal talent, and if possible, owning the inventors, rather than just the inventions.[124] Orton feared that Stearns' attorneys had insufficiently considered "shutting out competition" when they wrote the Duplex patent application, leaving it open to easy evasion. Orton proposed a safeguard: Western Union would employ an electrician to invent and patent "as many processes as possible for doing all or any part of the work" covered by the Stearns patent.[125]

For this job, Orton hired a former telegraph operator whom he praised as "probably the best electro-mechanician in the country": Thomas Alva Edison.[126] While employed as an operator, Edison had experimented in the machine shop with improvements to the telegraph. In 1869, he formed a partnership with two editors of *The Telegrapher*, Frank Pope and James Ashley. In an early exhibit of what became a notorious habit for spreading his talents more broadly than his patrons wished, he simultaneously collaborated with the Gold & Stock Company. The disappointed Pope and Ashley claimed Edison was "utterly unreliable." Orton later explained that Edison's disloyalty and disregard for agreements suggested he had "a vacuum where his conscience ought to be."[127] Orton met Edison in early 1871, when managers of the Gold & Stock Company introduced him to their "ingenious friend" whose inventions and talent were significant assets in negotiations for control of the Gold & Stock.[128] While

[123] Orton to Stearns, 24 September 1873, WUC, Christopher Beauchamp, "The Telephone Patents: Intellectual Property, Business and the Law in the United States and Britain, 1876–1900" (University of Cambridge, 2007), 22.

[124] Israel, *From Machine Shop to Industrial Laboratory*, 122.

[125] William Orton to J. B. Stearns, 2 December 1874, WUC.

[126] Paul Israel, *Edison: A Life of Invention* (New York: John Wiley, 1998), 49.

[127] Ibid., 66.

[128] Tracy R. Edson to William Orton, 13 January 1871, in Thomas A. Edison, *The Papers of Thomas A. Edison*, ed. Reese V. Jenkins, 5 vols., vol. 1 (Baltimore: The Johns Hopkins University Press, 1989), 237; Israel, *Edison*, 62–3.

Edison began to ply his talents on behalf of Western Union, he simultaneously maintained a complex arrangement with George Harrington, a former ambassador and government official who speculated in automatic telegraphy. Harrington formed a partnership with Edison in 1871 and set up a shop for him in Newark, where Edison spent $40,000 of Harrington's money.[129] Harrington and several other investors intended Edison's inventions to be employed in their new venture, the Automatic Telegraph Company. The brilliant Edison concurrently served two masters: the Gold & Stock, a Western Union subsidiary, and the Automatic, its competitor.

In 1873, Edison accepted Orton's charge to invent patentable improvements to the Stearns Duplex. He signed a contract with Western Union's chief electrician, George Prescott, making them "joint inventors" on new duplex patents.[130] Edison promised he could develop "bushels" of duplex designs, and the seventeen he delivered included duplexes that could send two simultaneous messages in opposite directions, and diplexes that could send two simultaneous messages in one direction.[131] Edison then combined his duplex and diplex designs to create the Quadruplex, which could send four concurrent messages on a single wire. Edison was "almost wild" about the promise of the Quadruplex, which he celebrated as even greater than his advances in automatic telegraphy.[132] Orton praised the Quadruplex as "more wonderful than the Duplex" in an announcement to stockholders of "pending" negotiations for Edison's patents.[133] By the end of 1874, Western Union was on the verge of launching the Quadruplex on its lines, when Gould and Eckert's raid on Edison and the multiplex telegraph began.

Edison had managed his spending ineptly, and the depression in the wake of the Panic of 1873 squeezed him as his income fell and the cost of operating his shop rose. To keep his shop open, he gave up his house and moved his family into an apartment. In December 1874 his debts to Harrington came due.[134] "I need 10, 9, 8, 7, 6, 5, 4, 3, or 2,000 dollars – any one you

---

[129] Complaint in the case of Atlantic and Pacific Telegraph Co. against George B. Prescott, The Western Union Telegraph Company, Lemuel W. Serrell, and Thomas Edison, WUC.

[130] Thomas A. Edison, *The Papers of Thomas A. Edison*, ed. Reese V. Jenkins, 5 vols., vol. 2 (Baltimore: The Johns Hopkins University Press, 1991), 233.

[131] Israel, *Edison*, 79–80.

[132] William Orton to Anson Stager, 15 December 1874, WUC.

[133] Western Union Annual Report, 14 October 1874, WUC.

[134] Israel, *Edison*, 99–101.

would like to advance," he wrote to Orton.[135] Orton gave Edison $5,000, which Edison later claimed was for an order of twenty Quadruplex instruments but Orton insisted was an advance on the patent for the Quadruplex, which Edison "invented expressly for Western Union."[136] On Christmas day, Edison and Prescott sent a memorandum to Orton proposing to sell the design to Western Union for $25,000 plus monthly royalties per instrument.[137]

While working on the Quadruplex, Edison had continued his automatic telegraphy experiments for Harrington, his partner J. C. Reiff, and the Automatic Telegraph Company. The Automatic Company was built on possibilities – *if* the company could negotiate railroad agreements and *if* Edison's automatic telegraph could be effectively deployed, it would be a formidable rival to Western Union. The only certainty about the Automatic was that it flirted with insolvency. Reiff conspired to arrange a secret sale of his company to Western Union in July 1874, but Orton rejected the overture. "I have no time to plan subterfuges nor to practice finesse," he scolded Reiff.[138] However, subterfuges and finesse were the particular strengths of Jay Gould, and in the plight of the Automatic he found an opening against Western Union.

In late December 1874, Orton left on a trip to Chicago without an agreement with Edison in place, undoubtedly intending to conclude negotiations when he returned, evidently not appreciating the financial desperation of Thomas Edison, the audacity of Jay Gould, and the perfidy of Thomas Eckert. Orton left Eckert to manage Edison, unaware that Eckert had already allied with Gould. Edison later admitted under oath that Eckert brought Gould to his Newark lab for demonstrations of the automatic and Quadruplex systems.[139] Duly impressed, Gould opened negotiations with Reiff, Harrington, and Eckert.

On the night of December 30, they struck a deal: Gould would purchase the Automatic Company – including Edison's automatic patents – for

[135] Edison to Orton, 7 December 1874 in Edison, *The Papers of Thomas A. Edison*, 360.
[136] Edison, Deposition in the case of Atlantic and Pacific Telegraph Co. against George B. Prescott, The Western Union Telegraph Company, Lemuel W. Serrell, and Thomas Edison, WUC. Orton's addition was in the deposition's margin in Orton's handwriting.
[137] Memorandum for William Orton, 25 December 1874 in Edison, *The Papers of Thomas A. Edison*, 366.
[138] Defendant's Exhibits 33a and 33d, in the case of Atlantic and Pacific Telegraph Co. against George B. Prescott, The Western Union Telegraph Company, Lemuel W. Serrell, and Thomas Edison, WUC.
[139] Klein, *The Life and Legend of Jay Gould*, 200.

the A&P, Edison would become the A&P's electrician, and Eckert would become the A&P's president. The arrangement hinged upon Reiff's assurances that Edison's earlier contract with Harrington superseded his agreement with Western Union. Late that night, Eckert brought Edison to Gould's house on Fifth Avenue. Edison showed Gould his agreement with Western Union's Prescott and a receipt for the $5,000 advance Orton had given him. Gould paid them no heed and offered Edison $30,000 for four patents he would soon file, handing him a $10,000 check on the spot.[140] Fully aware of Western Union's claim, Gould ordered his Washington lobbyist to file Edison's patents immediately, before Western Union's managers "had an idea of what was going on."[141]

When Orton learned of Eckert's betrayal, he countered Gould's capture of the Quadruplex with a legal assault against the A&P. Republican powerbroker Roscoe Conkling represented Western Union in court, while Gould hired the notorious trial lawyer Ben Butler, a Radical Republican Congressman who had been a leader in the impeachment of Andrew Johnson. Western Union won the first battles of the legal war, preventing the deployment of the Quadruplex on A&P lines.[142] This rendered Edison's automatic telegraph useless, since it relied on the Quadruplex. While Edison busily attempted to invent an improved, noninfringing Quadruplex, Orton publicly proclaimed that the A&P's threat to compete with Western Union was akin to an attempt to bore a two-inch hole with a gimlet – doomed from the start. Edison promised Gould that his inventions would prove "that it makes a great difference who has the handling of the gimlet."[143] Boasts aside, however, Edison apparently decided that telegraph warfare held no interest for him and declined the job of head electrician at the A&P to return to full-time inventing.[144] It is a testament to Edison's value that by the fall of 1875, less than a year after his alleged treachery, Orton had lured him back to work at Western Union.[145]

Eckert assumed the presidency of the A&P, joined by three of his top aides from Western Union. He found the lines of the unprofitable A&P in a "very inefficient condition." Despite Western Union's deep pockets and

---

[140] Plaintiffs Testimony in Chief, in the case of Atlantic and Pacific Telegraph Co. against George B. Prescott, The Western Union Telegraph Company, Lemuel W. Serrell, and Thomas Edison, WUC; "Articles of Agreement," 4 January 1875, in Edison, *The Papers of Thomas A. Edison*, 526.

[141] Jay Gould to William Chandler, 5 January 1875, Chandler Papers.

[142] Norvin Green, Memorandum for General Swayne, n.d. 1882, WUC.

[143] Edison to Gould, 26 July 1875, in Edison, *The Papers of Thomas A. Edison*, 521.

[144] Israel, *Edison*, 103–4.

[145] Meeting of the Western Union Executive Committee, 4 December 1875, WUC.

nearly two decades of experience destroying competitors with profitless rates, Eckert adopted a "determined and vigorous policy" to grow the business through rate reductions.[146] Sure enough, Western Union matched the cuts with rates described in the press as "ruinous."[147]

If the only purpose for owning a telegraph company was to profit by sending telegraph messages, Gould was a fool to invest in the A&P and launch a rate war against Western Union. If, on the other hand, the purpose of owning *stock* in a telegraph company was to profit by buying and selling shares at advantageous moments, Gould was a genius. It is all but certain that Gould aimed to profit in the stock market and eventually force Western Union to buy him out.[148]

In Gould's investing career, he repeated a strategy of buying small, weak properties, using them to attack larger, stronger firms, and speculating in the stock of both. The game often ended when Gould sold his upstart company to his opponents at a premium. With only a slight change of details, investment banker Henry Clews' account of Gould's modus operandi in his railroad operations describes his telegraph strategy as well. Gould's method was to buy several "bad roads, put them together, give the united roads a new name, call it a good, prosperous line, with immense prospects in the immediate future, get a great number of people to believe all this," and then sell inflated stock. If the venture failed, Gould would sometimes buy it back from disappointed investors at a steep discount, pump it up again and repeat the process.[149]

Even before Gould absconded with Edison and Eckert, he had ventured into manipulating telegraph stock prices. Orton had reached a secret agreement with him in March 1874 for Western Union to buy a majority of A&P shares, but the proposed deal resulted "only in an active speculation in the stock, mainly for [Gould's] benefit." A second consolidation negotiation proved similarly futile.[150] Now Orton looked upon the A&P rate war as yet another attack by Gould-led short-sellers on Western Union's stock price. The "blowing of the bears" would soon cease, and then, Orton concluded, there would be no more talk about

[146] Eckert to Helen Gould Shepard, 16 May 1893, Helen Gould Shepard Papers.

[147] *New York Tribune*, 6 February 1875, 6.

[148] Klein, *The Life and Legend of Jay Gould*, 197; Grodinsky, *Jay Gould, His Business Career, 1867–1892*, 150.

[149] Henry Clews, *Twenty-Eight Years in Wall Street* (New York: Irving Publishing Co., 1888), 625.

[150] William Orton to Hugh Allan, 5 September 1875, WUC.

how "the great Atlantic & Pacific" with its comparatively small amount of mileage and capital would "destroy the Western Union."[151] Orton, though, had misjudged his foe. The rate war was only an opening gambit in a multipronged attack.

Gould's interest and influence in the railroads set him apart from previous telegraph competitors. Orton claimed he had "no fears" that the A&P could break Western Union's relationship with the Pennsylvania Railroad, but within three months Gould had convinced Tom Scott to put A&P lines up on his entire road.[152] Gould similarly used Western Union's troubled relations with the Baltimore & Ohio Railroad – compounded by a rate war between the B&O and Vanderbilt's New York Central Railroad – to convince John Garrett to connect the contested B&O wires to A&P offices.[153]

Gould encouraged attacks on Western Union in the press as well. Gould's attack on Western Union coincided uncannily with an aggressive campaign against Western Union by the New York *Daily Graphic*, the first daily newspaper to feature pictures.[154] A pair of brothers, Charles and James Goodsell, founded the *Graphic* in 1873 after failing with *The Financier*, a weekly business journal that exposed market "evils" like "stock-jobbing" and "conspiracies" to manipulate markets.[155] *The Financier* had long targeted Western Union, which it called a "monstrous monopoly" among the worst of over-capitalized firms.[156] "Anti-Monopoly, Anti-Blood-Sucking Capitalists is what the people want," James Goodsell told Ben Butler.[157]

Daily assaults on Western Union became more fervid as Gould's rate war began. *The Graphic* branded Western Union the "national leech" sucking the life "directly out of the veins of American enterprise."[158] The Goodsell brothers carried their campaign to Washington as well, delivering copies of their attacks on Western Union to every member of Congress.[159] Orton contended that the Goodsells were "for sale" and Western Union could have had the "friendship of the *Graphic*" if he had

---

[151] William Orton to Edward Allen, 30 January 1875, WUC.
[152] William Orton to Anson Stager, 23 January 1875, WUC; Klein, *The Life and Legend of Jay Gould*, 201.
[153] William Orton to Anson Stager, 20 November 1875, WUC.
[154] Joshua Brown, *Beyond the Lines: Pictorial Reporting, Everyday Life, and the Crisis of Gilded Age America* (Berkeley: University of California Press, 2002), 67.
[155] "Prospectus," *The Financier*, 6 January 1872, 3.
[156] *The Financier*, 12 October 1872, 275.
[157] James Goodsell to Benjamin Butler, 25 February 1874, Benjamin Butler Papers.
[158] "The National Leech," *New York Daily Graphic*, 4 February 1875, 684.
[159] J. C. Reiff to William Chandler, 24 February 1875, Chandler Papers.

been willing to "pay the market price."[160] There is no definitive evidence that Gould paid for the *Graphic*'s support, but surviving correspondence connects the Goodsells to several of Gould's close associates.[161] Circumstantial evidence is against them. The New York *Times* exposed the brothers in late 1875 as dishonorable swindlers, describing their schemes as "black-mailing brought to a science."[162]

Gould added Congressional pressure to his assault in the winter of 1875. Gardiner Greene Hubbard had not relented in his crusade to create a postal telegraph system to compete with Western Union, though he had made little progress. In late 1874, Hubbard found a "strong ally" in Gould and the Atlantic & Pacific Company.[163] Gould personally wrote checks to Hubbard in the winter of 1875 to support his campaign.[164] Nor was Hubbard Gould's only man in Washington. Gould retained William E. Chandler, a Republican lobbyist who was "the pinnacle of his profession."[165] Chandler received almost daily "blue jays" – short, handwritten notes on light blue stationery – from Gould, giving specific orders for a legislative attack.[166]

Gould continued to rely on Congressman Ben Butler, who assisted Gould both as counsel on the Quadruplex patent case and in legislation favorable to the A&P.[167] Butler's primary motivation may have been venal, but his animosity toward Western Union was genuine. In 1867, Butler had clashed with Orton over Western Union's refusal to open its files to the House committee investigating Lincoln's assassination.[168]

---

[160] Orton to Henry Weaver, 22 November 1875, WUC.

[161] Ben Butler was allied with the Goodsells going back at least to 1874 and contributed pieces to the *Graphic* in 1875 (requesting his name be left off); J. C. Reiff was in contact with the Goodsells and told Chandler about it; Gardiner Hubbard was also in touch with the Goodsells. James Goodsell to Benjamin Butler, 25 February 1874, Butler Papers; J. C. Reiff to William Chandler, 24 February 1875, Chandler Papers; Charles Goodsell to Gardiner G. Hubbard, 9 March 1876, Hubbard Papers.

[162] "J. H. and C. M. Goodsell, The Modern Way of 'Founding a Newspaper,'" *The New York Times*, 20 November 1875, 1.

[163] Gertrude Hubbard to Gardiner Hubbard, n.d. 1875, Hubbard Papers.

[164] Gould considered paying Hubbard in stock instead of cash in January, and two letters in January and February refer to $1,000 cash payments. It is difficult to imagine that these were the *only* payments that Hubbard received. Jay Gould to William Chandler, 15 January 1875, Chandler Papers; Gould to Chandler, 17 January 1875, Chandler Papers; Gould to Chandler, 22 February 1875, Chandler Papers.

[165] Margaret Susan Thompson, *The 'Spider Web': Congress and Lobbying in the Age of Grant* (Ithaca, N.Y.: Cornell University Press, 1985), 170.

[166] Leon Burr Richardson, *William E. Chandler, Republican* (New York: Dodd, Mead & Company, 1940), 163.

[167] Jay Gould to William Chandler, 5 December 1874, Chandler Papers.

[168] William Orton to C. A. Tinker, 7 April 1868, WUC.

In 1874, Butler tangled with Western Union again when a battle in Congress erupted over his attempt to appoint the new collector of the Boston customs house. To thwart his opponents, Butler publicly exposed their confidential telegrams. Orton held Butler's clerk, a former Western Union employee dismissed for fraud several years earlier, responsible for the theft of the messages.[169] For his part, Butler had no scruples about stealing the messages of his political opponents, claiming that he could read anybody's telegrams if he had "a fancy" and that he never put anything on the wires that he "did not expect to be read by everybody."[170] According to Western Union, Butler's "fancy" required bribery and fraud.

Gould and Eckert designed a three-pronged legislative attack on Western Union, and with Butler serving as their point man in Washington, created a bill to order.[171] Their agenda included the repeal of the Page Patent, regulation of the interchange of business between telegraph companies, and an act authorizing the Post Office to contract with other telegraph companies. In 1868, Congress had granted a special patent for a telegraph induction coil to Charles Grafton Page, an inspector in the U.S. Patent Office. The Congressional act was a ploy to stake an American claim on the coil, which had also been claimed by a European inventor.[172] Page died shortly after Congress awarded the patent, and his widow offered it to Western Union for $500,000 – a staggering sum for a patent. Page's attorneys claimed that the patent covered the electromagnetic circuit breakers employed in virtually *all* the telegraphs in the United States. In the most dire predictions for the patent's effect under Western Union's control, every line in the country might be "compelled to submit to consolidation upon such terms" as Western Union might dictate, new construction would cease, and innovation in telegraphy would be limited to only technologies that Western Union "should see fit to permit or license." Yet the patent's validity remained in doubt, and Western Union bought a half-stake for only $24,000 and a pledge to seek royalty payments and sue infringers. In 1875, the first two infringement suits neared trial, and Western Union filed a new suit against the A&P.[173]

[169] The clerk, George B. Cowlam, appears under shadowy circumstances in several places in Orton's letterbooks. William Orton to Anson Stager, 5 March 1874, WUC.
[170] Butler to W. E. Curtis, 30 September 1876, Butler Papers.
[171] Jay Gould to William Chandler, 8 January 1875, Chandler Papers.
[172] Israel, *From Machine Shop to Industrial Laboratory*, 135.
[173] William Orton to O. S. Ferry, 17 February 1875, WUC; Robert C. Post, *Physics, Patents, and Politics: A Biography of Charles Grafton Page* (New York: Science History Publications, 1976), 180.

For Gould and every other Western Union competitor, reversing the Page Patent was imperative; interchange regulation was potentially even more important.[174] An interchange law would require Western Union to accept the message of any other company and carry it at a regular prorated tariff in the same order as all other messages. The regulation would neutralize the advantage of Western Union's national network; a customer could send a message on the A&P without the need for an A&P office at the destination. A&P could thus skim the cream from the telegraph market and leave the rest.

Butler introduced a postal telegraph bill that matched Gould's design. He circumvented the House Committee on Post Offices and Post Roads, in which Western Union exercised powerful influence, by submitting his bill instead to the House Committee on the Judiciary, which he chaired. Hubbard ally and Massachusetts Republican Henry Dawes had already launched a House Judiciary Committee investigation into Western Union's relationship with the AP, so Butler made the unpopular dual monopoly a target in his bill. *The Daily Graphic* noted that thanks to the "slavery of the press," every single AP newspaper but the *Herald*, known "to be restive in its chains," ignored the introduction of Butler's bill.[175] The bill included the interchange provisions that Gould sought for the A&P, but took its attack further than Gould had advocated.[176] Butler emphasized the dangers posed by the AP and Western Union's control of the news and commercial intelligence.[177] He proposed requiring that the gathering and transmission of commercial news be conducted by separate companies and forcing the telegraph companies to charge uniform rates to all press associations for like service – a policy that Orton himself had long advocated.

Butler's attack alienated the AP editors Gould needed to drum up public opposition to Western Union. Gould sought to sever the anti-AP measure from the bill, but too late.[178] Western Union's lobbyists kept Butler's bill off the floor of the House until the February adjournment. An attempt to repeal the Page Patent also made no progress. The *New York Sun* claimed Butler's legislation had been nothing but a "big stock speculation in Wall

---

[174] Gould to Chandler, 10 January 1875, Chandler Papers.

[175] "The Slavery of the Press," *New York Daily Graphic*, 15 January 1875, 553.

[176] "A bill to establish certain telegraphic lines in the several States and Territories as post-roads, and to regulate the transmission of commercial and other intelligence by telegraph," H. R. 4470, 43d. Congress, 2nd Session.

[177] Dorsey, Senate Report No. 624, 43rd Congress, 2nd Session, 2.

[178] Jay Gould to William Chandler, 22 February 1875, Chandler Papers.

Street, at the head of which stood Jay Gould."[179] Through rate cuts, the Atlantic & Pacific had secured "much public favor," but Gould's attacks on Western Union's political flank had failed.[180]

By the summer of 1875, Eckert was seriously ill with pneumonia, and Gould was losing patience with the unprofitable A&P. Orton gleefully speculated that the "Atlantic &Pacific sponsors" were realizing they had "a corpse on their hands" and would soon surrender to Western Union.[181] The pressure on Gould mounted. Western Union reached an accord with the Southern & Atlantic Telegraph Company, the A&P's principal Southern ally, taking it out of the A&P system, "crippling" the A&P's Southern facilities, and incurring a major loss of "prestige before the public." The A&P would have to invest in new lines just to regain the lost connections rather than expanding into new territory.[182]

Gould appeared ready for peace. The A&P and its allies agreed to suspend the ruinous rate war and restore prices.[183] Representatives of Western Union and the A&P reached a tentative merger agreement and Western Union's stock price surged when newspapers reported rumors of the deal. *The New York Times* suggested that the *Tribune* – widely believed to be under Gould's influence – was responsible for the merger rumors in an attempt to "bull" Western Union stock.[184] Indeed, Gould and his allies at the Union Pacific had been quietly buying shares of Western Union.[185] Once the price had settled at a new high, Gould and his partner Sydney Dillon blocked the deal by demanding 40 percent more than had been agreed upon – undoubtedly selling their shares of Western Union *before* scuttling the merger, and perhaps adding a short position on Western Union as well.[186] Gould's peace had been a feint. By the end of 1875 rumors swirled on Wall Street that the A&P would renew the telegraph rate war, though Gould privately assured Orton that

---

[179] "Butler's Big Stock Job: The Secret History of the Telegraph Bill – A Wall Street Scheme," *New York Sun*, reprinted in the *Journal of the Telegraph*, 15 March 1875, 89.
[180] Reid, *The Telegraph in America*, 585.
[181] Orton to Stager, 15 July 1875, WUC.
[182] Orton to Stager, 16 July 1875, WUC. By the following summer, Western Union had purchased a majority of Southern and Atlantic stock and leased all its lines.
[183] Orton to Hugh Allan, 5 September 1875, WUC.
[184] "Who Is Behind the Scenes?" *The New York Times*, 8 August 1875.
[185] Klein, *The Life and Legend of Jay Gould*, 202.
[186] Meeting of the Trustees of the Atlantic and Pacific Telegraph Company, 31 August 1875, WUC; William Orton to Edwin Morgan, 3 September 1875, Edwin Morgan Papers.

he would not cut rates and would consent to any "practicable scheme for the reduction of expenses."[187]

Western Union was already making deep cuts, particularly to labor costs. Growth in the telegraph market remained robust even after the Panic of 1873. Despite the depression, the number of messages transmitted each year rose steadily. In the first year after the panic, Western Union's profit declined 9 percent, but by the middle of 1875, profits were up 29 percent from their low point and 17 percent higher than before the panic.[188] Deflation had meanwhile pushed down the price of labor – wages across the economy fell by an average of 25 percent during the depression.[189] Over Orton's objections, the executive committee formulated a sliding scale to reduce Western Union's payroll. Orton's salary dropped by 25 percent and all other salaries reduced in declining proportions – down to a 5 percent cut for those earning at least $600 per year.[190] The sliding scale cuts outraged employees, who used Western Union wires to organize meetings – and invite the press – in several cities to condemn the policy. "What has become of the proposition to make the employees' interest identical with the employers?" a contributor wrote to *The Telegrapher*, noting that there would be no protest were the company "poor and not earning money by the millions."[191] The "impertinence" of many of the complaints annoyed Orton, particularly a vow by Peoria employees to resist becoming "slaves to monopoly." Orton warned the Peoria employees that Western Union would certainly not be willing to perpetuate slavery after its abolition during the recent war. To a colleague he added that if the "slaves to monopoly" did not "succeed in escaping," he would happily see that their "emancipation" was "promptly declared."[192] Despite employee anger at the sliding scale, Orton maintained in his private correspondence that Western Union was nowhere near as profitable as critics supposed.

The A&P took advantage of the wage cut controversy by publicly announcing that it would not follow Western Union's lead of taxing its employees "to secure dividends to its stockholders."[193] The A&P resumed

[187] Orton to Stager, 29 December 1875, WUC.
[188] Annual Report of the Western Union Telegraph Company, 30 June 1891, WUC.
[189] Jerry Markham, *A Financial History of the United States: From Christopher Columbus to the Robber Barons, 1492–1900*, 2 vols., vol. 1 (Armonk, N.Y.: M. E. Sharpe, 2002), 296.
[190] Meeting of the Western Union Executive Committee, 7 December 1875, WUC.
[191] "Justice, Injustice, and their Results," *The Telegrapher*, 25 December 1875, 309.
[192] William Orton to Anson Stager, 18 December 1875, WUC.
[193] "The Reduction of Salaries," *The Telegrapher*, 18 December 1875, 304.

the rate war in early 1876, cutting its tariffs by 20 percent. Orton believed it was "not only fallacious but wicked" for the rivals to waste money just to hurt each other, but he followed the A&P rates down.[194] In March, Western Union's panicked directors skipped the dividend. When payments resumed in June, critics accused the company of distributing a dividend that it had not earned.[195]

Despite the mounting cost, Orton preferred to try to outlast the A&P rather than reward Gould's tenacity with a generous buyout.[196] Perhaps Orton was determined to follow Hiram Sibley's old rule not to "buy a telegraph line from anybody but the sheriff."[197] However, Gould would not abandon the A&P as long as it served as a tool in his stock market operations. The A&P announced a plan to increase its capital from $10 million to $15 million, raising new money for operations through stock sales while making the company a bigger pill for Western Union to swallow in a merger. A&P insiders took $4 million of the new stock at a cut rate of 20 percent of par, though a shareholder suit against this alleged stock watering temporarily enjoined the capital expansion. The stock exchange opened its own investigation into charges that the additional capital had no legitimate purpose except to depress the price of Western Union.[198]

Gould redoubled his effort to disrupt Western Union's railroad partnerships, securing contracts with several key roads, including the Pennsylvania and the B&O.[199] A&P employees began to string wires on the B&O right-of-way, and Western Union, which claimed to own the poles, sent men to rip down the A&P wires as quickly as they could be put up. Western Union dragged the battle into the courts, securing injunctions against both the B&O and the A&P.[200] The legal wheels turned slowly, emboldening other railroads to show a "growing disrespect" for their contract obligations.[201] Orton hoped for an amicable settlement with the B&O that would demonstrate the "binding force" of Western

---

[194] Orton to Harrison Durkee, 10 January 1876, WUC. This was a turn for Orton, who had been more willing to "burn the district" in previous battles that were less damaging to Western Union.

[195] Meeting of the Board of Directors, 8 March 1876, WUC; William Orton to James G. Bennett, 8 June 1876, WUC.

[196] Orton to R. W. Russell, 23 May 1876, WUC.

[197] Norvin Green to Hiram Sibley, 27 February 1885, WUC.

[198] "Misfortunes Accumulating," 1 June 1876, *Journal of the Telegraph*, 164.

[199] Reid, *The Telegraph in America*, 586.

[200] Western Union Executive Committee Meeting Minutes, 15 November 1876, WUC.

[201] William Orton to C. J. U. Gwinn, 19 March 1877, WUC.

Union's railroad contracts.[202] This desire for a friendly outcome led Western Union to volunteer free service to the B&O during the railroad strike of 1877, but still the B&O would not come to terms.[203]

In every aspect of telegraph business, from boards of trade to press reports to hotels and resorts, the A&P put Western Union on the defensive. In some areas, such as press reports, Orton allowed the A&P to take business until its wire capacity became so overloaded that service problems discouraged customers.[204] But the A&P won several small victories. For example, the A&P supplanted Western Union's exclusive right to operate in Washington's elite Arlington Hotel, so incensing Orton that he had the A&P thrown out of the prestigious Willard's Hotel in retaliation. The Centennial celebration of 1876 also became a battleground. Western Union offered to provide telegraph service to the event grounds in Philadelphia and a cut of the gross to the Centennial fund.[205] To Orton's chagrin, the A&P won exclusive rights with a bid three times higher, blocking Western Union from serving the site. Western Union messenger boys had to pay admission just to make their deliveries and were forbidden from taking replies.[206] Edison alone had a larger exhibition space than Western Union's planned display of telegraph technology, "that most wonderful product of American genius."[207] Thanks to the A&P's exclusive contract, visitors to the Western Union exhibit could admire the machinery but not send any telegrams.[208]

Competition with the A&P drove Western Union to develop a brand identity. Managers had long assumed that most customers paid little attention to which company carried their messages, and the principal advantage Western Union offered consumers was having the most convenient telegraph office for any given location. But with the A&P garnering so much public attention and sympathy, Orton began to take notice of the assortment of faded Western Union signs, many of which advertised only a generic "Telegraph Office." Lettering should be uniform, he determined, and all signs should bear the name "Western Union" in the same white letters on a blue background, with no shading, and no variant

---

[202] William Orton to E. D. Morgan, 4 April 1877, WUC.
[203] William Orton to John Garrett, 21 July 1877, WUC.
[204] Orton to Stager, 3 February 1877, WUC.
[205] Orton to William Bigler, 5 December 1875, WUC.
[206] Orton to Henry Weaver, 29 June 1876, WUC.
[207] Orton to Henry Pettit, 21 February 1876, WUC, Orton to Henry Pettit, 8 February 1876, WUC.
[208] William Orton to A. T. Goshorn, 17 July 1876, WUC.

colors or lettering.[209] "'The little blue and white sign' of the Western Union Co. is a trade mark [*sic*] of great value, and we can not afford to let the value deteriorate by failure to keep our signs reasonably fresh," he advised a subordinate.[210] Upon learning that A&P messengers in Chicago wore uniforms, Orton decided Western Union messengers in major cities should wear uniforms as well.[211] This element of the brand came at no added expense to Western Union – the company required messenger boys to pay for their own uniforms.[212]

Though Western Union showed no signs of breaking, Cornelius Vanderbilt declined sharply. He died on January 4, 1877, and his business empire passed to his son William Henry Vanderbilt. William faced not only a battle with Jay Gould, but also a confrontation with his brother Cornelius, who publicly contested their father's will and dragged the family's affairs through the courts.[213] After the Commodore's death, Gould escalated his battle against Western Union. The conservative William reportedly lacked the "backbone" of his famous father, and, Gould probably reasoned, could be forced into a favorable settlement.[214]

Gould's skill at market manipulation is unquestionable, but it was his stamina that proved unstoppable. Gould reorganized the A&P, stacking the deck with railroad bosses – Garrett of the Baltimore & Ohio, Hugh Jewett of the Erie, Collis Huntington of the Central Pacific, C. K. Garrison of the Missouri Pacific – and two experienced market operators, English investor James R. Keene and Gould's friend Russell Sage. The A&P defeated the court challenge to its capital expansion and issued $5 million in new stock, increasing the total by 50 percent. Gould launched the most drastic rate cut yet, dropping the price for ten words to twenty-five cents in all the territory east of Omaha, a bold step that an industry insider again described as "suicidal."[215] Gould publicly declared that rate reductions were a blow against the Western Union monopoly on behalf of the public welfare – a publicity technique he had also employed

[209] William Orton to W. J. Holmes, 12 October 1876, WUC.
[210] William Orton to Stager, 5 August 1876, WUC.
[211] William Orton to Stager, 23 January 1877, WUC.
[212] Downey, *Telegraph Messenger Boys: Labor, Communication and Technology, 1850–1950*, 65.
[213] Wheaton J. Lane, *Commodore Vanderbilt: An Epic of the Steam Age* (New York: Alfred A. Knopf, 1942), 324.
[214] Grodinsky, *Jay Gould, His Business Career, 1867–1892*, 151.
[215] Reid, *The Telegraph in America*, 587.

during his battle to control the Erie Railroad, which challenged the New York Central monopoly.[216] Yet the public would not embrace the notorious Jay Gould as a monopoly killer. Even Western Union's long-time antagonist, the *New York Herald*, questioned whether Gould's expansion of the A&P was in "good faith," suggesting it was more likely intended to increase the price of consolidation or perhaps to "bear" Western Union stock so "schemers" could buy low and then sell at a great profit when they withdrew their opposition. Whatever the plan, the *Herald* speculated, Gould would "reap a harvest," while "the senders of messages would be the ultimate victims."[217]

Western Union's managers concluded Gould's target was Western Union's stock price, or even control of Western Union itself – there would be no permanent competitor. The contest was a "bitter war" made by "reckless and unscrupulous rivals" whose goal was to force discouraged Western Union shareholders to sell out and allow "the enemy" to "come into control."[218] Indeed, by the summer of 1876 Gould was making inquiries to potential allies on Western Union's board, suggesting he would soon be in control of *both* the A&P and Western Union.[219]

To weaken Western Union's stock price, Gould again pressed his attack on several fronts. Hubbard's postal telegraph campaign in Congress resumed. Levi Dowley, a small Western Union shareholder fronting for Gould's "clique," sued Western Union for an injunction against payment of the dividend on the grounds that Western Union had not earned it. Dowley's suit failed, but he and the Gould clique launched a second legal attack the following year. Orton sent letters of protest to newspapers that printed Dowley's accusations, insisting that Western Union was the victim of a speculator's scheme and had paid the dividend with net profits that were not "required for any other purpose."[220] But this last claim rang false: Western Union continued cutting expenses, curbing new expenditures, and canceling what even Orton deemed "very desirable new construction" and "important reconstruction."[221]

Conditions for a bear attack could not have been more favorable for Gould. Rate wars, dubious dividend payments, and the enduring depression

[216] Grodinsky, *Jay Gould, His Business Career, 1867–1892*, 152.
[217] "Atlantic and Pacific Telegraph," *New York Herald*, 23 February 1877, 6.
[218] William Orton to James Gamble, 19 July 1877, WUC.
[219] Russell Sage to Edwin D. Morgan, 10 July 1876, Edwin D. Morgan Papers.
[220] William Orton to the Editor of the *Times*, 10 March 1877, WUC.
[221] William Orton, Memoranda for Mr. Prescott, 6 April 1877. According to some sources, Western Union did not even earn its dividend. See Grodinsky, *Jay Gould, His Business Career, 1867–1892*, 153.

sent railroad stocks tumbling in 1877. In July the nation appeared on the verge of revolution. B&O Railroad slashed wages by 20 percent without cutting its dividend, igniting the Great Railroad Strike, which shut down railroads across the nation. The federal and state governments dispatched militias, and the ensuing clashes claimed one hundred lives and destroyed $10 million in property.[222] Amidst the turbulence, Gould's "gang of cla-quers" derided Western Union's financial condition in the press and the number of short-sellers mounted sharply; in a certain sign of speculation, Western Union was daily one of the most heavily traded issues on the New York Stock Exchange.[223] "There never was such a raid made on a really good stock," Western Union Vice President Norvin Green confided to a friend."[224] But Western Union kept paying its dividend, and with weaker holders already shaken out, the stock price held fast and then gradually advanced.

The end of the telegraph war came late in the summer of 1877, but tele-graphic competition may have had little to do with the peace. In the spring of 1877, William Vanderbilt negotiated an end to the railroad rate wars, signaling to Gould – whether intentionally or not – that unlike his father, the younger Vanderbilt would appease rivals for the sake of peace.[225] Within days of the end of the railroad rate war, rumors emerged that Gould had purchased substantial stakes in several of the railroads between Chicago and Council Bluffs, where Gould's Union Pacific began. Vanderbilt's Eastern roads depended upon feeder roads from the West, and he could not afford to allow Gould to acquire control and strangle his business. For both men, control of the telegraph was not the only prize in their contest, nor even the most important. The heavily capital-ized railroads remained Gould and Vanderbilt's primary interests. The jewel in Vanderbilt's crown was not Western Union but the New York Central, and the truly damaging rate war was not on the wires, but on the Eastern roads.

[222] Heather Cox Richardson, *West from Appomattox: The Reconstruction of America after the Civil War* (New Haven, Conn.: Yale University Press, 2007), 178.

[223] See for example, "Financial Affairs," *The New York Times*, 31 July 1877, 6. Western Union's daily volume in July hovered close to twenty thousand shares, or more than 5 percent of all outstanding shares. In April 1877, daily volumes of thirty-five thousand shares traded were seen. Only the Lake Shore Railroad had a consistently greater trad-ing volume.

[224] Norvin Green to W. O'Brien, 3 April 1877, Norvin Green Papers (FHS).

[225] Grodinsky, *Jay Gould, His Business Career, 1867–1892,* 153.

In May, the Michigan Central Railroad emerged as a critical prize in the war.[226] Vanderbilt, Gould, and Gould's associate Sydney Dillon all owned large stakes in the Michigan Central; National City Bank's Moses Taylor held the balance of control. Vanderbilt wanted control of the Michigan Central, which paralleled his Lake Shore lines, but Taylor resisted. In June, Vanderbilt conceded his proxies to Taylor, who elected a slate of directors. Gould realized that the Gould–Dillon shares could give Vanderbilt the control of the Michigan Central at the next election, and thus they constituted a precious bargaining chip. On the Michigan Central, Gould was the kingmaker. He could use the shares as leverage to force a favorable end to the telegraph issue, offering Vanderbilt control of the Michigan Central in exchange for buying the A&P.[227]

In mid-summer 1877, Gould authorized Eckert to negotiate a consolidation with Western Union.[228] An emissary from the Western Union board assured Eckert that an agreement would "be equitable to all stockholders and enable both companies to earn and save a large sum of money beyond what is possible" in competition.[229] Committees from both companies met secretly on August 14 at the offices of the Union Trust Company. A leak brought a passel of reporters, but neither a long session during the day nor an evening session in Vanderbilt's suite at the Windsor Hotel produced an agreement.[230] The committees met again the next evening and into the night,[231] while Vanderbilt remained in his suite, and Gould lurked in a corner outside the conference room, talking quietly with Frank Work, a Western Union director and Vanderbilt captain. The negotiations *outside* the conference room were undoubtedly more influential than those carried on inside. At half past ten, Gould sent a note to Vanderbilt and the two men talked in the hall. An hour later, Gould disappeared into Vanderbilt's suite for a private conversation. After this tête-à-tête, the negotiating committees announced that they had reached an agreement.[232]

---

[226] Klein, *The Life and Legend of Jay Gould*, 204.
[227] Grodinsky, *Jay Gould, His Business Career, 1867–1892*, 157.
[228] Jay Gould to Edwin D. Morgan, 31 July 1877, Edwin D. Morgan Papers.
[229] Executive Committee Meeting of the Atlantic and Pacific Telegraph Co., 9 August 1877, WUC.
[230] "Telegraph Consolidation, 15 August 1877, *The New York Times*, 2.
[231] Executive Committee Meeting of the Western Union Telegraph Co., 21 August 1877, WUC.
[232] "The Telegraphs Consolidated," *The New York Times*, 21 August 1877, 1.

The treaty ending the first telegraph war was not a consolidation, which might have opened the field to new competitors, but a pooling arrangement.[233] Western Union and the A&P would share their receipts for twenty years, with 87.5 percent to go to Western Union. This was similar to pooling arrangements railroads used as shelter from competition, but the telegraph pool differed because Western Union actually owned its new partner. Western Union purchased slightly more than half of the A&P from Sage and Keene at twenty-five cents on the dollar, a 25 percent premium over the market price.[234] The companies entered a state of semi-consolidation, operating separately but with enough unity to reap the benefits of their agreement. Rates in the East, driven down during the telegraph war, doubled at most points just days after the pooling arrangement began.[235] Managers drew up a list of redundancies and immediately began shutting A&P offices and laying off employees.[236] Orton was unapologetic for firing the A&P's employees, deeming it "unjust for the successful Company to discharge its employees who have rendered a faithful service." He maintained a haughty disdain for his vanquished rival. "If boasting were an essential element of success," he responded to a plea for the job of an A&P office manager, "the Atlantic &Pacific should have been a most prosperous corporation." To the victor went the spoils, and A&P employees had chosen the wrong side of the war.[237]

Western Union's victory, however, proved to be hollow. The vision of a "paying" unified system, pursued by Hiram Sibley, created by consolidation in 1866, and doggedly defended by William Orton, seemed once again ascendant. A slew of rivals had been eliminated: the Atlantic & Pacific, the Franklin, the Bankers' & Brokers', the Pacific & Atlantic, the Southern & Atlantic, the American District, the Automatic, the Gold & Stock – all were either defunct or adjuncts of Western Union. In Orton's own words, they had disappeared "into the maw of the 'Great Monopoly.'"[238] At the end 1877, virtually the entire American telegraph system was once again administered from the colossal new Western

---

[233] Speculation about pooling to avoid attracting new competitors was discussed openly in the press. "The Rival Telegraph Companies," *Boston Daily Globe*, 15 August 1877, 5.

[234] Klein, *The Life and Legend of Jay Gould*, 204–5.

[235] William Orton, Memoranda for General T. T. Eckert, 25 August 1877, WUC.

[236] It was actually to the advantage of the A&P to close as many offices as possible, since it reduced its share of the expenses without reducing its portion of the pool. This became a point of contention between the two companies. Western Union Executive Committee Meeting, 24 October 1877, WUC.

[237] William Orton to George W. Mead, 12 October 1877, WUC.

[238] William Orton to John Van Horne, 23 December 1871.

Union headquarters in lower Manhattan. But at the next election of the Michigan Central Railroad directorate, Vanderbilt revealed he controlled a majority of shares, confirming that horse-trading with Gould had ended the telegraph war. Western Union had largely served as a pawn in a contest for railroad territory that one historian called "a great game of chess."[239] The company's stock had been a vehicle for speculators and the "war" had largely been a fiction because it remained in Gould's power to wage or not to wage as his railroad and securities manipulations required. The final pooling arrangement was essentially a payoff, legitimizing a competitor that Orton had long insisted was utterly illegitimate.

For the telegraphing public, the war had offered the short-term benefit of rate cuts, but rates increased again after the Windsor Hotel Agreement. In the meantime, competition and low rates probably took some of the wind from the sails of telegraph reformers in Congress, while Gould had used telegraph reform itself as simply another arrow in his quiver. There would be no telegraphic competition, and the enriching of A&P shareholders ultimately came at the expense of telegraph customers. What's more, for any keen observer, but especially for Jay Gould, a valuable lesson emerged: Western Union's greatest asset, the barrier to entry posed by railroad rights-of-way, had been revealed as a vulnerability. Gould would soon press home his advantage.

---

[239] Thomas Childs Cochran, "The Legend of the Robber Barons," *Entrepreneurial History* 1, no. 5 (1949): 5.

7

First Time Tragedy, Second Time Farce

In the fall of 1877, the Western Union Telegraph Company mastered time itself. At noon on October 30, an electrical signal from the Naval Observatory in Washington sped through two hundred miles of Western Union lines to an electromagnet fixed atop a flagpole standing two hundred fifty feet above Broadway in lower Manhattan. At the instant the signal arrived, the magnet released a ball, three and a half feet in diameter, sending it tumbling down the twenty-foot staff. Cities throughout the world provided similar public displays of correct local time. In New York a "time ball" had been hand hoisted and dropped from the roof of the customs house in the 1850s, and the navy yard provided an evening gun, but the time ball at the pinnacle of Western Union's towering headquarters offered greater visibility and accuracy. Mariners in the harbor and observers as far away as the New Jersey side of the Hudson River synchronized their clocks and pocket watches to Western Union's "standard time."[1] Despite the trappings of scientific exactness, the time ball was so prone to delay and disruption by inclement weather that newspapers published a daily report on what time the ball had *actually* fallen. Yet this minor nuisance did little to distract from the

[1] "Standard Time by Telegraph: The Western Union Time-Ball," *The New York Times*, 18; September 1877, 2; "Western Union Time-Ball," *The New York Times*, 30 October 1877, 8; "Important Telegraph Events of 1877," *Journal of the Telegraph*, 16 January 1877, 17; Norvin Green to S. R. Thamblin, 27 February 1880, WUC. The ball went into service in September, but the first published reports of its daily drop do not appear until 30 October. On the first day, "standard time" was actually five seconds ahead of schedule. "Standard time" was for local *New York* only. The railroads introduced time zones in 1883.

time ball's popularity as a symbol of "civic modernity" enabled by the telegraph.[2]

Looking up at Western Union's massive granite fortress, twice the height of most of its neighbors, a casual observer stopping to set his watch by telegraph time might imagine that Western Union was indomitable, but the "Great Monopoly" that controlled 90 percent of the telegraph industry and was much maligned for its concentrated power over American communications was in a parlous state. The unfinished tower stood as a symbol of both the heights Western Union had achieved and the precariousness of its position. More than two years after the imposing headquarters opened, the building's tower remained incomplete. The falling time ball announced noon, but the tower reported no other time because there were only four "staring blank spaces" where a great clock had been intended. In the epic telegraph war against the Atlantic & Pacific Company (A&P), Western Union could spare no funds to complete the grand edifice.[3]

Telegraph competition should have been an object lesson in the merits of a laissez-faire political economy The war with the Atlantic & Pacific Telegraph Company had reduced telegraph rates and created new facilities without government interference or taxation, at least until a deal was struck. But in the end, if this phantasmic telegraph competition had had any salubrious effects, they were felt most keenly in Jay Gould's stock portfolio. The competition with Gould's A&P had revealed Western Union as less powerful than the railroad tycoons and speculators who owned it.

"When combination comes in at the door, this political economy of competition flies out of the window," journalist and enemy of monopoly Henry Demarest Lloyd wrote of Western Union. "It is a political economy of persons, not of the people."[4] C. Osborn Ward, a writer and labor activist, similarly criticized the enrichment of the "almost invisible minority" of Western Union's large shareholders. "Shall the interests of forty millions be ignored to gratify a handful of forty?" he asked in his 1878

---

[2] Alexis McCrossen, "Time Balls: Marking Modern Times in Urban America, 1877–1922," *Material History Review* 52, Fall (2000).

[3] By the end of 1878, the clock was still not completed, and a new manufacturer was being sought. "Standard Time by Telegraph: The Western Union Time-Ball," *The New York Times*, 18 September 1877; Meeting of the Western Union Executive Committee, 20 November 1878, WUC.

[4] Henry Demarest Lloyd, "The Political Economy of Seventy-Three Million Dollars," *Atlantic Monthly*, July 1882, 75.

Labor Catechism.[5] In truth, "forty" was an overestimate. Gould and three or four of his partners had stage-managed the entire A&P charade, and William H. Vanderbilt and a handful of his allies had capitulated and paid them off. Perhaps no more than a dozen men had determined the fate of the American telegraph.

The game of industrial chess that Vanderbilt and Gould played with the nation's telegraph network proved so enriching for Gould that he decided to play a second match. In the second round, pressure from Gould probably cost Western Union its investment in a technological advance that would eventually dwarf the telegraph: the telephone. Though this was an unintended consequence of Gould's attack, it spelled the beginning of the end of Western Union's control of American telecommunications.

A historian of telephone technology has noted that observers often assume that "the 'end use' of a new technology is embedded in the technology itself," but the path from invention to deployment is seldom so straight.[6] There was little about the early telephone that suggested it had a purpose analogous to the telegraph, much less that telephony would *supplant* telegraphy.[7] The two histories, though, are intertwined. The telephone was born in the cradle of resistance to telegraph monopoly and followed a similar line to widespread use. Western Union dominated its early history, though the telegraph giant famously missed the chance to buy Bell's patent for $100,000.[8] Early experimenters with telephony did not seek to create a rival to the telegraph, but to develop an instrument in the area where innovation held the most promise for reducing the cost of telegraphy itself: multiplexing.

Duplex and Quadruplex telegraphs demonstrated that multiplexing, which increased wire capacity by simultaneously transmitting multiple

---

[5] C. Osborne Ward, *A Labor Catechism of Political Economy. A Study for the People. Comprising the Principal Arguments for and against the Prominent Declarations of the Industrial Party, Requiring That the State Assume Control of Industries* (New York: Trow Printing Co., 1878), 100.

[6] W. Bernard Carlson, "Entrepreneurship in the Early Development of the Telephone: How Did William Orton and Gardiner Hubbard Conceptualize This New Technology?" *Business and Economic History* 23, no. 2 (1994): 161.

[7] This idea is actually more absurd given the rise of email and SMS, both of which suggest that it was the inconvenience and cost of sending telegrams that made the telephone superior, not because users necessarily preferred the personal contact of a phone call.

[8] See, for example, Thomas Childs Cochran, *200 Years of American Business* (New York: Basic Books, 1977), 78. Cochran credits Western Union managers for quickly realizing they had made a "mistake," rather than suggesting that they were actually pursuing a different strategy.

messages on a single wire, could be both practical and profitable. Elisha Gray, an inventor and founder of Western Electric, the equipment manufacturer for Western Union, believed the next breakthrough would be a telegraph capable of transmitting tones – an acoustic form of multiplexing.[9] Gray developed an "Electro-Harmonic Telegraph," which he claimed could send as many as nine messages simultaneously over a single wire five hundred miles long.[10]

Alexander Graham Bell, a teacher of the deaf and expert in acoustics, also experimented with harmonic multiplexing in the early 1870s. In 1872 Gardiner Greene Hubbard, the long-time enemy of Western Union, invited Bell to teach at a school for the deaf attended by Hubbard's daughter, Mabel. Hubbard showed keen interest in Bell's experiments with harmonic telegraphy. After Western Union's purchase of the Stearns Duplex patent demonstrated that multiplex technology potentially had great economic value, Bell determined to perfect and patent his own system.[11] Bell installed a prototype of his device in Hubbard's Washington home in the spring of 1875, and Hubbard arranged for a demonstration for William Orton. Bell erroneously believed that the A&P had recently paid Edison $750,000 for the Quadruplex patents, and that Western Union, seeking to make up "lost ground," would pay a similar sum for his multiplexing harmonic telegraph.[12] Orton thought Bell's design inferior to Gray's, but he invited Bell to bring his apparatus to Western Union for testing.[13]

In New York, Bell and Western Union electrician George Prescott experimented with Bell's device. Despite poor signal strength, Bell reported that his telephone "did work" and impressed Prescott.[14] A few days later, Bell met with Orton. In a letter to his parents, Bell vividly

[9] Gray was a founder of Gray & Barton, along with Western Union's Anson Stager. In 1872, Western Union's equipment shop and Gray & Barton were merged into Western Electric. For a company history, see Stephen B. Adams and Orville R. Butler, *Manufacturing the Future: A History of Western Electric* (Cambridge, U.K.: Cambridge University Press, 1999).

[10] James D. Reid, *The Telegraph in America and Morse Memorial*, 2d ed. (New York: John Polhemus, 1884), 643.

[11] Bruce, *Bell: Alexander Graham Bell and the Conquest of Solitude*, 93.

[12] Alexander Graham Bell to Alexander Melville and Eliza Symonds Bell, 5 March 1875, Alexander Graham Bell Papers.

[13] W. Bernard Carlson, "The Telephone as Political Instrument: Gardiner Hubbard and the Formation of the Middle Class in America, 1875–1880," in *Technologies of Power: Essays in Honor of Thomas Parke Hughes and Agatha Chipley Hughes*, ed. Michael Thad Allen and Gabrielle Hecht (Cambridge, Mass.: The MIT Press, 2001), 33.

[14] Alexander Graham Bell to Alexander Melville and Eliza Symonds Bell, 18 March 1875, Alexander Graham Bell Papers.

related how Orton had made him wait in the anteroom of his office until he had finished his business for the day and then beckoned Bell inside. The hard-nosed corporate president and the naive young inventor sat side by side on a couch. Orton threw his feet up on a chair and told Bell of his high regard for Elisha Gray. Western Union would commit its "great power" to Bell or Gray, and the side it favored would become the stronger party. He mused that no invention was worth more than $100,000, particularly Bell's "crude" telephone. Moreover, Western Union would never cooperate with Gardiner Greene Hubbard. Days later, the two men met again and Orton declared Western Union would buy a worthy device but refused to say whether he favored Bell over Gray.[15]

Orton's rough treatment of Bell and refusal to cooperate with Hubbard is easily explained. Hubbard had often argued before Congress that innovation would hasten cheap telegraphy, and Orton generally dismissed miraculous technological advances as impracticable or fraudulent. However, Thomas Edison's ambitions had recently allowed Jay Gould to steal the Quadruplex from Western Union, and Orton probably believed he could manage Bell more easily if he separated him from the striving Hubbard. Regardless, the harmonic telegraph captured Orton's interest, and he set Thomas Edison (who returned to Western Union in the summer of 1875) to work developing commercially viable versions.[16]

Bell, meanwhile, departed from multiplex telegraph and began to experiment with sending human speech rather than harmonic tones. He successfully transmitted speech for the first time in June 1875 and filed for a patent in February 1876 – barely ahead of Gray. That summer, Bell proudly displayed his telephone at the Philadelphia Centennial Exhibition, claiming it was both less expensive and more effective than Elisha Gray's. As a demonstration, Bell transmitted soliloquies from *Hamlet* across the exhibition hall.[17]

Yet the question remained whether the telephone had any practical, marketable application. Mounting financial problems for both Hubbard and Bell gave the matter some urgency. Bell's assistant, Thomas Watson,

---

[15] Alexander Graham Bell to Alexander Melville and Eliza Symonds Bell, 22 March 1875, Alexander Graham Bell Papers. George B. Prescott claimed that after this incident, Bell's permission to use Western Union wires was withdrawn by Orton, but some experiments continued anyway. See George B. Prescott, *Bell's Electric Speaking Telephone: Its Invention, Construction, Application, Modification and History* (New York: D. Appleton & Company, 1884), 444.

[16] Paul Israel, *Edison: A Life of Invention* (New York: John Wiley, 1998), 138–9.

[17] James A. Mackay, *Sounds out of Silence: A Life of Alexander Graham Bell* (Edinburgh: Mainstream, 1997), 138–9.

recalled that Hubbard's wife, Gertrude McCurdy, was anxious to see Bell marry her daughter, Mabel, and insisted that Bell sell the telephone outright.[18] Hubbard apparently believed that Bell's best hope was to sell or lease his invention to a telegraph company, perhaps even in the hope that with the new technology Western Union would finally "reform itself" and provide the cheap telegraph service that Hubbard had long demanded.[19] So firm was the telephone's connection to the telegraph in Hubbard's mind that in demonstrations of the device at the Hubbard home, Hubbard allegedly pronounced "What hath God wrought" as a test phrase.[20] Nor was Western Union the only potential telegraph customer. Unlike Morse thirty years before, Bell had access to vast enterprises that could deploy his device at scale. In June 1876, Hubbard received permission from the A&P to begin testing the telephone on their lines – a course that Orton had warned Bell would incur the wrath of Western Union.[21]

If Orton ever rejected an offer to buy Bell's telephone, the event would have taken place in the fall of 1876 or winter of 1877. Watson recalled that Hubbard and Bell offered Orton all their patents for "the exorbitant sum of $100,000," and Orton "somewhat contemptuously" rejected the offer.[22] Norvin Green, Orton's successor, told Congress in 1883 that it was he who had turned down Hubbard's $100,000 offer.[23] The contradictions in the several stories of the event suggest protracted negotiations rather than the rejection of a single offer.[24]

Orton must have been chagrined that circumstances required him to negotiate with Hubbard, a man whom he had often accused of trying to destroy Western Union. Though Orton and Hubbard had been cordial

---

[18] See, for example, Bruce, *Bell: Alexander Graham Bell and the Conquest of Solitude*, 227.

[19] Carlson, "Entrepreneurship in the Early Development of the Telephone," 175.

[20] Mackay, *Sounds out of Silence: A Life of Alexander Graham Bell*, 133.

[21] D. H. Bates to Gardiner G. Hubbard, 26 June 1876, Hubbard Family Papers.

[22] Thomas A. Watson, *The Birth and Babyhood of the Telephone* (American Telegraph and Telephone Information Department, 1913), 23.

[23] *Report of the Committee of the Senate Upon Relations between Labor and Capital, and Testimony Taken by Committee* (Washington, D.C., 1885), 882.

[24] In Hubbard's letters, a pair of minor references suggests an ongoing negotiation, including a letter to his wife in October 1876 in which Hubbard hinted that with Bell's growing success, they could "get on without Mr. Orton." Gardiner G. Hubbard to Gertrude McCurdy Hubbard, 16 October 1876, Hubbard Papers. Hochfelder concludes from letters in the AT&T archive that the negotiation lasted about a year, from October 1876 to December 1877. See David Hochfelder, "Constructing an Industrial Divide: Western Union, AT&T, and the Federal Government, 1876–1971," *Business History Review* 76, no. 4 (2002): 709. Much of this evidence was also reviewed by Michael Wolff in Michael F. Wolff, "The Marriage That Almost Was," *IEEE Spectrum* 13, no. 2 (1976).

in the past, by 1876 their personal relationship had soured. Orton likely knew Hubbard was cooperating with Gould and the A&P. Gertrude McCurdy Hubbard warned her husband that Orton was a "powerful and unscrupulous enemy" who would use "every means in his power" to "crush" Hubbard.[25] In 1876, Orton severed Western Union's relationship with an attorney whom he accused of giving "countenance and comfort to, the so-called Postal Telegraph scheme of Mr. Gardiner G. Hubbard."[26] Norvin Green claimed in 1890 that but for Orton's "repugnance" for Hubbard, Western Union would have acquired the telephone at a bargain price.[27] Nonetheless, surviving letters from the fall of 1877 show that Hubbard negotiated directly with Orton.[28]

Though his personal dislike of Hubbard may have figured into it, Orton's apparent rejection of Bell's telephone was likely for tactical reasons. Orton was cautious about adopting new technology. *The Telegrapher* criticized Western Union for having a policy "to decry inventions as of no importance or value" until they were developed by other companies that Western Union subsequently swallowed up.[29] In one important respect, the telephone *was* of little value to Western Union: after years of investment in telegraph multiplexing, the telephone reduced line capacity by once again requiring a single line to be committed entirely to a single transmission – a major backward step.[30] Though Orton did once refer to the telephone as "a children's toy,"[31] he undoubtedly recognized that it had great potential. When he penned his "children's toy" remark he had been paying Edison to design telephone variations for more than two years. In a renewed negotiation with Orton in September 1877, Hubbard

---

[25] Gertrude McCurdy Hubbard to Gardiner Hubbard, n.d. 1875, Hubbard Papers.
[26] William Orton to Anthony Pollok, 16 September 1876, WUC.
[27] Norvin Green to Henry H. Bingham, 6 June 1890, WUC.
[28] Gardiner Hubbard to Gertrude McCurdy Hubbard, 15 September 1877, Hubbard Family Papers. Gertrude staunchly opposed cooperation with Orton, whom she deemed "capable of any meanness or wickedness and a foe to the end." Gertrude Hubbard to Gardiner Hubbard, 17 September 1877, Hubbard Papers.
[29] "The Western Union Telegraph Company and Inventions and Inventors," 13 February 1875, *The Telegrapher*, 40.
[30] Carlson, "The Telephone as Political Instrument," 39–40.
[31] This expression appears in William Orton to George S. Ladd, 10 January 1878, WUC. The same phrase appears in a document that purports to be a Western Union committee report that rejects the telephone, dated from November 1876. Michael Wolff reprinted this "report" and claimed it appeared in several engineering journals, but he believed it to be a fake, and I am in complete agreement with him. It is also worth noting that even in the Ladd letter, Orton orders one hundred sets of telephones and warns that the success of the apparatus will depend upon its improvement and its cost – hardly a dismissal of the technology. See Wolff, "The Marriage That Almost Was," 47–8.

told his wife that Western Union managers had a "high appreciation of the value of telephones."[32] Gertrude Hubbard enviously described how Western Union supplied Edison with "unlimited means for electrical instruments, chemical collections of minerals, and whatever can aid him," plus "a stenographer at his side taking down every new idea or experiment." She surmised that Western Union intended to make a telephone that would supplant Bell's patent.[33]

Over and over, the history of the telegraph demonstrated that controlling a patent did not guarantee success. In the 1850s Western Union had no rights to the Morse patent, but through a series of alliances and consolidations, it absorbed the first-movers in the industry and absorbed the Morse lines. This provided a dual lesson for assessing the telephone: first, Western Union might eventually control the Bell patent even without buying it early on. Chauncey DePew, who became a director of Western Union in 1881, recalled that Orton had talked him out of investing in Bell. "Bell could not succeed with his device, even if it worked," Orton told DePew in 1876. "We would come along and take it away from him."[34] Second, if Western Union bought the Bell patent, a competitor might still circumvent it, as Western Union tried to do by employing Edison to design telephones. Furthermore, Orton's experience with Edison, Gould and the Quadruplex underscored the risk of investing large sums in patents – at minimum, the expense of defending patents in court could erase years of profits. Orton predicted that litigation over the telephone patent would be "so costly both in time and money" that it would slow the device's introduction and likely "destroy the value of all interest."[35]

William Orton did not live to see if his telephone strategy was the right one. Orton suffered recurring bouts of ill health, and twelve years at the helm of Western Union took a toll. The fight with Gould and the A&P had perhaps a greater impact than any previous competition. In March 1878, after much urging from his friends, Orton announced he would spend the summer in Europe on his first extended leave.[36] On Sunday,

---

[32] Gardiner Hubbard to Gertrude McCurdy Hubbard, 15 September 1877, Hubbard Papers.
[33] Gertrude McCurdy Hubbard to Mabel Hubbard Bell, 23 November 1877, Hubbard Papers.
[34] DePew's story was reprinted in the *New York Herald Tribune* on 1 August 1926. I have quoted from Wolff, "The Marriage That Almost Was," 48.
[35] William Orton to Samuel S. White, 1 March 1878, WUC.
[36] Meeting of the Western Union Board of Directors, 13 March 1878, WUC.

April 21, Orton attended the Church of the Holy Apostles, where he served as a vestryman, and then took an afternoon drive in Central Park. In the evening, he complained of exhaustion, retired at ten, and suffered a massive stroke. He never regained consciousness and died the next morning.[37] Orton was fifty-two years old and left a wife and eight children. Though he stood for more than a decade at the head of a company that made millions for investors, Orton was one of a growing breed of salaried managers, not a capitalist. He was reportedly worth less than $100,000 when he died.[38]

Western Union's directors eulogized Orton's energetic leadership and personal integrity, as did the New York press. Several reports cited Orton's demise as a warning against the dangers of professional overexertion. "His death was sudden and plainly due to the strain of long-continued overwork, unbroken by the relaxations of rest which are essential to health and long life," admonished *Harper's Weekly*.[39] Western Union suspended executive business so that managers and directors could collectively attend Orton's funeral. The board commissioned a portrait of Orton for the president's office but politely declined a sculptor's offer to create colossal statues of Orton and Morse to stand in the front of the Western Union building.[40]

Norvin Green, a vice president who specialized in railroad contracts, became Western Union's new president.[41] Green, a sixty-year-old country doctor and Kentucky Democrat, had risen to prominence as the leader of the Southwestern Telegraph Company, part of the "Six Nations" cartel that led to Western Union's monopoly. Green was a consummate insider, and he had a far greater appetite for speculation than Orton. (This trait did not always serve him well – Green lost much of his wealth from

[37] "William Orton: Sudden Termination of a Busy and Useful Life," *The Journal of the Telegraph*, 1 May 1878, 129–31.
[38] A variety of reports suggest that Orton was worth around $75,000. See, for example, "William Orton, Sudden Death by Apoplexy of the President of the Western Union," *Chicago Daily Tribune*, 23 April 1878, 2. Agnes Orton launched a series of appeals to the company for various payments she believed were due to the family. Orton's lack of personal wealth, despite his elevated position at Western Union and among New York's elite, is actually typical of the growing salaried managerial class and the separation, beginning in the railroad companies, between owners and management. See Chandler, *The Visible Hand*, 87.
[39] "William Orton," 11 May 1878, *Harper's Weekly*, 370.
[40] Special Meeting of the Western Union Board of Directors, 23 April 1878, WUC; Western Union Executive Committee Minutes, 29 May 1878, WUC. These spaces had originally been intended for Morse and Franklin.
[41] Norvin Green to Mills, 31 August 1878, Green Papers (FHS).

the Southwestern Telegraph in a speculative venture.)[42] As president of Western Union, Green had access to a mountain of inside information, and he made quick use of it: in his first three years as president, he made $300,000 "in operations in the stock."[43]

With Orton gone and the A&P war over, Vanderbilt reversed Orton's policy of reinvesting earnings in improving and expanding the network and buying back watered stock. Green and Vanderbilt agreed to issue a major dividend in stock, rather than cash, thus increasing the company's outstanding capital and greatly enriching large shareholders. Beyond pleasing investors, the capital expansion had strategic aims: Green noted that the resulting "moderate rate of dividend" would reduce attacks on Western Union as "an extortionate monopoly." It would also, by expanding Western Union's notional capitalization, make the company a bigger pill for the government to swallow if it "should take the lines."[44]

The New York *Daily Graphic* mocked Vanderbilt for cashing in Western Union's surplus – "cutting the melon" in the financial parlance of the day. A cartoon depicted Commodore Vanderbilt's heir sitting on top of a giant "Western Union Melon" held in place by Green. In his right hand, Vanderbilt wielded "Le Sabre de Mon Pere," with stock speculators beneath him, eagerly waiting for a piece. Jay Gould sat to one side, a sheaf of Western Union stock certificates tucked beneath his arm. When plans for the stock dividend were canceled a few days later, the *Graphic* depicted Vanderbilt slipping on the shattered hunks of Western Union and flying akimbo through the air – "too ripe!"[45] But the stock dividend had merely been forestalled, not abandoned. In June 1879, Western Union shareholders received a 17 percent stock bonus, and a hike in the cash dividend from 6 to 7 percent. Orton's policy of investing earnings in the institution rather than payouts to investors had come to an end.

Just before he died, Orton had tried to secure Western Union's telephone interests without Bell. In November 1877, he had organized the American Speaking Telephone Company, an affiliate under Western Union management that combined several telephone patents and licensed them to

---

[42] Norvin Green to Joseph Richardson, 1 May 1876, Norvin Green Papers (FHS).
[43] Norvin Green to George Douglass, 11 June 1881, George Douglass Papers (U.K.).
[44] Norvin Green to W. H. Vanderbilt, 27 August 1878, Green Papers (FHS).
[45] "Getting Ready to Cut the Melon," New York *Daily Graphic*, 30 October 1878; "Too Ripe!" New York *Daily Graphic*, 4 November 1878.

the Gold & Stock Company.[46] The placement of Western Union's telephone interest in the Gold & Stock is telling: Gold & Stock operated
Western Union's private line business, suggesting that managers saw the
promise of the telephone in dedicated intrabusiness lines, rather than in
long-distance intercity communication. In early 1878, Western Union
proposed for the Bell interest to join forces by pooling telephone patents,
thereby avoiding what promised to be costly and protracted patent litigation. The Bell interest insisted on Bell's claim as "sole inventor" and
demanded half the stock of the new company; Western Union would
not "for a moment admit" to such a claim.[47] When negotiations failed,
a contest commenced. In one of his last acts as president, Orton ordered
the ground floor of the former A&P headquarters – which stood vacant
across Broadway from the Western Union building – filled with an exhibition of telephones to attract customers to the curious new device.[48]

Over the next two years, Western Union's business grew to fifty-six
thousand telephones in fifty-five cities.[49] Bell competed fiercely in commercial centers, but Western Union took the lead in New York and Chicago
while Bell hung on to the advantage in New England.[50] In August 1878,
Bell Telephone sued American Speaking Telephone in Massachusetts for
infringing on Bell's patent. Still, the two companies continued to discuss
a potential consolidation of their interests and nearly concluded a settlement in early 1879. However, Hubbard feared that in a combined company Western Union would try to protect the telegraph by suppressing
the telephone.[51]

In fact, Western Union's managers intended to promote the telephone
not as an independent technology, but only because they thought it best
used in combination with the telegraph. Norvin Green stressed that the
telephone was a natural "Auxiliary of the Telegraph," ideal for use in
"factories, mines and small towns and communities where the amount of
business did not employ the full capacity of the wires or pay the salary of

---

[46] "Articles of Association" for the American Speaking Telegraph Company, 17 November
    1877, WUC.
[47] Norvin Green to Charles A. Cheever, 12 February 1878, WUC.
[48] William Orton, Memoranda for Mr. Chandler, 23 March 1878, WUC.
[49] American Speaking Telephone Company Board of Directors Quarterly Meeting Minutes,
    11 June 1878; Carlson, "Entrepreneurship and the Early Development of the Telephone,"
    182. Carlson estimates Bell sold about half as many telephones during the same time
    period.
[50] Christopher Beauchamp, "The Telephone Patents: Intellectual Property, Business and the
    Law in the United States and Britain, 1876–1900" (University of Cambridge, 2007), 47.
[51] Hochfelder, "Constructing an Industrial Divide," 712.

an operator" – a talking "automatic" telegraph. Green did not imagine that ceding such poorly paying nodes to the telephone posed a threat to the telegraph's dominance of long-distance communication. Besides, the telephone had obvious disadvantages: it kept no record, and the natural "probabilities of mistakes and misunderstandings" in conversation combined with imperfect transmission led to "important errors" that were "impossible to trace." Why would anyone prefer to communicate using an inaccurate and unverifiable alternative to the telegraph?

If the telephone were an "auxiliary to the telegraph," Western Union had no strategic interest in pouring resources into competition with Bell. A prudent cooperative agreement would make a "sweep" of telephone patents and keep them out of the hands of competing telegraph companies. Green believed such an alliance held greater value to Bell than to Western Union because in his view Western Union's Edison telephone was superior.[52] In fact, Bell employed a copy of Edison's transmitter but had a stronger claim on telephony in general – in effect neither company had a working telephone that did not infringe on the other's patents.[53] In addition to the great expense of a litigation that might leave both parties with legally inoperable systems, there was also the danger that legal action would expose the telephone's secrets, revealing the weak points in the patents and, Green feared, advertising "to inventors the very little things they had to get around to make a new Telephone that would not infringe."[54]

On November 10, 1879, National Bell Telephone and Western Union reached an accord. Under the agreement, Western Union exited the telephone business, and in exchange, Bell promised to stay out of long-distance communication. Bell received all of Western Union's telephone patents and agreed to pay Western Union 20 percent of revenue on telephone rentals, royalties, and licenses. Western Union sold Bell its fifty-six thousand subscriber telephones and granted rights-of-way – with appropriate compensation – on Western Union pole lines. Most importantly, Bell agreed to an exclusive connection: all telegraph messages from Bell would go to Western Union. Green insisted this exclusive agreement was advantageous for both companies, as any potential competitor against Bell in telephony would naturally seek Western Union as a partner.[55] The agreement also barred Bell from transmitting news, market

---

[52] Norvin Green to George Gifford, 18 August 1879, WUC.
[53] Beauchamp, "The Telephone Patents," 48–9.
[54] Norvin Green to W. H. Forbes, 2 July 1879, WUC.
[55] Norvin Green to George Gifford, 19 July 1879, WUC.

quotations, or telegraph messages in competition with Western Union or its subsidiaries. As Green had predicted, the consolidation was a boon for the Bell Company – its stock rose from $50 to $995 when news of the agreement broke.[56]

For Western Union the agreement with Bell marked a retreat rather than an alliance, a treaty with equal rewards for two firms that were hardly equal. Bell's patents could probably not have defeated Western Union's telephone claims in court, and after twenty-five years of crushing smaller competitors, "'The Great Monopoly' should have found the tiny Bell Telephone Company to be easy fodder."[57] The most compelling reason for Western Union's withdrawal from telephony came not from within the company, but from without. The looming threat to Western Union in 1879 was not the fledgling Bell Telephone Company, but the opening of a new attack by Jay Gould.

The joining of the A&P and Western Union in 1877 was a squeamish affair. Perhaps the ferocity of the competition left too much bitterness between the rivals for easy conciliation; at Western Union resentment surely lingered toward Thomas Eckert and his lieutenants for their treachery. The two companies did not merge into a single management but remained separate firms with pooled expenses and profits. Though Western Union owned the A&P, tension persisted between the two managements; they overstated their claims that the firms formed "one harmonious system." A shareholder lawsuit challenged the arrangement, and Western Union refused to make any payments to the A&P while the suit was pending.[58] Eckert remained the president of the A&P, but now he was employed by the managers he had conspired against. Gould had insisted as a condition of the consolidation that Eckert would be General Manager of the new system. This did not occur, leaving Eckert "in a compromised position."[59]

---

[56] Contract details may be found in George P. Oslin, *The Story of Telecommunications* (Macon, Ga.: Mercer University Press, 1992), 229.

[57] George David Smith reviewed Western Union's success in beating Bell in several major urban markets: Western Union bought out Bell agents, cut prices, offered access to its lines, "lenient terms of credit, indemnification against losses in patent suits, and lower-priced telephone equipment." This was an impressive set of advantages. See George David Smith, *The Anatomy of a Business Strategy: Bell, Western Electric, and the Origins of the American Telephone Industry* (Baltimore: The Johns Hopkins University Press, 1985), 38.

[58] Western Union Executive Committee Minutes, 17 April 1878, WUC.

[59] Thomas Eckert to Helen Gould Shepard, 16 May 1893, Helen Gould Shepard Papers. J. D. Reid confirmed in the 1884 edition of *Telegraph in America* that Eckert had been promised this post. See Reid, *Telegraph in America*, 579.

Gould later claimed that his personal friendship for Eckert and disappointment that he failed to make him the General Manager of Western Union led him to create a new telegraph company. "I made up my mind that I would put this man at the head of as big a company as I had taken from him," he testified to the Senate Committee on Relations Between Labor and Capital.[60] This tall tale was typical of the enigmatic Gould, who concealed his motives to prevent rivals from anticipating his actions. Eckert recounted a similarly fanciful story about how he told his friend Gould of an idea he had for a telegraph company that would lease private lines to individuals and businesses along the Eastern seaboard, and Gould spontaneously wrote him a check for a million dollars.[61]

Despite Eckert's fond recollections, it is unlikely that Gould launched a new telegraph company for sentimental reasons – more likely Gould had William H. Vanderbilt's railroad interest in his sights. Gould had long sought a link between Chicago and Omaha to circumvent the Iowa Pool, the name for the three railroads that carried traffic east from Gould's Union Pacific. During the winter of 1879, Gould secretly acquired the Wabash Railroad, a broken and financially troubled road with service between St. Louis and Toledo that represented an end run around the Iowa Pool. Suddenly, Vanderbilt faced a dangerous competitor to his eastward rail traffic and wondered whether Gould would seek negotiations or launch a rate war. For the second time, Gould had positioned himself to use a competing telegraph company as leverage with a Vanderbilt, and he believed this Vanderbilt to be an easy mark.[62]

Though Western Union had eliminated its most substantial competitor by buying the A&P in 1877, a number of opposition telegraph lines persisted. The Continental Telegraph constructed a seaboard line from Boston to Washington, but its absurd capitalization of $950 per mile of line was the hallmark of a contractors' scheme – it would build overpriced lines until no more stock could be sold and then declare bankruptcy. There was also the threat of smaller local lines, which sprang up "here

---

[60] *Report of the Committee of the Senate upon the Relations between Labor and Capital*, 5 vols., vol. I (Washington, D.C.: U.S. Government Printing Office, 1885), 1069.
[61] Thomas Eckert to Helen Gould Shepard, 16 May 1893, Helen Gould Shepard Papers. This story bears an amusing commonality to several other yarns in which Gould suddenly produces a checkbook and writes out absurdly large drafts. J. D. Reid also repeated the story that the American Union "had its origin in one of those marvelous friendships which now and then relieve the cold and hard features of ordinarily life." See Reid, *Telegraph in America*, 578.
[62] Maury Klein, *The Life and Legend of Jay Gould* (Baltimore: Johns Hopkins University Press, 1986), 235.

and there" and stole some business, but not enough to make them worth buying and creating "additional inducements for further filibustering" from aspiring entrants. Instead Green adopted Sibley's policy of "burning the district," using Western Union's A&P affiliate to drive rates down and bankrupt competitors.[63]

The Central Union Telegraph Company may at first have appeared to be one such nuisance competitor. It constructed a line from Oswego to New York City and would have garnered little notice but for a rumor that Gould and Russell Sage had encouraged the creation of the line as a stock speculation. Green naively believed that Gould and Sage did not have "any idea of trying the experiment over" of pouring money into an opposition company "with a view of making it back out of the market."[64] The banker Henry Clews recalled in his memoir that even when it was clear that Gould intended to parallel Western Union's primary lines and push rates down until he reached another settlement, Green would not believe it.[65] Underestimating Gould again proved a grave error.

In a sign of impending trouble, Eckert resigned as president of the A&P in March 1879.[66] In late April, Gould incorporated the Union Telegraph Company with ten million dollars in nominal capital. Gould took half the shares and gave the remainder to David Homer Bates, the former superintendent of the A&P, and Charles Tinker, an Eckert ally who had once been Western Union's manager at Washington and now superintended the Baltimore & Ohio (B&O) telegraph lines. Because neither man was wealthy, Gould presumably provided them with the funds for their investment. The Central Union Telegraph formed the core of the new enterprise.[67] On May 15, Gould incorporated the American Union Telegraph Company in New York with a great capitalization of $13 million, adding as supporters Sage and Sidney Dillon, partners in his first raid on Western Union. The second telegraph war was about to begin.

Western Union's first response to a renewed challenge from Gould was dismissal. "No man knows better than Jay Gould ... that an opposition

---

[63] Norvin Green to Jeptha Wade, 16 December 1878, Green Papers (FHS).
[64] Norvin Green to Jeptha Wade, 16 December 1878, Green Papers (FHS).
[65] Henry Clews, *Twenty-Eight Years in Wall Street* (New York: Irving Publishing Co., 1888), 629–30.
[66] For reasons that remain unclear, the A&P board – now under the control of Western Union – convinced Eckert to remain at his post until the end of the calendar year, but though he served out this term, he had already started working for Gould. See Klein, *The Life and Legend of Jay Gould*, 277.
[67] Julius Grodinsky, *Jay Gould, His Business Career, 1867–1892* (Philadelphia: University of Pennsylvania Press, 1957), 203.

telegraph in this country can not be made a success as a business enter-prise," Norvin Green declared.[68] The rapid growth of American Union, however, soon forced Green to admit that Gould's attack was no bluff, though he publicly insisted that the American Union's "impossible" plan to build a national network in two years was strictly a put-on.[69] In either case, Green maintained that the American Union was "not a legitimate business enterprise," would not conduct "an honorable competition," and was intended as "a stock-jobbing drive at the market value of Western Union securities."[70] Whatever Gould's plan, appeasement or an offer to consolidate would reinforce a dangerous precedent. If Western Union paid Gould handsomely for the American Union as it had for the A&P, Green feared a similar scheme would appear "every two or three years." Green preferred to fight and demonstrate the futility of an "opposition telegraph" until the American Union's backers grew "sick and tired" of losing money.[71]

Exhausting Gould and his partners, as ever, would not be easy. Western Union had the advantage of exclusive railroad contracts that gave the telegraph company free transportation for maintenance and construc-tion, rights-of-way for lines, and rent-free railroad telegraph offices that came staffed with cheap, part-time railroad telegraph operators. Moreover, Green reported that Western Union owned the telegraph lines on 95 percent of all the railroads in the country.[72] To build an opposition network, a competitor would have to neutralize this railroad advantage, but an assault on Western Union's railroad position was precisely what Jay Gould intended. Indeed, it had already begun.

Gould's first attack was on the legal basis of Western Union's telegraph contracts themselves, and began nearly a year before the launch of the American Union. The Telegraph Act of 1866 granted telegraph compa-nies the right "to construct, maintain and operate lines of telegraph" in the "public domain" and "over and along" any "military or post-roads" of the United States." The plain intent of the legislation was to promote competition by making it easier for firms to access rights-of-way, and Congress subsequently defined "all railroads or parts of railroads" as

[68] Norvin Green to Hugh Alan, 27 June 1879, WUC.
[69] Norvin Green to Work, 27 September 1879, Green Papers (FHS).
[70] Norvin Green to Hiram Sibley, 30 September 1879, WUC.
[71] Norvin Green to Hiram Sibley, 19 August 1879, WUC.
[72] "Minutes of a Hearing Before the Committee on Railroads, United States Senate," 28 January 1879, WUC.

post roads.[73] Yet application of the statute remained ambiguous. The law did not dictate whether railroads with exclusive telegraph contracts were *entitled* to open their rights-of-way to competing telegraph lines or were *obligated* to do so. Moreover, telegraph regulation had been left largely to the states, and telegraph companies were state-chartered corporations; the Telegraph Act presented an expansion of federal power and potentially an intrusion on states' rights. Its constitutionality remained untested.

In 1877, the U.S. Supreme Court weighed in on the Telegraph Act in *Pensacola Telegraph Co. v. Western Union Telegraph Co.* In *Pensacola*, the court reviewed an 1866 monopoly granted by the state of Florida to the regional Pensacola Telegraph. The company carried Western Union messages to Pensacola for the exorbitant sum of $1 for fifty miles. C. L. LeBarron, a local businessman and Pensacola Telegraph's principal owner, tried unsuccessfully to sell the line to Western Union in the late 1860s. Pensacola's port swelled in importance, and in 1872 the railroad on which the telegraph line ran asked Western Union to build a new line to provide cheaper service. With characteristic probity, Orton expressed reluctance to "destroy the value" of Pensacola Telegraph and felt "morally bound" to purchase it instead, offering to pay the full capital price of $5,000, though Western Union could reproduce an identical line for substantially less.[74] Since LeBarron held a state-granted monopoly, he demanded $20,000. Western Union refused, ignored the state-granted exclusive, and built a line on the railroad right-of-way, ruining LeBarron's business.[75]

When the case reached the Supreme Court, Western Union won a sweeping judgment that gave Gould an unexpected opening. The Court determined that the telegraph constituted "commerce" and upheld the constitutionality of the Telegraph Act. Because the telegraph carried commercial communication between the states, it doubtless fell under "the controlling power of Congress" and merited federal protection from "hostile State legislation." Florida's exclusive grant to the Pensacola Telegraph Company attempted to "regulate commercial intercourse between its citizens and those of other States" and violated federal supremacy over interstate commerce. Monopoly grants or any other attempts to exclude foreign telegraph corporations were thus unconstitutional.

Pensacola proved to be part of a broader movement in the Court in the late nineteenth century to expand protections for interstate commerce

---

[73] Congress, Session I, Chapt. 230. Revised Statutes, Title LXVI, Chapt. 9, Sec. 3964, 773.
[74] John Van Horne to George Mumford, 8 June 1872, WUC.
[75] William Orton to Roscoe Conkling, 12 April 1878, WUC.

and prevent states from using acts of incorporation and grants of monopoly to exclude foreign corporations or prevent consolidations.[76] Writing in dissent, Justice Stephen J. Field called the curtailing of state authority to exclude foreign corporations "novel and startling" and warned that it would make "state control" of corporations "impossible."[77] The effects of the *Pensacola* decision were threefold. First, the Supreme Court sharply limited state power to regulate or exclude telegraph corporations. This transfer of power from the states to the federal government helped to shield national corporations from state and municipal laws intended to promote local interests. Second, and more directly, the *Pensacola* decision determined that any telegraph company could operate on any post road – not merely those in the public domain – provided it had a "right of way *secured by private arrangement with the owner of the land.*"[78] Telegraph companies thus could not invade railroad rights-of-way without the consent of the railroad, and Western Union's railroad allies could keep their roads closed to competing telegraphs. The *Pensacola* decision was "like sucking honey from a rag," Orton had gleefully written to Western Union's counsel, "the further you get in, the sweeter it grows."[79] However, *Pensacola* could also be interpreted in quite another way: the decision suggested that although a railroad could not be *forced* to violate its exclusive telegraph contract, it could *voluntarily* open its right-of-way to competing telegraphs.[80] This created a rich opportunity for Gould: a competitor seeking to duplicate Western Union's network on the major railroads would only have to provide a greater incentive than the free service Western Union had promised. If the telegraph competitor *already* owned an influential interest in the railroad, as Gould did, he could violate existing exclusive contracts virtually at will. *Pensacola* took away the most powerful weapon in the Western Union legal arsenal: the injunction against violations of its exclusive contracts.

[76] Morton J. Horwitz, *The Transformation of American Law, 1870–1960: The Crisis of Legal Orthodoxy* (New York: Oxford University Press, 1992), 79.

[77] Henry O'Reilly noted happily that no one could ignore the Telegraph Act of 1866 now that it prevented states from interfering with the telegraph. Henry O'Reilly, "Importance of the National Telegraph Law," manuscript notes, 1878, O'Reilly Papers (RHS).

[78] *Pensacola Telegraph Co. v. Western Union Telegraph Co.*, 96 U.S. 1 (1877). Emphasis is mine.

[79] William Orton to Porter Lowrey, 11 April 1878, WUC. Subsequent cases that depended on *Pensacola* as precedent include *Telegraph Company v. Texas* (105 U.S. 460 [1881]), *Western Union Telegraph Co. v. Ann Arbor Railroad Co.* (178 U.S. 239), and *Western Union Telegraph v. Pennsylvania Railroad Co.* (25 Sup. Ct. Rep. 133).

[80] Grodinsky, *Jay Gould, His Business Career, 1867–1892*, 202.

The legislative wrangling *Pensacola* produced strengthened Gould's position. *Pensacola* infuriated U.S. Senator Charles Jones, who had argued the case on behalf of Pensacola Telegraph. After his defeat in court, Jones challenged Western Union in the Senate. In April 1878 he introduced a bill authorizing railroad companies to maintain and operate telegraph lines and to combine their lines with other railroads, while forbidding railroads from entering exclusive right-of-way contracts with telegraph companies.[81] This was an open invitation to railroads to enter into competition with Western Union. Whether the law was necessary for railroads to operate commercial telegraphs was not a settled question. The *ultra vires* doctrine that limited corporations to the commercial activities explicitly granted in their charters eroded in the postwar period, but railroads going into telegraphy could still expect *ultra vires* challenges.[82] New York's Senator Roscoe Conkling, a powerful supporter of Western Union and occasionally its paid legal counsel, hampered the progress of the Jones bill in the Senate – it appeared that Western Union's lobby had once again "fixed" the company's problems.[83]

Gould, of course, had already secured a highly effective lobby of his own. Congressman Ben Butler, who had worked for Gould during the first telegraph war, circumvented the committee roadblocks Western Union's lobbyists constructed against Jones' bill in the Senate by proposing a similar measure as an amendment to the Army appropriations bill under consideration in the House. What came to be known as the "Butler Amendment" authorized railroads to operate commercial telegraph lines under the terms of the Telegraph Act of 1866.[84] Butler claimed the provision would create "wholesome competition" in telegraphy.[85] *The Boston Globe* estimated that railroads entering the telegraph business would cost Western Union two-thirds of its receipts.[86] The House approved the Butler Amendment and passed the appropriations bill on February 8.

[81] Jones introduced the bill on 15 April 1878. 45th Congress, 2nd Session, S. 1093.
[82] Horwitz, *The Transformation of American Law, 1870–1960*, 77.
[83] *Congressional Record*, 45th Congress, 2nd Session, 1151.
[84] The Amendment's complete text is as follows: "And telegrams are authorized to be transmitted by railroad companies which may have telegraph lines, for the Government and for the general public at rates to be fixed by the Government according to the provisions of the Revised Statues...." The appropriations bill is H. R. 6145. Congressional Record, 45th Congress, 3rd Session, 973.
[85] Congressional Record, 45th Congress, 3rd Session, 973.
[86] "Uneasiness of Telegraphic Officials, Caused by the Butler Amendment," *Boston Globe*, 7 February 1879, 1.

On February 13, the Senate Committee on Railroads opened a hearing on the proposed Jones bill and the relationship between the Associated Press and Western Union. Norvin Green, still reeling from the passage of the Butler Amendment in the House, charged that there was no "earthly need" for railroad telegraph legislation. Western Union's counsel, Porter Lowrey, brazenly argued that the *railroads* posed the real threat of a "complete and offensive monopoly" over the telegraph.[87] The legislation was a "scheme" to depress the value of telegraph stocks, and honest country stockholders were losing money to the speculators.[88] Green acknowledged that Western Union was "alluded to as a mammoth monopoly" but insisted that even "strong corporations have poor stockholders." According to Green, a "very large part" of Western Union's stockholders were "widows and orphans,"[89] a claim that the *Daily Graphic* spun into a front-page cartoon of Green standing before the "Western Union Orphan Asylum," begging to stay the axe of the Butler Amendment.[90]

At the behest of Western Union's reliable friend, Senator James G. Blaine, the railroad committee postponed a decision and called for the creation of a special commission to investigate telegraph competition and the constitutionality of the postal telegraph.[91] Butler claimed he had won a great victory for "cheap the transmission of intelligence… for the people."[92] Western Union's Senate allies amended the Butler Amendment to explicitly require railroad companies to assent to the Telegraph Act of 1866, potentially subjecting their lines to a future government takeover.[93] Because the railroads depended upon telegraphy for operations, they would thus become a powerful constituency against nationalization of the telegraph. The Butler Amendment became law shortly after American Union Telegraph incorporated in May 1879. Gould's way was prepared.

---

[87] *Minutes of a Hearing before the Committee on Railroads*, 2d, 13 February 1879, 28.

[88] Ibid., 16–17.

[89] Ibid., 3.

[90] "A Pathetic Plea," *New York Daily Graphic*, 28 February 1879, 805.

[91] "Congress and the Telegraph: Action of the Senate and House on the Bill of Senator Jones…" *Journal of the Telegraph*, 1 March 1879, 66.

[92] Benjamin Butler, "Interview," 27 February 1879, Butler Papers.

[93] The Butler Amendment as originally written did not require railroads to give their written assent to the Telegraph Act of 1866. In assenting, the railroad companies formally accepted the Act's provisions for a government buyout of telegraph lines. Western Union's managers may have feared the railroads would be granted the right-of-way provisions without being subjected to a potential buyout. Revised Statutes, 46th Congress, Session I, Chapter 35, 23 June 1879.

Western Union's domination of railroad rights-of-way had made it appear unassailable. But Western Union was like an ancient city that had invested all its resources in building high walls: however impregnable it appeared, if the walls could be breached, the city would fall. With new legal leverage in hand, Gould began his attack. Before American Union officially launched, Gould once again donned the mantle of the antimonopolist. American Union promotional pamphlets promised the company would relieve "the public from the burdens imposed by monopoly." No more would the people be "at the mercy of [Western Union's] continued extortions." The pamphlets announced the American Union's strategy was to "explode" Western Union's anticompetitive railroad contracts.[94]

After the incorporation of the American Union in May 1879, newspapers reported that Gould had gone West with a cadre of railroad men and a "huge pile of railroad and telegraph maps and other important-looking documents." The purported object of the trip was to "perfect new schemes of connection" for Gould's Western railroads, but also to secure a telegraph connection with John Garrett's B&O for a network "in opposition to Western Union."[95] By summer a proxy war erupted between American Union and James Shaw's Continental Telegraph in New Jersey. Shaw, an ally of Western Union, sent his men to cut down poles allegedly constructed illegally by American Union. Gould's lawyers secured warrants for Shaw's arrest in several towns. Western Union arranged for bail services to keep Shaw out of jail and ensure his "successful contest."[96] American Union offered a $2,000 reward for proof that Continental workmen were behind the dismantling of American Union lines and proclaimed that Continental was "known" to be under Western Union's control.[97]

Meanwhile, *Pensacola* and Gould's legislative wrangling was paying off. The major victory for American Union that summer, indeed the key to "exploding" Western Union's railroad contracts, was not the guerrilla war in New Jersey but a court case in Indiana. In 1870, the Wabash Railway and Western Union had entered into a typical contract: Western Union erected lines and operated them; Wabash provided operators and offices, maintained the lines, and committed to Western Union "the

94 "List of Offices of the American Union Telegraph Company," n.d. [c. 1880], WUC.
95 "Jay Gould's Western Trip," *The New York Times*, 16 May 1879.
96 Norvin Green to Drexel and Morgan, 1 August 1879, WUC.
97 "List of Offices of the American Union Telegraph Company," n.d. [c. 1880], WUC.

exclusive right of way along the road."[98] The Wabash had since been mortgaged, foreclosed, and purchased out of receivership by a successor corporation. That corporation, now under Gould's control, denied that Western Union's exclusive right-of-way was still in force or had even been legal in the first place. Under Gould's direction, the Wabash permitted the American Union to build lines on its right-of-way. At Western Union's request, the federal circuit court ordered construction halted until a hearing on the legality of the contract, giving Gould an opportunity to test *Pensacola*. Gould's lawyers argued that Western Union sought to use the court "to enforce a covenant openly and avowedly to discourage that competition and freedom of trade which public policy so warmly encourages."[99] The argument was an arrow shot straight into Western Union's Achilles' heel.

The decision in the Wabash case proved more devastating to Western Union than Gould's attorneys could have hoped. Judge Harlan agreed that the court could not sustain an injunction to protect Western Union's exclusive right-of-way. But he also ruled that the exclusive contract violated the Telegraph Act of 1866. The Supreme Court's *Pensacola* decision established the federal government's supremacy in telegraph regulation, so Harlan looked to the only relevant federal law – the Telegraph Act – and read in it a clear public policy preference for open rights-of-way and telegraph competition. The railroad could not exclude from the right-of-way any telegraph company that assented to the terms of the Telegraph Act provided the new lines would not materially damage or obstruct existing lines. The intent of the federal telegraph law, Harlan explained, was to open post roads to all telegraph companies. As the Supreme Court had ruled in *Pensacola* that state legislatures could not grant monopolies in violation of the Telegraph Act, certainly private railroad corporations could not do so either.[100]

After more than a decade of ambiguity, the courts had given the Telegraph Act of 1866 a definitive interpretation: the law demanded a

---

[98] H. S. Green and Wager Swayne, *The Western Union Telegraph Company V. The Wabash Railway Company, Et Al.: Argument for Defendant Railway Company* (Chicago: Press of Beach, Barnard & Co., Legal Printers, 1879), 5.

[99] Ibid., 22.

[100] "United States Circuit Court. District of Indiana. *Western Union Telegraph Co. V. American Union Co. Et Al,*" *The American Law Register (1852–1891)* 28, no. 3 (1880). There were two glaring ambiguities in this decision. First, Harlan offered no definition of what constituted material interference with an existing line. Second, there were no established mechanisms for condemnation for telegraphic purposes, though Harlan indicated that such condemnation required compensation.

competitive telegraph industry, and the federal government had the authority, even against hostile state legislation and exclusive private contracts, to encourage such competition. Railroads had the right to invite rival telegraph lines onto their rights-of-way, and, if they would not do so, the rights-of-way could be forced open by condemnation. American Union, a creature of railroad magnates to begin with, was perfectly designed to take advantage of the leverage newly granted to railroad operators. In November American Union announced that the B&O's John Garrett had joined the company's directorate. The American Union's executive committee, consisting of Garret, Gould and Russell Sage, had come to resemble a railroad war council.[101]

In January 1880, American Union officially opened for business. Gould's new telegraph company sprouted with extraordinary swiftness. In little more than seven months the American Union connected all the major cities from New York to Omaha with twelve thousand miles of wire. To build lines, Gould established another firm, the Central Construction Company. Though it had its own $5 million capital, Central Construction was entirely the creature of American Union, which dictated where it built lines and then took possession of them "at fair valuation."[102] American Union's construction took place at a rate never before seen in the telegraph industry. Gould had launched his A&P campaign five years earlier with a small network of lines already in place, but the American Union sprouted from scratch. Gould and his partners supplied "abundant capital," and according to one observer, "The lines went up as if by magic."[103]

Under the terms of the Butler Amendment, the B&O, Wabash and several other railroads assented to the Telegraph Act of 1866, expanded their telegraph operations, and pledged them to Gould's American Union.[104] In Canada Gould threatened Western Union's exclusive connections to the Montreal Telegraph Company – a surviving member of the 1850s telegraph cartel – and the Dominion Telegraph Company, which had formerly been a partner of the A&P. Western Union managers had long encouraged the Montreal and Dominion companies to consolidate to prevent their rivalry from being used to the advantage of a Western Union

[101] American Union Telegraph Company Directors Meeting, 3 November 1879, WUC.
[102] American Union Telegraph Board of Directors Meeting, 31 October 1879, WUC. Washington Connor was the president, and the executive committee included Joseph Owen, James Owen, and G. P. Morosini, Gould's personal assistant.
[103] Reid, *Telegraph in America*, 578.
[104] "The New Telegraph System," *New York Tribune*, 17 January 1880, 8.

competitor looking for Canadian allies. After merger talks failed in 1879, the Dominion Company ignored its exclusive contract with Western Union and connected to the American Union.[105] Gould subsequently leased the entire Dominion Telegraph, doubling the size of the American Union's network and creating a trunk line to Chicago via Canada, bypassing Western Union's exclusive rights-of-way in the states.[106]

Having already formed alliances with two of the most powerful Eastern railroads, the B&O and the Pennsylvania, the American Union launched an attack on Western Union lines on the Western roads under Gould's control. The Kansas Pacific Railroad ignored a contract requiring the transportation of Western Union men and materials and used a switching engine to forcibly rip Western Union wires off the poles. Western Union sought relief in federal court and won an injunction, yet rumors abounded that American Union had secretly installed batteries along the railroad – at a moment's notice, the American Union could flip a switch and take over the lines from Chicago to Kansas City in an electrical coup d'état.[107] No sooner had the Kansas Pacific been quieted than the battle flared again on the Union Pacific, which was also under Gould's control. Western Union's A&P affiliate controlled the lines on the Union Pacific railroad by lease. The railroad abruptly took possession of the A&P lines, cut off the A&P offices, and declared it would take messages from all telegraph companies. The Kansas Pacific and B&O did the same despite injunctions against them.[108] In just a few days, the American Union had created a spine for its network across the West.

Western Union had little to gain by attempting a war of force in which the railroads had all the advantages, so the mêlée moved into the courts.[109] In the legal battle, Western Union fared better. By the beginning of May a victory in the United States Circuit Court reinstated the company's control over many of the stolen lines.[110] Green dismissed Gould's attempt to build a system by snatching railroad lines as a mere "short lived robbery," but he warned his patron, William H. Vanderbilt, that Gould's real aim was "to break" Western Union's stock price. Green had been

---

[105] Norvin Green to Hugh Allan, 27 June 1879, WUC.
[106] Norvin Green to Hugh Allan, 10 July 1879, WUC.
[107] "Telegraph War," *Chicago Daily Tribune*, 27 February 1880, 7.
[108] "A New Way to Establish a Telegraph System," *Journal of the Telegraph*, 16 March 1880, 86. A court injunction prevented American Union from disturbing the Western Union lines on the Union Pacific Railroad.
[109] "The Rival Wires," *Chicago Daily Tribune*, 5 March 1880, 5.
[110] "The Telegraph War – Another Victory for the Western Union Telegraph Company," 1 May 1880, *Journal of the Telegraph*, 135.

"reliably informed" that Gould and his allies had sold Western Union short, and their theft on the railroads, even once legally repudiated, might be "enough to serve their purpose."[111]

There can be little doubt that from the beginning Gould planned to win his war in the stock market.[112] In December 1879, Green was certain that Gould was using the threat of American Union's impending attack to buy Western Union while its stock was down; then in March, Gould's party appeared to be selling Western Union short.[113] A month later Green believed that an attempt by John Garrett and J. C. Reiff to stir up legislation against Western Union in Congress validated rumors that the Gould party was once again accumulating Western Union.[114] Soon the financial press reported that Vanderbilt had sold one hundred thousand shares to Gould and was "clearing out" of Western Union altogether, which both men denied.[115] But Green privately admitted that the lack of Vanderbilt's support for the stock gave the bears control of the market. Gould was a "great fool" if he was not buying Western Union, but Green believed unequivocally that Gould *was* buying, that he intended to get control of Western Union, and that he had created American Union entirely for this purpose.[116]

Green claimed that the "real effect of the opposition" was materially less substantial than the public assumed.[117] Unlike in the previous competition with Gould, costly rate competition was limited, and Western Union used the A&P to match the American Union's cuts.[118] Green urged Western Union's directors to keep up the fight, but he faced opposition from entrenched investors who owned large portions of his company. In addition to the cautious younger Vanderbilt, several large Western Union holders were interested above all in maintaining steady dividends.[119] This conservative faction presented a weakness for Gould to exploit – if he could control enough Western Union stock to elect new board members and tip the balance in favor of a settlement with American Union, he could end the

[111] Norvin Green to William H. Vanderbilt, 27 February 1880, WUC.
[112] Klein, *The Life and Legend of Jay Gould*, 278.
[113] Norvin Green to Gardiner G. Hubbard, 1 December 1879, WUC.
[114] Norvin Green to Augustus Schell, 23 April 1880, WUC. Green, or more likely, Vanderbilt, posted Schell at Willard's Hotel at the time to lobby full-time against threatening legislation.
[115] Klein, *The Life and Legend of Jay Gould*, 278.
[116] Norvin Green to Duff, 1 June 1880, Green Papers (FHS).
[117] Norvin Green to Duff, 1 June 1880, Green Papers (FHS).
[118] Norvin Green to General Superintendents, 6 December 1879, WUC.
[119] Grodinsky, *Jay Gould, His Business Career, 1867–1892*, 270.

telegraph war with a settlement between two boards that were *both* under his influence, in essence making an agreement with himself that would no doubt be favorable. He had done just that in merging the Kansas Pacific and Union Pacific railroads, "negotiating" an agreement with himself in which Kansas Pacific stock purchased at 11 percent of par was exchanged for Union Pacific stock at 96.[120] Such an agreement between American Union and Western Union would not only enrich Gould, it would make him the new owner of a reestablished telegraph monopoly.

Contrary to Green's prediction that Gould could not afford to wait, American Union had gained so much ground that Western Union's position had perceptibly weakened. Gould had expertly built a national network virtually overnight and projected further expansion.[121] American Union controlled lines on more than a dozen major railroads – a decisive advantage despite court battles and rumblings that Western Union would use the Page Patent to sue the railroads out of the telegraph business.[122] By the end of 1880, American Union operated with only a narrow loss – an astonishing feat for such a new and fast-growing firm.[123] Gould opened still another front, attacking Western Union's alliance with the Atlantic cable companies that operated as a monopoly cartel. Gould publicly railed against the cable monopoly and announced he was forming a cable company of his own. In just forty hours he raised $7 million in capital for the new American Telegraph & Cable Company – a greater sum than most overland telegraph companies had raised from investors in their entire existence.[124]

Western Union's position on Wall Street steadily worsened. The competition with American Union devoured profits; the directors reduced the annual dividend; the stock price tumbled; and many Western Union insiders, fearing a protracted fight, sold their shares. But Gould kept buying, until by the end of 1880 he had the largest single stake in Western Union.[125] Green later told New York state legislators that Gould, the "great leader" of the bear party, had duped the many speculators who believed Western Union would tumble still lower. The short-sellers thought they were following Gould, but "the wily leader doubled on his tracks," and the pack

[120] Green warned of Gould's plot using these numbers on the railroad merger. Norvin Green to W. O'Brien, 23 September 1870, Green Papers (FHS).
[121] American Union Telegraph Company Directors Meeting, 23 August 1880, WUC.
[122] Grodinsky, *Jay Gould, His Business Career, 1867–1892*, 280.
[123] Ibid., 275.
[124] Reid, *Telegraph in America*, 292.
[125] Grodinsky, *Jay Gould, His Business Career, 1867–1892*, 278.

of sellers did not see him "as he passed back, picking up the chickens they were dropping." By the time speculators realized Gould was *buying* Western Union, not selling, Gould was already "cozily ensconced in his den enjoying his chicken supper, sauced with 100,000 shares."[126] Western Union's share price had almost doubled from its low during the A&P war after the restoration of the monopoly in 1877. Gould's new war had taken 25 percent off the price of the stock, giving him an opportunity to buy back in at a substantial discount. At 78 per share, Gould's 90,200 Western Union shares were worth $7 million.

Green had no idea just how far Gould had come into the ownership of Western Union and that the war was already lost. Vanderbilt had been selling his holdings in Western Union and using the proceeds to buy into Western railroads, including forty thousand shares of Union Pacific, moving him closer to the Gould party. Vanderbilt met with Gould periodically to discuss railroad matters, though he later denied that they spoke about the telegraph in anything more than a passing way. Vanderbilt's Union Pacific holdings also led him to meet with Gould's colleague Sidney Dillon, who suggested that Gould was ready to harmonize their telegraph interests. Eager to end the strife, Vanderbilt sent a surrender note to Gould, who came the same afternoon to Vanderbilt's mansion with railroad magnates Sage, Dillon and Frederick Ames in tow.[127] Two days of "stormy" negotiations ensued.[128] Vanderbilt told Gould that Western Union stockholders had become "very uneasy" with declining profits and he had been under "a great pressure" to act.[129] As the largest Western Union stockholder and the most influential American Union stockholder, Gould was in an enviable negotiating position. If Vanderbilt refused to sell, Gould might take control of the company's board and settle the issue from the inside. Instead Gould offered a generous deal that enriched all the parties involved.[130]

In the agreement, Western Union paid $15 million in new stock to American Union shareholders, about *twice* what American Union had cost to build. The settlement included the absorption of the A&P – still

---

[126] Norvin Green, "Proposed Telegraph Legislation: Argument of President Norvin Green at Albany against the Proposed Anti-Consolidation Act," 16 February 1881, *Journal of the Telegraph*, 49.

[127] "Vanderbilt on the Witness Stand in Connection with the Telegraphic Consolidation," *Chicago Tribune*, 2 June 1881, 3.

[128] Klein, *The Life and Legend of Jay Gould*, 280.

[129] "Vanderbilt on the Witness Stand in Connection with the Telegraphic Consolidation," *Chicago Tribune*, 2 June 1881, 3.

[130] Klein, *The Life and Legend of Jay Gould*, 280.

operated by Western Union as a separate company – for another $8.4 million in new Western Union stock. Western Union shareholders received a $15 million stock dividend allegedly representing retained earnings that had financed line construction. Vanderbilt's son had "handed over a large part of the value which his father had created, to his father's arch-foe – Gould."[131]

Though the agreement was secret, the news leaked and Western Union's stock surged on the market. Investors were pleased; critics of the telegraph monopoly were not. *The New York Times* greeted the rumors of consolidation with the front-page headline, "Another Vast Monopoly."[132] The *Chicago Tribune* declared the merger was "unparalleled in the annals of stock-jobbing" and decried "Jay Gould's friendly contracts and negotiations with Jay Gould." Gould's "telegraphic aqua pura," the *Tribune* added the following day, would contain more than $30 million in watered stock.[133] In New York, outrage spread wide among the downtown merchants, and the Cotton Exchange and Produce Exchange formed committees to explore forming a new opposition company. The Merchants' Telegraph Company in Chicago raised half a million dollars in stock subscriptions.[134]

The most potentially damaging response came in the courts. Green assured Gould that the merger would "go smoothly" but recommended fortifying "with every care and precaution against any attack of the stock increase in the court."[135] Within days shareholder Rufus Hatch filed for an injunction against the merger. Hatch had a long history of conflict with Gould, but he made his court challenge against the merger in the name of public demand for cheaper telegraph rates. American Union had promised to confer "upon the community the blessing of cheap telegraphy" while earning healthy dividends besides, but this "engine with which to break up the monopoly" had been unjustly and illegally shut down, Hatch charged, and the businessmen of the United States would not submit to paying the outrageous rates that the enlarged Western Union would require to pay dividends on its bloated capital.[136] The judge

[131] Grodinsky, *Jay Gould, His Business Career, 1867–1892*, 281.
[132] "Another Vast Monopoly," 12 January 1881, *The New York Times*, 1.
[133] "A Chapter in Telegraphs Unparalleled in the Annals of Stock-Jobbing," *Chicago Tribune*, 13 January 1881, 6; "Water," *Chicago Tribune*, 14 January 1881, 2.
[134] "The Telegraph Schemes," *The New York Times*, 22 January 1881, 8.
[135] Norvin Green to Jay Gould, 13 January 1881, WUC.
[136] Rufus Hatch, "Affidavit of the Plaintiff," Rufus Hatch against American Union Telegraph Company, Western Union Telegraph Company, Atlantic and Pacific Telegraph Company and others, 19 January 1881, WUC.

denied Hatch's request for an injunction, leaving the "question of practical monopoly of telegraphy" to the legislature instead.[137]

Gould immediately cemented his control over Western Union, making Eckert the united company's General Manager. Green remained president, perhaps because of Gould's confidence in his leadership, but more likely because Green had proven an able defender of Western Union in Congress. Gould rewarded Green after the consolidation with access to American Cable Construction Company stock. Green subscribed to $50,000 in cable stock, asking that his name be kept off the books and almost certainly paying much less than the nominal price. A year later, Western Union leased the cable company, paying 5 percent annually on its nominal capital stock – a handsome return for insiders who bought below par. Green also requested another $750,000 for "friends" of Western Union.[138] Shareholder suits against Western Union became another speculative opportunity for Green and other insiders. Green bragged that he had taught the pressers of "speculative injunctions" that "others could play in their little game" of timing transactions according to court proceedings. Green made at least $100,000 from such speculation in the first six months following Gould's takeover.[139]

Gould rebuilt Western Union's board of directors and senior management, removing most of the Vanderbilt clique and installing his own allies, such as Dillon and Sage. The last of the "telegraph men" who had numbered among the industry's pioneers also departed. Gould ousted O. H. Palmer, Western Union's former treasurer and a stalwart since the firm's Rochester days. Green explained to Palmer that he was not of "material service" as an investor, nor had he any influence in "important Railroad contracts," and Gould wanted a seat for railroad titan Collis Huntington. There was no room for Palmer unless a new vacancy came up and no "big railroad man or a moneyed mogul" wanted the seat.[140] Western Union was now in the hands of the railroad capitalists.

Gould later claimed his victory over Vanderbilt and capture of Western Union was virtually accidental. "Well, the Western Union [stock price] went down and I bought a large interest in the stock," he told a committee of Senators in a voice so soft that they repeatedly asked him to speak up. "I found that the only way out was to put [the telegraph companies]

[137] "Telegraphic Litigation," *Journal of the Telegraph*, 16 February 1881, 51.
[138] Norvin Green to Jay Gould, 28 January and 31 January 1881, Green Papers (FHS).
[139] Norvin Green to George Douglass, 11 June 1881, George Douglass Papers (U.K.).
[140] Norvin Green to O. H. Palmer, 31 January 1882, Green Papers (FHS).

together – that an opposition could not sustain itself, and I bought a very large interest in the Western Union, and out of that grew the present state of things."[141] In the "present state of things," Gould controlled Western Union and made its granite skyscraper his personal headquarters. His ninety thousand Western Union shares doubled in value after the announcement of the American Union consolidation. In the merger he exchanged his American Union and A&P for still more Western Union stock. In all, Western Union's capital increased to $80 million – more than twice what it had been when Orton finished squeezing the water from the stock shortly before Gould's first attack in 1875. Yet Western Union's network had increased in mileage by only a little more than 50 percent during the same period, and the new mileage constructed by the American Union had been designed to duplicate Western Union lines.[142]

In the end, Gould's scheme to grab Western Union did little to improve telegraph service. In the three years in which he built American Union, competed with Western Union, and then merged the two companies, Western Union's average toll barely declined while the cost per message slightly increased.[143] There was little benefit to telegraph users, who ultimately paid the dividends on the new Western Union shares that Gould paid to himself and his partners in exchange for the competitor they created. The American telegraph remained expensive, its use largely limited to commercial customers who could afford to pay steep rates.

It can be justly argued that as a finance capitalist, Gould was ahead of his time, that his rivals despised him primarily because he beat them at their own game. But Gould had also made a mockery of a supposedly self-regulating capitalist system reliant upon competition, trust, and some notion of fair play. In 1866, the presidents of the three largest telegraph companies urged Congress to keep out of the industry on the grounds that a public telegraph would be "inferior and terribly destructive," but private enterprise lent the telegraph "that spirit of self support which gives sinew to the national character, and vigor and manhood to the citizen."[144] This romantic vision of self-sufficient, competitive entrepreneurs

---

[141] *Report of the Committee of the Senate Upon the Relations between Labor and Capital,* 1069.

[142] Western Union 1891 Annual Report, WUC.

[143] Average tolls for 1879–1882 were $0.386, $0.385, $0.384, and $0.382. Average costs per message were $0.252, $0.256, $0.258, and $0.260. Western Union 1891 Annual Report, WUC.

[144] "Letter from the Postmaster General," Ex. Doc. No. 49, 39th Congress, 1st Session, 12.

may have applied to antebellum proprietary capitalists, but as a pioneering finance capitalist, Gould played a different game altogether. He built an entire telegraph network to serve as little more than bait to lure bigger prizes in the stock market and his railroad empire. He manipulated the press, co-opted telegraph reform as a way to damage Western Union, and quite probably controlled telegraph stock prices. He was a virtuoso to be sure, but his art was a swindle. Gould's critic Henry Demarest Lloyd described his con: "Swinging his legs from a back-tilted chair, he would tell his friends that Western Union was a worthless bundle of expiring patents, uncertain contracts, and old wires, and that he should not buy a share above sixty."[145] But the price never fell to sixty, and Gould had been buying Western Union all along. Telegraph competition had been nothing but a fiction, written in Gould's own hand.

---

[145] Lloyd, "The Political Economy of Seventy-Three Million Dollars," 78.

8

Octopus of the Wires

The trope of the robber baron has had a longer stay in the popular imagination than in historical scholarship. Seminal works such as Gustavus Myers' *History of the Great American Fortunes* and Matthew Josephson's *The Robber Barons* defined the genre in the early twentieth century.[1] Josephson's epic of corruption and thievery is still in print after three quarters of a century, and popular histories often recycle his rich yarns.[2] Academic historians, however, have relegated the robber barons to legend, downgrading them from selfish, power-hungry brutes to merely "semipiratical entrepreneurs" and then transforming them into industrial statesmen.[3] The robber baron archetype suffered some obvious problems, not least of which was the dramatic, Manichean picture of a society in which the "public" was manifestly "good" while industrial titans were manifestly "bad" and immune to social sanctions and cultural norms.[4] Such villainy has no place in contemporary business history, which

---

[1] Gustavus Myers, *History of the Great American Fortunes*, III vols., vol. III (Chicago: Charles H. Kerr & Company, 1909); Matthew Josephson, *The Robber Barons; the Great American Capitalists, 1861–1901* (New York: Harcourt Brace and Company, 1934).

[2] For a recent entry in this category, see Jack Beatty, *Age of Betrayal: The Triumph of Money in America, 1865–1900* (New York: Alfred A. Knopf, 2007).

[3] Chester McArthur Destler, "Entrepreneurial Leadership among the 'Robber Barons': A Trial Balance," *The Journal of Economic History* 6, Supplement: The Tasks of Economic History (1946): 46.

[4] Thomas Childs Cochran, "The Legend of the Robber Barons," *Entrepreneurial History* 1, no. 5 (1949): 6; Four years later in *Railroad Leaders*, Cochran expanded his examination of the influence of culture in business behavior and dismissed the robber baron story entirely, expanding the role that managers or "professional entrepreneurs" played in great business enterprises. See Thomas Childs Cochran, *Railroad Leaders, 1845–1890* (Cambridge, Mass.: Harvard University Press, 1953).

suspends moral judgment, all but ignores intentionality, and demotes the omnipotent barons to little more than a supporting role. In the "organizational synthesis,"[5] the corporation itself and newly empowered salaried executives such as Western Union president William Orton became the stars of the show. The bill of lading and standard accounting procedures played a greater part in determining the course of industrial development than secret deals and stock manipulations. Perhaps a few moguls acted with mercenary motives, but larger trends toward centralization and deployment of technological advances determined the outcome. Titans like Gould were little more than a bridge between traditional merchant capitalism and the modern multiunit enterprise. They were ahead of the curve, but they did not dictate the trajectory. They built the railroads that drove the revolution, but the revolution was bigger than they were.[6]

The transition in industrial history from the realm of caricatures, rumors, and tall tales to an empirically based organizational synthesis was a great advance in scholarship, but it does not tell the whole story. Gilded Age corruption, both financial and political, was real, and corporations were at the center of many of the worst abuses. As historian Richard White has recently written about the tangled web of subsidies, debt schemes, and stock manipulations on the Western railroads, "Corruption was never so simple as businessmen seeking to improve their bottom line; the corrupt often prospered at the expense of the firms they ran. Corruption produced winners and losers and tangible results."[7]

What was true of the railroads was true as well for the telegraph – the manipulation of Western Union stock for the enrichment of its large shareholders had tangible results. Gould's competitive threat may have forced Western Union to streamline its operations and, for a time at least, to reduce tariffs and consequently open the telegraph to a broader public, but a real, *permanent* competition rather than merely a speculative one could have achieved the same outcome. The machinations that

---

[5] Louis Galambos, "The Emerging Organizational Synthesis in Modern American History," *Business History Review* 44, no. 3 (1970); Louis Galambos, "Technology, Political Economy, and Professionalization: Central Themes of the Organizational Synthesis," *Business History Review* 57, no. 4 (1983).

[6] Alfred D. Chandler, *The Visible Hand: The Managerial Revolution in American Business* (Cambridge, Mass.: Belknap Press of Harvard University Press, 1977). For an excellent overview of Chandler's influence twenty years after *The Visible Hand*, see Richard R. John, "Elaborations, Revisions, Dissents: Alfred D. Chandler, Jr.'s The Visible Hand after Twenty Years," *Business History Review* 71, no. 2 (1997).

[7] Richard White, "Information, Markets, and Corruption: Transcontinental Railroads in the Gilded Age," *The Journal of American History* 90, no. 1 (2003): 43.

determined when the telegraph companies would compete and when they would merge had more to do with market speculation and leverage over railroads than the efficient transmission of messages. Vanderbilt, Gould, and their colleagues raked in profits from buying and selling telegraph securities, but telegraph customers and ultimately the enterprise itself paid for it.

Jay Gould had already secured a despicable place in the popular imagination when he completed his takeover of Western Union in 1881. At the news of Gould's victory *The New York Times* declared there was nothing left to celebrate on Washington's birthday, since "free government" had "lasted only a century, and Mr. Gould is now on the point of completely and forever destroying it." "His Majesty Jay Gould" dominated the railroads and could manipulate the stock market at will. He allegedly controlled two – perhaps even three – of the seven papers that managed the Associated Press (AP), and now Western Union gave him power over the news itself.[8] An 1881 cartoon in *Puck* depicted Gould and William Vanderbilt torturing Uncle Sam on a rack fashioned from a telegraph pole, wires, and two locomotives. A New York *Times* headline tarred Western Union as the "Octopus of the Wires" in 1883.[9] In 1884, it was widely believed that Gould had used Western Union to hold back election returns and make a fortune in the market.

The historians who popularized the robber baron mythology enthusiastically repeated popular allegations against Gould. According to one account, Gould "scanned the telegraph, or manipulated it, as an open book to the secret of all the marts."[10] Western Union president Norvin Green resolutely denied the potential for any such "scanning." Gould, he claimed, never went near the operating room. More than three million messages per month passed through Western Union's offices, but not more than one complaint per year fairly accused the company's employees of exposing the contents of a private message. Nine-tenths

---

[8] "His Majesty Jay Gould," *The New York Times*, 23 February 1881, 4. Maury Klein has argued that Gould controlled the *World* for only a brief period of time, that he had no proven influence over the *Tribune*, and that he did not control a third AP paper. See Maury Klein, *The Life and Legend of Jay Gould* (Baltimore: Johns Hopkins University Press, 1986), 394.

[9] "The Two Philanthropists," *Puck*, 23 February 1881, 8; "The Octopus of the Wires," *The New York Times,* 3 August 1883, 3.

[10] Matthew Josephson, *The Robber Barons: The Great American Capitalists, 1861–1901* (New York: Harcourt Brace and Company, 1934), 208.

of Atlantic cable messages were transmitted in cipher and could not be "scanned" even if they were exposed.[11] Gould's detractors similarly accused him of fabricating news to influence the stock market, protect capital, and thwart "labor and radical movements at every opportunity." According to one purveyor of robber baron tales, Gould used the telegraph to prejudice "the mass of the public against any movement or agitation threatening the complete sway of capital."[12] In fact, no conspiracy was necessary to prejudice the public against labor radicalism. Although Gould strengthened Western Union's relationship with the AP, he did not – indeed, could not – control the press syndicate, at least not directly.[13]

Though Gould probably did not use Western Union for the nefarious purposes so often reported in the press, there is nonetheless little doubt that he used the company for his personal gain – primarily through his maneuvers in Western Union stock.[14] In 1882 the Gould-dominated board reversed Western Union's twelve-year policy of funding construction with retained net earnings – henceforth profits would be appropriated for dividends, and construction funded with assets from the bulging company treasury, such as surplus Western Union shares and telephone stocks.[15] There was nothing illegal about the new policy, but it amounted to a raid on the company piggybank and again signaled that construction was no longer the highest priority. The dividend increased to 7 percent per year, which Green regretted in later years, admitting it was "not so easy" to return to lower payments. Green acknowledged that the gush of cash paid to shareholders left him with funds "scarcely sufficient to

---

[11] Green to the Editor of the *Evening Post*, 24 November 1882, WUC.

[12] Gustavus Myers, *History of the Great American Fortunes*, III vols., vol. III (Chicago: Charles H. Kerr & Company, 1909), 90.

[13] Menahem Blondheim discusses Gould's aborted effort to bring Western Union into the news business. This was probably less an evil scheme than an attempt to rationalize Western Union's relationship with the several warring syndicates. By 1885, the joint New York AP and Western Associated Press had formed a secret trust with the opposition United Press, creating a complete news monopoly in which Gould played no part at all. See Menahem Blondheim, *News over the Wires: The Telegraph and the Flow of Public Information in America, 1844–1897* (Cambridge, Mass.: Harvard University Press, 1994), 164–8.

[14] Klein has attempted to redeem Gould's reputation by showing that he ran Western Union effectively in the 1880s, earning and paying regular dividends. However evidence suggests that Gould's personal wealth was his primary concern, and Western Union's financial and material condition both declined during the period. See Klein, *The Life and Legend of Jay Gould*, 474.

[15] Green to David A. Wells, 6 August 1885, WUC.

provide for the new constructions" required to keep up with railroad extensions and growing business.[16]

During Gould's tenure Western Union also reduced investments in research and development, leading to a "conspicuous failure to advance the telegraph art."[17] In the 1870s, Western Union had launched multiplex telegraphy and contributed to the development of the telephone. In the 1880s, however, the company abandoned in-house research and charged the electrician's office to pursue patent violators instead.[18] The company all but ignored areas in which telegraph innovation was most in demand, such as underground wiring for crowded municipal wires or automatic telegraph devices that might democratize telegraphy. Western Union relied principally on the same Morse technology that had been in service for decades, and only the threat from long-distance telephony in the early twentieth century finally forced the company to return to significant investments in research and development.[19]

Despite the popular perception of Gould as a fearsome overlord wielding Western Union against the people, Western Union's dominance of the nation's communications declined during the 1880s. Gould's capture of Western Union from Vanderbilt raised the fearsome possibility that Gould would use the company to expand his power on Wall Street, but the opposite ensued. Gould's commercial empire was embattled on several fronts in the 1880s, including Western Union. For all his might as a market operator, Gould could not stop speculators from manipulating Western Union's stock just as he had, nor prevent new competitors from trying to compel him to buy them out. Western Union's lobby continued to undercut reform efforts in Congress, but not even Gould could stop the campaigns for cheaper telegraphy. Perhaps most dangerously, the Octopus of the Wires could not contain the resentment and frustration of the operators who made the iron wire speak.

Not since the 1870 operators' strike had Western Union or any other telegraph company faced a significant challenge from organized workers. The failure of 1870 discouraged unionism – Western Union crushed the strike

---

[16] Norvin Green to James F. Demarest, 31 March 1884, Norvin Green Papers (FHS).
[17] H. H. Goldin, "Governmental Policy and the Domestic Telegraph Industry," *The Journal of Economic History* 7, no. 1 (1947).
[18] Paul Israel, *From Machine Shop to Industrial Laboratory: Telegraphy and the Changing Context of American Invention, 1830–1920* (Baltimore: Johns Hopkins University Press, 1992), 146.
[19] Ibid., 158.

and destroyed the Telegraphers' Protective League (TPL) along with it. Operators who returned to work took the "ironclad oath" not to participate in "combinations" against the company. Rumors of a "blacklist" banning organizers from employment at any Western Union office were probably true.[20] Even *The Telegrapher*, once the voice of the National Telegraphers Union and later an independent operators' journal, folded in 1877 and merged into *The Journal of the Telegraph*, Western Union's official newspaper.

After a decade of quiet, however, two conditions made it all but inevitable that telegraph workers would again begin to organize: the growth of labor unionism across American industry and the steady decline in wages at Western Union. The harsh economic conditions of the 1870s and the Great Railroad Strike of 1877 touched off a groundswell of labor activism. The 1880s saw hundreds of thousands of workers engaged in tens of thousands of labor actions. One historian's description of the socially regressive pressures heaped upon workers after the Civil War epitomized the plight of the telegraph operator: "the permanency of wage labor, the physical and mental exhaustion inflicted by the factory system, and the arrogant exercise of power by the owners of capital."[21]

Despite Jay Gould's characterization of telegraphy in 1883 as a "nice, genteel occupation," telegraphers had a litany of complaints.[22] An operator's job was exhausting, both in large urban offices in which message traffic was relentless, and in small rural railroad offices where a telegrapher's duties often included selling tickets, handling baggage, and signaling trains. "There are few old men in the telegraph business," an operator told a Senate committee in 1883. "Either he dies young, or he is compelled to quit the business to save his health."[23] Operators complained about long night shifts, and they particularly despised working on Sunday, a service they believed to be more important to the telegraph company than to the public. Unlike most manual laborers, telegraph operators generally received a monthly salary and no overtime, a formula that operators supposed encouraged their exploitation. A frequent complaint held that "common laborers" digging ditches earned more than

[20] Vidkunn Ulriksson, *The Telegraphers: Their Craft and Unions* (Washington, D.C.: Public Affairs Press, 1953), 37.

[21] Leon Fink, *Workingmen's Democracy: The Knights of Labor and American Politics* (Urbana and Chicago: University of Illinois Press, 1983), 4.

[22] *Report of the Committee of the Senate Upon the Relations between Labor and Capital*, 5 vols., vol. I (Washington, D.C.: U.S. Government Printing Office, 1885), 1084.

[23] Ibid., 116.

operators if they worked the same hours. Even worse, operator wages fell steadily after the 1870 strike. Though the 1870s were a deflationary decade – consumer prices fell by more than 20 percent – operator wages fell by perhaps twice as much during the same period. According to operator testimony to Congress in 1883, the average monthly operator salary was $54 for commercial operators and $39 for railroad operators, down from around $100 in 1870. These declines resulted from Western Union's wage-reducing "sliding scale." Though Western Union employed only one-fifth of all operators directly – two-thirds were railroad operators only indirectly in Western Union's service – the giant company fixed the standard of labor and other firms "followed its lead" on wages.[24]

Western Union operators saw a direct connection between their labor, the rewards paid to capital, and the prices paid by the telegraphing public. While operator compensation declined, telegraph investors grew rich through large dividend payments and the generous buyouts Western Union paid to new competitors. The invention of multiplex telegraphy had increased the carrying capacity of telegraph lines, reducing capital costs per message, but none of this increase in profitability accrued to operators. Operators saw the outsized return on Western Union's watered stock and the vast sums paid to competitors as penalizing their wages directly – labor paid for the sins of finance capitalism.[25]

By 1881, telegraph operators had formed two labor unions: the conservative Brotherhood of the Telegraph and the United Telegraphers of America, which became the first telegraphers union to affiliate with the Knights of Labor. In the summer of 1882, the two unions merged to form the Brotherhood of the Telegraph of the United States and Canada, District Assembly 45 of the Knights of Labor.[26] The booming Knights reached more than 700,000 members by 1886 and represented a major shift from elite craft unionism to industrial unionism combining both skilled and unskilled workers. The Knights warned against the "alarming development and aggressiveness of great capitalists and corporations," which left unchecked would "inevitably lead to the pauperization and hopeless depredation of the toiling masses."[27] This view aligned with the perception among operators that capital was steadily grinding

---

[24] Ibid., 103–5.
[25] Ibid., 135–40.
[26] Edwin Gabler, *The American Telegrapher: A Social History, 1860–1900* (New Brunswick, N.J.: Rutgers University Press, 1988), 159–61.
[27] George E. McNeil, *The Labor Movement: The Problem of Today* (New York: The M. W. Hazen Co., 1892), 485.

down wages, overworking and impoverishing operators. The Knights also offered a strategic advantage over the TPL, the secretive, elitist craft union responsible for the failed strike of 1870. The TPL had excluded women and railroad telegraph operators, leaving Western Union two large sources of strike-breaking replacement labor. The Brotherhood of the Telegraph shared the Knights' principle of including all the workers in the industry, male and female, skilled and unskilled. The Brotherhood included not only commercial operators, but also railroad operators and even telegraph linemen.[28]

The agenda of the Brotherhood of the Telegraph reflected demands that operators had made for years: eight-hour day shifts and seven-hour night shifts, equal pay for equal work for female operators, and overtime for Sunday work and long shifts. After robustly growing to 150 assemblies in the United States and Canada, in July 1883 the Brotherhood presented a list of grievances to managers at Western Union, several smaller telegraph companies, telephone companies, and electric-light companies.[29] The leaders of the Brotherhood insisted that a strike had not been their aim, that they combined only for "self-protection" and with "the knowledge that they were quietly being worsted by the company, gradually growing downward as to the salaries and general treatment."[30] Western Union managers, who had most certainly been monitoring the growth of the union, denied that the Brotherhood legitimately represented their employees and refused to consider the list of grievances.

On July 19, 1883, three hundred operators walked out of the Washington Western Union office and the Great Strike began. For two weeks the strikers fared well – three-quarters of commercial operators in "the principal commercial towns and cities" left their jobs.[31] The union claimed two thousand new members in the first weeks and six thousand by the third week, a significant portion of the perhaps twenty thousand telegraph operators in the United States and Canada. The Brotherhood claimed to represent 90 percent of Western Union's workers.[32] Nor was Western Union the only firm affected. At least two other firms that workers

---

[28] *Report of the Committee of the Senate Upon the Relations between Labor and Capital*, 101.
[29] Electric-light companies were included because they employed linemen. Ibid., 110.
[30] Ibid., 178.
[31] Norvin Green to Proctor Scott, 29 November 1886, Green Papers (FHS).
[32] This figure is based on an 1883 estimate from a Brotherhood leader. *Report of the Committee of the Senate Upon the Relations between Labor and Capital*, 102, 12.
(112)

struck, the American Rapid Telegraph and the Bankers' & Merchants,' acceded to the union's demands for higher wages and overtime pay for Sunday work.[33]

Despite a substantial loss of business, Western Union kept the wires alive with a combination of nonstriking "pigeons" and unemployed and retired telegraphers. As the duration of the strike stretched from days to weeks, the conflict became a battle of endurance, a contest that favored the corporation with its vast resources. In early August, the Brotherhood called for railroad telegraphers to strike as well, but the movement failed. The tide had turned against the union.[34] A committee of employees met with Western Union's general manger T. T. Eckert, but he refused to negotiate.[35] On August 17, the strike collapsed in an unmitigated defeat for the operators.

The strikers blamed the union leadership for strategic and tactical errors and publicly accused the Knights of Labor of inadequate support. Terence Powderly, the leader of the Knights, claimed in his autobiography that the clandestine Brotherhood was only loosely connected to the Knights and Powderly – who opposed union secrecy – did not learn about the strike until the wheels were already in motion. He tried to persuade the Brotherhood to forestall the walkout but had no power to interfere in the union's affairs.[36]

Though costly for both parties, labor fared worse in the strike than Western Union. The strikers lost $150,000 in wages, and a quarter found they had no jobs to which they could return because Western Union made the temporary "plugs" permanent. Labor leaders claimed Western Union's financial losses totaled more than $2 million.[37] Green believed the strike's total cost to Western Union was less than $1 million,[38] but acknowledged the contest was "very desperate and expensive." Still he *insisted* fighting the strikers had been "absolutely necessary to maintain the right of the stockholders to manage their own property,"[39] and the hundreds of thousands of dollars lost in the strike were "the best financial investment"

---

[33] McNeil, *The Labor Movement: The Problem of Today*, 391.
[34] Gabler, *The American Telegrapher*, 13–21.
[35] Ulriksson, *The Telegraphers*, 47.
[36] Powderly claimed that he foiled a plot by a radical to bring a successful conclusion to the strike by dynamiting the poles in front of the Western Union building. Terence V. Powderly, *The Path I Trod*, ed. Harry J. Carman, Henry David, and Paul N. Guthrie (New York: Columbia University Press, 1940), 106–12.
[37] McNeil, *The Labor Movement: The Problem of Today*.
[38] Green to H. W. Blair, 10 January 1884, WUC.
[39] Norvin Green to Proctor Scott, 29 November 1886, Green Papers (FHS).

Western Union had ever made. Green told a reporter after the strike, "General Eckert tells me he will get one-third more work out of a man each day, and that is economy."[40] Despite such boasts, the Knights did not shrink from further contests with Jay Gould. In 1885, the Knights forced Gould to recognize a union contract on the Missouri-Pacific Railroad and "we made Jay Gould recognize us" became a rallying cry that attracted hundreds of thousands of new members. This victory, however, was short lived: Gould crushed the 1886 Great Southwest Strike, one of the first in a series of defeats that devastated the Knights of Labor.[41]

Despite Green's claims of "economy," the Great Strike inspired greater opposition to Western Union monopoly in the press than at any previous point. This ironically may have worked against the strikers. *The Nation* suggested the strike relied too much "on the sympathy of the public and the unpopularity of the Company," fooling strikers into believing that "the business men of the country were really on their side."[42] The *New York Herald*, Western Union's most persistent foe, railed against the corporation day after day in its pages, as did dozens of other newspapers across the country. "The telegraph business in this country is already in the hands of a huge and unscrupulous monopoly, and the tendency is toward further monopoly," claimed the *Memphis Appeal*. Several papers speculated that the strike had drummed up so much support for a government telegraph that Gould had engineered the whole episode as a way to sell Western Union to Congress for "an enormous price."[43] A study of editorials in the wake of the strike found 123 notices in 79 different newspapers in favor of government telegraphy.[44] The Senate Committee on the Relations Between Labor and Capital, which had been formed in 1882 to investigate the industrial conditions responsible for the alarming number of strikes in the United States, interviewed telegraph strike leaders, rank and file operators, and Jay Gould and Norvin Green.

For operators, telegraph reformers in Congress, and the telegraphing public, the chief problem in the industry remained the chronic lack of significant competition – the Western Union "monopoly." There could be

---

[40] "Views of President Green," *Boston Globe*, 22 August 1883, 4.

[41] Lawrence Goodwyn, *The Populist Moment: A Short History of the Agrarian Revolt in America* (New York: Oxford University Press, 1978), 35–6.

[42] "The Last Stage in the Telegraphic Strike," *The Nation*, 9 August 1883, 110.

[43] Dozens of editorials favoring the postal telegraph were reprinted in *Report of the Committee on Post-Offices and Post-Roads, United States Senate, on the Postal Telegraph*, (Washington, D.C.: U.S. Government Printing Office, 1884), 86, 92.

[44] "Postal Telegraph Facilities," September 1890, WUC, 41–43.

no telegraph competition, a striker told the Senate committee, "because the one great corporation, the Western Union, swallows all competing lines as fast as they are constructed."[45] Bell Telephone Company president William H. Forbes later described how Western Union's competitors each posed "for a time as a public benefactor, organized to fight the Western Union," winning public sympathy and rights-of-way under this pretext. However the results were always the same: "The footsteps of all lead into the Western Union cave; not one has ever returned."[46] The Pacific & Atlantic, the Atlantic & Pacific, and the American Union had all promised to break the Western Union monopoly, and the latter two firms built credible competing national networks. But the major stockholders in all three companies had found generous buyouts more compelling than liberating the nation from the telegraph monopoly. It is not surprising, given Gould's success in creating competitors and selling them to Western Union, that other entrepreneurs tried the same ploy after Gould took over in 1881.

Mutual Union Telegraph emerged as a new competitor almost immediately after Gould's successful raid on Western Union. Mutual Union had been formed in the 1870s by a pair of Washington, D.C., investors who – despite a lack of experience in the industry – sought to profit by operating on Eastern interurban trunk lines, rather than entering a general competition with Western Union. After American Union merged into Western Union in early 1881, Mutual Union's backers seized upon popular anger toward the restored telegraph "monopoly" as an opportunity to expand. The diminutive company's capital increased from $600,000 to $10 million; in two years the company established railroad contracts and built more than twenty-five thousand miles of wire in twenty-two states. Two prominent Western Union managers served successively as general manager of the fledgling enterprise, which grew without launching a rate war or a "noisy" public relations campaign. Mutual Union, like its predecessors, appeared to be a legitimate new competitor in the industry – until the "crookedness set in." Like so many telegraph and railroad companies before it, Mutual Union employed a contractor to build its lines and doled out large sums of stock in payment, which was not permitted by

---

[45] *Report of the Committee of the Senate Upon the Relations between Labor and Capital*, 127.
[46] Quoted in Ray Ginger, *Age of Excess: The United States from 1977 to 1914* (New York: The Macmillan Company, 1965), 34.

its corporate charter. Western Union added to the company's legal problems by suing it for infringing on the Page Patent.[47] Under pressure from the litigation, the company's stock became a target for stock speculators, including Gould, who intended to foil the Mutual Union threat by acquiring enough stock to control the rival firm.

Edward Bok worked as an office boy at Western Union at the time, and in his Pulitzer-prize winning autobiography, he described taking notes for Gould and learning about his stock machinations firsthand. Bok could not resist following Gould, whose moves in the market were "tallied precisely with the rise and fall of Western Union stock" because, Bok noted, "Jay Gould had the cards all in his hands."[48] When rumors on Wall Street suggested Gould had acquired enough stock to control Mutual Union, Western Union president Norvin Green denied knowing anything about it, while Mutual Union managers claimed that purveyors of the fraudulent news intended to bull Western Union stock.[49] But Bok remembered knowing "exactly whence this rumor emanated" – Gould's office.[50] According to Bok, Gould kept buying Western Union, and as the rumors spread that Gould controlled Mutual Union, Western Union rose by 15 percent. Finally, Gould publicly announced that he and his "friends" – several Mutual Union insiders – controlled more than half of Mutual Union's stock and a million dollars of the company's bonds. A "working compact" gave Western Union control over Mutual Union's management, and its bonds finally started paying interest.[51] A year later Western Union formally leased Mutual Union's lines, paying 1.5 percent on its $10 million in nominal capital. Because Gould had acquired much of Mutual Union's stock for less than 10 percent of its nominal value, Western Union – Gould's own company – paid Gould better than 15 percent per year on his "investment" in Mutual Union stock. Western Union also guaranteed a 6 percent payment on Mutual Union's five million

[47] James D. Reid, *The Telegraph in America and Morse Memorial*, 2d ed. (New York: John Polhemus, 1884), 602–4.

[48] Edward W. Bok, *The Americanization of Edward Bok: The Autobiography of a Dutch Boy Fifty Years After*, ed. W. David Lewis (New York: Charles Scribner's Sons, 2000), 97. Bok describes the speculation as being in American Union, but this is almost certainly an error. He recalls working for Gould at the Western Union building at 195 Broadway, which Gould moved into only after merging American Union and Western Union. Bok left Western Union in 1882, shortly after riding Gould's coattails in the market. Thus it is almost certain that Bok was actually describing Gould's speculation in Mutual Union.

[49] "Mutual Union and Western Union," *The New York Times*, 23 March 1882, 8.

[50] Bok, *The Americanization of Edward Bok*, 98.

[51] "Gould Controls the Telegraph," *The New York Times*, 31 March 1882, 8.

dollars in bonds, much of which Gould had acquired at prices well below par. The lion's share of Western Union's $450,000 in annual payments to former investors in Mutual Union probably went directly into Gould's pockets.[52]

One piece of Mutual Union eluded Western Union's grasp: John Garrett's Baltimore & Ohio Telegraph, a subsidiary of the Baltimore & Ohio Railroad (B&O). At nearly every opportunity Garrett had allied the B&O with whichever telegraph company threatened Western Union. In 1879, the B&O joined Gould's American Union but remained a separate property and pulled away when American Union and Western Union merged. Garrett leased B&O to Mutual Union when it challenged Western Union, and now that Mutual Union was gone he announced plans to launch his own general opposition. He hired away Western Union managers and operators and created a unique type of telegraph company that was an auxiliary to the B&O Railroad with no stock of its own. The railroad retained control of B&O Telegraph, which was actually a system of twenty-six companies, one per state.[53] Having no common stock on the market made B&O immune to Gould's favorite line of attack.

Western Union managers believed that only cash infusions from the B&O Railroad kept B&O Telegraph alive, and the competition would last only long enough for the B&O to pressure Western Union to offer a lucrative buyout.[54] But Gould would not consent to pay off competitors the way he had twice forced Western Union to do for him unless the transaction was personally profitable. Western Union managers were determined to wipe out the B&O and prevent the appearance of "a new opposition to buy off every year."[55] Just as Western Union had used its Atlantic & Pacific subsidiary to undercut the prices of American Union, the company now used the leased Mutual Union to undersell the B&O.[56]

In late 1884, John Garrett died and control of the B&O passed to his son Robert. Robert Garrett carried on the telegraph fight, but shareholders in the railroad company grew concerned about the diversion

---

[52] Gould claimed in 1882 that fifty-two thousand shares of Mutual Union had cost "something less than $500,000." The *Times* reported he had invested about a million dollars in Mutual Union's bonds, which were not paying interest and were probably available at well below par. See "Gould Controls the Telegraph," *The New York Times*, 31 March 1882, 8; "Mutual Union Wiped Out," *The New York Times*, 11 February 1883, 5.

[53] Reid, *Telegraph in America*, 758–60.

[54] Norvin Green to James Demarest, 26 August 1884, WUC.

[55] Green to A. W. Campbell, 30 December 1886, Green Papers (FHS).

[56] Green to Powell and Plympton, 8 January 1885, WUC.

of railroad funds into the telegraph venture. Throughout 1885, rumors swirled on Wall Street of consolidation between the combatants. Garrett grew anxious to unload the B&O on Western Union, perhaps because he had poured his own money into the scheme to quell criticism from the railroad shareholders.[57] Green reported that Garrett's "vain ambition for a telegraph system" had embarrassed B&O Railroad and now Garrett was losing control of his company amidst rumors questioning his sanity.[58] In 1887, Henry Ives, a B&O Railroad investor and stock operator known as the "Napoleon of Wall Street" tried to sell B&O Telegraph to Western Union, but he asked too high a price and lacked clear authority to sell the company.[59] When Garrett retreated to Europe that summer, a cadre of B&O Railroad shareholders led by J. Pierpont Morgan – who was also a Western Union director – sold the B&O telegraph system to Gould for $5 million in Western Union stock.[60] Garrett, receiving word of the negotiations, cabled from Paris that he would return immediately, but the deal closed while he was still at sea.[61]

The B&O war cost Western Union dearly. Traders battered the company's stock for several years, cutting its value in half. The directors reduced and then suspended the dividend. Gould snapped up shares when the price fell and sold when it climbed, taking great advantage of inside information all the while.[62] Green followed suit, providing confidential information to friends about the future of Western Union stock while actively trading on his own account, sometimes using the purchased stock itself as collateral in lieu of paying money upfront.[63] At times, this backfired. Green took Western Union stock without paying any margin before the announcement of the Baltimore & Ohio merger, and when the stock unexpectedly fell on the news, Green scrambled to cover the loan.[64]

----

[57] Green to C. J. U. Gwinn, 8 July 1885, WUC.

[58] Green to Russell Sage, 17 March 1887, Green Papers (FHS); Klein, *The Life and Legend of Jay Gould*, 385.

[59] Norvin Green to Henry S. Ives, 8 July 1887, WUC.

[60] Special Meeting of the Western Union Executive Committee, 6 October 1887, WUC.

[61] "Robert Garrett's Health," *The New York Times*, 11 October 1887, 1.

[62] For example, in November 1884 he took Western Union stock when it was depressed. In February 1886, Green denied that Gould, Sage and their partners were out of Western Union, but admitted they had "reduced their holdings when the stock was ten percent higher." Green to M. Greene, 20 February 1886, Green Papers, (FHS).

[63] Green's letterbooks in the Western Union Collection reveal very little of such activity. His private letterbooks at the Filson Historical Society, however, are full of such correspondence.

[64] Norvin Green to S. and L. Wormser, 18 October 1887, Green Papers (FHS).

As a Gould property, Western Union suffered when Gould's other stocks fared poorly on the market. In 1888, investors learned that Gould had been paying unearned dividends on his Missouri-Pacific Railroad, and the stocks in Gould's roads plunged, taking Western Union down with them. While the Missouri-Pacific crash held the price down, Gould's partners loaded up on Western Union, and Green wished he could buy more himself. He probably found a lender to back his play, because six months later, he was once again trying to cover speculative losses in his Western Union account.[65]

Despite the active telegraph competition throughout the 1880s, Western Union could not escape the opprobrium of monopoly. Gould's place at the head of the company made Western Union appear more dangerous than ever before, and perhaps deservedly so. Allegations that Gould used the telegraph to interfere in American politics were outlandish, and yet Gould's payments to telegraph reformers during his battle with Western Union suggest that Gould had a taste for conspiracy. The most dramatic accusation of Gould's political abuse of the telegraph came in 1884, when *The New York Times* claimed he had tried to steal the presidential election for James G. Blaine. The anti-Gould newspapers harped on Gould's support for Blaine before the election and some began referring to the senator as "Jay Gould Blaine."[66] The AP compiled the returns from the close contest between Blaine and Democrat Grover Cleveland, so the election news inevitably passed through the offices of Western Union. *The New York Times* declared that Gould deliberately held back returns from New York State – where the race was extremely tight – for several hours. Gould's alleged goal had either been to help the Blaine campaign steal the election by fraud, or else to speculate in the stock market by issuing false reports of Blaine's victory and selling stocks short until the news of Cleveland's victory was released and the market declined.[67] Threats of mob violence against Gould and Western Union worried Green enough to request police protection for his company.[68]

To disprove the charges, Green invited newspaper mogul Joseph Pulitzer for a demonstration of the handling of election bulletins and introduced Pulitzer to Western Union's many Democratic officers and

---

[65] Norvin Green to J. Milliken, 23 March 1888, Green Papers (FHS); Norvin Green to J. Seaver Page, 28 September 1888, Green Papers (FHS).

[66] Klein, *The Life and Legend of Jay Gould*, 336.

[67] "A Dangerous Game," *The New York Times*, 7 November 1884, 4.

[68] Norvin Green to Stephen B. French, 6 November 1884, WUC.

clerks.[69] Even in private, Green insisted that three-quarters of the "men on the Executive floor supported and voted for Cleveland," including the Treasurer, who "always voted the Republican ticket." A majority of company operators and clerks had marched in a Cleveland procession with a Western Union banner.[70] If Gould truly did try to steal the election for Blaine, he did so without the knowledge of Western Union's president or its employees.

Publicly, Green railed against the impracticability and injustice of persistent postal telegraph schemes just as his predecessors had for decades. In an 1883 article against the postal telegraph in the influential *North American Review*, Green warned that government telegraphy was a slippery slope that would lead to public ownership of the railroads, warehouses, grain elevators, and even bakers' shops.[71] Green made such claims so often that they exhibited a rehearsed quality – he repeated passages from his *North American Review* article verbatim in both official correspondence and Congressional testimony. In other ways, though, he was showing more flexibility.

In 1887, Congress passed the Interstate Commerce Act, one of the first significant pieces of big business regulation. Historians have vigorously debated which interest was most responsible for the law – Southern and Western farmers, merchants and manufacturers, and railroad executives have variously been assigned responsibility. The Commerce Act restricted discriminatory railroad rate practices and banned freight pools, but the commission the act created proved largely ineffective.[72] Though the Supreme Court had determined in the *Pensacola* decision that the telegraph constituted "interstate commerce," the Interstate Commerce Act addressed only the railroads. Congress subsequently debated legislation to bring the telegraph under the Interstate Commerce Commission's supervision.

After years of opposition to government interference of any kind, Western Union leaders now *embraced* the principle of telegraph regulation, as they had tactically at times in the past. Green believed putting the

[69] Norvin Green to Joseph Pulitzer, 7 November 1884, WUC.

[70] Norvin Green to Abram Hewitt, 8 December 1884, Green Papers (FHS).

[71] Norvin Green, "The Government and the Telegraph," *North American Review* 137, no. 124 (1883): 425.

[72] Skowronek criticized this regulatory regime as a failure because the numerous interests it represented could not possibly produce a coherent public policy. For his criticism and a review of historical arguments on the source of the bill, see Stephen Skowronek, *Building a New American State: The Expansion of National Administrative Capacities, 1877–1920* (New York: Cambridge University Press, 1982), 125–31.

telegraph under the authority of the Committee on Interstate Commerce would kill the postal telegraph at last.[73] A "very conservative law of regulation" would "settle the telegraph question." Railroad leaders similarly encouraged regulation to stabilize freight rates and bring order to their "increasingly chaotic industry."[74] Western Union managers' notion of "very conservative" included a strong objection to any provisions that would give the government the power to set rates. "The only question is as to what 'regulate' means," wrote Green in 1888. Congress had no right to "fix the price of a barrel of flour in New York, which has been shipped from Minneapolis, or a hogshead of tobacco from Kentucky," so it had no right to fix the price of a telegram "concerning these products."[75]

Green had good reason to hope for conservative regulation, because support for a government telegraph appeared to be gaining momentum. In the 1880s the National Board of Trade and Transportation embraced the postal telegraph. The National Board counted more than 20 major commercial organizations among its members, including the conservative New York Chamber of Commerce. Testifying on behalf of the Board before Congress, F. B. Thurber reported that English business organizations – such as the London Chamber of Commerce – considered the postal telegraph in their country a success and were universally opposed to returning to private management. Thurber argued that Western Union's bloated capital and dividend obligations and the lack of competition in the industry made for overpriced service that limited the use of the telegraph. Cheaper rates would bring the telegraph into universal use. "The argument that but a small part of our population now use the telegraph is not argument at all," he insisted. The leaders of "the great railway corporations of the country" controlled Western Union, and "in the matter of transmitting intelligence," their interest diverged from that of the "general public."[76]

Green's acknowledgement of the potential benefits of conservative regulation may also have reflected the need to respond to the growing consensus that the telegraph was a "natural" monopoly. Gould employed a familiar doublespeak about the telegraph "monopoly": Western Union was not a monopoly, yet there could be no legitimate competition in the

---

[73] Norvin Green to John G. Moore, 25 February 1888, Green Papers (FHS).
[74] Norvin Green to C. G. Peters, 8 March 1888, Norvin Green Papers (FHS). Gabriel Kolko, *Railroads and Regulation, 1877–1916* (Princeton, N.J.: Princeton University Press, 1965), 4.
[75] Green to J. D. Caton, 2 February 1888, WUC.
[76] F. B. Thurber, "Postal Telegraph Facilities," 11 March 1890," WUC, 16–29.

telegraph industry. Gould told a Senate Committee in 1883 that his experience running the American Union Telegraph had taught him "that an opposition could not sustain itself" – though there is little evidence that American Union was unsustainable. On the other hand, Gould admitted that competition was "necessary as a factor to prevent excessive charges in business enterprise." He reasoned that Western Union had no exclusive franchise to perform the nation's telegraphing, and a business without an exclusive franchise was not a monopoly. Any day some "John Doe" or "Richard Roe" could come along and enter the telegraph business. In a free market, monopoly was "practically impossible."[77]

To most observers outside of Western Union's influence, it was competition, not monopoly that was "practically impossible." Gardiner Greene Hubbard, the indefatigable telegraph reformer, agreed with Western Union managers who held that opposition companies were generally speculative ventures designed to goad Western Union into overpaying for their property. In 1884, Hubbard appeared before the Senate Committee on Post Offices and Post Roads and argued that the consolidation of the Mutual Union demonstrated that monopoly was inevitable as long as the telegraph remained in private hands. Hubbard predicted – correctly – that the B&O would meet the same fate: Western Union would buy the B&O with new sums of watered stock and force the public to pay the dividends.[78] Competition was a fraud, and only the federal government could cure the ills of the telegraph industry. "My proposition is that the telegraph business is, and of necessity must be, a monopoly," Hubbard told the Senators. Wherever consolidation was possible, "there competition is impossible."[79]

The new "natural monopoly" critique of the telegraph held that *because* there could be no competition, Western Union should not be left alone to conduct the nation's telegraph business. Henry George, a popular antimonopolist who had run afoul of Western Union in the 1860s, told the Senate Committee on the Relations Between Labor and Capital that the telegraph industry was "in its nature a monopoly." A single firm would always undersell or absorb its competitors.[80] In 1887, political economist

[77] *Report of the Committee of the Senate Upon the Relations between Labor and Capital*, 1069–73.
[78] *Report of the Committee on Post-Offices and Post-Roads, United States Senate, on the Postal Telegraph*, 55.
[79] Ibid., 57. The last problem would later be solved by the empowerment of a government antitrust function.
[80] *Report of the Committee of the Senate Upon the Relations Between Labor and Capital*, vol. 1, 468.

Henry C. Adams proposed in an influential essay, "The Relation of the State to Industrial Action," that a "principle of increasing returns" governed certain industries, dictating that consolidation would generate greater value. "Such businesses are by nature monopolies," he wrote. To believe that "competition can secure for the public fair treatment in such cases, or that laws compelling competition can be enforced" was pure self-deception. In industries subject to natural monopoly, Adams concluded, the only options were "an irresponsible, extra-legal monopoly, or a monopoly established by law and managed in the interest of the public."[81] The Senate Committee on Post Offices and Post Roads reached a similar conclusion and recommended expanding the work begun by the Interstate Commerce Act with a bill to regulate the telegraph. "The power to control these corporations must rest somewhere," Texas Democrat John Reagan wrote in his report to the Senate. "Shall we leave it to be exercised at the discretion of a few persons whose interests are adverse to those of the great body of the people, and without the restraints of the law?"[82]

Western Union's weakened competitive and political position helps explain the outcome of the final significant contest in the telegraph industry, a competition with the silver tycoon John W. Mackay. At the age of nine Mackay immigrated to New York from Ireland as a steerage passenger. His father died shortly after he arrived, and he helped support his family by selling newspapers and shining shoes on Park Row, across the street from the site where the Western Union building would one day stand.[83] Mackay went West and worked his way into a fortune as a miner. He was already prosperous when he became a partner in Nevada's Comstock Lode and became popularly known as the "Bonanza King." Why Mackay suddenly became interested in the telegraph in the 1880s remains a mystery.[84] According to legend, Mackay's wife, who preferred to live in Europe, accrued exorbitant cable bills, drawing Mackay's attention to the high cost of transatlantic telegraphy – and doubtless to the potential profits, too.[85] Mackay partnered with James Gordon Bennett,

[81] Henry C. Adams, "Relation of the State to Industrial Action," *Publications of the American Economic Association* 1, no. 6 (1887): 64.
[82] Senate Report No. 434, 50th Congress, 1st Session, 1–2.
[83] Ethel Manter, *Rocket of the Comstock: The Story of John William Mackay* (Caldwell, Idaho: The Caxton Printers, 1950), 18.
[84] John B. Taltavall, *Telegraphers of to-Day: Descriptive, Historical, Biographical* (New York: John B. Taltavall, 1893), 163.
[85] Manter, *Rocket of the Comstock*, 200.

Jr., the editor of the *New York Herald*. For nearly two decades the *Herald* had chafed at the Western Union monopoly and the high prices charged by the Atlantic cable cartel, and after Gould's takeover in 1881, Bennett became his "most persistent tormentor" in the press.[86]

Gould himself had challenged the Atlantic cable monopoly by forming the American Telegraph and Cable Company, but in 1882, Gould's cable joined the cartel, restoring the monopoly. The cartel connected exclusively with Western Union, which enjoyed an effective monopoly on domestic connections to European communication. Bennett convinced Mackay to help him create the Commercial Cable Company to force lower cable rates and frustrate Gould.[87] With Mackay's money the Commercial Cable Company laid two new Atlantic cables in 1884. The cable cartel launched a ferocious rate war that gradually pushed prices down from seventy-five cents per word to twelve cents.[88] Western Union refused to carry messages for Commercial Cable to other points in the United States, making Mackay's competing cables an expensive dead end. To solve this problem, Mackay started buying small, struggling domestic telegraph companies, much like Hiram Sibley had when he created Western Union thirty years earlier. Mackay's consolidation plan centered on the Postal Telegraph Company, a troubled New York firm. Mackay reorganized and renamed the Postal Telegraph and Cable Company with $20 million in capital stock and bonds.[89]

The term "postal telegraph" had been associated with proposals for a government telegraph. Because Mackay designed his domestic company to feed his Atlantic cables, speculation abounded that he hoped to establish a network and then sell it to the government. Postal Telegraph offered a cheap uniform rate of 25 cents, presumably to "appeal to what was supposed to be a wide public desire for postal telegraphy under government control."[90] George S. Coe, a manager of the Postal, promised Congress in 1884 that his company had been created to do the public service cheaply, and "with the aid of the post-office deliveries in large cities,"

---

[86] Klein, *The Life and Legend of Jay Gould*, 313.
[87] James M. Herring and Gerald C. Gross, *Telecommunications: Economics and Regulation* (New York: McGraw Hill Book Company, 1936), 22.
[88] Oscar Lewis, *Silver Kings: The Lives and Times of Mackay, Fair, Flood, and O'Brien, Lords of the Nevada Comstock Lode* (New York: Alfred A. Knopf, 1947), 106–7.
[89] Reid, *Telegraph in America*, 773.
[90] Ibid., 775. Manter makes the same claim and suggests that Postal Telegraph George S. Coe was assigned to the duty of negotiating a government buyout. See Manter, *Rocket of the Comstock*, 206.

Postal Telegraph could transmit "the greater part of the correspondence now carried by the United States mail."[91] Green believed that the Postal's interest in a government contract or buyout was really just a ploy to convince Western Union to buy the company instead.[92] Western Union nearly bought Postal Telegraph in 1885 but would not pay more than the physical value of the lines, dooming the deal.[93] Mackay reorganized Postal Telegraph in 1886, placing it under the able command of A. B. Chandler, one of Western Union's top managers. Postal Telegraph nonetheless continued to struggle. Thanks to the rate war, the cables earned no profits, while the Postal's land lines pulled perhaps $15,000 a month from Mackay's pocket.[94] Mackay admitted to an associate, "The best thing to do is to sell out the whole plant to the Western Union, ticker and all."[95]

But just at the moment when Postal Telegraph appeared ready to tumble into the maw of Western Union, the "Great Monopoly" assented to a duopoly instead. In 1888, the Atlantic cable war ended with an agreement setting cable rates at twenty-five cents per word, one-third of what they had been before Mackay began the fight four years earlier and well below the rates preferred by the cable pool. Mackay spurned offers to lease his cable to the cartel. All the challengers before him had waved the banner of antimonopoly and then dropped it at a plum opportunity to sell, but Mackay held his ground. The twenty-five cent rate he forced on the cable pool remained in place until the introduction of transoceanic radiotelegraphy decades later.[96] Perhaps Mackay's success in the cable war inspired him to hang on to his landlines.

By 1889 Postal Telegraph reached so many points in the United States that it competed effectively with Western Union. In New York, Mackay built a sixteen-story tower three blocks north of Western Union's headquarters, announcing the permanence of his firm in a manner unlike any previous competitor.[97] In 1889, Western Union and Postal-Telegraph negotiated agreements on rates and rebates and the amicable settlement of future disputes, creating a duopoly that lasted until Western Union absorbed Postal Telegraph in 1931.

---

[91] *Report of the Committee on Post-Offices and Post-Roads, United States Senate, on the Postal Telegraph*, 147.
[92] Norvin Green to R. J. Bright, 22 December 1884, WUC.
[93] Green to James Demarest, 31 July 1885, WUC.
[94] Green to John Pender, 2 July 1887, WUC.
[95] Quoted in Lewis, *Silver Kings*, 108.
[96] Herring and Gross, *Telecommunications: Economics and Regulation*, 22.
[97] Lewis, *Silver Kings*, 108.

Early on the morning of July 18, 1890, a small fire began on the sixth floor of the towering Western Union headquarters on Broadway. Some operators later speculated that the blaze had been set by "Old Man Kav," an apparition who haunted the upper stories beneath the hulking mansard roof, mischievously tangling wires and disrupting circuits. More likely some wires had short-circuited and ignited the gutta-percha insulation in the surrounding lines. Within a few minutes, the fire spread to the operators' room. City firefighters arrived in time to rescue several stranded employees from the roof and contain the conflagration above the sixth floor. By noon they had quenched the fire entirely, but the top three floors suffered severe damage. The fire destroyed more than five hundred telegraph instruments and most of the batteries. The twelve hundred wires that streamed out of the seventh-floor balcony fell silent.

The smoking, ruined top floors of the Western Union building had been a nexus of American communications. Half the messages that arrived in the operating room each day were not destined for New York, but only passed through this central hub. The cotton, produce, gold and stock exchanges depended upon fresh information provided by Western Union. The domestic lines that fed the Atlantic oceanic cables terminated in the Western Union building. The AP had its main offices there, and the fire destroyed them too. Not since the blizzard of 1888 knocked down so many wires that New York was briefly cut off from the rest of the world had the nation's commercial activity been in such grave danger of suspension. Western Union's employees scrambled heroically to resuscitate the telegraph, and within hours they had cobbled together a semblance of normal business conducted via satellite offices around New York and across the Hudson in Jersey City. Though general delays lingered for days, the commercial exchanges and AP were already back on the wires by the time the afternoon papers announced their disruption.[98]

The aesthetic grandeur of the Western Union headquarters proved a casualty of the fire. The building had been designed to be fireproof, and so Western Union had insured neither the structure nor the equipment inside. A few days after the fire, the company announced that the arching mansard roof with its iron balconies and soaring clock tower were to be torn down and the upper floors rebuilt to match the simpler granite façade of the lower floors. The building would rise monotonously for ten

[98] "Fire Stops the Telegraph," *The New York Times*, 19 July 1890, 1; "The Wires Are Working," *The New York Times*, 20 July 1890; "Fire at Western Union Headquarters," *Illustrated American*, 9 August 1890, 134–7.

stories and then stop abruptly at the cornice, standing forty feet shorter than it had when its tower first reached above the city's skyline in 1875. The remodeling of the Western Union building reduced one of the world's first skyscrapers to just another undistinguished commercial high-rise in a budding forest of similar buildings.

The diminution of the Western Union building befitted a company that was itself diminished. New competition had emerged in the telegraph industry, including what proved to be a permanent rival, and the fast-growing American Bell Telephone had taken a share of the telecommunications market. Western Union had entered the 1880s with the derisive nickname "Great Monopoly" and remained one of the nation's largest companies, but the massive railroad corporations and emerging industrial "trusts" had taken its place as the leading corporate bogeyman. The destruction of the iconic tower occurred just as Western Union began a long march down the road to irrelevance, and eventually to failure. For three decades Western Union had been a pioneering, innovative firm that covered the country with wires and forged a new industry, but in the 1880s it stalled in its climb.

Why did Western Union settle for a duopoly with Postal Telegraph after more than thirty years of pursuing a monopoly? There are several possible answers. For ten years the press had battered Gould for attempting to control the telegraph, and perhaps he hoped to deflect criticism by leaving a docile competitor in the field. New competition had followed every major consolidation since 1866, and the contests with the Mutual Union, B&O and Postal Telegraph had all been triggered by Western Union's merger with American Union. Perhaps Gould realized that a stable duopoly paradoxically offered better protection against competition than a monopoly. Moreover, Western Union stock had suffered from broad market declines, bear attacks on all Gould's companies, and the suspension of the dividend during the battle with the B&O. Perhaps Gould did not believe Western Union was prepared for a drawn out fight with an enemy whose principal investor had pockets as deep as his own and no railroad interest that Gould could use as a bargaining chip. "There's no beating John Mackay," Gould reportedly said. "If he needs another million or two he goes to his silver mine and digs it up."[99] The telephone also posed a threat as its popularity grew and it took an increasing share of the intraurban telegraph business.[100] Perhaps this external competitive challenge to the industry encouraged a new commitment to internal stability.

99 Ibid., 106–7.
100 Herring and Gross, *Telecommunications: Economics and Regulation*, 4.

Although all these factors probably contributed to the decision not to challenge the Postal Telegraph, one other factor may have been more potent than all the others: the persistent danger that the government would step in and dismantle Western Union if it pursued a monopoly.

In late 1889, Postmaster General John Wanamaker launched the last great postal telegraph crusade. Wanamaker, a Philadelphia merchant and department store pioneer, headed the Post Office Department from 1889 to 1893. He noted that several Postmasters General had recommended that the post office assume responsibility for telegraphing and that "uniform testimony" before Congress indicated that lower rates and improved facilities led to wider use and greater revenue for the telegraph. Wanamaker concluded that telegraphy was "the legitimate work of the post-office" and that the people were right to "stoutly demand telegraph facilities at postal stations."[101] Gardiner Greene Hubbard joined the campaign, which lasted throughout Wanamaker's tenure as Postmaster General and garnered great popular support. By the end of the 1890s, the Farmers' Alliance and Industrial Union, the National Grange, the Knights of Labor, the Railway Union, the American Federation of Labor, the International Typographical Union, the People's Party, and the Prohibitionists had all included government ownership of the telegraph in their platforms.[102]

Though the plan never included buying private telegraph lines, each year Wanamaker's scheme grew more ambitious, including forcing lower rates by regulation, creating a cheap telegraph service in connection with existing post offices, and finally leasing lines, instruments, and operators to transmit messages at fixed government rates. An iteration of Wanamaker's plan even included taking control of the telephone system along with the telegraph.[103] Ultimately, Wanamaker's campaign followed the same pattern as all those that had preceded it. Western Union publicly insisted the government plan was misguided, corrupt, and certain to fail, while managers privately attempted to rework the plan so that it would be advantageous to Western Union or better still, kill it in committee.

---

[101] John Wanamaker, "Postal Telegraph Facilities," 11 February 1890, WUC.

[102] Frank Parsons, *The Telegraph Monopoly* (Philadelphia: C. F. Taylor, 1899), note on 12–13.

[103] U.S. Post Office Dept. and Daniel C. Roper, *Government Ownership of Electrical Means of Communication. Letter from the Postmaster General, Transmitting, in Response to a Senate Resolution of January 12, 1914, a Report Entitled "Government Ownership of Electrical Means of Communication,"* (Washington, D.C.: U.S. Government Printing Office, 1914), 25–8.

The financial panic of 1893 terminated whatever momentum Wanamaker had built up – retrenchment became a greater priority than public control of telegraphy. In 1899, a leading Progressive, Prof. Frank Parsons, attempted to relaunch the postal telegraph movement with a two-hundred-page indictment of Western Union titled *The Telegraphy Monopoly*. Parsons noted that it had become an article of faith among industrial and agricultural reform organizations that the government should own and operate the telegraph – along with the telephone and the railroads. Despite this growing constituency in favor of a postal telegraph, however, the issue excited little new interest in Congress. The diminutive Postal-Telegraph and Cable Company provided a modicum of competition in telegraphy, and, more importantly, the telephone presented an alternative. The Great Monopoly was not considered monopoly enough to fall under the sway of the Sherman Anti-Trust Act of 1890. Despite Western Union's tepid support for conservative regulation, Congress passed only measures to regulate railroad telegraphs constructed in fulfillment of legislation granting the railroads land and loans.

The federal government did not institute general telegraph regulation until the Mann–Elkins Act in 1910.[104] After the death of Jay Gould in 1892 and Norvin Green in 1893, George Gould became the principal Western Union stockholder and Thomas T. Eckert ascended at last to the presidency of the company. Even more than his predecessors, Eckert "milked" Western Union for profits rather than reinvesting in growth. As the telephone giant AT&T ascended, Western Union declined.[105] In 1909, the two companies joined together when cash-starved Western Union sold to AT&T its holdings in New York Telephone, and George Gould sold his 30 percent of Western Union to AT&T. This "marriage" reignited Congressional opposition to concentration in telecommunications. The resulting Mann–Elkins Act at last brought the telegraph and telephone under ICC regulation, requiring rates that were "just and reasonable."[106] AT&T felt increasing pressure from federal regulators who worried a truly "great monopoly" in telecommunications had been created. Fearing an antitrust suit or a government takeover of the industry, AT&T divested from Western Union in 1914.

---

[104] Herring and Gross, *Telecommunications: Economics and Regulation*, 210.
[105] George P. Oslin, *The Story of Telecommunications* (Macon, Ga.: Mercer University Press, 1992), 263.
[106] Alan Stone, *Public Service Liberalism: Telecommunications and Transitions in Public Policy* (Princeton, N.J.: Princeton University Press, 1991), 183–6.

After a brief period of prosperity following its separation from AT&T, Western Union performed poorly during the Great Depression and never truly recovered.[107] Western Union's independent existence ended in 1994, when First Financial Management bought the company in a bankruptcy auction. First Financial merged with First Data Corporation the following year. In January 2006, First Data Corporation revealed plans to relaunch Western Union as a public company providing the domestic and international money transfer service that had been its principal product since the 1980s. On January 27, 2006, just after the announcement of the company's rebirth, Western Union terminated its telegram business. Despite the present-day ubiquity of the Western Union brand, money transfer is a competitive industry, and Western Union has long ceased to be a monopoly.

As Western Union president Russell McFall boasted in his speech to the Newcomen Society in 1971, Western Union had played a major part in "making history," and not just technological history (as McFall believed), but that of capitalism itself.[108] "The Great Monopoly" had helped to shape a new corporate order, and powerfully reinforced it. But the historical significance of the rise of the great American corporations – and particularly Western Union – had been observed long before. "We are making history," Jay Gould had told the Senate Committee on Relations Between Labor and Capital in 1883 in testimony rejecting the idea of legislative action against the telegraph monopoly. "We are all working together, the rich man and the poor man, all working together to make our republican institutions a success in the world."[109]

Gould was an artful manipulator of political language, and his invocation of rich and poor working in harmony to better the republic was at least disingenuous, if not pure flimflam. After all, his testimony came just a month after his company crushed the largest strike in the history of the telegraph industry. Nonetheless, his choice of the term "republican institutions" is intriguing. The Founders of the United States had considered communication to be so vital to the health of the republic that they enshrined a postal service in the Constitution as one of the few specifically enumerated responsibilities of the federal government. In the 1840s,

---

[107] David Hochfelder, "Constructing an Industrial Divide: Western Union, AT&T, and the Federal Government, 1876–1971," *Business History Review* 76, no. 4 (2002): 724–5.

[108] Russell W. McFall, *Making History by Responding to Its Forces* (New York: Newcomen Society in North America, 1971).

[109] *Report of the Committee on Post-Offices and Post-Roads, United States Senate, on the Postal Telegraph*, 1092.

the telegraph had narrowly missed joining the Post Office Department. As the principal stockholder in the dominant *private* telegraph firm, Gould's appeal to republicanism was indeed ironic. If the Western Union telegraph monopoly reflected any political philosophy, it was the triumph of economic liberalism *over* republicanism.[110] It was Western Union, and not the government telegraph proposed by reformers, that represented a departure from traditional norms of American political economy.[111]

In the decades when great corporations first emerged, Western Union ceaselessly lobbied Congress and campaigned in the press to promote the idea that private economic interests were best suited to promote the public good. However, Western Union offered an economically liberal answer to a question traditionally posed in republican terms: In the vast United States, what type of communication would promote a well-informed and unified citizenry? The liberal answer provided by corporate telegraph managers and their allies in Congress and the press had several obvious advantages. The private telegraph system had been built and maintained with tacit government aid, but at virtually no cost to the treasury. Competition encouraged high-quality service and reasonable rates, spurred new innovation, and prevented corruption. Private initiative had made the American telegraph the fastest communication network in the world.

However appealing the liberal model might have been, it obscured both the market reality and a no less imperative set of competing political principles. Although Western Union offered the distinct advantage of protecting the public purse, the benefits of competition were limited, because The Great Monopoly bought off its challengers. Marginal improvements that might be attributed to competition – extension to new regions, reductions in interurban rates – could just as well have been achieved through policy requirements – as indeed they were in the Post Office. More importantly, what might be regarded as republican principles of communication were ignored and delegitimized. A republican system might have emphasized universal service to all regions regardless

---

[110] I have adapted this formulation from John Lauritz Larson, *Internal Improvement: National Public Works and the Promise of Popular Government in the Early United States* (Chapel Hill: The University of North Carolina Press, 2001), 263.

[111] Mark Lloyd has recently argued that communications policy is "at the center of the structure of the U.S. republic," and the concession to a private telegraph was "the first serious crack in the structure of American governance." See Mark Lloyd, *Prologue to a Farce: Communication and Democracy in America* (Urbana and Chicago: University of Illinois Press, 2006), 12, 19.

of potential profitability, low rates to allow small businesses and private individuals to access the telegraph, and a policy for news transmissions that encouraged a free and diverse press instead of monopoly syndicates like the AP. True, this possibility exists only in the records of opposition to private telegraph and in historical imagination, but that makes it no less real.

The public policy that created a private telegraph monopoly gave the power of fast communication only to those who could pay for it. Not surprisingly, Western Union best served large private interests similar to itself – railroads, other large corporations, financial markets, and press syndicates. In a more than superficial sense, the telegraph could even be said to have been a condition necessary for their creation, initiating a self-reinforcing loop. Only the wealthy could afford the telegraph, so only the wealthy used the telegraph, and they defined the uses *they* chose as the telegraph's legitimate purpose. As a business matter, there was little injustice in this arrangement, but as a matter of public policy, the persistence of Western Union indirectly determined who had the power of fast communication in the new, telegraph-enabled industrial economy and who was excluded from speaking. Moreover, though the policy preference for private telecommunications was not irreversible, the precedent that Western Union set and fiercely defended had a lasting impact. As sociologist Paul Starr recently noted in his history of the American media, "Once the twig was bent, the tree started to grow in a particular direction – private interests accumulated, ideological defenses developed, and what was once an open question became a hardened institutional reality."[112]

No alternatives were possible as long as public policy was secondary to the interests of capital. Western Union blocked telegraph reform and shaped the public discourse on the telegraph problem to protect private investment – and overinvestment – in telegraphy. In the 1850s telegraph entrepreneurs determined the best way to ensure the value of their investment was to form an anticompetitive cartel – the North American Telegraph Association. In the 1860s, a single-firm monopoly promised better returns, so monopoly became the goal of telegraph managers. In the 1870s, Jay Gould and his allies recognized the opportunity to win big in the stock market by competing with Western Union and speculating in its stock, and so competition briefly reemerged. Between the founding

[112] Paul Starr, *The Creation of the Media: Political Origins of Modern Communications* (New York: Basic Books, 2004), 165.

of the first telegraph firms and the maturing of Western Union, there certainly was a revolutionary change in the management of large firms, but this managerial revolution was not responsible for the policy of monopoly. Individual greed – embodied most visibly by Jay Gould – played a large part in determining the fate of telegraph competition, but Gould did not create the telegraph monopoly; he merely exploited it.

The history of the Western Union telegraph monopoly reveals how a new political economy emerged once private property became detached from individuals and small proprietorships and concentrated in industrial corporations. In short, it is a story of the transition from people making money to money making money. Western Union demonstrated how a corporation could be more than a mere mechanism for growth and profit: it could be a political actor, it could shape the communications habits of a nation, it could define the links between markets, and it could influence the distribution of news – and in certain circumstances, the content, too. Instead of adhering to existing public policy, Western Union managers argued for a new public policy and defined the public interest in Western Union's terms.

The rise of the American telegraph industry is a story of entrepreneurship, innovation, and managerial revolution, but it is first and foremost a story of the preservation of capital and the production of dividends. The inexorable logic of generating a return on capital explains the consolidation of the telegraph industry, the high prices for messages, limited service outside of cities, and even managers' troubled relationship with employees. Western Union's monopoly may, in fact, have made the American telegraph network the largest and fastest in the world, but this was never the company's true purpose. The strategy to monopolize the industry was in the service of protecting Western Union's investments in patents, lines, equipment, and right-of-way contracts. It was a strategy above all to protect its capital, in an era that may be defined by that ideal.

Manuscript Collections

Bell, Alexander Graham. Alexander Graham Bell Family Papers, Library of Congress, Washington, D.C.

Butler, Benjamin. Benjamin F. Butler Papers, Library of Congress, Washington, D.C.

Caton, John Dean. Papers of John Dean Caton, Library of Congress, Washington, D.C.

Chandler, William E. Papers of William E. Chandler, Library of Congress, Washington, D.C.

Clowry, Robert Charles. Papers of Robert Charles Clowry, Library of Congress, Washington, D.C.

Cornell, Ezra. Ezra Cornell Papers, Cornell University Library, Ithaca, N.Y.

Field, Cyrus W. Cyrus W. Field Papers, New York Public Library, Humanities Manuscripts and Archives, New York, N.Y.

George, Henry. Henry George Papers, New York Public Library, Humanities Manuscripts and Archives, New York, N.Y.

Green, Norvin. Green Family Papers, University of Kentucky Library, Lexington, Ky.

Green, Norvin. Norvin Green Papers, Filson Historical Society, Louisville, Ky.

Green, Norvin, Uncataloged Green Family Papers, Filson Historical Society, Louisville, Ky.

Gross, William L. William L. Gross Papers, Western Reserve Historical Society, Cleveland, Ohio.

Hubbard, Gardiner Greene. Hubbard Family Papers, Library of Congress, Washington, D.C.

Manning, William Andrew. William Andrew Manning Papers, Western Reserve Historical Society, Cleveland, Ohio.

Marble, Manton. Papers of Manton Marble, Library of Congress, Washington, D.C.

Morse, Samuel F. B. Papers of Samuel Finley Breeze Morse, Library of Congress, Washington, D.C.

O'Reilly, Henry. Henry O'Reilly Papers, New-York Historical Society, New York, N.Y.

O'Reilly, Henry. Henry O'Reilly Papers, Rochester Historical Society (held by Rochester Public Library), Rochester, N.Y.

Post, George Browne. George B. Post Architectural Record, New-York Historical Society, New York, N.Y.

Shepard, Helen Miller Gould. Helen Miller Gould Shepard Papers, New-York Historical Society, New York, N.Y.

Sherman, John. Papers of John Sherman, Library of Congress, Washington, D.C.

Sibley, Hiram. Hiram Sibley Family Papers, Rochester University, Rochester, N.Y.

Sibley, Hiram. Hiram Sibley Family Papers Addition, Rochester University, Rochester, N.Y.

Wade, Jeptha Homer. Jeptha Homer Wade Family Papers, Western Reserve Historical Society, Cleveland, Ohio.

Washburne, Elihu Benjamin. Papers of E. B. Washburne, Library of Congress, Washington, D.C.

Western Union Telegraph Company Records, Archive Center, National Museum of American History, Smithsonian Institution, Washington, D.C.

Index